SELLING THE CONGO

MATTHEW G. STANARD

Selling the Congo

A HISTORY OF EUROPEAN PRO-EMPIRE PROPAGANDA AND THE MAKING OF BELGIAN IMPERIALISM

UNIVERSITY OF NEBRASKA PRESS | LINCOLN & LONDON

Library of Congress Cataloging-
in-Publication Data
Stanard, Matthew G.
Selling the Congo: a history of European
pro-empire propaganda and the making
of Belgian imperialism / Matthew G. Stanard.
p. cm.
Summary: "Examination of pro-empire
propaganda advanced by Belgium during its
colonial rule of the Congo" —Provided by publisher.
Includes bibliographical references and index.
ISBN 978-0-8032-3777-3 (hardback: alk. paper)
1. Belgium—Colonies—Africa—Public opinion—
History—20th century. 2. Public opinion—
Belgium—History—20th century. 3. Propaganda,
Belgian—History—20th century. 4. Congo
(Democratic Republic)—Colonization.
5. Congo (Democratic Republic)—
History—1908–1960. I. Title.
JV2818.S73 2011
325'.3493096751—dc23
2011023628

Set in Sabon by Bob Reitz.

To the memory of William B. Cohen

Contents

Illustrations

Preface

In 1984 my family moved to Brussels, Belgium; my brothers and I attended an international school in Waterloo where we could see the Butte du Lion—the monument to Wellington's victory over Napoleon—from some of the school's top-floor classrooms. One day, my science classmates and I went on a field trip to the Royal Museum for Central Africa in Tervuren. As a recently expatriated American preteen, I was ignorant of Belgian politics, society, and culture, but I still remember wondering: Why was this absolutely enormous museum about central Africa located in the middle of little Belgium? I also remember that during the several years my family lived in Belgium, I heard about the Zairian government's repeated demands that artifacts and other materials be repatriated to central Africa, and the Belgian government's steadfast refusal to do so. I was puzzled why Belgium would care so much about African artifacts from such a faraway place to the point of sticking tenaciously, for years, to an apparently unethical position.

Fifteen years and five changes of address later, I was sitting in a graduate seminar on European imperialism with Bill Cohen at Indiana University–Bloomington in spring semester of 2000. The year previous I had left my lobbying job in Washington DC to go to graduate school to study European history and especially modern European imperialism. Although my time in Belgium was key to developing an interest in European history that eventually led to graduate school, I had zero intention of studying Belgium's history or Belgian imperialism. Yet as the semester unfolded that spring and as I researched pro-empire expositions, I found that while much had been written about how British and French colonies affected their respective metropoles, precious little had been published on the Congo's effects on Belgium. I ended up writing a seminar paper on the colonial section of the 1958 Brussels World's Fair and Belgians' views of their empire. My interest in the reverberations of overseas empire continued in the years after 2000, with a focus on Belgium; the appeal of the subject only intensified as I discovered the many ways in which the empire had "come home" as well as the surprising degree to which Europeans promoted imperialism among their countrymen and women. Along the way, the question kept posing itself as to the nexus among information produced about the colonies; the root causes of imperialism; and empire's echoes in European politics, society, and culture. What could we tell about the nature of empire by looking at those who deliberately promoted overseas expansion and at their motivations for doing so? Was propaganda evidence of an imperialistic spirit? Or did it indicate the contrary, since so many people apparently needed convincing? Did pro-empire messages succeed or fail, or succeed only in part, or did they instead lead to unplanned outcomes? The result of all this questioning is the following study of pro-empire propaganda in Belgium, its genesis and sources, and its effects.

Along the way, I have incurred many debts. Support from the Belgian American Educational Foundation for study in Belgium was crucial for the bulk of the research that went into this work. Indiana University–Bloomington provided support in a number of ways, including a Chancellor's Fellowship, a Doctoral Student

Grant-in-Aid of Research from the Research and University Graduate School, and Hill and Dissertation fellowships from the Department of History. A Wolfsonian-Florida International University Fellowship provided the opportunity to research in The Wolfsonian archives in Miami Beach in 2006–7, and various research stipends from Berry College helped along the way.

In Belgium the staffs at the Cinémathèque Royale, the Archives Générales du Royaume, the Archives de la Ville de Bruxelles, and at the Bibliothèque Royale de Belgique Albert Ier were wonderful. Patricia Van Schuylenbergh and the staff at the Royal Museum for Central Africa were particularly helpful during my many days there, as were Françoise Peemans and Pierre Dandoy at the Archives africaines at the Ministry of Foreign Affairs. This work could not have been accomplished without the help of Berry College Memorial Library, especially Xiaojing Zu, but even more so the tremendous resources of the Indiana University libraries, especially Rhonda Long and the rest of the Document Delivery Services staff in Bloomington.

A number of other individuals were fundamental to this book's completion. Noemi Sarrion has supported me in the most important ways, for many years now. Jim Diehl and Phyllis Martin, whose help has been invaluable, have been tough, critical, and inspiring mentors over the years. Both Bill Schneider and Jim Le Sueur generously agreed to work with me beginning in 2003 and have been supportive ever since. The faculty and staff of the Indiana University Department of History and the Berry College Evans School of Humanities, Arts, and Social Sciences have been unfailing in their support over the years, and I especially thank George Alter, Carl Ipsen, David Pace, George Brooks, Chad Parker, Alexia Bock, Larry Marvin, Jon Atkins, and Christy Snider. My parents, Doug and Bonnie Stanard, have always been encouraging and were crucial when it came to the logistics involved in multiple research stays in Belgium. I also was lucky to enjoy innumerable stays, dinners, and conversations at "Hotel Spangenberg," Meredith and Adolf Spangenberg proprietors. Every time I am in Brussels, Jean-Luc Vellut is unfailingly welcoming, generous, and helpful. My debt to the many other students of European and African history is evident in the book's notes. Thanks also is due to Heather Lundine and her team of readers at University of Nebraska Press and the others who read, listened to, or commented on earlier versions of parts of this study, many of whom are named above. Special thanks to Jeremy Hall, Diane Land, Andrea Lowry, and Kelly Petronis, all of whom read the entire manuscript. Amanda Haskell and Amber Spann helped out with notes and references. Of course any errors or omissions are my fault alone.

My advisor at Bloomington, Bill Cohen, passed away unexpectedly in November 2002, while I was in Brussels on an extended research trip. To me, and to many others, he was a giant: always enthusiastic, at times delightfully inscrutable, and funny when he wanted to be. Above all, he was a prodigiously talented scholar, and he inspired me to try to do my best as a historian. I still miss him very much. I can only hope that he would have enjoyed reading this little study about Belgian imperialism. It is dedicated to him and his memory.

Abbreviations

AA	Archives africaines, Ministère des affaires étrangères/Ministerie van Buitenlandse Zaken
AGR	Archives générales du royaume/ Algemeen Rijksarchief
AIA	Association internationale africaine
AIC	Association internationale du Congo
AICB	Association des intérêts coloniaux belges
AUCAM	Association universitaire catholique pour l'aide aux missions
BCB	*Biographie coloniale belge/Belgische koloniale biografie*
BCK	Compagnie du chemin de fer du Bas-Congo au Katanga
CAPA	Centre d'accueil pour le personnel africain
CCACC	Centre congolais d'action catholique cinématographique
CCN	Cercle colonial namurois
CCS	Commission Coloniale Scolaire
CID	Centre d'information et de documentation du Congo Belge et du Ruanda-Urundi
ECS	École coloniale supérieure
EIC	État Indépendant du Congo/Onafhankelijke Congostaat

Foréami	Fonds Reine Elisabeth pour l'assistance médicale aux Indigènes du Congo Belge
Forminière	Société internationale forestière et minière du Congo
FRAIUTO	Fondation royale des amis de l'Institut universitaire des territoires d'outre-mer/ Vriendenfonds van het Universitair Instituut voor de Overzeese Gebieden
Inforcongo	Office de l'information et des relations publiques pour le Congo Belge et le Ruanda-Urundi/Voorlichtings- en Documentatiecentrum van Belgisch Congo en van Ruanda-Urundi
INUTOM	Institut universitaire des territoires d'outre-mer
MRAC	Musée royal de l'Afrique centrale/Koninklijke Museum voor Midden Afrika
NOVA	Nieuwe Organisatie voor Verkoop en Aankoopsbevordering/Nouvelle organisation favorisant ventes et achats
OC	Office colonial
OCIC	Office catholique international du cinéma
POB/BWP	Parti ouvrier belge/Belgische Werkliedenpartij
PSR	Parti socialiste révolutionnaire
Soprocol	Société auxiliaire de propagande coloniale
ULB	Université libre de Bruxelles
UMHK	Union minière du Haut-Katanga
UN	United Nations

SELLING THE CONGO

Introduction

One July afternoon in 2000, a group of people, including former colonials, walked through the Cinquantenaire Park in Brussels and halted before the simply named Colonial Monument. The monument's foreground depicted a young African lying down, representing the Congo River. On the left a European soldier combated the slave trade, while figures on the right represented another colonial soldier tending to a wounded comrade. The large central panel portrayed the African continent, "henceforth open to civilization," and a group of soldiers surrounding King Leopold II. Atop the monument a young woman represented the country of Belgium, "welcoming the black race."[1] Two members of the group advanced solemnly toward the memorial and, kneeling, placed wreaths to honor the memory of the nation's colonial pioneers.[2]

Similar scenes continue to be enacted at other monuments across the country. In June 2003 a "national ceremony to honor the flag of Tabora" commemorating the World War I victory in German East Africa began at Namur's Leopold II monument.[3] On 24 June 2005 a large equestrian statue of Leopold II was reinaugurated in Brussels after a restoration in time for the country's 175th anniversary, at which a small group from the Association des anciens et amis de la Force publique du Congo Belge (Association of Veterans and Friends of the Belgian Congo

1. Vinçotte's Colonial Monument in Cinquantenaire Park
(photo by the author).

Armed Forces) honored Leopold II by presenting the colors.[4] All these people were paying homage to imperialism at just a few of the dozens if not hundreds of imperialistic monuments that still dot the Belgian landscape five decades after the Congo's independence. These memorials are remnants of the country's colonial past, former propaganda pieces created to rally public support for the Belgian empire in central Africa. The large body of pro-empire propaganda produced in Belgium is the subject of this book.

Because the term "propaganda" has taken on numerous meanings over the years, a brief word on its definition is in order before examining the case of Belgian imperialistic propaganda. As a result of the mobilization of enthusiasm and censorship that accompanied World War I, propaganda "came to be a pejorative term; all governments installed propaganda offices, and all of them falsified news."[5] The word became more suspect after the totalitarianism of Nazi Germany and the Soviet Union became better understood. Goebbels and Hitler believed Germany had lost World War I in the realm of information production and created propaganda with little regard for the truth. Even Communists turned against the Soviet system, as the extent of the interwar show trials and Stalin's cult of personality became better known.[6] These developments led many to equate propaganda with outright lies. Nevertheless, to understand propaganda as only untrue is to misconstrue the term. Propaganda is the production and dissemination of information to help or hinder a particular institution, person, or cause, and the actual ideas, concepts, and materials produced in such an effort. As Garth Jowett and Victoria O'Donnell define it, "Propaganda is the deliberate and systematic attempt to shape perceptions, manipulate cognitions, and direct behavior to achieve a response that furthers the desired intent of the propagandist."[7] Propaganda might be biased or partial, but it is not necessarily false. For example, particular government, missionary, and private films deliberately misrepresented the situation in Belgium's colony or events in its history to make particular points, thereby qualifying those films as propaganda. But often films were tendentious rather than deliberately misleading, having as their goal the instruction of the audience along the lines of a particular ideology.

Many also understand propaganda as primarily a state product.[8] Yet it can issue from a variety of sources, such as during World War I when not only governments but also various elites produced propaganda. In Italy, for instance, the army controlled the press and information at the front; the government produced information directed at foreign audiences; and civil, financial, and industrial elites worked in concert with both.[9] The same

was true for propaganda in favor of overseas empire: it emanated from a variety of sources, including the state and colonial
administrations, commercial interests, missionary orders, and
individuals. A distinction is to be made, however, between propaganda and advertising—the latter of which endorses products and, in the case of imperialism, comprised narrowly focused
promotional materials by specific enterprises.

This study of pro-empire propaganda and the making of Belgian imperialism is centered on five major media of propaganda
that reached the mass of the population in the metropole, with
an emphasis on the period of twentieth-century Belgian state
rule. The first chapter demonstrates how in 1908 Belgium inherited not only a colony from Leopold II—along with its bur-
densome legacy of abuses—but also a tradition of pro-empire
propaganda that set much of the tone for information produced
during subsequent decades. The bulk of the book then examines
five media of propaganda: expositions, museums, education in
favor of empire, monuments, and colonial cinema. The chapter on expositions explores the major Congo exhibits at Belgian
world's fairs, of which there were five between 1908 and 1960,
and then ventures further to examine smaller and much more
numerous colonial exhibits throughout the country. Similarly,
the chapter on colonial museums and their curators goes beyond
the now-infamous Congo museum in Tervuren to uncover what
other permanent collections of Africana in Belgium preserved,
represented, and displayed. These two chapters highlight how
expositions and museums were particularly powerful propaganda because they complemented each other, with museums'
permanent displays of power reinforced by expositions' temporary messages. Public education, the subject of another chapter, added force to these two powerful media at the university,

secondary, and primary school levels, in particular when the Ministry of Colonies entered the classroom to educate school-children directly. Two final chapters explore two differing ways Belgians represented the empire: in the more traditional media of stone and bronze, namely, colonial memorials in the metropole, and in the new medium of film.

Certain means of communication for information about the colony have been excluded, for various reasons. Literature is included only in cases when something was written primarily as a tool to promote the colony or imperialism, as opposed to a work of pure fiction.[10] Thus an analysis of *bandes dessinées* (comic strips), such as *Tintin au Congo*, is excluded.[11] African artwork is considered within the confines of the expositions, museums, and other sites in which Belgians displayed it. Photographs are likewise taken into account only insofar as they played a role in other media.[12] Because they rarely bore imperial imagery, Belgian postage stamps, banknotes, and coins are excluded, as are the many commemorative colonial medals that were cast, which circulated infrequently.[13] Dozens if not hundreds of streets and squares were named after colonials, but a study comparable to Robert Aldrich's essay on colonial street names in Paris would require an additional study, the conclusions of which likely only would reiterate many of those in the chapter on monuments.[14] The study does not delve into radio because examining the few transcripts available, such as those of White Father Léon Leloir's broadcasts in the 1930s, might skew the evidence, considering so many others are irretrievable.[15] The book also leaves out commercial advertising and packaging that may have promoted products from the Congo, because they were not geared toward promoting the colony as such. Although Belgium administered the League of Nations mandates Ruanda and Urundi (later UN

Trust Territories) as colonies, the Congo remained the primary focus of the kingdom's overseas imperialism; thus propaganda attempting to "sell" the Congo to the metropolitan population is the main object of inquiry.

Imperialistic Propaganda and the Nature of Belgian Empire

A more profound understanding of pro-empire expositions, museums, education, monuments, and film forces us to revise our views of the nature of Belgian imperialism in a number of ways. The examination of imperialistic propaganda that follows shows, for instance, that there was a surprising number of people cheering on the empire in the metropole and that arguably a colonial culture arose in the country as well. To say that a colonial culture developed is to assert that the Congo was more than an economic, diplomatic, or political concern of an elite. In an era of universal primary education, high literacy rates, an extended franchise, and mass entertainment, colonies overseas entered into people's everyday lives in multiple ways. Some people became aware that their livelihood or those of family members were dependent on colonial commerce. Others became conscious of the empire in multiple forms, consented to it, and in many cases actively supported it.[16]

The notion of enthusiastic imperialism in Belgium flies in the face of the literature on the Belgian Congo, which has long depicted Flemings and Walloons as indifferent to overseas empire.[17] This interpretation goes all the way back to Belgium's takeover of the Congo in the first place: when the state took control of the colony in 1908, it did so with virtually no imperialistic tradition and no groundswell of support for empire. The Kingdom of Belgium had become independent only in 1830 after centuries of being a *victim* of imperialism within Europe. Ultimately, it was the country's second monarch, Leopold II, who was responsible for the empire. He expressed early on his desire for a colony and pursued the issue with fervor as king until he finally secured an African territory through diplomacy, playing on great power rivalries.[18] That Leopold was the driving force was evident immediately; when the United States and the European powers acknowledged the Congo as a colony in 1885, called the État Indépendant du Congo (EIC), they recognized it as Leopold II's *personal* colony, which it remained for more than two decades until he ceded it to Belgium under pressure.

It seems strange that a small, neutral state with no imperialistic traditions governed an African empire for many decades after Leopold II turned it over. Traditional interpretations explain that Belgian imperialism was not a mass movement and that Walloons and Flemings were "reluctant imperialists" who arrived late and only halfheartedly to the game of European imperialism.[19] According to this view, after 1908 the colonial edifice rested on three pillars: the church, the state, and capital.[20] Church leaders supported colonialism because of the special status, privilege, and freedom of action it provided for Catholic orders like the Scheutists, Trappists, and Capuchins. Because of secularization in Europe and because the colonial administration discriminated against American, British, and Scandinavian Protestant missions, this was a particularly desirable situation. The state, dominated by the French-speaking middle classes, supported imperialism for nationalistic purposes and because it acted "as a field of exclusive power" for the francophone bourgeoisie.[21] As for the private capital in the Congo, this was one of Leopold II's prime legacies, and colonial industry and finance were closely intertwined with the state.[22] For instance, the state participated in all three large colonial concerns formed in 1906:

Union minière du Haut-Katanga (Mining Union of Upper Katanga, UMHK), the Compagnie du chemin de fer du Bas-Congo au Katanga (Railway Company of the Lower Congo in Katanga, BCK), and Société internationale forestière et minière du Congo (International Forestry and Mining Company of the Congo, Forminière). The largest banking-industrial corporation in Belgian history, Société générale, dominated all three firms; after 1908 no government wished to overthrow this system of private interest and administration.[23]

Because a semblance of altruism was useful in many ways, Belgians of all backgrounds and politics played up the notion that "on the whole, Belgians were not in the least interested in the foundation of a Belgian colony."[24] But pro-empire propaganda reveals that this attitude did not remain unchanged, and the label "reluctant imperialists" greatly underestimates the extent to which ordinary people came to understand and support the colony. Belgians not only sustained the empire in significant ways, but many became convinced imperialists, evidenced by widespread, enduring, and eagerly embraced propaganda in favor of the Congo.

Yet grassroots support for imperialism is not reflected in present-day popular culture, and the term "reluctant imperialists" has stuck. Only very recently has research into Belgian imperialism begun to chip away at the long-standing scholarly consensus that empire did not resonate at home.[25] One reason for this is because most work continues to focus on the Leopoldian era at the expense of the Belgian state-rule period. Peter Bate's 2004 film *Congo: White King, Red Rubber, Black Death* and reactions to it represent examples of the near obsession with the comparatively briefer Leopoldian period.[26] Bate's film, like Adam Hochschild's popular *King Leopold's Ghost*, mostly

retells Morel's Congo campaign against the atrocities of the Leopoldian period, relegating the half century plus of Belgian rule
to a postscript.[27] A recent article by Vincent Viaene on colonial
culture restricts itself to the period before 1905.[28] Studies on the
state-rule period generally have focused on economics, politics,
international relations, and crises at the expense of culture. Guy
Vanthemsche's excellent synthesis on Belgium and the Congo,
for instance, addresses domestic politics, international relations,
and economics from Leopoldian rule through the postcolonial
era but only occasionally delves into the empire's social and cultural ramifications.[29]

Preoccupation with the extreme violence of the Leopoldian
period has caused Belgian imperialism to be viewed as an extraordinary, almost exotic episode, because the period after
1908 — which lasted far more than twice as long as Leopold's
reign — is lazily lumped together with the specter of Leopold II's
calamitous colonial rule.[30] The press has sensationalized Belgian
colonialism by depicting it as the worst of modern European imperialisms. In a now-familiar refrain, Michela Wrong exaggerated that "no colonial master has more to apologise for, or has
proved more reluctant to acknowledge and accept its guilt, than
Belgium. On the roll-call of Africa's colonial and post-indepen-
dence abusers, it undoubtedly holds unenviable pride of place."[31]
Such hyperbole has found its way into academic discussions,
such as when Robert Edgerton wrote in *The Troubled Heart
of Africa*, among other factual errors: "Once European powers
took possession of the Congo, its people were almost perennially
hungry, and its mineral wealth enriched only politicians and foreign corporations."[32] Although foreigners did grow rich on the
country's mineral wealth, millions of Congolese simply were not
perennially hungry from 1885 to 1960. In *The New Republic*,

David Bell conflated Leopoldian and Belgian rule to discredit a Belgian law that might have targeted Israeli prime minister Ariel Sharon as a war criminal (the law was later changed). Bell characterized Belgium's rule in the Congo as "a crime of genocidal dimensions" and wrote that after Leopold II's acquisition of the Congo, "Over the next several decades, Belgium exploited its colony's riches, particularly rubber, with unparalleled ruthlessness, causing the deaths of millions of Africans forced into virtual slave labor."[33] Yet the rubber boom ended well before the 1908 reprise.[34] What is more, the atrocities committed during Belgian rule — and to an extent during Leopold's reign — were not without parallels.[35] French administration in neighboring Moyen-Congo, like the EIC, depended on concession companies, which led to horrific abuses.[36] The insurrection against U.S. rule in the Philippines after the Spanish-American War led to the deaths of more than two hundred thousand Filipinos. From 1904 to 1907 Germans in South-West Africa killed 75–80 percent of the Herero and nearly 50 percent of the Nama peoples.[37] In the British case, neglected famines in India in the eighteenth and nineteenth centuries killed millions.[38] In 1943 around three million died in Bengal when "Churchill's government rejected Viceroy Wavell's pleas for shipping to be diverted from the immediate war effort to send food aid to Bengal," thus revealing "the sham of British claims to be administering India efficiently."[39] Following this were the many tens of thousands of people killed at the 1947 partition of India and the brutal crackdown in Kenya in the 1950s, to mention just two more examples.[40]

Particularly egregious to many critics is that Belgians today supposedly know little of their colonial past, a result of what Adam Hochschild called the "Great Forgetting." According to the popular press, "the Congo is Belgium's forgotten skeleton" in the closet.[41] Critics repeatedly have attacked today's Royal Museum for Central Africa as an illustration of this forgetting, calling it a relic. It is true that between 1908 and 1960 there was a great deal of forgetting of atrocities in the EIC, and also that most colonial-era scholarship on central Africa emphasized a positive history.[42] But the assertion by Wrong and others that there has been no acknowledgement or serious investigation into the country's colonial past is belied by the record of original, archive-based scholarship over the past half century.[43] Jean Stengers began producing important original contributions even before the Congo's independence. Since 1960 the Royal Academy for Overseas Sciences has printed numerous archives-based studies, and Belgian scholarship includes major works by Jean-Luc Vellut, Daniel Vangroenweghe, and probably hundreds of master's theses on the colonial period.[44] Hochschild's work itself relied heavily on Jules Marchal's volumes based on official archival sources that he researched and wrote beginning in the 1980s. Ludo De Witte's *The Assassination of Lumumba* drew on official archives to unveil the state's complicity in Lumumba's death, provoking a parliamentary inquiry.[45] Foreign scholars working on Leopoldian or Belgian imperialism have had their works translated into Dutch and French, reaching Flemish and Walloon readers.[46]

All the same, there are few studies of imperialistic propaganda and colonial culture in Belgium, with limited examples on specific media like film, expositions, or individual events such as the 1897 Tervuren colonial exposition.[47] Although there has been growing interest in the subject, in particular from a cultural perspective, there has been no systematic examination of Belgian pro-empire messages, their producers, or what they tell us about the nature of Belgian imperialism and the country's colonial culture.[48] We also do not know much about the Belgian case because research into imperialistic culture in Europe only lately has turned to the lesser powers of Italy, Germany, Belgium, the Netherlands, Spain, and Portugal, as most major works address the French and British empires.[49]

Causes and Effects of Pro-Empire Propaganda

Aldous Huxley wrote, "Social and political propaganda . . . is effective, as a rule, only upon those whom circumstances have partly or completely convinced of its truth. . . . The propagandist is a man who canalizes an already existing stream. In a land where there is no water he digs in vain."[50] In the Belgian case, there was an unexpectedly large stream and a number of people digging. Missionary orders, private capital, and the state all promoted the colony, with the volume and staying power of government-directed propaganda suggesting that of the three the state had the greatest stake in the empire. Among the most fervent advocates of empire besides church, capital, and state were colonial veterans; what was most singular about the veterans' passion was the sacredness with which they regarded Leopold II and dead pioneers of the EIC period. Those nationals who died in Africa before 1908 became objects of cult worship, complete with their own myth and symbols, which underpinned the colonial mission. Alongside colonial veterans were numerous individual enthusiasts, curators, scientists, educators, and pro-empire groups; thus historians should add a fourth pillar to explain what propped up Belgian imperialism: key, active segments of the metropolitan population. Both the state's preeminent position among the three pillars and the population's important role in promoting empire change our understanding of why this small, neutral state with no colonial tradition took over and ran an empire for more than half a century.

Many Belgians saw propaganda as essential to defending their hold on an enormous colony. True, the colonial administration needed functionaries and settlers and naturally wanted nationals to fill those positions. But fear also underlay much of the propaganda. From the outset of Leopold II's expansion into central Africa, some feared other European powers would move into borderlands of the immense Congo and take over the colony in part or in whole.[51] The EIC, which in many respects comprised little more than armed pillage, depended heavily on foreign soldiers; the EIC's armed forces, the Force publique, recruited many if not most officers from nations with smaller militaries like Italy, Norway, Denmark, and Sweden.[52] During the colony's earliest days, most doctors there were non-Belgian, primarily Italian.[53] Even the most powerful colonial businesses could not recruit enough Belgian workers, for example UMHK, especially in its early years.[54] This apprehension heightened when new foreign challenges arose, for instance interwar German irredentism.[55] The fact that fear played such an important role in accelerating imperialistic propaganda and sentiment—thereby strengthening Belgium's resolve to hold on to the colony that largely fell into its lap by accident—shows the importance both of emotions in decision making and of the domestic origins of international relations.[56]

The heavy emphasis on propaganda directed at youth and the fear of the loss of the Congo suggest that despite the colony's retrospectively tranquil and secure appearance, to the minds of enthusiasts and administrators, colonial rule was not a fixed thing but rather an open-ended process of becoming. Some see the period of 1908 to 1960 as one of consensus and calm in central Africa, bookended in the metropole by "some sudden high temperatures, at the moment of discussions on annexation and, fifty years later, through the crises of decolonization."[57] According to this view, colonial rule was disturbed only at the end by what Jean Stengers has called the Congo's "precipitous decolonization."[58] Yet any status quo in international relations or domestic affairs—imperial or otherwise—is never static or given, but rather exists and perdures through a process of making and re-creating. In this instance, propaganda aimed to correct a perceived lack of imperialism among Flemings and Walloons to secure colonial rule.

Measuring the impact of propaganda on attitudes, beliefs, prejudices, and everyday lives is notoriously fraught with indeterminacy.[59] What can be ventured is that Belgian pro-empire propaganda had mixed results. Historians of the new imperial history contend that Britain, France, and other nations were imbricated with empire (read: infused with, overlapped by, steeped in empire), because they brought the colonies back home to the metropole in the form of government propaganda, expositions, colonial novels, and commodities. In the Belgian case, propaganda did not lead society to become totally "steeped in" or "imbricated" with empire. If one considers the shock and unpreparedness with which Belgians greeted Congo's independence, we ought to conclude that propaganda successfully conveyed the concept of an everlasting colonial presence in Africa, if not necessarily love for the Congo. Yet evidence to the contrary is more persuasive. Congolese leaders wrested their independence from Belgium without much of a fight (comparatively speaking) in 1960, less than two years after the doors closed on what was perhaps the greatest staging of empire in Belgium's history at the 1958 universal exposition. Few people living in Belgium felt deep emotional attachments to central Africa, if the small number who emigrated there and the quick handover of power

in 1960 are any indication. In important ways pro-empire propaganda — similar to such efforts in France, Britain, and elsewhere — was unsuccessful in creating gut connections to the
Congo, save among the comparatively small number who lived
there. Perhaps this was due to the fact that half of the population
was in some sense excluded: it was overwhelmingly men who
promoted the colonial idea in Belgium and exalted male figures
in the process, suggesting either a desire to maintain a privileged
zone of action or women's greater remoteness from the colonial
idea, or both.

Yet if pro-empire movies, education, museums, monuments,
and other media were biased against women and did not create a deep-seated emotional connection to the Congo, they did
develop a significant if limited colonial culture. In one respect,
pro-empire messages sustained the nation and state by propa-
gating a myth surrounding Leopold II and fostering an imagined Belgian community. Memorials and museums intersected
with more transient forms of propaganda like expositions and
movies in what Tony Bennett has called the "exhibitionary complex," whereby permanent museums and ephemeral expositions
complemented one another.[60] Various media of propaganda cut
across class and language divisions to articulate nationalistic
messages that made the Congo a project around an acclaimed
version of history that rewrote the past and made the country
out as a legitimate, humanitarian colonizer. This rewriting of
history invented an imperial tradition concentrated on Leopold
II, recasting him as a prescient, ingenious, and generous colonial
ruler. This myth had long-standing consequences for Belgians'
understanding of their past, suggesting propaganda was exceed-
ingly successful. This centering of the country's imperial past
around Leopold II was ironic in that it was the very infamy of his

horrific EIC administration that was decisive in the 1908 hand-over of the colony.

Although pro-empire propaganda did not bring about a visceral attachment to empire, it did create or reinforce a denigrating image of Africans. Although many argued for an interpenetration of colony and metropole, Belgians and Congolese did not grow close during the colonial period. Enthusiasts and the state emphasized technological benefits, European education of Congolese children, industrialism, and agricultural advancement through European methods, all the while denying the value of indigenous culture, society, and economy. They often accomplished this by comparing and contrasting Belgian civilization with African backwardness. Colonial expositions supposedly offered "a voyage to the Congo," transporting fair goers "into the bush"; in reality, they presented a distorted view of central Africa for mass consumption. Authorities were deeply concerned about the presence of Africans in Belgium and enacted a policy of control and exclusion that segregated the colony and its peoples from the metropole. Because they kept their colonial subjects away from Belgium, the ability of Congolese to contest Belgian depictions was limited.

Belgians maintained control over places in the metropole where one could access the Congo, such as the Musée du Congo Belge (Museum of the Belgian Congo). This museum was what Mary Louise Pratt has termed a "contact zone," a place where "peoples geographically and historically separated come into contact with each other and establish ongoing relations, usually involving conditions of coercion, radical inequality, and intractable conflict."[61] Belgians controlled such restricted zones of contact with their colonial subjects as a means of illustrating their control over the Congo, eulogizing Leopold II, praising the work of colonial pioneers, and justifying imperialism. The museum at Tervuren was more about power and rewriting history than displaying the colony objectively. Curators asserted their place in society by creating and dispensing supposedly scientific knowledge about the Congo, while nonscientific ends such as the popularization of imperialism motivated their work. The propagation of a feeling of control and legitimacy seems to have worked such that A. A. J. van Bilsen's 1955 proposal for the emancipation of the Congo *within thirty years* became a scandal, many considering the time frame utterly unrealistic.[62] Not only did this reaction indicate the colonizers' paternalism, it also revealed a serious aversion to losing the Congo due in part to the decades-long efforts to sell the populace on the idea that the country's so-called tenth province was integral to Belgium.

Paternalistic Belgians successfully produced a primitive Other while simultaneously defining themselves as advanced. In Timothy Mitchell's concept of "Oriental disorder," nineteenth-century British colonialism in Egypt produced an order that was "conceptual and prior," which in turn created and in fact needed the Oriental for comparison.[63] Likewise one sees how Belgian pro-empire education, expositions, museums, and other media juxtaposed European order with a supposed African chaos, suggesting that Europeans' need for an Other to create their own order persisted well into the latter half of the twentieth century. This of course does not mean they provided an accurate depiction of the colony or that Congolese remained silent. To get at what Congolese thought or how they reacted to the dominant discourse requires "reading records against their grain," as Gyan Prakash has put it, to lay bare the "marginalization of 'other' sources of knowledge and agency" inherent in the project to encapsulate the Congo in the metropole, whether that marginalization occurred consciously or not.[64] By investigating the records in this way, one can glimpse alternate discourses, successful and unsuccessful, such as how Congolese at times spoke out against depictions of themselves or called for greater participation in colonial discourses.

Nonetheless, Congolese perceptions and reactions remain secondary in this story of how metropolitan propaganda shaped perceptions of Africans and colonialism. It was at home among their compatriots, not in the colony among the Congolese, that the vast majority of Belgians learned about the empire. It is important nonetheless to avoid viewing metropole and colony as separate entities only temporarily drawn together. As Ann Laura Stoler and Frederick Cooper have argued, one can instead employ a paradigm in which nation-state and empire comprise one analytical framework.[65] Gary Wilder's rethinking of French history between the two world wars argues that that country's overseas empire was not an add-on but rather an integral component of the Third Republic and the French imperial nation-state.[66] This type of analytical reframing forces us to rethink European history fundamentally. At the same time, there is the danger that by erecting a unitary imperial framework for analytical purposes, scholars buy into the imperialistic rhetoric of empire and a fictional unity of overseas European empires that is not borne out by the historical record.[67]

In the Belgian case, a unitary imperial analytic needs to be complemented by more traditional approaches because the Congo, along with Ruanda-Urundi after 1920, was in significant ways "merely" an overseas possession of the state. The number of Belgians living in the Congo was always very small.[68] Fewer than 50 Belgians resided in the Congo in 1886 at the outset of Leopold II's imperial adventure. This population grew to 17,700 by 1930, at which point it began to decline, reaching around 11,400 by 1934.[69] Despite post–World War II economic prosperity and the government's 1949–59 ten-year plan for economic development, which boosted the number of Belgians in the Congo, there were fewer than 89,000 living there at the highest point of settlement, on the eve of independence in 1959, representing less than 1 percent of the metropolitan population.[70] The Congo is comparable in this regard to the British and French tropical colonies, or the Italian empire in eastern Africa: a 1931 census revealed only 4,188 Italians living in Eritrea four decades after Italy seized it as a colony and only 1,631 in Italian Somaliland, which had become a colony in 1905.[71] The Congo was fundamentally different than Algeria, which held around 1,000,000 colonists by 1954; Southern Rhodesia, which contained 200,000 by 1955; and even Libya, where nearly 90,000 Italians resided by 1938.[72]

Other factors kept metropole and colony profoundly separated: Belgian missionaries during the EIC period only slowly took up Leopold II's offer to proselytize; recruitment for private and government work in the colony was always problematic; long German occupations disrupted metropole-colony relations; and few Belgians ever settled in the Congo as agriculturalists.[73] As years passed, more and more *colons* (colonists) lived in cities increasingly segregated from Africans.[74] Similar to other European colonists, Belgians living in the Congo were overwhelmingly male.[75] Government rules restricted both emigration and tourism, and thus travel companies that would have benefited from the tourist trade to central Africa had to fight against heavy regulations restricting Belgians from enjoying even brief stays in the Congo, as was the case in other colonies as well.[76] In 1957, when travel to and from the colony was easiest, only ten thousand tourists made the trip, a 15 percent increase on the previous year.[77] Some have claimed that virtually every Belgian family had a friend or family member who lived in the Congo during the state-rule period.[78] But this certainly was not the case. When the European population peaked in the Congo in the late 1950s, more than a third of Belgians in the metropole indicated they did not know a single European, let alone a Belgian, who had spent any time in the colony.[79]

The fact that few Africans from the Congo ever traveled to Europe also limited Belgians' exposure to the colony. In the late nineteenth century some people brought Congolese to Belgium to educate them, but this practice quickly ceased.[80] Authorities tightly controlled Africans temporarily located in the metropole, even if a few managed to slip away and settle there permanently and even if some returning colonials brought Congolese home as servants.[81] If in England "most working- or middle-class people probably never saw a single black face socially or at their work from the beginning of their lives to the end," this was even truer in Belgium.[82] The contrast with France is striking: while a half million French colonial subjects came to Europe during World War I, perhaps no more than two dozen Congolese fought for Belgium in Europe, and some—like Paul Panda Farnana—fought only because they were temporarily in Belgium and caught off guard by the outbreak of war.[83] That visits of Congolese "*évolués*" in the 1950s were major press events—even the subject of a special film—indicates the rarity of their presence.[84] Expositions, museums, education, monuments, films, and other forms of propaganda were therefore crucial in shaping people's views.

Toward a Broader View of Colonial Culture in Europe
Although this is a comparative study in limited ways, it informs our understanding of modern Europe and the history of

imperialism by opening up the possibility for more comparative approaches toward investigating colonial cultures in Europe. Such a method is needed because even the most significant research arguing imperialism's deep influence in Europeans' everyday lives approaches the question within the confines of individual national experiences with little reference to practices and effects in other places.[85] Tony Chafer and Amanda Sackur's *Promoting the Colonial Idea* showed how the empire shaped French culture, from street names to science.[86] Pascal Blanchard and Sandrine Lemaire's *Culture coloniale* and *Culture impériale* placed the empire at the heart of the French republics.[87] Robert Aldrich's *Vestiges of the Colonial Empire in France* demonstrated the penetration of the colonies into the very fabric of France.[88] Nicola Cooper showed how French authorities legitimized the southeast Asian empire by depicting it as compensation for the loss of the first French empire and promoted the *mise en valeur* (development) of the colonies to shore up French prestige.[89] Paralleling such scholarship on France is a multitude of studies on Britain and a growing number regarding Germany and Italy.[90] Yet for all the talk of thinking or working "beyond the nation," few have escaped the nation-state paradigm to consider colonial culture in transnational perspective—that is, to consider the possibility not of French, British, Italian, or other colonial cultures but rather a *European* colonial culture. The field of European colonial propaganda and its relation to the development of knowledge about Africa is in need of a comparative examination, and a first step is to move beyond France and Britain to incorporate considerations of the lesser European empires, including the Belgian case.[91] By drawing comparisons with Belgium's neighbors, this study represents an important step in that direction. It shows that information production about the colony in

Belgium oftentimes paralleled and even imitated similar efforts in France and Britain, and vice versa. The fact that Belgians embraced official and unofficial propaganda puts the Belgian case closer to the French than to the British experience.[92] At other moments, however, Belgian pro-empire messages were distinct and reflected a unique experience. At key points, this study returns to comparisons and contrasts to add to our understanding of European imperialisms from a comparative perspective.

Extending beyond France and Britain also breaks down barriers between the two antagonistic camps of interpretation in the current debate over empire and European culture. Practitioners of the confusingly labeled "new imperial history" or "new colonial history" argue that European culture was imbricated with or steeped in empire during the New Imperialism and that overseas empire had fundamental consequences for European concepts of citizenship, race, masculinity, and femininity.[93] Some have gone so far as to consider the issue settled and to suggest that we should begin to explore what comes "after the imperial turn."[94] On the other hand, there are those like Bernard Porter who argue that overseas empire affected Europe superficially at most. Porter asserts that in the British case, "There was no widespread imperial 'mentality.' . . . Imperial culture was neither a cause nor a significant effect of imperialism."[95] Building on the literature on the French and British empires and moving beyond the limits of individual nations and their colonial experiences, as this study does in places, can close the gap between these two intractable positions in useful ways.

Examining pro-empire messages about the Congo provides novel insights into what Herman Lebovics terms "the back workings of colonialism and imperialism on the metropolitan countries," in particular because of the uniqueness of the Belgian empire.[96] Belgium did not conquer its overseas possessions, rather it inherited them. Unlike most other imperial powers in the modern era, it had no long-standing colonial tradition, and its imperialism abruptly transformed at the outset of the twentieth century with the 1908 shift from Leopold's personal rule to state administration. And Belgium and the Congo can tell us about the connection between nation and empire. The idea has gained currency among historians that the nation should not be considered static, as has the concomitant that one cannot view overseas empire as something "out there" that impacted the nation "back home." The Belgian kingdom is a recent creation rather than some sort of eternal nation. The country is divided by language (French, Flemish, and since 1920, German); a strong Flemish movement repeatedly has challenged the nation-state's viability—not only on linguistic but also social, political, economic, and ideological grounds.[97] Few historians would argue for the immutability or eternalness of the Belgian nation, and thus it offers an important contrast.[98]

Comparing and contrasting the sheer volume of pro-empire propaganda in Belgium also demonstrates that European governments did not produce propaganda only in times of crisis such as war and that it was not only dictatorial, fascist, totalitarian, or communist regimes that employed it, but also liberal democracies. This confirms Jo Fox's work on British and German film that showed how propaganda was an enduring tool even in parliamentary democracies.[99] Much of what we know about modern propaganda derives from scholarship on World War I, which has skewed our understanding of its production.[100] David Welch, for example, has written that "whereas the democracies disbanded rather shamefacedly their wartime propaganda machines, the totalitarian and fascist regimes drew different lessons from the wartime experience, having few qualms about establishing 'propaganda ministries' for disseminating ideological propaganda both at home and abroad."[101] Although the conflict's victors might have dismantled their wartime propaganda offices, they did not stop propagandizing, which in terms of promoting imperialism continued not only through World War II but up to decolonization. John MacKenzie's *Propaganda and Empire* and Thomas August's *The Selling of the Empire* initiated this line of argument some twenty years ago by showing that pro-empire propaganda did not stop after the burst of European expansion at the end of the nineteenth century but persisted well into the interwar period and even until the 1960s. The Belgian state ramped up pro-empire propaganda after being liberated from German occupation in 1918, and this pace only increased into the 1950s until the loss of the Congo in 1960. The ubiquity of propaganda efforts, official and unofficial, in France, Britain, Belgium, and elsewhere suggests that this pro-empire device was an integral and necessary component of overseas rule in the twentieth century as governments and others attempted to manufacture consent in societies of mass politics.

To sum up, this study examines imperialistic propaganda and what it tells us about the nature of Belgian imperialism as well as the causes and effects of pro-empire propaganda, all the while keeping in mind how the Belgian case informs what we know about colonial culture in Europe more generally. Although the focus is the post-1908 state-rule period, that era is largely informed by the prior reign of Leopold II—the imperial mastermind who in 1885 unbelievably secured the great powers' recognition of a colony eighty times the size of Belgium and then set about exploiting it ruthlessly. Although a master propagandist who drew on all his talents to influence public opinion and maintain his control over the Congo, Leopold II ultimately failed, because international and domestic pressure forced him to surrender his prized African possession in 1908. He died one year later, unloved. However, perhaps Leopold the propagandist surpassed even himself as imperialist. Within a few short decades of his death, he was to be celebrated and even worshipped unabashedly as a great king — as Leopold the Colonizer, the genius who almost single-handedly built an undying empire. This was only part of the flood of information produced in the twentieth century, which grew out of many of the themes set forth during the Leopoldian period, to sway the masses in favor of their new empire. Already by 1908 Leopold II and his collaborators had set the stage for what was to follow.

One

The Inheritance

Leopold II and Propaganda about the Congo

The Kingdom of Belgium, independent in 1830, saw Leopold II ascend the throne to become its second king in 1865.[1] He was an intelligent and ambitious dynast who became a colonial genius in 1885 when the European powers recognized his authority over the vast État Indépendant du Congo extending over Africa's Congo River basin. The autocratic rule he instituted in the Congo reflected his aristocratic upbringing and an atavistic mindset. Nineteenth-century change posed problems for his Old Regime Weltanschauung, to which the colony proffered multiple solutions: it allowed him to escape what he felt was a stifling political and geographical situation as the constitutionally constrained sovereign of a tiny, neutral country where liberalism was ascendant and socialism threatened and where language divided both masses and elite.[2]

His colonial policies also were rooted in older models, especially the Dutch model of the Indies, meaning that the goal was not development or "civilization" but economic exploitation to enrich and strengthen the metropole. Ultimately, his vicious abuse of the Congo and Congolese brought his rule there under increasing scrutiny and criticism by the 1890s. Despite his aristocratic background, Leopold was not averse to working with "ordinary" Belgians who supported imperialism, or to producing propaganda to sway the masses and influence public opinion in order to salvage his personal rule in the Congo. Much research so far has examined Leopold II's voluminous deceptive counterpropaganda. Yet if one takes a broader view to encompass not only disinformation but also pro-empire propaganda like cinema and individual events such as the 1897 colonial exposition, one obtains a better idea of imperialistic propaganda during the Leopoldian era as a whole and also how messages created from 1885 to 1908 served as a backdrop for the period that followed. To understand the propaganda the monarch and his collaborators produced, it is useful to begin with a survey of Leopold II's imperial venture, its supporters, and the opposition it provoked.

Imperial Reveries and Stark Realities

Leopold II ascended the throne in 1865 with a full-fledged dream of acquiring a colony. Returning from a trip to Athens in 1860, he had presented Minister Frère-Orban with a block of marble from the Acropolis inscribed, "Il faut à la Belgique une Colonie [Belgium must have a colony]." The following year, he had asked a Belgian naval officer, "Do you know of an island in Oceania, the China Sea or the Indian Ocean that would be suitable for us?"[3] His father, Leopold I, had launched small, unsuccessful colonial ventures to Central America and elsewhere, but Leopold II believed colonial expansion was crucial for his small state's well-being. During his first decade in power, he explored many potential—and potentially profitable—colonial acquisitions, including a plan to lease the Philippines from Spain, all the while working within a mental framework shaped in part by the country's geographical movement and its emphasis on economic geography.[4]

Yet Leopold II's colonial future lay in central Africa, a region to which he turned only after 1875; his ability to eventually secure a massive colony there reflected shrewd, determined, and secretive diplomatic maneuvers. In 1876 he convened a geographical conference in Brussels at which he assumed the leadership of the newly formed Association internationale africaine (International African Association, AIA) to promote Belgian involvement in central Africa while disingenuously pleading altruistic motives to the delegates: "Do I have the need to say that in convening you in Brussels, I have not been guided by any egoistic views? No, Sirs, if Belgium is small, she is happy and satisfied with her sort; I have no other ambition other than to serve her well."[5] By 1878 he persuaded other powers to join him in financing a Comité d'études du Haut-Congo (Committee for Study of the Upper Congo), of which he covertly took control by 1882 and recast as the ostensibly international and neutral Association internationale du Congo (AIC). Using the AIC, Leopold funded explorers to central Africa who persuaded African leaders to sign treaties assigning political control to the association. Through a series of bilateral treaties at the time of the Berlin Conference (1884–85), the United States, Germany, Britain, and other powers (excluding the Ottoman Empire) recognized the AIC as an independent, neutral, and free-trade state under Leopold's control called the État Indépendant du Congo.[6] With the Congo as his own territory, Leopold became both king of Belgium and roi-souverain (king-sovereign) of the EIC, even though the two states were unlinked in any way save a shared sovereign.

Recognition was one thing; effective occupation and exploitation, another. Leopold II's desire to control the Congo, profit from it, and expand its borders conflicted with expansionist European powers as well as local interests, including those of the so-called Arabs trading inland from Africa's eastern coasts. The result was a repressive, martial, abusive regime.[7] Initially the EIC comprised a costly military operation carried out by administrators and explorers alongside the Force publique, made up of European officers and African soldiers. For Leopold, the high costs of exploration, occupation, and economic exploitation were exacerbated by low levels of exports and an absence of import duties, as required by treaty. When this system quickly drained the monarch's considerable personal fortune, he declared EIC monopolies on all raw materials, confiscated all "vacant" lands in the Congo, granted huge concessions to European companies, prohibited Africans from selling goods such as elephant tusks to private traders, began to extract ivory and natural rubber, and taxed exports. The economic policy of the EIC became the extraction of maximum amounts of raw materials at the lowest possible cost, leading to the savage exploitation of human, animal, and plant life in the Congo. Concessionary companies operating outside any legal structure and staffed in many cases by "men who had already shown their instability and lack of principles in Europe" forced Africans to collect wild rubber and other products, using brutal tactics that included summary execution, kidnapping, mutilation, torture, whipping, and the burning of villages.[8]

News of abuses that reached Europe and the United States sparked attacks on Leopold II and his administration, such as Mark Twain's *King Leopold's Soliloquy*. In Britain, E. D. Morel founded the Congo Reform Campaign in 1904, arguing that because the international community had recognized Leopold's African rule, that same community ultimately was responsible for what went on there. Morel's tireless efforts bore fruit: opposition grew first in Britain, then the United States and other countries, and finally in Belgium. The Socialist Party, which

came into being the same year as the EIC (1885), produced innumerable propaganda brochures with titles like *La politique
coloniale: Caoutchouc et mains coupés*, denouncing king, colonialism, and capital.[9] By the first years of the twentieth century,
Leopold faced the real threat of losing the Congo.

Leopold, who had proven his ability to dissemble and sway
diplomats' minds in the period leading up to 1885, now conducted a campaign to win over foreign and domestic opinion
as Morel and others sustained their attacks against him. In his
effort to control news and project a particular image, the king
benefited from the fact that information from the Congo was
hard to come by. Travel to and communications with central Africa were difficult; Europeans seldom went there; and few Congolese traveled to Belgium. The gulf that separated Belgium from
the Congo reveals an important metropole-colony dichotomy
reflected in much writing about the Belgian Congo and modern
European imperialism in general. Historians investigating the
"imperial turn" in the history of modern European imperialism
have lately criticized "older models of empire" and "the per-
sistence of 'home' and 'empire' as segregated domains and of
imperialism as a force with directional vectors rather than as a
spatialized terrain of power."[10] Leopold's campaign of propaganda and the Belgian case suggest that older models of empire
are still relevant. The EIC propaganda campaign was a clear case
where a sovereign introduced ideas from a segregated domain
(the Congo) into another (Belgium) in order to persuade people
to his point of view. The EIC administration literally separated
the Congo from Belgium—and vice versa—in important ways,
such as restricting African travel to Belgium. Although a number
of Belgians brought Congolese to Belgium to educate them, this
practice effectively ended by 1897. Thereafter, with exceptions

only running into the low hundreds, no Congolese came to Belgium before 1960 except for those Belgian authorities allowed to travel to Belgium for a limited time.[11] The production of propaganda in Belgium from 1885 to 1908 counters the idea that metropole and colony were not segregated domains. This is not to suggest that considering colony and metropole within one analytic field is not a valuable approach; to the contrary. Rather this is to argue that as studies of imperialism progress, they should be open to a variety of approaches in exploring imperialism generally and colonial culture, new and old.

Belgium, Meet Congo

Leopold's propaganda took several forms. The EIC administration in Brussels placed leaflets into train compartments across Europe, formed the front organization Fédération pour la défense des intérêts belges à l'étranger (Federation for the Defense of Belgian Interests Overseas) to refute antagonists, and created a secret press bureau to influence opinion in Belgium and abroad. The EIC published *La vérité sur le Congo* to put forth its viewpoint; not dissimilar to contemporaneous practice elsewhere in Europe, it also fed information and funds to journalists to shape public opinion.[12] In anticipation of the release of his own commission of inquiry report, Leopold supplied the British press with a summary more favorable to his administration put out by the West African Missionary Association, a group of Irishmen allegedly living in Brussels.[13] Even when Leopold II used funds from the Congo to add to his legacy as Roi-Bâtisseur (King-Builder) by completing Brussels's long-unfinished monument Arcade du Cinquantenaire in 1905, he did so with front men so as to not draw attention to himself or his Congo profits.[14]

Individuals and groups in Belgium came to the defense of

imperialism in central Africa, whether in concert with Leopold or not; by doing so they too helped introduce Belgium to the Congo.[15] Many of these were members of the so-called colonial lobby, which was not so much an organized association as it was an informal group favoring Leopold's Africa venture and its eventual takeover by Belgium. Alphonse Jules Wauters, publisher of *Mouvement Géographique*—unofficial journal of the EIC—was an early promoter, both through works he authored and the journal he edited. The goal of the journal at the time was "not only to reach the professor, the officer, the tourist, but . . . also . . . to interest youth of our schools and our universities in geography. . . . It will seek to penetrate into the lives of families."[16] Charles Lemaire—a Congo pioneer, faithful Leopold ally, and future director of Belgium's Colonial University—helped found the Société d'études coloniales (Society of Colonial Studies) in 1894 in Brussels, which along with subsidiary groups in Ghent, Liège, and elsewhere, promoted the Congo through conferences. Already by 1895 the Société d'études coloniales had around three thousand members.[17] Another enthusiast, André-Charles-Napoléon Van Iseghem, is representative in a number of ways of early zealots who were converted to the imperialist cause. Born in Ghent, Van Iseghem was educated as a lawyer and became involved early on in Belgium's nascent colonial lobby. His first trip to the Congo in 1896 made him a pioneer of tourism there and formed the basis of his book *Au Congo belge en 1896*. He studied the best means by which Belgium could assume control of the Congo and participated in the lively social life surrounding departures for and returns from Africa, including numerous banquets that confirm Roger Shattuck's labeling of the era as the "Banquet Years."[18] Van Iseghem returned to central Africa before the outbreak of war in 1914 and, already in his forties, served a number of roles in the then-Belgian colony, including district commissioner, before retiring from active service in 1921 at the age of fifty-five.[19]

During the 1890s Van Iseghem worked closely with Albert Thys, who was one of the foremost promoters of imperialism in central Africa and one of many among the procolonialists who favored the empire but not the emperor. Born the son of a country doctor in Dalhem in 1849, Thys graduated from the École royale militaire (Royal Military Academy) and École de guerre (Military College) and undertook a career as an army officer. At the age of twenty-seven he joined the military household of Leopold II, and soon thereafter he became secretary for colonial affairs in the king's cabinet. He played a key role in the construction of the first Congo railway linking Matadi to Stanley Pool and either founded or was a central figure in a number of major colonial enterprises including the Compagnie du Congo pour le commerce et l'industrie (Company of the Congo for Commerce and Industry), the Compagnie du Katanga (Company of Katanga), and the Banque d'outremer (Overseas Bank).[20] He fell out with his king in the early 1890s over the latter's Congo policies and resigned his EIC post, remaining a believer—with a vested financial stake—in the importance of the colony to Belgium's future. He tirelessly promoted the Congo to the point that by 1897 he already had given 355 talks or conferences to stimulate Belgian interest on the issue.[21] Many others joined Wauters, Thys, and Van Iseghem to promote imperialism in Africa, men such as Georges Hennebert, who gave around eighty speeches in 1907–8 alone to promote Belgium's annexation of the Congo.[22]

Leopold, his allies, and anti-EIC imperialist enthusiasts also showed off the colony in the metropole to interest Belgians in empire. Although historians have had a difficult time piecing together Leopold II's objectives, in part because he burned many of his papers, it is clear he intended from the outset to turn the colony over to Belgium.[23] The fact that pro-empire displays, and not just counterpropaganda directed at Morel and others, began in Belgium during the EIC period refutes those who have argued that the king was involved in the Congo solely for personal gain. Leopold II's prodigious efforts to interest his European subjects in the Congo indicate his intention to leave the Congo to his heir and the Belgian state.

One of the main methods used to promote the empire was expositions of the colony in the metropole, of which there were dozens in the years after 1885. Capitalizing on its location and extensive railway system, Belgium was among the most prodigious hosts of *expositions universelles* or *wereldtentoonstellingen* (world's fairs) during the modern period inaugurated by the 1851 London Crystal Palace Exposition; the Congo almost always figured prominently at these exhibitions.[24] What was to become a long tradition of exhibiting Africa and Africans in Belgium began with a modest Congo pavilion at the first Belgian-hosted universal exposition, in 1885 in Antwerp. Supporters of Leopold II's enterprise built a pavilion to introduce Belgians to colonial opportunities, even if the EIC did not contribute toward its creation.[25] Instead the Royal Geographical Society of Antwerp and its president Henri Wauwermans — a Leopold loyalist — created the Congo section, comprised of three parts: one on exports; one on potential imports, especially crops; and one on ethnography.[26] The section on ethnography included Chief Masala of Vivi and twelve other Congolese on display in a *"negerdorp"* (negro village) or *"village congolais"* (Congolese village), posing for photographs for the fifteen thousand visitors that made their way through each day.[27] This and subsequent displays of Africa and Africans in Belgium built on a long history of European spectacles of so-called exotic peoples from Africa or the Americas dating back to the fifteenth century. By the late 1800s, Europeans were putting Africans on tour, displaying them at expositions universelles, and placing them into what were essentially human zoos.[28] And Europeans were not alone in this. The organizing committee for the 1893 Chicago World's Fair tried to bring in pygmies from the Congo; only when a recruiter died in Africa did they settle for belly dancers and Buffalo Bill's Wild West show.[29] Organizers of the 1904 St. Louis World's Fair repeated the effort with greater success, obtaining Ota Benga, a pygmy from the EIC who afterward ended up in the monkey house of the Bronx Zoo.[30] As one world's fairs scholar put it, "Virtually every Western nation with overseas territories, however slight they might be, participated in imperial sections of exhibitions; even the Americans by the end of the [nineteenth] century lauded the idea of empire at World's Fairs, mimicking their European forebears with grim effectiveness."[31] Even non-imperialistic states such as Switzerland put Africans on display for metropolitan audiences, showing how this had become an almost universal practice in western Europe and the United States by the turn of the century.[32]

The 1894 Wereldtentoonstelling, also in Antwerp, introduced themes that were to mark procolonial propaganda in Belgium for decades to come. The 1894 event promoted empire, colonial commerce, and Leopold's rule by way of a "remarkable" pavilion to which organizers gave a touch of authenticity by having it guarded by African soldiers.[33] In addition to ivory sculpture; displays of imports and exports like rubber, copal, and cotton; as well as a diorama of railroads and caravan routes, the Belgian missionary group Mouvement antiesclavagiste (founded 1888) exhibited materials on the fight against the Arab slave trade in the Congo, including antislavery publications and dreadful slaving instruments such as "*la cangue*, pitchforks, chains, iron collars, wrist and ankle shackles." The Mouvement antiesclavagiste also showed captured Arab booty and portraits of Belgian heroes from the battles against slavery.[34] Another Congolese village in 1894 housed a number of Force publique soldiers and an ethnically heterogeneous group of 144 Congolese—"a sample of the largest number possible of peoples"—along with mules, cows, and pigs, as well as building materials from the Congo.[35] In the village, the Congolese could be seen "attending to their normal occupations" and were measured and photographed for science.[36] Colonial enthusiasts judged the displays a great success.[37] The fair emphasized the successful campaigns against Arab slave traders as an artful defense of Leopoldian actions in the Congo, a defense often repeated in the following decades to justify Belgian rule; this was artful because Leopold's colonial state initially sought accommodation with the Arabs—including Tippu Tip—and only entered into battle with them when they rebelled against European encroachments in central Africa. In 1894 one could also already detect pride in Leopold II and Belgian sacrifice as well as mindfulness of the envy of great powers: according to *Le Mouvement Antiesclavagiste*, other European powers were "jealous of the success of the Belgians in the Congo," whose accomplishments provoked other states "to invade all the rest of the African continent."[38] This stress on others' jealousy was to be a recurrent theme in succeeding decades, alongside effusive praise for Leopold II, for colonial pioneers, and for the so-called antislavery campaigns.

Three years after the Antwerp fair closed, a colonial exposition held in conjunction with the 1897 Exposition Internationale de Bruxelles took exhibiting of the Congo to a whole new level. In order to draw particular attention to his EIC, in 1897 Leopold had the colonial exhibits created apart from the World's Fair grounds, at a special site just outside the capital on royal domains in Tervuren. The main site for the inanimate exhibits in Tervuren was the Palais des Colonies, which visitors entered through a Salon d'Honneur filled with European-created chryselephantine sculptures that "functioned as both a promotional tool advertising the material riches to be gained from the imperial project, and as a naturalising mechanism employed in order to help efface the controversial nature of King Leopold II's Congo enterprise."[39] Visitors then passed through rooms dedicated to ethnography, imports, transportation, and exports, especially coffee, cocoa, and tobacco. An underground tunnel connecting different wings of the building displayed an assortment of Congolese fish in enormous tanks filled with formaldehyde.[40]

The most special attraction was located outside the Palais des Colonies on the surrounding grounds: more than 250 Congolese in several *"villages nègres"* (negro villages) as well as a *"village civilisé"* (civilized village) that was distinguished from the former by housing "civilized" Congolese.[41] These villages helped draw at least 1,200,000 visitors to Tervuren, not all of whom were civilized. Because some people were inclined to give the Africans food to eat, exhibition organizers erected a sign that read, "Do not feed the blacks. They are already being fed."[42] Seven Congolese died as a result of poor housing and living conditions, although the deaths of individuals brought to Europe for ethnographic exhibits were not unusual at the time.[43] One visitor complained, "Even though in general these natives seem neither too repulsive nor too frightful, they are there, parked as animals are in contests, flesh to white onlookers whose curiosity is not itself devoid of a certain ferocity."[44] Still, one can point to a report from the colony about how one returning Congolese had nothing but positive things to say about his experience, even if one should question the reliability of such a report from an African to a colonial official.[45]

The 1897 Tervuren fair saw the birth of another means of propaganda, namely, procolonial cinema. Supporters of empire in Belgium, like those elsewhere in Europe, recognized early on motion pictures' ability to stir people's interest in overseas territories.[46] Unlike efforts to counter Morel's Congo reform movement, which were instigated by Leopold II and his EIC administration, it was private investors and colonial enthusiasts who drove the initial foray into colonial cinema; in fact, EIC headquarters in Brussels never sent a single official film crew to the Congo to make motion pictures.[47] At the Tervuren colonial expo, visitors could stop at the Zoographe film pavilion that was the work of Optique belge, a group organized and financed by Albert Thys and others within the emerging colonial lobby.[48] One publication reported, "The animated views that will march past there [in the Zoographe] represent picturesque scenes of the black continent and are the indispensable compliment to a visit to the natives camped in the pretty villages of the lake."[49] In the end, despite reference to the "black continent," the Zoographe only showed films made in Europe because the crew sent to the Congo had not produced any useable film, and therefore Optique belge had to purchase motion pictures to show.[50] The projected films included shorts that director Alexandre actually filmed at the 1897 colonial fair itself, such as *L'arrivée d'un train à Tervueren* and *Les Congolais à Tervueren*.[51] On the whole, however, Optique belge was not profitable, leading investors to scrap it as early as February 1898.[52] Yet the Zoographe did show

that people would pay to see colonial films and that procolonialists thinking in the long term "wished to use the *cinématographe*
as a medium, in other words as an instrument of propaganda for
the Belgian colonial 'cause.'"[53]

The origins of another venue of imperialistic propaganda, the
Musée du Congo Belge, also date back to the Leopoldian period; like cinema, the museum got its start in conjunction with
expositions.[54] The EIC bestowed the very first significant ethnographic collection in Belgium's history to the Brussels Museum
of Natural History around 1885–86, and colonial officials as-
sembled the first major collection of Africana from the Congo
for the 1894 Antwerp World's Fair.[55] Yet similar to cinema, it
was the 1897 exposition that truly catalyzed the establishment
of a permanent museum. Leopold II did not plan the museum
to be a tool to rebut negative propaganda about the EIC regime,
as some have asserted.[56] Rather, he wanted to drum up support
for empire through a museum that would develop the colonial
sciences as well as provide a permanent window onto Africa.[57]
The Palais des Colonies, built for the 1897 exposition, reopened
to the public the following year as the Musée du Congo under
director Théodore Masui, who had been in charge of the 1897
temporary display and who would serve as director until succeeded by Emile Coart in 1899.[58] As collections grew under Coart's directorship, which lasted until 1910, Leopold II decided
to build a larger museum, also in Tervuren. Begun in 1904 and
finished by 1909, the Ministry of Colonies inaugurated the new
building in 1910 as part of the Exposition Universelle et Internationale de Bruxelles 1910.[59] Just as the Musée des colonies et
de la France extérieure (Museum of the Colonies and Exterior
France) in Vincennes emanated from the 1931 Exposition Coloniale Internationale de Paris, and the Field Museum of History

from the 1893 Chicago World's Fair, so too did the Musée du
Congo Belge arise from an *exposition internationale* (international exhibition).

Already by the new colonial museum's inauguration, the
country had hosted yet another world's fair. The 1905 Exposition Universelle et Internationale de Liège attracted seven million visitors to its 175-acre fairgrounds, making it the second
most visited universal exposition in European history to that
date.[60] The EIC participation in 1905 was comparatively minor
with a "discrete" Congo pavilion on an island in the river Meuse
that was built to look like the colonial governor's residence in
Boma and with displays including ivory sculptures, ethnographic objects, and an enormous (more than 262 square feet) color
relief map of the EIC.[61] Even though the colonial pavilion won a
number of awards, it does not seem to have elicited a great deal
of interest among fairgoers, perhaps due to a lack of African subjects on hand.[62] In one sense it is surprising that the 1905 exhibit
was so small and that Leopold II did not capitalize on the fair
to influence visitors and counter negative publicity surrounding
atrocities in the Congo. The colonial display in 1897 had proved
that he and his supporters were capable of putting on a huge
show, and by 1905 revenues from the Congo were flowing.[63] Yet
the EIC administration also was under increasing pressure. Leopold II could no longer play the British and the French off each
other after their 1904 Entente Cordiale, and opposition to his
rule had been mounting in Britain since E. D. Morel had formed
the Congo Reform Association in 1904. In fact, "Leopold feared
that the British might succeed in persuading the other powers to
intervene in the Congo."[64] At the same time as the fair, readers in
Britain were digging into Roger Casement's report on the Congo
atrocities, opposition had begun to mount at home, Leopold's

own commission of inquiry into abuses was on the ground in Africa investigating allegations, and many of the king's erstwhile collaborators had defected.[65] All this being said, when Leopold II fought back against his opponents, as seen earlier, he elected subtler approaches and employed clandestine propaganda. Thus, the uninspiring showing in 1905 might be attributed to a desire not to stir the pot. Covert press operations, not public exhibits, were Leopold's preferred method of counterpropaganda, and it would be a mistake to conclude that the main motivation behind colonial exhibits in Belgium during the EIC period was a desire to refute negative publicity.[66]

Early Imperialistic Propaganda: An Assessment

The period 1885 to 1908 saw the production of a surprising amount and variety of propaganda designed not only to rebut negative publicity surrounding the EIC regime but also to sway Belgian public opinion; on the whole it had limited success. The EIC administration covertly influenced public opinion through sham organizations and by plying journalists with cash. Leopold himself stashed money away to hide the extent of his Congo profits. Colonial zealots alongside the EIC used expositions, film, and a museum to drum up support for imperialism in central Africa.[67] By contrast, there were few commemorative plaques, monuments, or statues erected during the period that the Congo was Leopold's personal property. Only around ten Belgian monuments to imperialism in any form were built before 1908, and the construction of colonial monuments after 1908 was large scale in comparison. The EIC also made virtually no effort to influence children by means of formal education, and colonial education was nascent at best. Although there was no colonial fiction to speak of before 1908, all the efforts of Leopold and the colonial lobby had resulted in numerous publications, to the point that by the end of the nineteenth century, circulation of major imperialistic publications on the Congo and other colonies had reached perhaps as high as forty thousand.[68]

During this period, Belgian Catholic missionary groups engaged in little overt propagandizing—unsurprising considering that Belgian missionary activity in central Africa had only just begun by the first decade of the twentieth century.[69] French cardinal Lavigerie's White Fathers, founded in 1868, had taken the lead in missionary work in what was to become the EIC, followed by the French Holy Ghost Fathers and Protestant missions from Britain, such as the Baptist Missionary Society; the United States' American Baptists and American Presbyterians; and Scandinavia. To heighten his control, Leopold II endeavored to exclude foreign missionaries and promote Belgian missionary work. But because of their unwillingness, the king had to lean on Belgian Catholic missionaries to become active in the Congo. The Scheut fathers—founded in Brussels in 1862 by Théophile Verbist, before Lavigerie established the White Fathers—were active in other areas of the world like Mongolia and China, but not in central Africa. Not until the king put direct pressure on the Scheutists did they take up work there in 1888. They were joined later by Trappists, Belgian Franciscans and Capuchins, the Sœurs de la charité de Gand, and others. The Scheutists publicized their new activities in *Missions en Chine et au Congo*, a journal designed to raise both awareness and funds. As these groups slowly gained a presence in the Congo, the number of their publications aimed at metropolitan audiences also increased.[70]

Although much information designed to influence people was produced after 1885, it is difficult to gauge what effects it had on public opinion. From Leopold's position, these initiatives were unsuccessful because international and domestic pressure finally compelled him to transfer authority of his African territory to the Belgian state in 1908 against his will and timetable in what became known as the reprise, after which the EIC became the Belgian Congo. Leopold and his successors maintained important powers in the Congo, but it became a colony of the Kingdom of Belgium. The failure of Leopold's efforts suggests the limited effectiveness of direct propaganda; even the anticolonial Belgian Workers' Party's acceptance of the reprise was due less to propaganda than to beliefs that the takeover would be cost free, or that it would be the best way to correct abuses there, or that giving it up would hurt domestic industry.[71] At the same time, whereas interest in the Congo in 1876 was nil, it had increased tremendously by 1908. "Between 1876 and 1878, as Catholic ultramontanes and anticlericals came to blows on the street, few Belgians paid attention to the Geographical Conference in Brussels. . . . Thirty years later . . . the Congo could cause the demise of two cabinets and become the central theme of a national electoral contest. During the intervening decades, the resonance of imperialism in Belgian public life had grown apace with the colonial 'party.'"[72] Propaganda in all forms did introduce themes that recurred after 1908. Organizers intended the exhibits not only to inform but also to persuade, and they promoted not only trade and other possibilities but also the idea that Leopold's rule was beneficial for Africa and Africans. Exhibit brochures extolled the king's "wonderful" effort to civilize central Africa, expositions stressed missionaries' freedom of action there and their role in educating African children, and exhibits and accompanying publications in Belgium and overseas emphasized the importance of the Congo to Belgium's future.[73]

The Belgian state faced major challenges when it assumed control of the Congo, and propaganda aimed at strengthening colonial rule emanated from a variety of sources. Belgians inherited the fear that the great powers might try to seize or divide up the Congo, a suspicion exacerbated by the fact that the EIC had been heavily dependent on foreign workers, officers, and administrators. The colonial administration perceived the lack of Belgians in the colony in 1908 as a problem and sought nationals to fill positions in the colonial administration and economy; that popular interest in the overseas empire remained low only worsened the situation. Other challenges included a legacy of abuses and exploitation; doubts as to the efficacy of reforms; and massive and virtually autonomous colonial corporations, such as UMHK, BCK, and Forminière, which Leopold II had created to protect his control and in which the state had large financial stakes. Between 1908 and 1960, the state and private capital, now along with the Catholic Church, were to form the three main pillars of support of Belgian imperialism in Africa. These three pillars, and other groups and individuals, produced propaganda on a wide scale to increase support for the imperial project and legitimize Belgian rule. One of the means of propaganda was imperial displays at Belgium's world's fairs and local exhibits of empire after 1908, continuing a practice begun during the EIC period; it is to those displays that the book now turns.

Two

Denying African History to Build the Belgian Nation

Imperial Expositions

In some ways expositions of the Congo in Belgium changed little over the several decades of Belgian involvement in central Africa. In 1897 King Leopold II organized a huge display of empire in the village of Tervuren, just outside Brussels, in conjunction with the World's Fair that year. At the time, revenues were flowing in from the EIC, and the king had not yet been vilified for his brutal imperial administration. Yet the barbarity of Leopold's African enterprise already was evident at Tervuren, where organizers placed Africans behind fences in faux villages and then, because people threw food at them, posted warnings that they should not be fed. As noted earlier, seven Congolese died, and still today one can visit their tombs outside the church in Tervuren's market square.[1] When six decades later Brussels hosted the 1958 World's Fair, organizers again placed a group of Congolese behind fences in a so-called village for observation as they went about their daily affairs. Once again visitors tossed food at those people, and some asked if they could see the color of the palms of their hands or take a look at their teeth. Although the treatment of Africans had not changed much, the depiction of Leopold II had. Whereas in 1897 Leopold II was a somewhat unpopular monarch on the cusp of becoming much maligned, the 1958 event hailed him as an ingenious hero, summed up by a bust of him at the entrance to the main Congo pavilion that praised him by means of its caption, attributed to him: "I undertook the work of the Congo in the interest of civilization."[2]

The full range of Belgian colonial expositions in the metropole, how they changed over time, the motivations behind them, who instigated them, and their depictions of the colony offer fertile ground for historical analysis. The Ministry of Colonies, private businesses, the church, and procolonial interest groups repeatedly promoted the Congo at expositions in Belgium after 1908. There was no Belgian parallel to the 1931 Exposition Coloniale Internationale in Vincennes, which was wholly dedicated to overseas empires, or to Britain's 1924–25 Wembley Exhibit. What Belgians did do was exhibit the Congo as part of world's fairs, of which they hosted five between 1908 and 1960, and at smaller exhibits throughout Belgium, many of which were put together by the government's colonial propaganda office or local colonial interest groups.

Examining colonial expositions necessarily entails asking whether they affected their target audience, namely, the public at large, and thus whether they are a useful object of study for gauging popular culture and imperialism's impact on Europe. Expositions were huge affairs attracting vast audiences, and some scholars believe grand colonial displays such as the 1931 Paris Colonial Exposition represented the apogee of metropolitan interest in empire and linked colonizer and colonies. Nicola Cooper concludes, "Most commentators agree that the 1931 Colonial Exhibition marked the apogee of France's colonial Empire. . . . For the duration of the exhibition at least, [it was] the primary focus of the metropolitan media and imagination."[3] Others take issue with this interpretation, including Charles-Robert Ageron, who asserted that "the peak of the colonial idea in France is situated not at all in 1931 (or 1939) but well after the Second World

War and the influence of the 'apotheosis of Vincennes' could not be taken as decisive."[4] Herman Lebovics believes moments such as the 1931 fair "might better be understood as triumphs of the will of their organizers to believe their own fables than as plebiscites measuring popular sentiment."[5] In the British case, Bernard Porter argues that imperial exhibitions were appealing not because of their ideological messages but because they were fun, quoting one worker who said, "The majority of visitors were more interested in the lighter side, which was extensive and hilarious." In other words, imperial exhibitions were "an excuse to dress up, go out, and have fun." While Porter believes that events like the Wembley exhibition may have had significant impacts on imperialist zealots, most people placed little importance on empire and took away little from such events.[6] The mixed effects in the Belgian instance offers an important comparative case study.

Whether effective or not, the Belgian state and devotees of empire enthusiastically exhibited the colony in deliberate ways to popularize the empire, particularly among youth, signaling both a continuity with the Leopoldian period and an eagerness for empire not normally attributed to Belgians. Repeated presentations of the empire for mass audiences reveal a striking similarity of practice with other European empires and demonstrate that comparatively unknown Belgian exhibits merit greater inclusion in the literature on European expositions of colonized peoples and places.[7] As will be seen, initial colonial displays in 1910 and 1913 distanced the Belgian administration from Leopoldian rule, whereas those of the interwar and postwar years glorified Leopold II and taught a history affiliating contemporaneous Belgian colonial rule with the EIC. Adam Hochschild writes of a "Great Forgetting" in Belgium; that is how Belgians discounted the violence of Leopold II's rule in the Congo and re-created themselves as benevolent and righteous rulers in central Africa.[8] This was not by chance, but due at least in part to a deliberate effort by the Ministry of Colonies and others.

Architectural, human, and other representations of the colony at expositions also reveal a Belgian practice of Orientalism. In terms of architecture and the Other, Zeynep Çelik has demonstrated the importance of architecture at nineteenth-century world's fairs and showed the exchanges between Islam and the West that refuted the "'silent' and 'frozen' status given to Islam in Western discourse."[9] Belgian expositions confirm Çelik's emphasis on such architecture but show that in the case of the Congo, Belgian discourse at world's fairs did keep Africans' status largely silent and frozen right up to the end of the colonial period. Uncontested before-and-after depictions contrasted Congolese disorder and backwardness with Belgian order and development, and denied the value of indigenous culture while exalting European civilization, right into the era of decolonization. Since Edward Said's *Orientalism* appeared, many scholars have chipped away at the extent of Western power inherent to Said's argument by unveiling or discovering the viewpoint of the subaltern and by privileging the study of cultural representations over analyses of the naked exercise of power. Belgian expositions reveal limits of the Other's ability to contest European depictions. They also reveal certain drawbacks if one investigates culture at the expense of consideration of literal power relations. Said's assertion that a paternalistic Europe produced a backward "Other" while simultaneously defining itself as advanced retains a good deal of its explanatory power.[10]

Wereldtentoonstellingen and Expositions Universelles

There was essentially no interruption of efforts to popularize the empire and persuade Belgians of the value of the colonial project after Leopold died in 1909.[11] The Exposition Universelle et Internationale de Bruxelles 1910 was the first Belgian world's fair after the turnover of the EIC to the state in 1908, and it marked the first display of the *Belgian* Congo at such an event. There appears to not have been any doubt as to whether to exhibit the Congo once again, signaling that Belgium was determined to put its overseas possessions on display in the metropole just as other European imperial powers did. Coming so soon after the 1897 and 1905 fairs, the 1910 event established Belgium as a major exhibiting power, yet contemporaneous fairs around the world diminished its impact. Some doubted the exposition's attractiveness and novelty, such as the *New York Times*, which asked, "How is it possible for Belgian industry and art to have improved materially since the last world's fair in King Leopold's realm, held at Liege in 1905?"[12]

Organizers of the 1910 event used the fair to promote a particular vision of Belgian imperialism, even if its effects were limited and its colonial displays were bland. Some wished that the 1910 World's Fair would have been reflective both of the country's new civilizing mission and the great Leopoldian legacy.[13] Yet Belgium's colonial displays were lackluster, or as the press secretary for the colonial section later put it, "rather modest."[14] This was especially true in comparison to the French colonial displays on the main fairgrounds, which included pavilions for Algeria, Indochina, Madagascar, Tunisia, and West Africa, as well as a Senegalese village with men, women, and children on site.[15] Belgian organizers, all of whom were men, opted to carry over the schema from Leopold II's 1897 Tervuren exhibit by creating a colonial section apart from the exposition's main site called the Section Coloniale, Parc de Tervueren, located at the new Musée du Congo Belge.[16] The museum put together most of the colonial displays, including forty-five thousand ethnographic objects, probably because the colonial section had to make do with "poor [*faible*] resources" and did not have access to funds available for exhibits on the main grounds in Brussels.[17] Larger colonial firms such as Compagnie du Kasai and UMHK dominated the section, although Catholic missions also had their own exhibits. The Ministry of Colonies provided informational brochures and a stand with statistics and monographs regarding animals, minerals, and other natural resources—"generally dry documentation" as one person close to the organization of the section put it.[18]

Different in 1910 was the lack of Africans on display resulting from the Ministry of Colonies' worries about a repeat of the difficulties of 1897 when seven Congolese deaths caused a scandal.[19] One publication recognized that even if any decent exposition had to have, "in addition to an old quarter [*quartier ancien*], an exotic village," there were in 1910 "moral difficulties [*difficultés morales*]" following the experience of 1897.[20] Thus the 1910 Section Coloniale largely comprised displays in the Musée du Congo Belge and in the old museum building from 1897, the Palais Colonial, with a few others across the Leuvensesteenweg at a Pavillon du Matériel Colonial.[21]

Despite its mediocrity, the fair promoted the Congo while distancing the colony from its EIC forebear. Speaking at its opening, Minister of Colonies Jules Renkin recognized past mistakes while stressing a reformed and improved colonial administration, in effect distinguishing himself from his EIC predecessors. King Albert, successor to his uncle Leopold II, struck a similar note that signaled a recognition of past errors and a newfound responsibility for the African empire's future.[22] This is not to say that the 1910 colonial section disavowed the Leopoldian legacy.

The entrance to the displays was marked by a quote from Leopold II in bronze letters highlighting his civilizing mission; already in 1910, museum staff had placed an ivory bust of Leopold II in the new museum building's prestigious Salle du Dôme.[23] But all the same, the new administration clearly set Belgian rule off from the worst excesses of the EIC regime.

The world's last universal exposition before the outbreak of World War I, the Exposition Universelle et Internationale de Gand 1913, represented both a continuation and a break with Belgium's earlier colonial exhibits at such events. Coming so soon after the 1910 exposition, the 1913 fair confirmed Belgium as a major world's fair host. The event's main goal was advancing Belgian industry and commerce, just as other nation-states promoted themselves when holding such events. It was only after World War II that fair organizers promoted the idea of Belgium as a center for Europe by means of a universal exposition, and in 1913 the drive for European unity was a long way off.

Belgian, French, and British displays dominated the Ghent fair, whose most distinctive building housed the Belgian Congo exhibits.[24] The colonial section represented a continuation, in the sense that it was largely organized and classified as it had been in 1910, but its expanded scope broke with earlier displays.[25] With the work that went into creating the grand presence of the empire at the 1913 fair, it would seem colonial authorities wanted to make up for the deficiencies of the 1910 showing. A call to participants disclosed an invigorated attitude: "For the first time . . . Belgium will reveal itself, to foreign eyes, as a *colonial power*. A *Congo Palace* there [in Ghent] will show the glorious effort realized by the Belgian people in its large African domain."[26] Organizers wanted a display that would demonstrate the progress of reforms since the 1908 turnover, distancing the administration from the previous regime: "The Palais des Colonies will occupy a considerable expanse and will testify to the rapid progress accomplished in our beautiful colony, thanks to the new impetus given by a wise administration."[27] Authorities allotted a large space on the fairgrounds for the Ministry of Colonies to build an enormous Palais du Congo to show that Belgium had become a great imperial power and to popularize the Congo among Belgians. As Minister of Colonies Renkin said at the pavilion's opening, "The Exposition coloniale . . . is a work of popularization intended to familiarize the general public with colonial questions."[28] The Palais, which recorded 248,292 visitors, was a huge circular building over fifty feet tall "in the style of an oriental minaret" that covered nearly two and a half acres and that dominated one end of the fair's Avenue des Nations.[29]

Visitors were able to experience all sorts of things within the Palais du Congo. Upon entering, the visitor first found him or herself in the Salon d'Honneur with its busts of King Albert and Queen Elisabeth, as well as ivory sculptures in display cases. Beyond, exhibits of central African products and activities in the colony filled the hallways encompassing the interior chamber; masks and elephant tusks hung from the walls; specimens and materials filled vitrines. One hallway was dedicated to agriculture; another, to colonial gear and equipment. At the behest of the Ministry of Colonies, private firms such as UMHK created many of the displays, providing samples of colonial products to emphasize imports and exports.[30] Visitors could inspect results from expeditions to the Congo in scientific, zoological, and ethnographic exhibits, and the ministry provided an information desk, maps, and tables of commercial statistics. Also prominent were a number of dioramas off the circular hallway illustrating steam power, industry, colonial agriculture, and Catholic

missions.[31] The ministry called on missionaries who had participated in the Tervuren exposition (probably in 1910) to create the
displays of the Catholic missions.[32] Thus the visitor found in the
Palais du Congo a broad introduction to colonial life.[33]

Although the many displays were impressive, it was a panorama by painters Paul Mathieu and Alfred Bastien—contracted
by the Ministry of Colonies and located in the building's central
chamber—that dominated the pavilion. The panorama "gave a
visual lesson in 'colonial progress' by means of simplistic contrasts that were supposed to be clear to everyone at first glance:
untouched jungles next to Matadi and Leopoldville; vine bridges
versus iron overpasses; and huts of natives next to factories of
the white people."[34] This lesson of contrasts was not lost on contemporaries and represented a standard device Europeans used
to teach themselves about the extraordinary progress of which
they believed themselves capable.[35] The Mathieu and Bastien
panorama educated while it entertained, showing fairgoers that
the Ministry of Colonies had moved out from under the long
shadow of Leopold II, had enacted reforms, and had already
achieved impressive results as a colonial power.

There was a noticeable shift in such depictions of the colony
after World War I, the first of which was at the 1930 World's
Fair. That year, Belgians shed their reluctance and began to
embrace the imperial adventure, if numbers of visitors tells us
anything.[36] The 1930 event was different from those in 1910
and 1913 in that it was a dual, or dueling, event: enough time
had gone by that Antwerp's claim to the next world's fair was
weakened, and it had to share the project with Liège in Wallonia.[37] Colonial themes were left to the larger half of the fair
in Antwerp that made the Congo a focus, as it had in 1885 and
1894.[38] In addition to the prominent Belgian Congo pavilion,

the French and Italian governments each created buildings for their colonies; Portugal united displays of Guinea, Angola, São Tomé and Príncipe, Timor, and Mozambique under one roof.[39] There was no Congolese village in 1930, although a Frenchman by the name of Fautenay set up a "negerdorp" in which Africans could be seen going about their affairs, including swimming in a pond.[40] Also, a detachment of Congolese soldiers visited the fairgrounds for Belgium's centennial celebrations.[41]

Once again in charge, the Ministry of Colonies depicted the empire similarly to how it had in 1913 — that is, in grandiose fashion within a stand-alone building on the fairgrounds.[42] The ministry had three interrelated goals: show a total picture of the colonial administration; establish that Belgium could colonize as well as or better than any other colonial power; and demonstrate all this to large international and domestic audiences.[43] Originally, businesses and other groups were to be excluded from the main building, and displays were to be restricted to official documentation from the Ministry of Colonies and humanitarian groups of its choosing — that is, those that had "aided the accomplishment of the civilizing mission."[44] In the end, officials allowed some business groups to exhibit, but they designed the pavilion to emphasize the administration as opposed to private commerce or settler colonization. Instead of favoring industry, which was more the focus of the Liège half of the fair, organizers wanted the Congo section to show "a veritable synthesis of the work undertaken by the Belgians in the Congo."[45] Whereas in 1913 only the busts of King Albert and Queen Elisabeth greeted visitors, a prominent bust of Leopold II joined them in the 1930 Salon d'Honneur.[46] The Ministry of Colonies adorned the exposition with works from Arsène Matton, the same sculptor who created statues for the Musée du Congo Belge; what they

2. Postcard of Congo pavilion at the 1930 World's Fair (author's collection).

represented— "Slavery in the Congo," "Humanity Bringing Belgium and the Congo Together," "The Conquest of the Congo by Belgium," "Evangelization"—bespoke the pavilion's themes.[47]

The government used the 1930 displays to teach a particular version of history that exuded confidence in the future while rooting Belgian imperialism in the past. To legitimize the empire of 1930 and highlight Belgian-led progress, an allegorical plaque in the Salon du Vieux Congo near the entrance highlighted historical milestones from the 1876 AIA to the 1914–18 military campaigns in eastern Africa. The official guide explained the thinking: "Actually, it is logical that the visitor, before seeing in the rest of the Palais what the Congo of 1930 is, receive first an impression of what the Congo was in 1885 and of its initial development. Thus will he, by this contrast, better understand the progress realized in the course of a half century of colonization."[48] Like the 1913 Mathieu and Bastien panorama, a key motif and technique of the 1930 exposition was the contrast between African backwardness and Belgian civilization. Inside the pavilion, visitors found two large statues: one was titled *De Slavernij*, and the other, *Het Christendom*. The former showed a turbaned Arab lording over a nude, enslaved African woman kneeling at his feet; the latter depicted a missionary protecting a young, free African while literally cradling an African baby in his arms.[49] Thus Belgian imperialism, through conquest, freed Africans from slavery. One diorama in the same pavilion contrasted indigenous society, which was marked by "war sowing destruction" and "slavery bringing man down," to "the Catholic religion raising up and freeing" Africans and African society.[50] Another showed in the foreground "war-making tribes," while in the distance European missionaries could be seen "bringing salvation" through Christianity.[51] The official guide's illustration of the Salon du Vieux Congo indicated in what part of the room fairgoers were to begin their visit and in which direction to proceed, suggesting officials tried to educate the public in a deliberate manner.[52]

The inclusion of a bust of Leopold II and other devices linking the colonial administration of 1930 to a supposedly long history of involvement in the Congo was an attempt to legitimize Belgian control over its colony. The Salon du Vieux Congo in 1930 presented an exhibit titled "The Origins of the Belgian Congo in 666 Images," which covered European actions in central Africa from Sir Henry Morton Stanley's crossing of the continent to the eastern Africa campaigns of 1914–18. In this "history and geography lesson through images," the official guide stated, "the political thought of the founder inspires and guides the plan." It went on to assert that, considering the progress made, Belgium exhibited the Congo in 1930 with "a legitimate pride."[53] Whereas in 1910 or even 1913 organizers appeared hesitant or doubtful when it came to expressing pride in their central African *œuvre*, by 1930 they were gaining confidence. Belgium—unlike Britain, France, and Portugal—had no long imperial history; enthusiasts perceived the empire to be under threat on multiple fronts during the interwar period, from German colonial claims to the international economic crisis. Seizing on Leopold II as a great figure—one is pressed to imagine a figure of comparable stature to whom the Belgians might have turned—provided the country with the one and only tradition with which it might bolster the legitimacy of its colonial rule. This rooting of present imperialism within a real, fictional, or exaggerated imperial heritage was not unique to Belgium. Nicola Cooper has pointed out how French textbooks of the interwar period legitimized that country's recently acquired "new" empire of the late nineteenth and early twentieth centuries: "The majority of school manuals were at pains to emphasize the historical precedent of more recent colonial acts and conquests, and to place these events within a French tradition of colonisation."[54] In France this tradition of colonization reached back to its first overseas empire that largely perished after the Seven Years' War. In Belgium in 1930 there was little assertion of a distinct post-1908 colonial history, and the Congo of the time was instead linked to the Leopoldian period. Exposition director Count van der Burch further developed the connection when he invoked the memory of Leopold II at the colonial section's inauguration.[55] These messages reached a very large number of Belgians as the section became "one of the most visited" of the exposition: one source claimed ten million visitors, whereas an official source placed attendance at around four million.[56] As with earlier fairs, it is hard to tell the breakdown of the figures between men, women, and children, but photographs do indicate mixed groups of attendees. Even if foreigners or repeat visitors represented a significant percentage of the attendance, these educational displays had a far reach in a country with a population of not even nine million in 1930 and indicate a surprisingly acute interest in empire.

Four final notes can be made regarding the 1930 fair. First, national competition drove the building process, such as when Belgian organizers refused to put the Congo display at a comparative disadvantage.[57] Indeed, the final placement of the pavilion at the end of one of the exposition's main arteries indicates the colony's importance in organizers' eyes. Second, it shows that world's fairs were driven not only by nationalism but also by job creation, a mundane point unappreciated in the literature on universal expositions. Individuals made a good business providing services, and with each new world's fair, regulars could be found offering their services to organizers.[58] Third is the role of missionaries in the fair. Whereas at earlier fairs the role of the church was small, it was more significant in 1930, and the Congo pavilion included a large display promoting the work of Catholic missionaries as well as dioramas and statues.[59] Nonetheless, this presence was due in large part to the substantial subsidies the Ministry of Colonies provided to missionary groups like the Sœurs de Notre Dame, who were based in Namur and operated missions out of Kwango in southwestern Congo. The record reveals a general reluctance among missionary groups to expend funds to publicize their work at the fair.[60] Finally, for all the money and effort, the Congo pavilion was anything but an authentic depiction of central Africa. By packing the entire colony into one building, organizers homogenized the Belgian empire in central Africa and downplayed its diversity, just as French organizers would do in the French West Africa section in Paris the following year.[61] Moreover the Pavillon du Congo had more an "Oriental" than a Congolese character; when the Ministry of Colonies offered the building to the governor general of the Congo for use after the fair, he declined because it was, he said, "not very adequate to the African climate."[62] The Eurocentric pavilion and lack of exchanges at the 1930 fair suggests that, in contrast to architecture at some nineteenth-century expositions, Belgian architecture at world's fairs largely succeeded at keeping Africans silent.[63]

A world's fair returned to the capital in 1935 in the form of the Exposition de Bruxelles on the Heysel grounds, a site covering more than 250 acres just outside the city.[64] Just as France (1889) and the United States (1876 and 1893) celebrated anniversaries with exhibitions, so too did Belgium in 1935 by marking the fiftieth anniversary of the birth of the EIC and the centenary of Belgium's first railway.[65] Yet economic depression crimped the 1935 Congo section and made it much smaller than either that of 1930 in Antwerp or the one Belgium created for the 1931 Paris Colonial Exposition.[66] The Ministry of Colonies' Office colonial (Colonial Office, OC) tried to give the colony a particularly important presence because of the EIC's fiftieth anniversary.[67] The colonial section comprised three buildings and their surrounding grounds located at the end of one of the fair's main thoroughfares, the Avenue Coloniale. The main and largest building was the Palais du Congo, which was abutted by two buildings built by private enterprises that formed its two wings.[68] In the middle of the garden courtyard in front of the Palais du Congo was the *Congolese Elephant*, a towering sculpture by Albéric Collin of an elephant being ridden by three Africans. Behind the elephant and just in front of the pavilion's entrance was an oversized bust of Leopold II.[69] Upon entering the Congo palace, visitors found themselves in the Salon d'Honneur faced by a bust of Albert I, who had died unexpectedly the previous year, and a faux-ivory bust of the current sovereign, Leopold III—both of which associated the colony with the monarchy.[70] The pavilion's several rooms housed models, photos, vitrines, dioramas, and statues, including displays of the Force publique, Catholic missions, colonial education, the Ligue du souvenir congolais (League of Congolese Remembrance), health services, the OC's *bureau de documentation* (documentation bureau), a Salon des Artistes, and a huge map of the Congo.[71] One publication likened a visit to the pavilion to "a voyage to the Congo without leaving Brussels."[72]

Private interests exhibited alongside the government by means of two pavilions built by the Société auxiliaire de propagande coloniale (Auxiliary Company for Colonial Propaganda, or Soprocol).[73] The first, called the Pavillon Soprocol, promoted tourism in the Congo. Colonial tourism, which the French and Italians also were promoting within their empires, represented an area of potential growth that unfortunately for Belgian steamship companies and tourist firms was hampered by strict regulations on travel to the colony.[74] In addition to a panorama of the Ruwenzori and Parc National Albert created by James Thiriar, the pavilion recycled the panorama by Bastien and Mathieu from the 1913 Ghent exhibition. It also included a tasting room for Congolese coffee, organized by the Association des planteurs de café, as well as colonial products including mattresses, explosives, chocolate, liquor, and motorcycles.[75] The pavilion's centerpiece was the Caravane Congolaise (Congolese Caravan) comprising a dozen or so life-size mannequins of African porters and their European boss transporting crates of goods. A second building, the Pavillon des Entreprises, housed private firms and showed off a "synthesis of the economic activity of the Colony."[76] Soprocol also built a restaurant on-site, the Restaurant Léopold II. The Ministry of Colonies encouraged these efforts, but budget restrictions and the Ministry's requirement that businesses pay their own way made it difficult to get private companies involved, despite the offer of a prime, rent-free location. In fact, colonial firms were generally disinclined to exhibit in the mid-1930s; as OC director Frans Janssen put it after the 1935 event, such private participation generally was "difficult," with the government often stepping in to defray costs.[77] Nonetheless, businesses' initiative in 1935 far outstripped that of missionary groups, which contented themselves to a subsidized presence in the main pavilion. In the end, the Ministry of Colonies ensured that all buildings and exhibits put up by all interests meshed with government displays to give the impression that the Congo section formed one bloc.[78]

As in the past, organizers intended the 1935 colonial displays to propagate a positive message to both foreign and domestic publics regarding Belgian progress in Africa.[79] The displays of raw materials production emphasized that a bright future lay ahead.[80] Organizers provided a supposed total picture of the colony, so that when the visitor left the pavilion, he or she would realize everything about the Congo, including its "mining, livestock rearing, agriculture . . . means of transportation utilized in the Colony . . . diverse industries and organisms."[81] Exhibits taught visitors about Belgium's civilizing actions, philanthropy, and moral accomplishments including improved health care, demonstrated in dioramas showing officials inoculating Congolese.[82] It is unsurprising that there was such a focus on health since it was one area in which Belgians invested heavily compared to other colonial powers. To spread these optimistic messages, the Ministry of Colonies arranged for the printing and distribution of thousands of guides, a special issue of *L'Illustration Congolaise*, and other printed materials.[83] There is no evidence of opposition to these displays, and there certainly was no antiexhibition such as the surrealist protest of the 1931 Vincennes fair.[84]

Although not a stated goal, displays in 1935 reinforced Belgian feelings of supremacy and paternalism toward Africans. As mentioned, Soprocol's Caravane Congolaise showed African porters under command of a white boss. A Stand de la Force publique in the main pavilion comprised six mannequins: two representing white officers and four, their black subordinates — half represented the Force publique of the *antiesclavagiste* (antislavery) era; the others, the Force publique of the 1930s. Missionary displays also included mannequins. Some represented white nuns tending to sick Africans in bed, while others were more allegorical, as two nuns comforted two Africans — one a sickly, thin child and the other an adult who was down on his or her knees.[85] The section also developed once again the common before-and-after theme of European colonial propaganda that depicted the colony before the advent of Belgian rule and then later, after magnificent results had been achieved. The recycled Bastien and Mathieu panorama reprised themes of African backwardness and Belgian-led progress first seen at the 1913 Ghent exhibition, and a display of the Banque du Congo Belge contrasted with a diorama depicting "a barter scene [*une scène de troc*]."[86] As Patricia Morton has shown, architecture at the 1931 Vincennes fair made the contrast between (superior) France and the (undeveloped) colonies "concrete," thereby justifying colonization.[87] Likewise, in Brussels four years later, backwardness legitimized and made necessary Belgian imperialism.

As a whole, the exhibits had a far reach: the Ministry of

Colonies recorded 3,237,250 visitors, a huge figure that suggests a popular imperialism in the country. The Office colonial noted school-age children's attendance and assigned colonials on vacation in Belgium to accompany school groups in order to make a greater impression, indicating the ministry's ongoing interest in influencing young people.[88] Although it is difficult to even approximate the breakdown of women, men, and children among the visitors, ministry records do indicate large numbers of children, and photographs show mixed crowds on the exposition grounds.

Perhaps some visitors were drawn by the Congolese who were on site in 1935, although paradoxically the modest presence of Africans revealed persistent metropolitan fears. Soprocol brought in Congolese and other "exotics" for visitors to observe, and the grounds of the Soprocol pavilion were "laid out as a colonial garden with Congolese huts in which, before visitors' eyes, natives offered fabricated exotic objects for sale."[89] France's colonial displays included a France d'Outre-Mer (France Overseas) pavilion, an "Oriental theater," Senegalese merchants, and a Moroccan souk.[90] The prospect of Africans on the fairgrounds unnerved government officials, including OC director Frans Janssen, who urged beforehand "to exercise a serious surveillance on these natives" and that "a very strict discipline will have to be observed to avoid any abuse that might take place."[91] While fearful of the presence of Africans in Brussels, Janssen and his colleagues did not let this get in the way of bringing their vision of the colony to the metropole. The Ministry of Colonies informed Belgians about their colony with an ostensible total picture of the Congo, emphasizing a bright future, raw materials resources, and philanthropy for needy Africans. Moreover, the budget constraints that diminished the displays apparently did not dampen the zeal of the almost 3,250,000 visitors who passed through the pavilion.

More than two decades would pass before the Congo and Congolese would return to the metropole for another world's fair; it seemed that when they did, the colonial authorities were anxious to make up for lost time. The 1958 Brussels Exposition Universelle was the largest and most extensive that Belgium hosted during the colonial period and its last to date.[92] It also was the first such event held since the end of World War II, the last being the 1939–40 New York World's Fair. Unlike earlier expositions, the 1958 event included significant pavilions from former colonies in Africa, including Morocco, Sudan, and Tunisia.[93] The Parc Heysel site of the 1935 fair was expanded to cover 500 acres, and among the dozens of pavilions was the centrally located, nineteen-acre Belgian Congo and Ruanda-Urundi section that included a seven-acre tropical garden, a *village indigène* (indigenous village), and seven "ultra-modern buildings."[94] It proved one of the more popular sections, drawing approximately one million foreigners and more than thirty million Belgians from all provinces.[95] In fact, the fair was such an attraction that hoteliers, restaurateurs, and café owners in the Congo spoke of a crisis that summer resulting from so many colonials leaving to visit Brussels, as the number of hotel clients in Leopoldville declined around 50–60 percent. "The restaurants are practically deserted," the leader of the restaurant, coffee shop, and hotelier union announced, ironically during his visit to Belgium that summer.[96] The global view of the empire of central Africa—presented in the seven pavilions by means of displays, maps, models, film projections, and an African village—led one observer to remark that "all the Congo was at Heysel."[97] Yet less than two years after the fair closed, the Congo achieved its independence.

What visitors saw when they visited the Congo section were supposedly authentic pavilions and exhibits that, as in past expositions, were conceived and constructed by Europeans, most if not all of whom were Belgian men.[98] Expo general commissioner Baron Moens de Fernig made plain whose intentions lay behind the exhibits when he assured an interviewer that everything had turned out "according to our wishes."[99] The plan included bringing a total vision of the Congo and Ruanda-Urundi to the exposition grounds. "In the seven pavilions that we will build," one planner put it in 1955, "all the activities of the Congo and of Ruanda-Urundi will be represented. [An] absolutely complete panorama of the modern Congo will be realized."[100] The committee in charge of the section sought authenticity through "a proper African atmosphere" and the use of "indigenous artistic motifs" in the decoration of the pavilions.[101] Similar to other expositions since World War I, the 1958 event rewrote history by rooting the Belgian Congo in the EIC and recasting Leopold II in laudatory terms. This led, in retrospect, to almost ludicrously Eurocentric representations. Leopold II was placed in a position of great honor via a bust of him at the entrance to the main colonial pavilion with the caption: "I undertook the work of the Congo in the interest of civilization."[102] Also Eurocentric was the display of 425 pieces of artwork in the Congo section, much of which was European created. Instead of commissioning African artwork, organizers drew on collections at the Antwerp ethnographic museum and the Tervuren museum; when they did decide to include indigenous art, they worked with provincial colonial governors, not African artists, to decide which items to procure.[103] Gardeners brought plants from the Congo for the artificially heated tropical gardens; planted a sign that read "Danger—Lions"; and used speakers to broadcast music and sound effects such as animal cries, birds singing, and "the noise of drums."[104] All of these displays cost money, and the Ministry of Colonies subsidized the section to the tune of one hundred million francs, or more than fifteen million 2011 U.S. dollars.[105]

As with past exhibits, the 1958 Congo section had an educative purpose that benefited from its popularity with visitors. Exhibits included educational displays; sculpture; tapestries; natural products (and corresponding methods of extraction or harvesting); models of locomotives, trucks, boats, even railroad stations; as well as slide, photographic, and film presentations. As at past fairs, maps figured prominently, such as in the Pavillon des Mines and the Palais Gouvernemental: the former featured a massive map of the Congo that lit up various mining areas, and the latter, a map that reached up to the high ceiling.[106]

Although the Congo pavilions in 1958 were not unlike national ones that used exhibits to lay out their cultures and industries, they differed in their extensive use of educational displays, sculpture, and models of humans that suggested an imperialistic vision of Belgian-led progress in central Africa.[107] For example, models represented women engaged in cotton cloth production and other Congolese in an outdoor market in the colony.[108] In the agriculture pavilion, the Comité cotonnier congolais (Congolese Cotton Committee) erected a model of Africans working with cotton, of which the *Revue Congolaise Illustrée* wrote: "One can see natives working in an indefatigable rhythm under a large blue sky. One sees them working in the forest plantations or in village surroundings, harvesting and sorting their snowy harvest, carried by elegant black women to the first counting house."[109] The writer perceived the model as if it were a real-life scene, as if they were not actually inanimate objects but Africans themselves, in smaller form. As in 1930 in Antwerp, at least one of the colonial pavilions in 1958 was designed for visitors to move along in a certain sequence to educate them in a particular manner, and the Ministry of Colonies again sought to instruct fairgoers with specialized publications.[110]

For the Congo section to educate, it had to attract crowds, and organizers did so by providing people with the experience of visiting Africa itself.[111] One visitor's impressions echoed a general sentiment when he wrote that in the Congo section, "we were ready to believe ourselves transported to the middle of the bush."[112] The Congorama in the Belgian Congo and Ruanda-Urundi pavilion theater combined a thirty-minute movie with sound, light, and visual effects to "plunge" the viewer into "the disturbing ambience of primitive life."[113] *Le Soir pour les Enfants*, a weekly supplement to the daily *Le Soir*, suggested students visit the Congorama but warned, "When exiting, be careful not to go cut down spears in the bushes of the Congolese village!"[114] The Congorama not only entertained but also taught Congolese history from the official Belgian state point of view. The creators (all of whom were Europeans) compressed seventy-five years of history into a synthesis of the Belgian *œuvre civilisatrice* (civilizing effort), from Henry Morton Stanley on through the 1950s — that is to say, "the principal stages that have conducted the Congo from the night of prehistory to the light of civilization." A prospectus declared that the viewer would participate "in the Rail Battle [Bataille du Rail], in the combats against the slavers, in the discovery of the mineral riches of Katanga, in the creation of the National Parks, etc. In one word, he will relive THE GREAT HOURS OF THE CONGO."[115] This narrative glorified Belgians' work in Africa while denying the history of the peoples of central Africa. The Congorama's power as an instructive device was considerable because it attracted so many viewers—officially around two hundred thousand; press reviews almost certainly extended its impact by lauding its production and attesting to its accuracy.

The tropical gardens of the Congo section included an atavistic village indigène, where around twenty artisans recruited by the administration worked under the eyes of the public, at least during the first three months of the six-month-long exposition.[116] Planners considered including live animals from the Antwerp zoo in the tropical garden displays, bringing to mind the 1894 Antwerp Exposition Universelle with its cows, pigs, and other animals exhibited alongside Africans.[117] Through their presentation of people brought from the colony, organizers created a particular spectacle, a human zoological garden. Although there were other villages at the 1958 fair, such as La Belgique Joyeuse and the Hawaiian village, the Congolese exhibit was different. La Belgique Joyeuse, for instance, was an artificial town built to reflect different architectural styles from the nation's past, where visitors participated in events alongside workers in dress from bygone eras. Africans in their village were for observation only, separated from visitors by a fence.[118] When King Baudouin—who followed his father, Leopold III, as Belgium's sovereign—visited the village indigène, he greeted the Africans only from a distance with a friendly but reserved wave of the royal hand.[119] While La Belgique Joyeuse had nine artisans at work, it also had dozens of cafés, souvenir shops, and restaurants, as well as two waffle stands; it was an area in which to eat, drink, and have fun. A visitor could not get a beer or waffle in the village indigène.

Moreover, the re-created Africa of the Congo section and the village indigène stood in stark contrast to virtually all other pavilions, heightening the appearance of backwardness,

Otherness, and what Timothy Mitchell calls "Oriental disorder."[120] In 1958 the Congo village was literally and figuratively located in the shadows of the supermodern, 335-foot-tall Atomium, whose nine steel spheres represented an iron crystal magnified billions of times. The straw huts and dirt ground of the village indigène—intended to depict the Congo not of the past but of the present—contrasted with the surrounding modern buildings. This disparity on the Heysel grounds and in news reports depicted Belgians as advanced and Africans as primitive, endorsing the former's control over the latter. Albert Dupagne's statue of a nude African couple at the entrance of the Belgian Congo and Ruanda-Urundi pavilion, with the Atomium in the background, contrasted humankind in a natural state (the Congo) and as master of nature (Belgium). National pavilions showcased national pride, characteristic architecture, and technological achievements, in certain cases resulting in some of the most modern buildings constructed to that point.[121] The contents of the Congo pavilions also presented a sharp contrast between "backward" Africans and "advanced" Belgians that justified Belgian rule. The agriculture pavilion juxtaposed the "condition of the primitive native" and his ancestral tools and utensils with Belgium, which had "brought Congolese agriculture to its current state of development."[122] The insurance, banks, and trade pavilion displayed an ironwork canoe in the pavilion's main hall to show "the trade of the past."[123] This canoe was not dissimilar (except in its ironwork construction) from those that visitors could see outside in the tropical gardens next to the village indigène. Roger de Meyer's *Introducing the Belgian Congo and the Ruanda-Urundi*, published in 1958, had before-and-after shots of an African in traditional and European dress respectively.[124]

The village indigène also dehumanized Africans, as an account of an encounter there in *Le Soir pour les Enfants* demonstrates:

> In the Congo village, a good woman (good but scatterbrained) just stopped in front of a space where a black is in the process of sculpting a bit of wood. At the side of the black is seated a young black boy [*négrillon*], two or three years of age, who is looking through a picture book. Neither one raises his head to look at the many visitors who have stopped out of friendship and curiosity to face them from the other side of a little open-work fence. Agitated, the woman cries out in a very loud voice that this "baby is truly adorable." You must have been able to hear her all the way to the Atomium. That is her first mistake. But it is not the worst. Because she now takes a candy bar out of her handbag. She breaks it in two with a brotherly gesture, and throws one half to land in between the knees of the boy. Right away, without the least hesitation, the boy throws the tidbit back over the fence without even looking up, with an air of noble contempt. Well done, little black boy [*petit Noir*]! You're in the right. The village congolais is not a zoological garden.[125]

But it was. The young boy threw the candy back over the fence without reflection, surprise, or even a glance, indicating this was not the first time he had faced such humiliation. In fact, treatment of the Africans was so bad that they would no longer stand for it; by mid to late July, they had returned to the Congo, the huts of the village more than likely remaining empty thereafter. The official reason given for their departure was that they were originally to stay in Belgium for a limited time only. The real reason: they were tired of the inhumane treatment at the hands of the public.[126] Visitors did not invariably toe the official line or demonstrate barbarous prejudices against Africans, but enough did to drive the people of the village indigène away.

The 1958 World's Fair therefore saw a level of opposition to the official discourse unprecedented for such an event in Belgium, if surprisingly muted considering the anticolonial developments elsewhere by that point, such as the Bandung Conference and Ghana's independence. Congolese in Brussels protested by meeting in secret during the time of the fair, spreading nationalist and proindependence sentiment. Following what the conservative press called a belated "discovery of the Congo" in the 1950s, Socialists and others met with Congolese at their residences in Belgium in 1958, spreading potentially subversive ideas.[127] The Socialist daily *Le Peuple* regretted the deliberate sequestration of visiting Congolese at Tervuren and lamented the lack of Africans at the Congo section's inauguration. Others opposed the dehumanizing treatment of Congolese, such as the visitor who tempered her enthusiasm for the tropical garden with the criticism that "the Congolese were parked there like livestock and exhibited as curious beasts."[128] In late July a writer for *De Standaard* protested the treatment of Congolese in his description of the situation that brought about their departure: "We went to see [the village indigène] with brutality, provocative pedantry and egoism that characterize modern life and the blacks were profoundly embittered by it. . . . We, the public, we have forgotten that the black also has a heart and pride, and that he wants to be something other than a curiosity. . . . This deplorable misunderstanding is but an omen of additional disillusions that await us in the Congo, but we have only ourselves to blame for it."[129] The well-placed criticism was too little and too late. As Catherine Hodeir has pointed out, "The pavilion of the Belgian Congo still participated in the old conception of the representation of the colonies . . . illustrating an already out-of-date paternalistic system of government."[130] Even skeptical observers such as those writing for *Le Peuple* could not help but be enthralled by the Congolese presence.[131] The 1958 event was the last of many expositions that subjugated Africans and deprived them of human qualities, a shocking throwback years after the defeat of biological racism in the heart of Europe and during a time of decolonization and of the civil rights movement in the United States.

Congolese on display in the village indigène were only several of hundreds of so-called évolués in Belgium from April to October; others included police officers, tourists, Catholic and Protestant brothers and sisters, journalists, dancers, musicians, and performers, in addition to the *mwamis*, or traditional kings, of Ruanda and Urundi.[132] Exposition managers put Africans to work as guides and interpreters; others engaged in typical crafts in the village indigène; while still others toured the country (always with Belgians) to observe local industry and culture. Women in the Catholic pavilion went about everyday tasks before the eyes of a non-African public, embroidering, making baskets, or doing needlework. Franciscan father Guido Haeson directed a singing group from Kamina called the Troubadours du Roi Baudouin who performed at the Heysel grounds, in Brussels, and in other big cities. Authorities brought in a detachment of the Force publique—picked according to athletic ability—to perform various spectacles and sporting events, during which they attracted substantial press coverage and throngs of onlookers. While members of the Force publique managed to tour the country and meet their colonizers, representations of them focused overwhelmingly on them as performers and soldiers under

white control, reaffirming who was master in central Africa. Another group was Changwe Yetu, a dance troupe comprising 120
dancers that Jean-Marc Landier had selected during a three-year
trip throughout the Congo and Ruanda-Urundi.[133] Similar to
the Congorama, Changwe Yetu performances had the effect of
taking audience members "into the bush."[134] Yet it is doubtful
Changwe Yetu brought ruler and ruled any closer. At the end
of their sojourn, the dancers asked Minister of Colonies Léon
Pétillon to extend their stay, writing, "Since our arrival, we were
given the task to follow all given orders for the success of the
program. Because of this, we have not had the spare time to have
a little contact with the Belgian people, their achievements, and
their lifestyle, what could have been for us and for our people an
invaluable enrichment."[135] Pétillon refused and they returned as
scheduled.

Belgian command over colonial subjects was not isolated to
the Changwe Yetu dancers, and organizers kept Africans under
strict control in the metropole, reflecting the long-standing anxiety about the presence of Africans in Europe that lasted right up
to the last years of European overseas empires.[136] The government housed Congolese in segregated quarters, mostly in the so-
called *village africain* (African village) or *Congolese dorp* (Congolese village) in Tervuren, officially the Centre d'Accueil pour
le Personnel Africain (Welcome Center for African Personnel,
CAPA). Organizers worried about interactions among Congolese
and Belgians, how and where Africans would be housed, as well
as where any Congolese tourists would stay. In the end, virtually all Africans brought to Belgium for the world's fair were
under tight control, either cloistered at the CAPA in Tervuren or
elsewhere, or under white supervision: a priest in the case of the
Troubadours du Roi Baudouin, Lieutenant Colonel Lescrenier

from Liège in the case of the Force publique detachment, and so forth.[137] Since the appearance of Edward Said's *Orientalism*, many scholars have chipped away at the extent of Western power in Said's argument by unveiling or discovering the viewpoint of the subaltern.[138] The Belgian instance of substantial command over colonial subjects as recent as the late 1950s warns us of the limits of such counterarguments.

As in 1930 and 1935, the World's Fair of 1958 magnified Leopold II's legend and closely associated the ongoing imperial project with him. In late June, procolonialists and Belgian and Force publique troops memorialized the king and "colonial pioneers who died in Africa for civilization" on the Journée belgo-congolaise (Belgian-Congolese Day). Speeches acclaimed Leopold for having had the vision to embark on an imperialism where no other European power had dared to tread—that is to say, for having begun the task of civilizing the vast unknown expanse that was central Africa in Europeans' eyes before Leopold "arrived" there. At the Congo pavilion's inauguration, Minister of Colonies Auguste Buisseret stated that Belgians "have the pride to have scrupulously accomplished in Africa the orders that the founder of our colony bequeathed to us."[139] Colonials thus yet again made claims on the past to exalt Leopold II.

Quinzaines Coloniales, 1925–39

While expositions universelles were the greatest displays of Belgian empire, they were not the only ones. Among others were a series of *quinzaines coloniales* (colonial fortnights) that the colonial administration's propaganda bureau, the Office colonial, staged in their Brussels offices from 1925 to 1939.[140] It was OC director Frans Janssen who really developed the use of quinzaines coloniales, which as their name indicates usually lasted around two weeks. François "Frans" Janssen, born in St. Josse-ten-Noode just outside Brussels in 1873, was to spend all of his forty-six-year career in public service. By the age of eighteen, Janssen already had begun work in the clerk's office of the Brussels Tribunal de commerce, or commercial court. By 1910 he had moved to the relatively new Ministry of Colonies, becoming a deputy chief clerk. He spent some time during World War I representing the Kingdom of Belgium in the Netherlands at Flushing (Vlissingen), service for which he later received the Croix de Chevalier de l'Ordre de Léopold and a deputy director position within the Colonial Ministry. Janssen was instrumental in the creation of the OC in 1924 and became a tireless advocate of imperialism. He also traveled widely to promote the Congo at expositions in Paris, Rome, Warsaw, and elsewhere, although there is no evidence he ever traveled to Africa, let alone the Congo. He directed the OC until his retirement in 1937, after which he remained active until his death in 1948 — for example, by filling the role of president of the Commission consultative de l'Office colonial (Colonial Office Advisory Committee).[141]

The primary goal of quinzaines coloniales was to develop economic ties between the metropole and the colony. Although imperialism was highly profitable to particular enterprises, colonial trade overall remained limited. This, and the fact that the colony never was a destination for much emigration and that government policy did not promote such settlement, meant that metropole-colony economic connections were tenuous.[142] Moreover, Belgium was in a particular situation compared to France, Britain, and the other European imperial powers in that it had inherited free-trade policies from the EIC and thus could not employ a system of "imperial preference" as others could.[143] So officials did what they could, namely, "1° Further colonial production and the import into Belgium of raw materials; 2° Further the export toward the Congo of products of national manufacture."[144] They called this the *interpénétration* (interpenetration) of the two economies. Quinzaines coloniales demonstrate that many believed in the idea, widespread at the time, that by buying more raw materials from the colony, one would put more money into the hands of colonial subjects, thereby expanding demand for finished goods from the metropole.[145]

With the advent of economic depression in the 1930s, the purported importance of quinzaines took on greater significance.[146] As the downturn persisted, the colony was depicted inconsistently—alternatively as a source of inexhaustible markets and resources for producers and consumers, and as a place of weak productivity and low fertility. For the 1932 Exposition des Produits du Congo, the head of the Association des intérêts coloniaux belges (Association of Belgian Colonial Interests), Gaston Périer, identified the Congo as a cure for the nation's economic ills: "The resources of our Colony are multiple and justify the absolute confidence that we maintain, despite the worries of the moment, as regards the tenth Belgian province that can and must play an important role in the recovery of national prosperity."[147] Minister of Colonies Paul Crokaert pointed to the "vitality of our Colony, its wealth, all its immediate and future resources and our profound faith in its assured future despite the current period of crisis and contemplation [*recueillement*]," a belief echoed by other ministers at similar exhibits.[148] Yet at one, a participant of the Compagnie agricole et industrielle du Congo (Agricultural and Industrial Company of the Congo), E. de Jaer, conveyed a somber tone of realism by criticizing the poor soils of the Congo and advising against all hopes of establishing plantations that required fertile land.[149]

Despite their ostensibly economic rationale, quinzaines coloniales became nationalist affairs that emphasized the country's
civilizing mission over the pursuit of profit.[150] In his opening
speech at a quinzaine for cutlery and small tools, Prime Minister and Minister of Colonies Henri Jaspar asserted that "the
economic equipment of Belgium should have the preponderance
in the Congo" and that "the Congo has important mechanical,
electric and agricultural industries that require sizeable equipment. It matters that the material be as much as possible of Belgian manufacture."[151] The desire to nationalize colonial imports
and exports repeatedly found expression at these events, indicating that the government wanted to get businesses involved in
the nationalization of imperialism and reflecting a long-standing
wariness of non-Belgian influence. Private business echoed the
administration's line, not only claiming the colony for Belgium
but also using quinzaines to associate colonial trade with patriotism and the civilizing mission.[152] Jaspar stressed that industry
had "the moral obligation to conquer the colonial market. In
working to develop our trade and our industry in the Congo, our
manufacturers do a task of enlightened patriots," an exhortation
that resounded in the press.[153] A speaker addressing Minister of
Colonies Paul Tschoffen at one inauguration wove textiles together with the civilizing mission: "In supporting cotton production as you do during these difficult moments that we are going
through, you accomplish, *Monsieur le Ministre*, an eminently
civilizing task."[154]

These attempts by the state to interest Belgian businesses
in colonial commerce revealed the fear that intensified Belgian interest in empire between the wars. Enthusiasts such as
Janssen feared producers were not paying enough attention to
the Congo and opportunities there, causing Belgium to lose

out to competitors, particularly Germany and Britain.[155] The quinzaines asserted that Belgium could, and should, compete with foreigners' products; one newspaper reported a particular event as "proof that our industry has set itself completely free from foreign tutelage, that it can fight on all markets."[156] As one administrator stated at an early quinzaine, the goal was in part to increase the number of colonial firms, but even more so to develop "a more constant contact between Belgian industrialists and the groups that work toward the industrial, commercial and agricultural development of the Congo."[157] The colonial press received Janssen's efforts positively; as one typical account put it, "We applaud without reservation the fortunate initiative of the Office Colonial that, to the favor of the successive expositions that it anticipates organizing, courageously undertakes the task to perfect the 'colonial' education of our merchants and industrialists."[158] In order to reduce their own outlays and to extend their promotional capabilities to the maximum, the OC tried to get business groups to pay for the quinzaines coloniales as far as this was possible, and several private groups or firms did pay for the bulk of different expositions.[159]

Yet the OC faced serious obstacles in promoting colonial commerce. For a 1928 tobacco exhibit, Janssen had a hard time getting any Congolese tobacco from any source whatsoever—metropolitan or African—and he had to turn to the Musée du Congo Belge, then finally to the government at Boma, to obtain samples. How would one promote Congolese tobacco when not even the association of tobacco importers had any on hand? Sometimes it was the OC that carried the weight for private enterprise, trade following the flag. While the OC drew both colonial firms and businesses not specific to the Congo to their offices in Brussels from both language regions, they had difficulty interesting many businessmen from the start, and some firms participated only out of a sense of duty. For a quinzaine on textiles, out of more than eight hundred *bulletins d'adhésion* (membership forms) the OC sent out, only forty companies participated. This lack of participation was tied to issues concerning the bottom line; when firms did not believe quinzaines affected profits, they often either took a pass or participated only if cajoled into doing so by someone in the OC. Few colonial firms saw the interpénétration of the Belgian and colonial economies as essential to their own interests.[160]

Janssen and his staff did not let such difficulties thwart the quinzaines, and eventually they reached large audiences. Janssen sent notes to his press contacts, and the OC disseminated press releases and invitations to senators, diplomats, journalists, businessmen, schoolteachers, mayors, colonial administrators, and colonial firms to attend event inaugurations. As quinzaines continued, promotion became more sophisticated, publicity increased, and the OC began publishing special brochures about exhibitors, their wares, and the OC's role in promoting colonial commerce. The propaganda office even tried to add a touch of authenticity by hiring Africans to form an honor guard for at least one event and made a particular effort to encourage visits by schoolchildren, noting student attendance.[161] Teachers wrote thank-you notes and used feedback cards to ask for materials like brochures or samples of colonial raw materials. One teacher thanked Janssen for sending materials and let him know that "the visit to the colonial exposition greatly interested the students thanks to the beautiful presentation of the exhibited objects and to the kind and clear explanations provided by the guide."[162]

As long as they lasted, the quinzaines also offered an

opportunity to praise Leopold II, such as when his portrait found its way into catalogues—"To him we owe our Colony," read the caption of one.[163] Busts of him often figured prominently, and speakers invoked his memory in their remarks. "We owe the colony to the genius of our great King LEOPOLD II to whom Belgium would never know how to have enough gratitude," declared one notable.[164] Such praise reached thousands of visitors from 1925–39, and the quinzaines probably successfully projected a positive vision of the colonial past. Such adulation ceased with the arrival of war and occupation in 1940, when ministerial staff at all levels was dispersed and the OC ceased its exhibits. After the war, the Ministry of Colonies was restructured, and the government did not hold any additional quinzaines coloniales.

Local Colonial Exhibits

In addition to quinzaines coloniales and wereldtentoonstellingen, there were innumerable local or specialized colonial expositions held across the country. The great number of temporary exhibits or displays within larger expositions after 1908 (a conservative figure would be seventy-five) makes an analysis of them a task fraught with hazards; the number of permanent colonial exhibits in Belgium and Luxembourg during this time period was at least twenty-four, not including those at the OC's offices and the Tervuren museum.[165] Many local displays were generic in nature, simply "colonial" expositions of one sort or another, while others addressed specific subjects, such as Antwerp's 1932 Koloniale Boekententoonstelling.[166] Local exhibits enticed, entertained, and informed people and increased their awareness of the colony, even if not all were outstanding or original. The publication *Mukanda* wrote of the 1925 OC exhibit at the sixth Foire Commerciale de Bruxelles, "It would be preferable to put a sign in the middle of an empty stand with the note: *Same thing as the last time.*"[167] The impact of certain exhibits is questionable because they were lost among innumerable others, such as the imperial stand at the Brussels International Fair, which was only one of countless exhibits that made up the fair every year.[168] The local press extolled these displays; exceptions aside, it seems that many if not most of them attracted large crowds.[169] For example, in 1925 the Chambre de commerce et de l'industrie de Namur (Namur Chamber of Commerce and Industry), the Ministry of Colonies, and colonial companies hosted an Exposition Coloniale de Namur that attracted more than one thousand people, which one publication described as "perfect. It gives a complete idea of our rich colony, of its vegetable and mineral resources, of the fertility of its ground, of the immensity of its territories."[170] Geographically, Brussels and Antwerp were major centers of expositions, the latter especially during the interwar period: the Koloniale Jaarbeurs van Antwerpen was held every year from 1924 until at least 1933, and again in 1955.[171] The exhibit of 1932, to take one year, focused on colonial imports; exports of finished goods to the colony; the OC; the Ministry of Foreign Affairs; the port of Antwerp; and colonial education, missions, and health. Antwerp was one of Europe's largest seaports and Belgium's main trade outlet; the 1932 fair reflected foreign trade's centrality to the well-being of the city, including both domestic and foreign exhibitors such as Krupp (Germany), MacKinnon and Cie (Scotland), Caterpillar (United States), and Méran Frères (France).[172]

A variety of different groups put on local exhibits, but local pro-empire groups and the Ministry of Colonies played the leading role. Some exhibits found their roots in individual enthusiasts who organized them to show off the colony and their own interest in Africa.[173] Missionary orders and private colonial enterprises, on the other hand, seem to have been less anxious to promote the colony locally on their own initiative. Religious groups organized a number of exhibits to promote missionary activity in the Congo, but not without controversy.[174] The Socialist government of the commune of Jemappes, for example, openly disapproved of a missionary section in a local colonial exhibit.[175] While the largest and best-financed colonial firms often seemed uninterested, some companies such as Forminière, Banque du Congo Belge (Bank of the Belgian Congo), or the Comité spécial du Katanga (Special Committee of Katanga) promoted imperialism indirectly by working with local groups and the Ministry of Colonies to supply items and samples for display.[176]

While the Ministry of Colonies' propaganda office played a preponderant role in many local shows, the initiative usually came from local groups, the OC supporting mainly larger expositions in big cities to avoid dissipating its resources.[177] The OC was supportive of private efforts, but because it did not have a large budget, it usually only assisted if it incurred no costs; it refused to participate if the exhibit served a private interest or pursued a profit.[178] Its main contributions were networking, materials procurement, and technical assistance, but in some cases, it did actively participate by setting up its own stand or loaning materials to local organizers who lacked colonial goods.[179] Coordination between the OC, colonial firms, and local groups expanded the range of forums and means by which the OC and local groups could promote colonial products, and thus the imperial idea.[180] The OC used its participation to arrange for follow-up information to be sent out, and as usual the OC was particularly interested in schoolchildren attendance.[181] In the end, local chambers of commerce, *cercles coloniaux* (colonial clubs), and others instigated most local exhibits after 1908 and did so to drum up interest in the colony, particularly among young people. We see a clear example of this grassroots support for imperialism in a letter from the Comité régional de Mons (Mons Regional Committee) to the Ministry of Colonies regarding Mons's 1928 colonial exposition: "Our goal is to make the advantages that we can obtain from the Congo stand out and to make propaganda for our colony by drawing the attention of the public and of the students of our schools to all that it has that is interesting."[182]

A few common themes united local exhibits of empire, despite their diversity. Similar to quinzaines, they stressed the economic benefits the Congo offered as well as the idea that the Congo could save the *mère patrie* (motherland) from potentially dangerous neighbors and from the vagaries of the world economy. The stress on the Congo as a source of economic strength for Belgium during the economic downturn began soon after World War I — that is to say, long before the depression hit.[183] Therefore, the concept of interpénétration was not a hasty reaction to economic hardship, but rather a basic premise of the colonial relationship after World War I.[184] Administrators echoed these ideas when they participated at local exhibits, such as at the Koloniale Jaarbeurs van Antwerpen in 1932 when oc director Frans Janssen, speaking in French and Flemish, said that the time had arrived to truly take control of the colony and its economy by developing the colony's raw materials to fulfill Belgium's needs and in turn by producing all the finished products needed by the colony. By deepening such economic links during the depression, Belgium would "remain the masters there after the crisis."[185] In this way, Belgian propaganda paralleled that being produced by the Conseil économique (Economic Council) of France's Conseil supérieur des colonies (High Council of the Colonies), which was formed in 1920, and Britain's Empire

Marketing Board, created in 1926. British imperial propaganda during the interwar years depicted the empire as a self-sufficient unit that could help Britain weather adverse economic conditions.[186] Local organizers wanted to prove the importance of the Congo for Belgium's future, or in their words, how "our Colony occupies and is susceptible to occupy in larger measure from the point of view of the supplying of the metropole with primary materials."[187] It is no surprise this theme received greater emphasis as the country moved closer to war in the late 1930s and then again after World War II. One publication reported passionately on the 1949 Foire Coloniale de Bruxelles: "All the products of the Congo and all their characteristics are shown there. . . . Numerous panels recall that 'The Congo is Belgian,' '40 billions of capital are invested, of which almost the totality are Belgian,' '300,000 Belgians of the metropole live off the Congo.'"[188]

Local expositions sometimes advertised colonial products but could not always find any of quality to promote. In the case of a 1928 international expo on coffee, the Ministry of Colonies decided it should not offer a tasting of Congolese coffees because they would be obviously inferior to others at the exposition.[189] Just as Frans Janssen in the late 1920s had a difficult time finding Congolese tobacco from any source—metropolitan or African—the OC could not locate any Congolese coffee for a 1946 exposition in Dendermonde.[190] Thus, a second theme of these local expositions was a pro-empire enthusiasm that sometimes surpassed realities.

Another theme of local expositions was the colony's link to Leopold II. A bust of the deceased king "dominated" a 1935 colonial exposition in Arlon that celebrated the fiftieth anniversary of the foundation of the EIC; another had figured prominently at the Foire Commerciale de Bruxelles in 1926; yet another did so at the post–World War II Exposition de Termonde; the list continues. According to one observer, Leopold II's bust at the 1949 Foire Coloniale de Bruxelles served to "remind our contemporaries all that Belgium owes to the creative genius of this great King."[191] Officials praised Leopold II at inaugurations, such as when Minister of Colonies Buisseret and others did so in their opening remarks at the 1955 Koloniale Jaarbeurs van Antwerpen.[192] Exposition brochures also lauded the king.[193] Exhibits honored the Belgian dynasty as a whole by including busts of other sovereigns.[194]

Local exhibits of empire provide a richness that furthers our understanding of procolonial forces and complements what we know about larger shows of empire at Belgium's many world's fairs. On the one hand, the repeated praising of Leopold II reinforced a positive rewriting of the past; on the other, the lack of products limited the impact of exhibits of raw materials such as coffee and tobacco. Although the Colonial Ministry played a major role even in smaller exhibits, the numerous involved local groups and enthusiasts disclose a depth of support that raw attendance numbers at universal expositions cannot reveal. Historians of colonial exhibitions who have by and large restricted their analyses to only the most prominent displays of empire in France, Britain, and elsewhere could study these and other cases in greater depth by moving beyond highlights such as the 1924–25 Wembley and 1931 Paris colonial expositions to consider the impact of local, city, and regional exhibits of empire.[195] British, French, and Belgian expositions at the national level, for example, contrasted European "civilization" and colonial "savagery," oftentimes by means of before-and-after techniques; it would be useful to explore if similar devices were used on the local level. If hybridity was avoided in 1931, as Patricia Morton argues, was this sustained or countered at local expositions? Did smaller exhibits of empire challenge official discourses, as the 1931 anticolonial exposition in France did? Whereas there were few Africans, Asians, or African Americans in Belgium before 1960, there were comparatively many in France and Britain.[196] Did this presence lead to altered discourses on the local level at smaller exhibits or to more contestations of the colonial order?

In sum, the state, missionary groups, and private interests all used expositions universelles after 1908 to sell a positive version of the colonial mission to the Belgian populace, particularly young people, and to a broader European or even global audience. They emphasized nation and dynasty; the benefits of European technology, education, and health care for Congolese children; agricultural advancement; and industrial growth, all the while denying the value of indigenous culture, society, and economy. Similar to other European imperial powers, organizers of Belgian colonial exhibits denied an African history by projecting a history of central Africa that began with Leopold II and continued with Belgian rule. Anonymous Africans mattered little in displays that showed Congolese as subjects, not as partners, in the imperial project. An inexhaustible technique was that of sharp contrasts, from Bastien and Mathieu's 1913 panorama to before-and-after photos of an African in De Meyer's 1958 *Introducing the Belgian Congo and the Ruanda-Urundi.* The use of contrasts between Africa before and after the arrival of Europeans was not just a Belgian phenomenon. British expositions also used them, and the French colonial exposition of 1931 developed a contrast between "metropolitan 'civilization' and colonial 'savagery'" as a tool to demonstrate French colonial order, as Patricia Morton has shown.[197] Most distinctive in the Belgian case was the atavism of the 1958 displays.

Three

Curators and Colonial Control

Belgium's Museums of Empire

When Frans Olbrechts became the fifth director of the massive Musée du Congo Belge in Tervuren in 1947, a position he was to hold until his death in 1958, he brought a fresher, more worldly, and arguably more learned background to the position than those of his predecessors.[1] Olbrechts was of a younger generation, raised when the Congo was integral to the Belgian experience. Born in Mechelen in 1899 and orphaned at a young age, Olbrechts was not even ten years old when Belgium took control of the Congo. After World War I forced him from the country, Olbrechts learned English at the Darlington Queen Elizabeth Grammar School. He later studied ethnology at Columbia University under Franz Boas, received his doctorate, and conducted field research in North America and West Africa — the latter with the encouragement of Henry Schouteden, the director of the Musée du Congo Belge at the time. In 1936 he published what was to become a noted ethnological text, *Ethnologie: Inleiding tot de studie der primitieve beschaving*, one of many publications over the course of his career.[2] According to one sympathetic writer, Olbrechts championed the role of the scientist in society, and this would seem to make his appointment as director of the museum all the more appropriate considering its dual scientific-popularization role.[3] Moreover, he advocated the study of African artwork as art and of its creators as artists, rather than merely ethnographic pieces and nameless producers, respectively.[4] There was much this polymath offered, yet one thing he did not: experience in the Congo. When appointed director in 1947, Olbrechts had never traveled to the colony at any point during his life; perhaps more telling as to the Tervuren museum as an institution, he did not travel there until 1955, eight years into his tenure and just three years before his death.[5]

The Musée du Congo Belge in Tervuren was one of a number of imperial museums or institutes tied to overseas expansion in Africa or Asia that came into being in the European imperial states. These included the Pitt Rivers Museum and the research-oriented Imperial Institute in Britain as well as France's Musée des colonies et de la France extérieure. Even the lesser imperial powers opened such institutions: Italy with its Museo Coloniale in Rome; a Deutsches Kolonialmuseum in Berlin; and in the Netherlands a colonial museum and later a colonial institute. All these establishments were not only scientific institutions but also sites of politics and power. As Sharon Macdonald has put it, "Politics . . . lies not just in policy statements and intentions (though these are important) but also in apparently non-political and even 'minor' details, such as the architecture of buildings, the classification and juxtaposition of artefacts in an exhibition, the use of glass cases or interactives, and the presence or lack of a voice-over on a film."[6] Yet no other colonial museum was quite like Belgium's Congo museum that remains still today, until now only somewhat altered, on the outskirts of Brussels.[7] As late as 1999, Jean Muteba Rahier could write that the display of Africana confirmed "a sort of nonmodern, noncivilized, frozen state of being characterized by a series of 'strange esoteric rituals' directly opposed to the ideals of modernity. Africa, as it appears, is filled with ahistorical societies in definitive need of colonization."[8] It might not be that Africa appeared ahistorical, as Rahier writes here, but rather that it appeared prehistorical. Begun during Leopold II's reign as part of his plan for a vast imperial complex in the village of Tervuren, after it was finished and opened just months after his death, it remained the only building that was ever completed. Nevertheless, it remained a mammoth colonial museum at the center of a tiny country with a huge overseas empire.[9]

Although a number of studies of the Tervuren museum have emerged in recent years, many take it and its displays at face value, and few have investigated the viewpoint of curators or visitors. Archival sources regarding the rationales behind the museum and considerations of the museum from the viewpoint of the visitor are critical complements to visual analyses of the museum. The Musée du Congo Belge was a contact zone between two geographically distant peoples, namely, dominant Belgians and their Congolese subjects.[10] The state, colonial enthusiasts, and private pro-empire groups used this contact zone not to get to know Congolese better, but rather to pursue other ends, which were reinforced as this permanent scientific and educational establishment intersected with more transient forms of propaganda, such as expositions. Nonetheless, "reading records against the grain" reveals alternate discourses, successful and unsuccessful, in the elaboration of the museum.[11] Not unlike expositions, the Musée du Congo Belge demonstrates that pro-empire propaganda in Belgium, as elsewhere, continued well into the twentieth century, even right up to decolonization. Indeed, this most striking of all the European colonial museums should be understood primarily as a tool of propaganda that explained and justified imperialism at the expense of science, exploration, and understanding. Moreover, the Musée du Congo Belge fostered Belgian nationalism by associating the colony with the Saxe-Coburg dynasty and by lionizing colonial heroes and Leopold II. And the government in Brussels prevented propaganda from being divided into Flemish and Walloon components by centering their efforts around the Tervuren institution, even if local efforts to create empire museums indicate an unexpected level of enthusiasm for the Congo after 1908.

Founding, Funding, and Visiting the Congo Museum at Tervuren

Standing about eight miles outside Brussels in the town of Tervuren and inaugurated in 1910, the Congo museum is an incredible if mixed achievement. Frenchman Charles Girault modeled the building after his Petit Palais, built for the 1900 Paris Exposition Universelle; it cost almost nine million gold francs — today's equivalent of about thirty-five million Euros.[12] The rectangular building is about 410 feet long and 246 feet wide, covering close to 30,840 square feet, with the Chausée de Louvain and an enormous *jardin à la française* (French garden) on either side.[13] The entrance for official visits was a large rotunda on the park side of the building topped by an almost ninety-two-foot-tall dome enclosed by enormous glassed-in bays, the glass of which contained the royal monogram.[14] Vitrines, sculptures, and exhibit pieces filled the long, high-ceilinged rooms inside, which ran almost the full length of the building. The interior formed a large unroofed court, the Cour d'Honneur. One student of Leopold II's rich architectural legacy has called the museum "one of the most unquestionable successes of the oeuvre of the Roi-Bâtisseur."[15] Yet his intentions for the museum were never fully realized. He originally envisioned the museum as but one part of a grandiose imperial complex to include an École mondiale

3. The Royal Museum for Central Africa (photo by the author).

(World College) for students from across Europe to study overseas administration, a Pavillon des Congrès Coloniaux to host
events, and a Salle des Exercises Physiques. Following his death,
the government quickly abandoned his plans, although not without protest from some of his former collaborators.[16]

King Albert I and Jules Renkin publicly inaugurated the new
Musée du Congo Belge on 30 April 1910.[17] Born in 1875 as the
nephew of Leopold II, Albert had just become the kingdom's third
monarch in December 1909. In contrast to his uncle, Albert actually traveled to the colony, spending a considerable time there just
months before Leopold's December 1909 death. During that trip,
the prince corresponded with Renkin, and they developed a good
relationship.[18] Renkin, who was thirteen years older than the new
king, was a lawyer, Catholic party politician, and government
minister who supported turnover of power in the Congo to Belgium. In October 1908 Renkin became the country's minister

of colonies, an office he held for a decade, far longer than any of his successors. In their speeches, Renkin and Albert recognized past mistakes yet spoke of an improved Congo administration, in this sense distancing themselves from their predecessors. They also conveyed the institute's dual mission of scientific research and imperialistic propaganda, a message that museum guides repeated.[19] Renkin underlined the museum's scientific role, even naming its scientific journal *Annales du Musée du Congo*.[20] He stressed that the 1910 exposition and the new museum aimed to move beyond past prejudices in order to promote goodwill, and to "excite in hearts the desire to collaborate with the great work of civilization, where Belgium, despite all hardships, will know how to show the profound imprint of her genius." The king sounded a similar note: "One colonizes today not as in the past—by importing arms, liquor and exploiting a country to excess—but by introducing in remote and primitive countries more dignified morals, sanctioned by Christian morality, and spreading there discoveries of science and marvels of modern technology. A colonizing people that understands its true interests is concerned above all for the well-being of the populations subjected to its guardianship."[21] Both spoke of the need to inform Belgians about the empire and about the civilizing mission, a necessity in a country that had no imperial history and that had just taken over an immense African territory. As the head of the museum's history department later put it: "The exposition rooms of the new museum of the Congo were adapted to the necessities of the moment: Belgium, which had just taken in hand the destinies of a vast territory offering enormous possibilities, needed to devote itself to bringing its nationals up to speed about African things."[22]

Scientific research, education, and the development of a colonial spirit formed the core of the museum's mission. In 1910 the institute's new director, who would serve in that post until 1927, was Baron Alphonse de Haulleville, a member of the pro-colonial lobby who promoted imperialism by means of works such as his 1898 *Les aptitudes colonisatrices des Belges, et la question coloniale en Belgique.*[23] To de Haulleville the museum was not only "a conservatory of objects but also a living and active school," whose goal was "to educate the masses." In addition to providing research facilities, de Haulleville believed the museum "had yet another mission: it must be an instrument of propaganda of colonial ideas. Presented according to scientific data, its collections speak to reason, at the same time that by their exhibition, as much seductive as objective, the results acquired thanks to the genius and energy of our race, they move the heart while eliciting noble enthusiasms and healthy emotions."[24] A guidebook indicated this further: "The goal of the Museum is to instruct, to create the colonial education of the visitors, to create and develop a colonial mentality in Belgium. . . . The Museum must be a permanent instrument of sound propaganda of the colonial idea; a living and active school."[25] This guidebook from 1925 was written by Joseph Maes, in charge of the museum's ethnographic section from 1910 to 1946 and arguably the person most responsible for shaping the museum at the time.[26] (Like his successor, Olbrechts, Maes joined the museum having never traveled to the Congo and only went there once, from May 1913 to mid-1914.[27]) Thus the institution's main goals were similar to the dual educational and research objectives that formed the "organizational basis of many of the larger museums established during the Museum Movement" in Britain in the latter half of the nineteenth century.[28] Curators in Britain at this time similarly "cast themselves in the role of benevolent educators," asserting their place in society by "dispensing rational and more particularly 'scientific' knowledge about the colonies and their indigenous people."[29] Tervuren museum administrators likewise sought to distinguish themselves by claiming control over information about the colony at the intersection of science and popular education.

It is important to ask how visitors reacted to the museum and its displays. This is a difficult question to answer for any museum because it is easier to assess museums' aims and goals than it is to scrutinize visitors' reactions. Moreover, museums cater to broad groups of people, and there is no such thing as the typical visitor, making the measurement of display effectiveness even more difficult.[30] This might be particularly problematic in the case of museums of non-Western objects and art.[31] Nonetheless, we can get a sense of the feeling that the museum may have elicited by means of a firsthand account of a 1910 visit by L. Vincart, who was probably a government official at some point:

> During the walk through of this wonderful building, the Belgian visitor . . . feels his emotions of national pride rising involuntarily . . . to be part of the people that counts among its sons the heroic victors over the Arabic slave drivers, and also the numerous undaunted heroes of the work of Evangelization. . . . And everywhere he is also reminded of the activity and the daring in the field of trade and industry equally, how the Belgians in the space of so few years—in only a fourth of a century!—can have transformed an unknown and unapproachable continent in all respects.[32]

Thus a visitor to the museum could swell with national pride as he or she learned about Belgium's transformative international role: spreading Christianity, combating the slave trade, and developing industry and trade.

To reach citizens of all classes, the museum was easily accessible thanks to free and unrestricted entry, a direct Brussels–Tervuren tramline, and the country's extensive railway system.[33] Just as British colonial museums defined "their publics as having a large working-class component," creating a policy "designed to unite all classes in the defense of nation and empire," so was there a similar rallying of the masses to the colonial cause at the Musée du Congo Belge.[34] And the masses responded. As the old museum building got ready to close in 1909, it received an incredible 450,000 visitors in its last eight months of operation, and the new museum received 182,500 visitors between 30 April and 15 August 1910.[35] Because the museum also served as the colonial section of the Brussels World's Fair that same year, it is unsurprising that attendance figures declined in the years immediately following. But by the 1920s, the annual number of visitors regularly exceeded 150,000, a level that it maintained in years after, exceptions being the years of World War II.[36] There were perhaps as many as six million visitors who went to the museum from 1910 to 1960, confirming a significant level of interest in imperialism among the general population. Although these might seem like small numbers, they represent a significant percentage of the Belgian population. In 1959, for instance, approximately 176,100 people visited the museum, representing just less than 2 percent of the total population. For very rough comparison purposes, the most popular museum in the United States in recent times, the Smithsonian National Air and Space Museum, attracted on average 7,648,754 visitors per year from 2002–4, or about 2.5 percent of the U.S. population.[37] So in this respect, the Belgian experience did not parallel that of Britain, where some scholars have argued that empire even reached to the level of "lived" in everyday practices in the metropole.[38]

Attendance at the museum in Tervuren would belie such an assertion in the Belgian case. At the same time, as comparative figures from the Smithsonian's number one museum demonstrate, more Belgians were interested in empire than perhaps previously believed.

How many of these visitors were male, how many were female, and from what kind of social backgrounds they were drawn are hard questions to answer. The few figures available that break down schoolchildren attendance by gender indicate an equal number of girls and boys.[39] In any case, the museum as institution reflected Belgian imperialism as a whole; in the museum as elsewhere, it was overwhelmingly men who promoted the colonial idea in Belgium and exalted male figures in the process, suggesting either a desire to maintain a privileged zone of action or women's greater remoteness from the colonial idea, or both.[40] Extending a gender analysis of the museum quickly reveals that it was a male creation: those who constructed the museum, administered it, and produced its displays were exclusively male, from the museum's directors and administrators, to artists such as A. Matton and Thomas Vinçotte who created sculptures for the collections, to those who collected specimens in the Congo. And this appears not to have changed with time.

Even if fundamentally the museum changed little, what men and women who followed Vincart's 1910 visit would have seen did not remain unchanging over the years, as one might infer from recent accounts.[41] Collections grew substantially as a result of the country's expositions universelles, which of course contributed from the very beginning since the institution's origins were in the 1897 Exposition Coloniale in Tervuren and Leopold II's desire to open a window onto Africa.[42] Girault's building, which also served as the colonial section of the 1910 Exposition

Universelle et Internationale de Bruxelles, replaced the previous Musée du Congo, which had been the Palais des Colonies for the 1897 fair. The 1935 World's Fair supplied a bust of Leopold II to the museum's Cour d'Honneur as well as an ivory bust of Leopold III and a large elephantine sculpture by Albéric Collin.[43] The 1958 World's Fair contributed a number of items to the museum's collections as well as the CAPA building. In this way, this permanent scientific and educational establishment intersected with more transient forms of propaganda like expositions. There also were reorganizations of exhibits such that by the post–World War II period the museum had changed the *salle du mémorial* (memorial hall) and also begun to display African artwork and European sculpture. It seriously downplayed colonial exports and imports for a number of reasons, from the fact that large companies dominated the colonial economy, to the Ministry of Colonies' cessation of promotion of settler colonization, to the need to accommodate growing ethnographic and scientific collections.[44] Nonetheless, the building itself saw only one significant alteration, when its inner arcade was enclosed to provide more exhibition space.[45] The underlying rationalization of the displays—that they present a total picture of the Congo—remained unchanging.[46] Jean Muteba Rahier attributed this to the fact that responsibility for the museum's rooms were divided among differing departments and sections.[47] Of course, a much simpler explanation for consistency in the museum's displays, if a less palatable one from a postcolonial viewpoint, is that the directors during the colonial period—Haulleville, Schouteden, Olbrechts, and Cahen—were satisfied with the exhibits as they were.

Another possible reason the museum did not change much is that it received inadequate funding, and it does appear it suffered from disregard in the colonial budget.[48] A 1931 government report indicated the museum lacked funds and noted that it received less money than similar scientific establishments in Belgium.[49] In the middle of his tenure as museum director in the mid-1930s, Henry Schouteden lamented to the minister of colonies that credits allocated to the museum were "so reduced."[50] In the run-up to the 1935 Brussels international exposition, OC head Frans Janssen wrote to the minister of colonies about the "abandoned" state of Tervuren, referring likely in part to the foundations of the École mondiale that had sat unfinished and unused since the government halted construction in 1910. While affirming his belief that Belgium possessed "the most beautiful world museum of African art and of artistic and scientific materials," he went on to write that Tervuren "is in the process of foundering [s'abîmer] and losing a part of its value. It is necessary to save it and begin again the projects of His Majesty Leopold II in their great lines."[51] Tervuren's town council wrote—albeit with some self-interest in a time of depression, since the museum meant business for local establishments—to the Ministry of Colonies in 1932 that the museum was notoriously cramped and that a majority of its collection was inaccessible to the public and risking deterioration.[52] With such a reduced budget, the museum was forced to accomplish what it did "with fewer personnel than the other large museums in Belgium."[53]

The financial situation improved so little after World War II that the new director of the museum as of 1947, Frans Olbrechts, could not support research on the ground in the Congo. "It is an amazing fact that a man who was at the time becoming the director of one of the great centres of African art and material culture did not think he could muster the support and the funds for African research. This situation in itself is ample proof that up to that time Belgium and her scientific institutions had no real interest in promoting scientifically based anthropological field studies in Central Africa. Only lip service was paid to such enterprises."[54] So Olbrechts went outside the Ministry of Colonies to raise money, creating in the mid-1950s the group les Amis du Musée du Congo Belge (Friends of the Museum of the Belgian Congo).[55] While a committee of lawyers, businessmen, and government officials directed les Amis, the low cost to join—the maximum cost for the lowest level of membership was only one hundred francs, about two dollars—allowed for a broad public audience.[56] Despite the dedication of those such as Olbrechts, one might ask how important the museum was to the Ministry of Colonies considering its problematic finances. Although the museum received substantial outlays to complete it in 1910 and afterward throughout the colonial period, its administration believed there was never enough funding, reflecting a situation not unusual within western European state bureaucracies in the twentieth century. Despite such pleas, this lack of funds apparently persisted at least until 1960, indicating it resulted not just from the economic difficulties of particularly trying moments in Belgium's twentieth-century history, such as two foreign occupations and a major economic depression.

Tervuren's Total Picture of the Colony

The curators at Tervuren had enough funds to promote scientific research and endeavor to develop a colonial spirit, and a number of key themes emerged as they did so during the colonial period. The museum's collections implied control over the vast Congo by constituting a means by which the museum and its domestic audience could control the colony by dissecting and classifying it and condensing its enormous territory into photographs, objects in vitrines, maps, sculpted figures, and explanatory captions, all conveniently located just outside Brussels.[57] Upon the 1908 take-over, the state took control of the museum's land and building, claimed the institution through a new name (Musée du Congo Belge), and placed it within the Ministry of Colonies. It did not rely on business, religious, or other outside interests despite the fact that the museum at times faced difficult finances. The Co-lonial Ministry tasked curators with the classification, analysis, and study of all Africana from the Congo arriving to the mère patrie in order to give visitors the impression that the Congo was one unit and therefore whole, understandable, and control-lable.[58] This was despite, or perhaps because of, the fact that the colony was a massive territory the size of western Europe that in-cluded many peoples coming from different cultures who spoke countless different languages. By collecting everything about the colony in one place, the state achieved a legitimacy comparable to that of scholars who relied on Africana to establish their cred-ibility on African subjects, such as William H. Sheppard, who used his collection of African artifacts to illustrate his public lectures in the United States. Just as "Artifacts were tangible proof of Sheppard's visit to the mythic capital and his meeting with its ruler," so were the museum's displays of Africana proof of the state's authority.[59] As George Stocking has shown, power relations are always inherent in collections of material objects because a museum's objects necessarily once belonged to some-body else and had to be acquired in order to be put on display, often by use of force. Simply put, objects that a museum places before viewers once belonged to somebody else.[60] Thus the very establishment of the museum in the metropole, the collecting and displaying of Africana for all Belgians, and the extent of the collections demonstrated "the power exerted by Belgian

individuals and institutions over the Congolese peoples."⁶¹ Much
material had been collected by means of armed conquest and
thus, "In this sense the colonial museum was 'a powerful and
handsome trophy' displayed on the wall of a small and still very
young nation."⁶²

   This central repository was an attempt at a total picture of
a unified Congo. This was similar to other representations of
European overseas territories that gave the impression of cohe-
sive empires, the clearest examples being colonial exhibitions
like Marseille (1922), Wembley (1924–25), and Porto (1934)
that depicted empires as units. Or on a much smaller scale there
were devices like a German colonial postcard series in a decorative sleeve that produced the illusion of a unified overseas empire. Whoever bought the postcard series could literally carry
the German empire around in his or her pocket.⁶³ The museum in Tervuren similarly endeavored to capture the entirety of
Belgium's empire in central Africa in one place. The museum's
rooms—in 1910 there were two rooms for anthropology, one
for political and moral sciences, four for social sciences, and
five for natural sciences—were organized to provide a complete
overview.⁶⁴ An observer's remarks in 1959 reveal that this en-
cyclopedic approach was sustained over the decades: "The two
sections that deal with invertebrates in our Museum . . . have for
a final goal the establishment of a faunal inventory [*l'inventaire
faunistique*] of the Belgian Congo, that is to say an exact summary of all Congolese faunae [*toutes les faunes congolaises*]. . . .
In mineralogy the 6,500 conserved specimens cover almost the
totality of mineral species found to date in the Belgian Congo
and Ruanda-Urundi."⁶⁵ Whether it is possible to produce a total
picture of a thing as complex as the enormous Congo is moot;
what is relevant, however, is that the museum staff accomplished

much of what they set out to do in this attempt to portray control over the overseas territory by classifying it, organizing it, and reducing it to controllable, discrete, tangible collectibles.

The museum presented a particular narrative of the Congo in which the colony's history became a strictly Belgian affair.[66] It was, to use James Clifford's term, a "majority museum," which is to say an institution that articulated "cosmopolitan culture, science, art, and humanism—often with a national slant."[67] Baron Alphonse de Haulleville's 1910 museum brochure *Le Musée du Congo Belge à Tervuren* began with an *aperçu historique* (historical overview) centered on Leopold II's "opening up" of central Africa to civilization, including a chronology of key events starting with the king's 1876 speech to the Brussels Geographical Conference. Although de Haulleville mentioned foreigners such as Welsh American Henry Morton Stanley, he emphasized the role of Belgian nationals. The museum's memorial rooms also stressed the Belgian nature of imperialism in the Congo. The two plaques in the salle du mémorial titled "Comité d'Études du Haut Congo 1879–1885" and "Association Internationale Africaine 1877–1885" eulogized Belgian pioneers only and excluded foreigners. Other memorials in the room included tributes to soldiers, such as to Lieven and Jozef Van de Velde, Captain Lucien Bia, and General Émile Storms, all of them Belgian. By the 1940s, at least, the museum had added a bust of Albert I and later added a statue of Leopold II.[68] This meant that with the exception of one Luxembourger (Nicholas Cito) all figures memorialized in the room were Belgian. There was no bust to Stanley or to any of the many Scandinavians, Germans, Italians, or other foreigners who had helped explore and conquer central Africa, and certainly no commemoration of the many Africans who died fighting for the EIC.

The museum became an even more nationalistic institution through a process of contestation and because of Belgian fears. An example of this process is a letter Josué Henry de la Lindi wrote in 1934 protesting one of the large wall maps of the Congo in the museum, specifically how it represented the past. The map had already been in place for many years, representing European geographical knowledge of central Africa as it existed around the year 1900 by showing the itineraries of two early explorers, both of them German. What changed in 1934 was the addition of a memorial to the museum commemorating the 1,500-plus Belgians who died during the EIC period. Henry himself was a colonial veteran of the Leopoldian era who had become a pro-empire activist—he owed his noble title "de la Lindi" to his victory against the Batetela in 1897. He asserted in his letter that Belgians had been the first to survey the areas indicated on the map, during the Arab campaigns of the 1890s. Henry wrote, "As the wall map is in some way the symbol of the works accomplished by our colonial heroes, it would be unfortunate, it seems to me, to leave incomplete this scientific monument raised to their memory, and even more unfortunate to attribute to the Germans works and a glory that are not due to them: the 1,500 names written to the side, instead of being glorified, would be outraged by it."[69] Henry's complaint can be understood as part of a movement in the interwar period toward commemorating Belgian colonial pioneers, probably due to increased nationalism in the wake of World War I. Also, fears arising from post–Versailles Treaty colonial claims by Germany and from the 1933 accession of Hitler to power might help explain the Tervuren museum "claiming" central Africa for Belgium.[70] Although National Socialist territorial goals in Africa were not great, Henry and like-minded enthusiasts did not know this at the time; they certainly did not ignore German irredentism that was voiced throughout the 1920s and early 1930s.[71] As is so often the case, perceptions and emotions spurred actions such as the museum's redrafting of the map, affirming recent scholarship arguing that emotions should be integrated into histories of the domestic origins of international relations.[72]

Throughout the aperçu of de Haulleville's brochure is similar praise for the roi-souverain who had engaged in a "colossal labor" to open the "mysterious continent to civilization," and de Haulleville happily quoted de Brazza's quip that the conquest of the Congo was a work of titans accomplished by pygmies. The aperçu repeatedly eulogized Leopold II and Belgian colonial pioneers, to the point that de Haulleville had to check himself: "More space would be necessary than that which we have at our disposal in this leaflet to recall all the actions of brilliance, all the courageous undertakings that assured the progress of the occupation of the Congo from 1885 to 1895." Like other colonial devotees and Leopold apologists, de Haulleville asserted that the antislavery campaign was a glorious page in Belgium's colonial past: "How to retrace that brilliant Arab campaign that is one of the most beautiful pages of our colonial history. It abounds with acts of courage, with acts of heroism." Referring to the Arab campaigns allowed him once again to laud Leopold: "The initiative and the merit of this result fall above all to Leopold II. The King was the great organizer of the Arab campaign [*campagne arabe*]. He never forgot his goal, which was to assure the triumph of civilization and to serve the nation [*patrie*]." Leopold's "patrie" here is Belgium, of course, not his other "patrie," the EIC. De Haulleville concluded by calling Leopold II the "inspired initiator" of "indomitable energy" who was not dissuaded by "pusillanimous counsels." The summary ends in telling fashion with the death of Leopold II in December 1909.[73] Enthusiasts at the museum, in this case de Haulleville, praised Leopold II for his generosity and perspicacity, just as others did at expositions, monuments, and elsewhere; this first museum guide asserted themes that were to be repeated throughout the colonial period: accomplishment, pride, sacrifice, the greatness of Leopold II, and military conquest.

The Musée du Congo Belge also served as an extended homage to Leopold II and the dynasty. Speakers and administrators invoked Leopold II at museum events and in museum guides; since around the time of the 1935 World's Fair, a large bust of him has been located in the heart of the museum, in the center of the interior court, the Cour d'Honneur.[74] In the museum's entrance, the Salle du Dôme, one could for years find a bust of Leopold II by Thomas Vinçotte carved entirely out of elephant tusks.[75] A larger-than-life statue of Leopold II dominated one end of the salle du mémorial even into the twenty-first century. Museum guides and temporary exhibits honored the dynasty more generally. As Jean Muteba Rahier has pointed out, printed museum guides associated the Tervuren project with the monarchy and nation by starting not with the new museum building in 1910 or the 1908 reprise or the 1897 colonial exposition or even the 1885 founding of the EIC, but rather with the "history of the domain and of the village of Tervuren."[76] This maneuver served to fix the museum "within the history of the Belgian dynasty—the major symbol of Belgian national identity. The Belgian colonial enterprise [was] in that way rooted within what the authors of the guides want[ed] to present as a long royal tradition going back to the twelfth century," a somewhat misplaced interpretation because Belgium happened upon the Congo (and the museum) fortuitously as the result of one of its sovereigns' deeds and misdeeds.[77] Henry Schouteden, who took over the position from Alphonse de Haulleville in 1927, served as museum director for nearly twenty years and invoked the royal lineage in the very first sentence of his 1947 guide when he wrote, "Charming village of the surroundings of Brussels, at the edge of the forêt de Soignes, Tervuren was formerly a royal residence."[78] The very earliest Belgian involvement in the Congo only went as far back as the 1870s, but the museum invited its visitors to consider the institution as being deeply wedded to the dynasty and therefore the Kingdom of Belgium. In 1955 the museum displayed gifts King Baudouin had received during his trip to the Congo that year, complete with a larger-than-life image of the king himself. In 1958 the museum director at the time, Lucien Cahen, and his staff put on an exhibition of historical documents to mark the fiftieth anniversary of the annexation of the Congo, at which, as at other such temporary exhibits during the colonial period, busts representing the dynasty (e.g., of Leopold II and Albert I) dominated. After Maurice Van Hemelryck, minister of the Belgian Congo and Ruanda-Urundi, opened the exhibit, Cahen tied the museum of 1958 to Leopold II's vision, stressing "that the exhibited documents retrace the history of the cession of the Congo to Belgium and testify to the continuity of thought of the previous sovereign and to his extraordinary vision of the future."[79] Therefore, promoting dynasty and nation was a key component of the museum's action, tracing back to de Haulleville's 1910 museum guide that emphasized Leopold II and the Belgian dynasty and that described rooms that downplayed non-Belgians' contributions.

The museum also lauded the military, somewhat surprising in a small, neutral country. Throughout most of the period 1908–60, the museum's history displays in the œuvre civilisatrice room, the *salle centrale* (central hall), and the salle du mémorial emphasized the military nature of imperialism in the Congo. By the post–World War II period, these rooms held vitrines showing exploration, the occupation of the Congo, the 1914–18 campaigns, and the antiesclavagiste era by means of "moving souvenirs" of the military campaigns led by Commandant (later Baron) Dhanis, Colonel Chaltin, Commandant Lothaire, Commandant Pierre Ponthier, and Aristide Doorme, among others.[80] In 1934 the museum added a "Mémorial à la mémoire des Belges morts au Congo avant 1908" to the salle du mémorial that showed the names of all Belgians killed in Africa during the Leopoldian era from 1876–1908. In 1959, on the eve of Congo's independence, the museum inaugurated a towering plaque in the same room to heroes of the "antislavery" military campaigns of the 1890s titled "Campagnes antiesclavagistes, Veldtochten tegen de Slavenhandel, 1891–1899." Those campaigns originated not so much in Leopold II's supposed humanitarianism but rather in conflicts with indigenous rulers. When Leopold II faced a shortage of manpower and funds in the late 1880s and early 1890s, his agents in the Congo came to an arrangement with Tippu Tip (Hamed bin Muhammed), the Swahili ivory and slave trader who had assisted H. M. Stanley in his transcontinental voyage in 1875–77. Tippu Tip had established a large trading empire in eastern Congo and was so powerful that Leopold II offered him the governorship of the EIC's eastern province in 1887. Yet this collaboration with Arab Swahili traders quickly broke down, and in 1892 European officers of the EIC began what came to be called the *campagnes antiesclavagistes* (antislavery campaigns) to defeat Tippu Tip's Arab Swahili forces (the so-called Arabs) on the ground. While Leopold II conveniently described the campaigns as a battle against slavery, in reality they were military campaigns to extend his control in eastern Congo. The antislavery-campaign plaque listed names of the many Europeans lying dead in Africa and depicted Leopold, Chaltin, Dhanis, and other military leaders in profile, contributing to the room's martial theme.[81] There were few memorials to nonmilitary men, such as administrators or religious figures; four exceptions were those to entrepreneur Albert Thys, geologist Jules Cornet, engineer Nicolas Cito, and administrator Count Renaud de Briey.[82]

In fact the colonial museum transformed over time into a national war memorial of sorts. Gaynor Kavanagh has described how, through reverses and setbacks, the Imperial War Museum in England became both a site of research and a memorial to the Great War.[83] By the mid-1930s, with the building of the Mémorial à la mémoire des Belges morts au Congo avant 1908 and the addition of the bust of Leopold II to the Cour d'Honneur and other memorials to the salle du mémorial, the Musée du Congo Belge similarly had transformed into a war memorial, this one to Leopold II's — and through the museum and other colonial propaganda, Belgium's — wars of conquest in central Africa. The addition of memorials from that point forward confirmed this, as did innumerable *trophées de guerre* (war trophies) from retired colonials, all of which informed visitors of "the heroic period of the Belgian occupation of the Congo and the valiant pioneers of that period."[84] Should there be any doubt of the Musée du Congo Belge as a memorial, one only need consult the periodical the museum launched in the mid-1950s, *Congo-Tervuren* (later *Africa-Tervuren*), the very first issue of which started a years-long series called "List of the Pioneers of the Congo Free State" to commemorate in print those who had died in Africa during the Leopoldian era.

While memorial plaques and commemorative busts conveyed

4. Bust of Leopold II inside the Tervuren museum (photo by the author).

explicit messages, the museum also controlled history in more surreptitious ways. The museum was a scientific center for scholars, and Sony Van Hoecke and Jean-Pierre Jacquemin have shown that it promoted a certain vision of the Congo through selective dissemination of research material. Regarding Marcel Luwel's takeover of the directorship of the moral and political sciences section from Frantz Cornet in 1949, they write, "Until then [1949], when one furnished documentation on Belgian Africa to interested parties, it was to permit them to write popularizing texts [*textes de vulgarisation*], often of apologetic connotation."[85] They continue with what is a damning account of the museum's scientific work: "Information was frequently concealed [*occulté*], in order to conform to official doctrine, which was supposed to support the colonial consciousness. In this context, the filtering of information destined for the exterior world was a necessity and, as we have seen, Luwel's predecessor scrupulously performed this task."[86] In 1910 Albert I had announced the museum's two-fold assignment of imperialistic propaganda and scientific research, and museum director de Haulleville had said the collections were to be "presented according to scientific data," in order "to speak to reason."[87] Yet to follow Van Hoecke and Jacquemin, the emphasis was on propaganda above all else. Not only did the museum overtly propagate a heroic, nationalist, and pro-Leopoldian imperialist vision in its displays, it skewed research into the Congo in the way in which it cooperated with or counteracted researchers. Through items such as the wall map representing the geographical knowledge of central Africa circa 1900 that Henry de la Lindi complained about, the museum communicated an ideological position under the cloak of scientific objectivity. In the end, ideology trumped science in a purportedly dispassionate, scientific institution. This fact—coupled with the shift from a focus on economics in 1910 toward memorializing Belgian colonial history; the exclusion of missions, medicine, education, or other church activities in its "total picture" of the Congo; and its backing of the necessity of Belgium's presence in Africa, discussed below—means that the museum must be understood above all else as a tool that promoted imperialism. Just as colonial humanism in French West Africa was contradictory at its core, as Gary Wilder has shown, so was the museum because of its dual goals: the pursuit of objective science and the promotion of the ideology of imperialism.[88]

The museum remained largely unchanged under Olbrechts's successor, Lucien Cahen, perhaps surprising considering Cahen was the only director of the museum during the colonial period to spend an extended period in the Congo. Son of a Belgian father and French mother, Cahen's first language was neither Flemish nor French, but rather English, as he lived in Britain until he was nine years old; he did not begin to study Flemish until becoming director of the museum in 1958. Cahen trained as a geologist at the Université libre de Bruxelles (Free University of Brussels) and first traveled to the Congo in 1937. Like many Belgian colonials who found themselves in central Africa in 1940, he saw his stay extended and ended up serving in the armed forces. It was not until 1946 that he returned to Europe, after which he entered into the service of the Tervuren museum, with a brief return to the Congo in 1948–49.

Despite his time in the colony, Cahen's museum continued to be an exhibit of Africa of the past rather than of the present.[89] Cahen himself noted in 1959 that one Congolese visitor criticized the museum because it showed "the Congo as it was and not as that which it is becoming."[90] The only major change in terms of the displays under Cahen's tenure to 1960 was the "creation of remarkable dioramas of African wildlife."[91] In fact, the museum in 1959 could be criticized for depicting the Congo as something static, as a fixed entity, rather than as something that was changing and that could become (and was becoming) something else. Yet in 1959 the museum was called the Musée royal du Congo Belge (Royal Museum of the Belgian Congo), not the Musée du Congo d'autrefois (Museum of the Congo of Bygone Days), representing to the metropole what was supposed to be the contemporary Congo. Soon after he became director, Cahen faced a wholly new situation, namely, the independence of the Congo, the results of which dominated much of his tenure, which lasted until 1977. But whether Cahen would have under-taken major changes in the museum's content and displays had the Congo remained Belgian is doubtful because he prioritized the equitable distribution of the museum's limited budget among its several departments over substantial reforms.[92]

Whether or not museum administrators such as Cahen in-tended to depict an unchanging Congo, this result also may have been an unintentional consequence of the choice of order and display. Nicholas Thomas has discussed this point in reference to a colonial display of Fijian material culture in the 1880s, not-ing that it led to "a sort of setting-out and rigidification of Fijian culture. Cultural products were aestheticised, placed together, ordered and reordered. The manipulation of diverse objects im-plies the apprehension and ordering of the totality they repre-sented, that is, Fijian society in its parts and aspects. The apical position of the governing elite gave them the vantage point from which the totality could be recognised."[93] The museum in Ter-vuren placed metropolitans in an "apical position" from which to grasp the totality of the Congo, which appeared backward and unchanging. From this position, the museum and its visitors belittled African artwork. When Edouard De Jonghe—director general of the department within the Ministry of Colonies under whose purview the Musée du Congo Belge fell and professor of colonial studies at the Catholic University of Leuven—wrote in the 1930s that basically all African art was decorative only and thus should be studied not as art but as ethnography, he reflected a widespread view.[94] The dates of European contact officially circumscribed historical research at the Musée du Congo Belge during the period of colonial rule: "The field of research of the history section starts in the year 1483, that is to say at the moment when the West discovered the Congo."[95] Research into African history was not supposed to take place within the historical section, but fell under other sections such as anthropology.

The museum's Eurocentrism, which was woven into the fabric of the museum itself, presented a Congo that was fixed, backward, and incapable of change, and provided no room for contestation or adaptation. Despite the fact that Congolese artistic production began to enter Belgium as art as early as the 1920s and 1930s and the fact that experts such as Gaston-Denys Périer began promoting the value of African art as art, it was Europeans who created the sculpture and other art pieces as such in the museum.[96] Pieces such as Charles Samuel's sculptures depicted the barbarism of African society before the coming of the Europeans. In the sculpture *Vuakusu-Batetela Protects a Woman from an Arab*, Samuel depicted an African woman at the mercy of an Arab, yet another instance of the use of the anti-Arab slavery narrative for public consumption as evidence of Leopold II's beneficent imperialism, a narrative whose repetition allowed it to attain the status of myth in Belgium's colonial history.[97] Other examples of European artwork were the original statues of gilded bronze that the Ministry of Colonies commissioned to adorn the

5. Postcard showing Charles Samuel's *Vuakusu-Batetela Protects a Woman from an Arab* in the Salle des Bois (author's collection).

alcoves of the museum's entrance hall. The fact that they remained on display into the twenty-first century led one scholar to write in 2000, "One could almost think that the Congo is still a Belgian colony."[98] The nine statues that the Ministry of Colonies ordered between the years 1910 and 1922 symbolized the beneficial results of Leopoldian and Belgian imperialism in central Africa. Among them were those created by sculptor A. Matton, including *Belgium Bringing Well-Being to the Congo*, *Belgium Bringing Security to the Congo*, and *Belgium Bringing Civilization to the Congo*. The statues indicated the meaning behind the museum and formed a framework for visitors over the decades.[99]

The museum's treatment of African artwork and material culture also imparted male dominance over females and Europeans' superiority over Congolese. As noted, those who constructed and administered the museum and filled its collections were

116

solely male. Museum sculptures such as Samuel's *Vuakusu-Bate-tela Protects a Woman from an Arab* and Matton's *Slavery* used the cliché of the defenseless, nude woman to depict the ruth-lessness of the male Arab slave trade, and other sculptures used other tropes of the female figure.[100] The museum subtly com-municated European superiority over Congolese by not naming Africans and by depicting them nude. James Clifford has argued that Western museums in the twentieth century organized all non-Western artwork into two categories, artwork or materi-al culture, what he calls the "anthropological-aesthetic object system," or the "art-culture system."[101] Because the Tervuren museum supposedly represented the entire colony, one would expect it to have encompassed Congolese artistic production in addition to material culture. It did not. Displays of artwork did not name individual African artists and instead showed works anonymously or as typical of a group. As mentioned, "art" in the museum comprised only Europeans' artwork, and this did not even begin to change until the 1950s. Contrariwise, curators did name European colonial heroes; when they pointed out the accomplishments of explorers, soldiers, and administrators, they identified them as individuals.[102]

What is more, representations of African people in sculptures, drawings, photographs, and paintings showed them most often partially dressed or nude, whereas depictions of Europeans al-ways presented them fully clothed. Many Congolese did go about partially undressed—from a European perspective—and in this sense the depictions cannot be considered unusual or misrepre-sentative. As Enid Schildkrout and Curtis Keim point out, many collectors and exhibitors of Africana actually hoped to cast a more positive light on the peoples of Africa, and there is little to no evidence that could lead us to conclude that museum officials at Tervuren were any different. So the issue is more complicated than the museum simply degrading Africans.[103] Museum directors Olbrechts and Cahen, for example, were not propagandists but serious scientists who sought to promote the advancement of knowledge about Africa.[104] The important point is that under the veil of scientific authenticity, within a site in which "All cues assure the viewer that this is the realm of objectivity," the museum communicated African inferiority.[105] For instance, sculptor Herbert Ward, whose work the museum featured, sought more to capture the spirit of Africa than achieve scientific authenticity. Yet the placement of his artwork within the frame of the museum lent it an authority it would not have had in an art gallery.[106]

Whatever the intentions, displaying Africans half clothed represented them to visitors as unchanging, because to visitors Congolese were always half clothed. Anonymity, or worse, classification of Africans as "types" fixed Congolese within racial categories, for as George Stocking points out, "The notion of 'type' was for the statistically unsophisticated a last refuge of the traditional notion of racial 'essence.'"[107] In reality, Africans and African styles changed and varied. Photographs of Congolese dressed in suits visiting the museum in the 1950s point to the speciousness of displays. One such photograph shows museum director Olbrechts and two Congolese in suits and overcoats studying casts of nude figures by sculptor Matton of *types indigènes* (indigenous types) modeled after living Africans, including busts and torsos from the front (neck, chest, and hips) and the rear (neck, back, arms, and buttocks).[108] We should not underestimate the impact of the Musée du Congo Belge in this regard. Museums can offer observers more direct, unmediated access to other cultures, places, and times than, say, a written account, and can give viewers the impression that they have apprehended a culture, place, epoch, or geographical location more entirely and truthfully than they might have learned elsewhere: "While knowledge obtained from textual sources may be seen to have an unsatisfying 'secondhand' character, an artefact and what it immediately represents can be seen directly."[109] Rather than engage with the Congo of the present and with the inherent risks that came with that approach, museum curators opted to take refuge in a simpler story, which is that Africans were "types," not people. Thus, it is unlikely the museum brought Belgians and Congolese closer.

The direct access to Congolese culture the Musée du Congo Belge supposedly offered only reinforced and supplemented efforts put forth by the Ministry of Colonies to popularize the overseas enterprise among Belgians elsewhere, and in many instances it reinforced the discourse produced by other parts of the administration. Just as the OC's displays of colonial products at expositions in the 1920s and 1930s highlighted the Congo's economic importance even before the onset of the Great Depression, so too did the Musée du Congo Belge emphasize this theme. Maes described the approach toward visitors in his 1925 museum guide:

> We would like to make [visitors] see among this classified and exhibited evidence the great inexhaustible wealth and the resources of our Colony, the possibilities of the future that await us there; show [visitors] the incalculable difficulties that had been surmounted and the unlimited devotion of the very first pioneers to the work realized . . . to penetrate in the large Belgian masses, the conviction that the future, the development and the prosperity of Belgium, are deeply [*intimement*] tied

to the progress of our colonial dominion and to the complete realization of the civilizing work of which we have assumed the responsibility.[110]

The author here touches on a number of themes recurrent in Belgian imperial propaganda, especially during the interwar years: the inexhaustible wealth of the colony, the great possibilities of the future, the devotion and accomplishments of the colony's founders, and the coupling of the nation's future to that of the colony's. The museum depicted Africa as critical to Belgium's future, all the while presenting an image of an unchanging Congo stuck in a distant past. Therefore, visitors found in the museum a perpetually justified, hopeful, nationalist imperialism. Belgium and the Congo conjoined symbiotically because Belgium's future depended on the Congo, which was permanently backward and thus always in need of Belgium.

Regarding visitors to the museum, the Musée du Congo Belge—similar to the OC with its quinzaines coloniales and the Commission Coloniale Scolaire (Colonial School Commission, CCS), discussed below—took particular interest in school-age children. Directors believed in the necessity of reaching children, and museum publications stressed the need to inform school teachers and induce children to visit.[111] A French visitor to the museum in 1924 remarked that "schoolchildren of all provinces of Belgium are brought to the museum as a reward and one does not neglect anything to complement their colonial education."[112] What is more, the museum ran Journées d'Études Coloniales (Colonial Studies Days) for geography teachers, dividing them into groups for tours of the collections, both those on display and on reserve.[113] During the last decade of the colonial period, a Mr. Van de Voort alone gave twenty-five talks per year to visiting groups of schoolchildren, indicating that pro-imperial propaganda was anything but slowing down in the 1950s. In the same decade, director Olbrechts had speakers from the CCS provide detailed guided tours to whole groups of students.[114]

Thus the comparatively fixed and steady Musée du Congo Belge complemented propaganda efforts at expositions, in the classroom, and elsewhere. Again, according to Tony Bennett, different media worked together in order to convey the messages of an ideology. Drawing on the work of Michel Foucault, Bennett argued, "Public museums instituted an order of things that was meant to last. In doing so, they provided the modern state with a deep and continuous ideological backdrop but one which, if it was to play this role, could not be adjusted to respond to shorter-term ideological requirements. Exhibitions met this need."[115] Here we can find another possible explanation for why the Congo museum at Tervuren changed so little during the colonial period: if the Ministry of Colonies needed to generate new or short-term messages, or change with the times, it possessed a tool in Belgium's many expositions universelles. The Musée du Congo Belge, in contrast, formed a steady, permanent backdrop. A component of this was a unifying nationalism in the sense that there was to be only one official museum of empire for the nation, which becomes even clearer when one considers the many local museums outside Tervuren such as the Musée africain de Namur (African Museum of Namur).

Wallonia's Own Window onto Africa?
The Musée Africain de Namur

There were innumerable smaller colonial museums in Belgium, most prominently the Musée africain de Namur, all of which suggest a surprisingly high level of interest in the overseas empire. Despite numerous grassroots efforts to put the colony on display in Belgium, the Ministry of Colonies managed to sustain one centralized, official display of Africa and Africana in the museum at Tervuren. The most significant challenger to Tervuren was a museum in Namur, today the Musée africain de Namur, which is only the latest iteration of a Congo museum in that city.[116]

One of the larger cities in Belgium, Namur also is the capital of Wallonia; as early as 1910, former colonials and local zealots there formed an association called the Société d'études d'intérêts coloniaux (Colonial Interests Study Society). That group and other colonial interest associations that came into being later, such as the Cercle colonial namurois (Namur Colonial Club, CCN), supported the museum and its local pro-empire events, such as the 1925 Exposition Coloniale. During its first three decades of existence, Namur's colonial museum at times barely survived. In 1912 the Société d'études d'intérêts coloniaux created the first durable exhibit of Africana in the city's Hôtel de Ville, called the Musée commercial et colonial de Namur (Commercial and Colonial Museum of Namur), whose vitrines highlighted colonial exports in order to promote economic ties between Namur and the colony and identify business opportunities in central Africa. Like the Tervuren museum in its early years, the early focus in Namur was economics; there were no ethnographic or geological displays, no African artwork, no memorial plaques.[117] A bombardment in 1914 destroyed the entire collection, and it was not until a 1925 colonial exposition that another permanent museum came into being, the Musée colonial scolaire (Colonial School Museum), this time located in the attic of the Athénée Royal de Namur.[118] Yet another "museum" in Namur was created in 1930, specifically a *section économique coloniale* (colonial economic section) in the Musée industriel (Industrial Museum) of the Association des anciens elèves de l'École industrielle de Namur (Alumni Association of the Industrial School of Namur), in the city's new bourse building largely put together and paid for by the Ministry of Colonies and comprising raw materials such as palm oil, sugar cane, rubber, coffee, and minerals, alongside refined colonial products such as soap and rubber products.[119] UMHK agreed to provide a sample of radium, demonstrating this firm's willingness to assist even smaller propaganda efforts within Belgium.[120] Despite the Musée industriel's imprimatur, one local colonial enthusiast, Adolphe Gérard, did not recognize its legitimacy and began in 1933 to take steps to create in an unused school another colonial museum, which in 1934 emerged as the Musée colonial belge (Belgian Colonial Museum) — later called the Musée d'art colonial de Namur (Colonial Art Museum of Namur).[121]

Gérard's group made repeated requests for assistance from the Ministry of Colonies, and the resultant correspondence reveals the official view of museums, imperial propaganda, and the role of the Tervuren museum. The OC denied an early request for funds because they thought Gérard might be duplicating the efforts of the Musée du Congo Belge.[122] Director Schouteden wrote to the minister of colonies that the Tervuren institution "should remain, as its creator, King Leopold II, wished for it to, the natural center in which documents relating to the Belgian Congo concentrate themselves for the greater good of scientific study and research."[123] Besides its function as the sole metropolitan repository for colonial documentation, Schouteden emphasized the Tervuren museum's already reduced budget and its rightful claim to available government funds. Schouteden, defending his position in the colonial bureaucracy and budget, was backed up by Edouard De Jonghe — responsible for the Tervuren museum within the Ministry of Colonies — who stated that the Namur museum would "in some way duplicate work with the Musée du Congo Belge," and that it should "exist as a regional museum" only, supported by private funds. "The department should thus intervene as little as possible in the organization, in the fitting out and in the functioning of the Musée d'Art Colonial de Namur," De Jonghe concluded.[124] This is not to say the OC and the Ministry of Colonies were opposed to colonial activities in Namur, to Gérard as a person, or to what he was trying to accomplish. The OC in fact supported colonial popularization efforts in Namur and other parts of the country as evidenced by the fact that they created a *petit musée permanent* (little permanent museum) of the colony in Charleroi at the cost of 5,017 francs, and sent more than 5,000 francs worth of materials to the Musée d'art colonial de Namur.[125] In just five years, the Loterie Coloniale (Colonial Lottery) paid Gérard's museum almost 36,000 francs for publicity, which was, in the end, basically charity for a museum that was failing to bring in visitors. Gérard's feelings that there was bias against him within the ministry, which he expressed on numerous occasions, were largely if not entirely groundless.[126]

While not opposed to local organizations trying to popularize the colony through other museums, there was something the colonial administration would not tolerate: a regional group arrogating for itself the role of representing the colony officially. The ministry pursued a policy of centralization wherein the Congo was to be represented by one entity, controlled from Brussels. According to OC chief Janssen, only official government services or qualified groups could do this: "To occupy oneself with 'Colonial Propaganda,' it is necessary to know before anything else government policy, national as well as colonial, and to have permanent contacts with active colonial and Belgian circles, of the most diverse kind." Janssen believed local groups needed to restrict themselves to basic undertakings they could afford themselves, such as conferences, and did not need to engage in more sophisticated labors such as steering young people toward colonial careers. "The initiators of the Namur movement do not appear to be qualified to fill a role that the oc already fulfills with extreme care and with well-established relationships."[127] Janssen asserted that propaganda and colonial instruction should be left to the experts, namely, the colonial administration in Brussels.

Gérard, however, repeatedly asserted that the Ministry of Colonies favored the Flemish over the Walloon region, pointing to the establishment of the Université coloniale (Colonial University) and the École de médecine tropical (School of Tropical Medicine) in Antwerp as evidence.[128] Writing in the *Bulletin de l'Association Coloniale Liègeoise*, Gérard decried a power-hungry capital exercising its functions to the detriment of the regions: "The colonial groups of the provinces have been for a long time treated as negligible quantities by the Capital. . . . The politics of the Capital is centralization *à outrance* [to excess]." He went on to suggest an interprovincial federation to defend regionalism.[129] His group in Namur was not the only one to be rejected by the Ministry of Colonies in this manner, and some of his peers echoed his points.[130] The oc rejected a proposal from the Koloniale en Maritieme Kring, Brugge (Colonial and Maritime Society of Bruges) to become a branch office of the oc, indicating both the Ministry of Colonies' evenhanded treatment of the regions and its desire to centralize control.[131] Perhaps to some, the Ministry of Colonies aggravated regionalism, but the important point is that the government in Brussels did not want to see propaganda efforts in the metropole split along Flemish-Walloon lines, preferring to center the nation around the Tervuren museum. It is worth noting that the French government founded a Musée des colonies et de la France extérieure at the 1931 Vincennes Colonial Exposition partially modeled on the Tervuren museum, in the sense that it was meant to serve as a central "clearing-house for information" on French imperialism.[132] Yet within six years, the 1937 Exposition Universelle revived another museum with a focus on ethnography and the overseas territories, the Musée de l'homme (Museum of Man) at the Trocadero, inheritor of the Musée de l'ethnographie (Museum of Ethnography) that eventually came to have auxiliary offices and operations in numerous French regions. In contrast, the Belgian government successfully pursued a tighter centralization of Africana in one museum.

Gérard's aggressiveness introduced deep dissension among the ranks of colonial enthusiasts in Namur, provoking a split.[133] Gérard continued with the Cercle d'étude et de propagande coloniale (Colonial Studies and Propaganda Society) and his museum, while his erstwhile associate Major Weber formed a new organization, the CCN. While this latter group received support among Ministry of Colonies staff, the ministry and others dismissed Gérard as causing too many problems, believing that he was indulging in "fantasies" regarding the situation of local colonial efforts in Namur.[134] Gérard's communications and activities reinforced these impressions, such as when he at one point threatened the ministry with a negative press campaign.[135] Despite his accusations of "a negative attitude of certain upper functionaries of the Ministry of Colonies," he did not stop trying to receive official backing for his museum.[136]

In the end, it appears Gérard was somewhat of a charlatan.

He claimed to be a certified geological engineer with substantial experience, when in fact he was not.[137] In addition to the Musée d'art colonial de Namur, he embarked on a number of colonial ventures, including not only an Entr'aide et propagande coloniale (Organization for Colonial "Mutual Assistance" and Propaganda) and the Musée d'art colonial belge (Museum of Belgian Colonial Art) but also a Section de Missiologie in 1935, and later a Musée colonial scolaire, a Bibliothèque coloniale provinciale publique (Provincial Colonial Public Library), a Concours Colonial Scolaire (Colonial School Contest) for Namur, a Congrès national pour le peuplement blanc au Congo (National Congress for White Emigration to the Congo), the journal *L'Art Africain*, an Association nationale des scouts coloniaux de Belgique (National Association of Colonial Scouts of Belgium), and a Mémorial aux Morts du Corps des Volontaires Congolais, none of which met with any long-term success. And Gérard's dealings were shady, if not outright criminal. He tried to overcharge the Loterie Coloniale for displaying lottery posters at his museum, and the Comité supérieur de contrôle (Superior Committee for Monitoring) found numerous questionable arrangements when it investigated his activities.[138] In the end, perhaps Gérard's protests about regionalism on the part of the Ministry of Colonies did not reflect legitimate grievances as much as they did his desire to make money.

In any case, Gérard failed in his efforts to put together a lasting museum in Namur. The Ministry of Colonies characterized the museum in 1935 as "having gotten off to a very bad start," and a 1935 photograph shows it in poor condition.[139] Press accounts from the late 1930s, well after the museum had had a chance to establish itself, criticized the museum's administration, and a 1939 report indicated it had few visitors.[140] War's return in

1940 destroyed the museum's collections, as it did those of the Association des anciens élèves de l'École industrielle de Namur, which were still being exhibited at the time.[141] After the war, Gérard tried to restart the museum, professing to the Ministry of Colonies his rights to restitution under law, but it instead fell to others to pursue a colonial museum in Namur after the liberation.[142] In 1951 Fernand Prinz, the CCN, and the town administration of Jambes (outside Namur) launched the Musée colonial scolaire de Jambes (Colonial School Museum of Jambes), which in 1955—then known as the Musée colonial de Jambes (Colonial Museum of Jambes)—moved to a school building at Parc Astrid, where it would remain until 1977, at which point the city government seized the building and dispersed the collections.[143]

Although the ambitions of their displays changed over time, the colonial museums in Namur formed a backdrop guiding the city's understanding of the colony by bringing private materials into public display. In 1912 the Musée commercial et colonial de Namur of the Société d'études d'intérêts coloniaux showed a permanent exhibition promoting the economic possibilities in the colony. Between the wars, the museum broadened its ambit to promote the colony more generally, not unlike the Musée du Congo Belge's more diversified message in the 1920s and 1930s. The Namur African museum that came into being after World War II had a general scope, including raw materials, photographs, maps, African sculpture, artwork, wildlife, musical instruments, weapons, and a small library.[144] These varying backdrops conveyed a number of ideas, including the aggrandizement of Leopold II. The first museum's inauguration in 1912 glorified Leopold II when the president of the Société d'études d'intérêts coloniaux characterized the late king as "a clairvoyant sovereign, of wise spirit, very well-informed of the nation's necessities," who had created a great colony in a quarter century "by remarkable prudence and wisdom, single-mindedness of views and a tenacity that never failed."[145] An account of the inauguration of the Musée colonial scolaire de Jambes in 1951 stated, "Above a magnificent leopard, the portrait of Leopold II the Great carries the day before a background of the national and colonial flags [s'enlève sur fond de drapeaux nationaux et coloniaux]."[146] Activity by Gérard and others from 1933 to the end of that decade represented provincial support for the colony, but there also were other factors in play. Because the Vlaamse Beweging (Flemish Movement) grew in strength beginning in the late 1920s, one might speculate that this intensified Gérard's envy regarding the Colonial University's and Musée du Congo Belge's location in Flanders and his desire for reciprocation. The economic downturn of the 1930s deeply affected the coal mining area of southern Belgium, the Borinage, which runs from around Mons eastward to Namur and beyond. This might explain in part the enthusiasm among some in Namur during the 1930s for the possibilities the colony might offer, but in any case it shows support for empire in the provinces. Just as at the Musée du Congo Belge, objects such as weapons donated by former colonials directly represented colonial conquest and control, even if one reason for the prevalence of weaponry in displays of African objects was their durability.[147] Finally, like the Tervuren museum, the Musée africain de Namur today serves as a war memorial in a sense, bearing a plaque to deceased colonial pioneers from the city.

Local Colonial Museums

Outside Namur, numerous other colonial museums came into being that displayed the empire according to the colonist's point

6. Memorial at Musée africain de Namur (photo by the author).

of view; many of them were smaller collections displayed by missionary orders. Mission motherhouses like those of the Sisters of Our Lady at Bunderen and the Brothers of Our Lady of Lourdes of Oostakker created small permanent showcases of materials from the colony, as did convents, monasteries, and Catholic schools. In most cases the materials were those that missionaries had collected from the particular areas in which they were active in the Congo. Although at times these collections were exhibited as *"missie-expos"* (mission expos), they were mostly for smaller audiences; most such displays were largely unknown to those not connected to the order either by membership, education, or otherwise. Although their audiences may have been restricted, the sheer number of such collections—and therefore missie-expos over the years—is surprisingly large, with ongoing research suggesting that there may have been upward of fifty-two such collections, housing many thousands of objects.[148]

High schools and universities in both the north and south of the country created their own small-scale colonial museums, indicating a widespread interest in the colony. Edouard de Jonghe created one of the first of these, at the University of Leuven, which sustained a particularly close relationship with the colony from its beginnings, leading eventually to the University of Lovanium's founding in 1954.[149] There also was a small museum at the Université libre de Bruxelles, and Baron Houtart of the university stressed the school's dedication to promoting the colony and colonial careers, writing to the Ministry of Colonies "that it would not be useless to bring about young people's contact with the colonial idea, life in the Congo, the progresses realized . . . as of their entrance to the University." Houtart wanted materials for the colonial museum that would "strike the spirit of the youth," and the ULB's Conseil d'administration (Administrative Council) asked the ministry to send experienced colonials to the university to give talks to students, requests to which the ministry responded with enthusiasm.[150] Other museums were put up at schools like the Athénée d'Ixelles (Ixelles High School), near Brussels, which created a Musée colonial scolaire to teach students about the Congo and Belgium's civilizing mission.[151] The colonial press praised this Ixelles school museum and urged the Ministry of Colonies to create similar exhibits throughout the country.[152] The Collège Saint-Michel (Saint Michael's School), also in Brussels, secured a small museum through the OC: "We [the school] have so many of our former students in the Colony, we have so many others who will go, and we would like to send many others there who would be able to find there a field for their activity."[153] The OC provided goods such as product samples, photographs, maps, even tropical plants from the Jardin Colonial de Laeken.[154] There were such displays in other cities, including a Musée scolaire colonial in Ghent and a permanent exposition at the Université de Liège (University of Liège), from 1930–39 at least.[155] For the latter, the OC provided diagrams, maps, photographs, and colonial product samples, as it did elsewhere. At Liège, "the walls of stairwells and corridors and three classes [were] fitted out with frames in the total number of 123, and two wall maps [were] placed on the landings. . . . A collection of 16 diagrams of the principal export products [was] conserved by the professor of economics."[156]

Local interest groups besides those in Namur also pushed for their own colonial museums, and again the OC provided materials like publications, photographs, movies, maps, and charts, often coordinating the provision of goods from colonial firms like UMHK and S. A. Bunge. As mentioned, the OC created a "petit musée permanent" of the colony in Charleroi; it also provided materials such as a wall map of the Congo and photographic enlargements for the Nieuwe Organisatie voor Verkoop en Aankoopsbevordering (New Organization Promoting Sales and Purchases, NOVA), which was a "Foire Commerciale Ambulante" (Traveling Commercial Fair) based out of Antwerp that beginning in the late 1920s toured a number of cities to promote the economy, including colonial commerce.[157] The Koloniale en Maritieme Kring, Brugge, which at one point offered to become a subsidiary of the OC, took steps in 1929 to create a *petit musée colonial* (small colonial museum) and public library. The OC provided them speakers, movies, and materials, in addition to offering technical assistance and paying for products to be shipped to them from colonial companies.[158] In these many cases across the country, there seems to have been no opposition to permanent colonial exhibits, and zero input from Congolese. If colonized peoples were able to contest Europe's creation of its Other at certain times in particular places as some scholars have argued, this was not the case in local Belgian colonial museums.

Curators at Tervuren conveyed to museum visitors a heavy dose of nationalism, even if unintentionally. The reinforcement of both national feeling and support for overseas imperialism at Tervuren was a secular project, as was the museum at Namur and smaller school museums. Early accents on the economic benefits of imperialism rapidly shifted to an emphasis on a total picture of the Congo that stressed successful conquest, colonial heroes, Leopold II, and African backwardness. We are only now finding out more about the creation of colonial museums by missionary societies, but it is likely they were smaller collections. And they certainly did not rival the Tervuren museum and probably not even other local colonial museums. In all cases, the administration deliberately and consciously fended off attempts to devolve their power over permanent and official display of the colony, such as happened in the case with Gérard in Namur. The fact that the Musée du Congo Belge reached millions of visitors during the colonial period made it a steady tool of nationalistic and pro-empire propaganda.

Four

Educating the Imperialists of Tomorrow

From the vantage point of 1908, the idea of someone writing a history of Belgian imperial propaganda in the classroom a century later would appear strange, for why would the state or anyone else need to educate Belgians about the Congo? Leopold II had established an empire in central Africa with little to no church, business, or popular support, relying on foreign and Belgian military and administrative agents; international criticism of his administration sparked the 1908 reprise, not popular clamor for empire in Belgium. Not until the EIC was two decades old did Leopold II's administration found a colonial educational institute, and not until 1905 did the Congo enter the primary school curriculum as a subject, even though the state had put in place its first curriculum for public primary education as early as 1880.[1] Leopold had wanted to build an École mondiale of colonialism in Tervuren to train students from across Europe, but the government declined to pursue the idea after he died.[2] Why would the Belgian state after 1908 need to educate its citizens about the Congo, considering that the colony had been explored, conquered, created, administered, and annexed without broad popular support?

Nevertheless, the Belgian state, colonial enthusiasts, and, to a limited extent, businesses and missionaries made significant efforts to popularize the overseas empire in classrooms,

efforts that reveal two key points about propaganda in education and the nature of Belgian rule in the Congo. First, the state
sought not only to nationalize its African administration, which
was to be expected, but also to nationalize the imperial project by means of education that would instill an imperial spirit
among the population. This profound desire to nationalize the
empire—emphasizing making the Congo *Belgian* rather than
necessarily *better*—belies the argument imperialists made that
Belgian rule in central Africa existed above all for the benefit of
the Congolese. At a fundamental level nationalism drove Belgian
imperialism. A second point is that colonial education after 1908
shows that the imperial state and its supporters viewed colonial
rule as insecure, at times even threatened from within. Despite
official and scholarly depictions of imperial self-assuredness and
portrayals of tranquility and prosperity in the Congo at expositions, in film, and elsewhere, "the maintenance of order was not
as easy as certain official commentary said it was."[3] Recent work
has unveiled latent conflicts just below the surface in equatorial
Africa in the 1930s, 1940s, and 1950s.[4] With a tenuous hold over
vast territories and populations, many officials perceived the
metropolitan population's lack of knowledge of or interest in the
Congo not simply as undesirable but as dangerous. Because not
many Belgians settled in the colony and few went there to visit,
only a small fraction of the population had firsthand knowledge
of the colony, let alone a significant acquaintance with it. Technological, cultural, and religious superiority were not enough
to run an empire; national faith in the colony was necessary as
well. Colonial rule was not static but rather something always
in a process of becoming, and the state and colonial enthusiasts
wanted to direct how that becoming would turn out by creating
a national faith in empire through education.

It is natural that imperialists concerned about the lack of a pro-empire spirit among the populace after 1908 would turn to education as a tool to inculcate the masses. As elsewhere in Europe, by the twentieth century the state required elementary education for all school-age children. As a result, "The elementary school became the principal institution through which the established order sought to preserve the status quo."[5] The status quo changed when Belgium took over the EIC, and instruction needed to change as a result. There was widespread concern among colonial veterans, officials, and enthusiasts after 1908 that there was an "indifference of the masses for colonial things."[6] In the 1920s, one author called for greater education in schools and universities on colonial questions, complaining that *university education ignores the Colony. Except for rare exceptions, university courses . . . do not even mention the Colony, talk neither of its progress, nor of its future, nor of the problems that pose themselves there.*"[7] Decades after the reprise, high-placed officials and others lamented students' ignorance of colonial matters, as well as the lack of such knowledge among the population at large.[8] Université coloniale director Norbert Laude criticized the lack of colonial education in primary and secondary schools, saying that students who entered the university demonstrated "a complete ignorance of the history and the geography of the Belgian Congo."[9]

On a more practical level, administrators and others worried that a lack of education restricted the number of candidates able to work in the colony. Thus the government, similar to those in Britain and France, directly targeted schoolchildren in the classroom with pro-imperial propaganda, an effort that only accelerated as Belgium and the colony moved toward their unanticipated break in 1960. This classroom propaganda buttressed pro-imperial messages emanating from world's fairs, the Musée du Congo Belge, and the OC's quinzaines coloniales, all of which emphasized indoctrinating children. Classroom propaganda reinforced messages from these other media: love of dynasty and nation, reverence for Leopold II and the pioneer period, and negative views of Africans.

Studies of the "mobilization of enthusiasm" for empire in classrooms in Belgium, Britain, and France have focused on school textbooks, and they can be a useful point of entry for understanding classroom propaganda. Yet they should not be studied at the expense of other media; for in Belgium, as in other states, there was comparatively little coverage of overseas territories in history textbooks.[10] A broader view of education points to a dramatic development in colonial education in Belgium: the Ministry of Colonies' ramped-up efforts to indoctrinate students directly through its own Commission Coloniale Scolaire. In fact, that there was an acceleration of pro-imperial propaganda in the classroom between 1945 and 1960 might help explain why Belgians were so shocked and dismayed in 1960 when the Congo achieved independence so suddenly. This propaganda drive suggests avenues for further research into understanding post-1960 Belgian attitudes toward their colonial history and viewpoints on the Congo today. In addition to textbooks and the CCS, school contests and extracurricular activities also transmitted an imperialistic ideology to young children, as did the Université coloniale in Antwerp and other programs of higher education, at least among an elite.

Colonial Education at University

The EIC had no higher colonial educational institution, and the government abandoned Leopold II's École mondiale at Tervuren before it even got off the ground. This contrasts with France, which had an École coloniale (Colonial School) by 1889, and the Netherlands' requirement of passing a colonial examination. It is more similar to the cases of Portugal (Geographical Society of Lisbon's Escola Superior Colonial, 1906) and Germany (Kolonialinstitut, Hamburg, 1908).[11] Instead, in Belgium, others provided higher colonial education. The Catholic University of Leuven initially provided a limited number of classes geared, above all, toward colonial trade and legal studies, but well before 1908 professors there began offering courses in medicine, agriculture, and engineering and began researching tropical diseases. In fact, the center for tropical medicine at Leuven became the kernel for the later École de médecine tropicale in Brussels.[12] Pro-empire groups that were both private and secular, such as the Club africain d'Anvers (African Club of Antwerp) or the Société d'études coloniales, also organized part-time "colonial schools" and programs of colonial education as early as the 1890s.[13] These groups largely comprised EIC officials, colonial businessmen, and returned veterans who recognized that too many EIC administrators came from the military, were foreigners (37 percent in 1908), or both.[14] Some believed that the public needed to be persuaded of the importance of the colony in order to develop greater mass support for empire.

After the Belgian takeover, Minister of Colonies Renkin turned to the need for skilled administrators and doctors in the colony, creating in Brussels the École de médecine tropicale and an École coloniale in 1910 and 1911, respectively.[15] Yet he also almost immediately sought to overhaul and re-create those institutions in order to foster a true school of higher learning for overseas administrators. This led to Renkin's successor, Louis Franck, overseeing the completion of a flagship colonial educational institution, the École coloniale supérieure (Colonial College, ECS), renamed the Université coloniale in 1923, on the outskirts of Antwerp.[16] As an auxiliary of the Colonial Ministry, the school's administration and teaching were overseen by a Conseil d'administration and a Conseil de perfectionnement (Council of Development), respectively, but the minister of colonies retained control over important decisions such as the nomination of the school's director and professors. Substantial contributions from the American Commission for Relief in Belgium as well as the city of Antwerp offset the costs necessary to set up such a school.[17] The university became a vehicle to nationalize the colonial administration, admitting only citizens and excluding Congolese and mulattos (even if photos of some classes show students of color).[18]

Part-time or unofficial colonial education programs continued to spring up, suggesting that many believed the university was insufficient to address Belgium's needs, perhaps because it educated only a small elite. Professors at the ULB offered courses on the colony as early as 1909.[19] Other schools formed their own programs, including the Université de Gand (University of Ghent, 1908), the École coloniale de Liège (Colonial School of Liège, 1936), the École coloniale in Tournai (Colonial School in Tournai, 1943), and the Section coloniale (Colonial Department) at the École provinciale d'agriculture (Provincial School of Agriculture) in Waremme after World War II.[20] Interest groups outside these schools also created colonial educational programs, such as the Union coloniale belge (Belgian Colonial Union) that instituted a Cours de Préparation Coloniale (Course of Colonial Preparation) for merchants and manufacturers that it hoped would have a multiplying effect among the population by indoctrinating "members of the teaching staff

who thus will be in a position to initiate Belgian youth into colonial service early."[21] By 1946 they claimed to have taught close
to 1,500 students.[22] The Ministry of Colonies did not object to
these programs, and in fact often subsidized them.[23] It was clear
that in the search for knowledge about the Congo, education followed imperialism, not the other way around. Belgian "colonial
sciences" like anthropology and ethnography, for example, were
centered on the Congo at inception.[24]

Much more significant was the network that grew out of colonial interests at the Catholic University of Leuven. Belgian bishops had founded an African seminary in Leuven to train missionaries for the Congo as early as 1886–87, which Scheutists
took charge of after acquiescing that same year to Leopold's
requests to proselytize in the EIC. After recovering from the dev-
astation of World War I, missionary orders built on their early
collaborations with Leopold II to make the city and university
an important site of colonial education for both missionaries
and laypersons. The driving force during the interwar years was
Jesuit Pierre Charles, who created groups to pursue his vision of
more self-reflective and deliberative missionary activity in the
Congo. Charles started the Semaines de Missiologie de Louvain
(Missiology Weeks of Leuven) in 1923 to gather specialists together to tackle difficult missionary challenges, publishing the
results of each session. In 1925 he formed the Association universitaire catholique pour l'aide aux missions (Catholic University Association for Aid to Missions, AUCAM), a counterpart to
the Flemish Missiebond, which it soon surpassed in activity and
importance. AUCAM sought to "create among Belgian university students a climate of enlightened sympathy with regard to
the missions and encouraged Catholic intellectuals to go and
practice their profession among non-Christian populations."[25]

The *Éditions de l'Aucam* published various works that promoted not only a more thoughtful missionary activity but also imperialism more generally.[26] Students and professors also formed dynamic colonial study groups such as the Koloniaal Universitair Centrum (Colonial University Center, formed 1937–38) and Koloniale Universitaire Studiekring (Colonial University Study Group, 1946), among others, paralleling a practice at other Belgian universities. Other individuals besides Charles, including Leuven professor and Ministry of Colonies official Edouard De Jonghe, were key animators of colonial learning at Leuven.

The decade of the 1950s was particularly important because colonial studies at Leuven reached their greatest height at the same time that there was a recognition in some circles of coming independence. By the 1950s many missionaries and others already had returned to teach at Leuven, and with the advent of cheaper and faster air travel, many professors made their way to the colony during the summer for research and to meet with researchers and former students. It should be noted that this was one-way traffic: not until the early 1950s did Congolese students begin to come to Leuven, and by the mid-1950s there were only about ten there.[27] In the same decade, Rector Honoré Van Waeyenbergh led an effort to bring structure to the rather disparate colonial education at Leuven by creating the Colonial Institute of the Joined Faculties. But by 1955 Professor Jef Van Bilsen's iconoclastic views on the Congo's future independence began having their effects, and the terminology of decolonization circulated among Leuven students. A sign of the times was the renaming of the Koloniaal Universitair Centrum, as the Kongolees Leuvens Universitair Centrum (Congolese Leuven University Center).[28] Although Leuven was anything but a "colonial" university, a veritable colonial movement grew out of the symbiosis between students and professors studying the colony in Leuven and those at institutions created by the university (and others) on the ground in the Congo. The education both at Leuven and through secular programs demonstrates that the state's Colonial University in Antwerp did not monopolize higher colonial education.

Even if other institutions provided colonial education, and if the University of Leuven became a node of colonial interchange, Antwerp's Université coloniale was exceptional in a number of ways. Colonial education was the reason for its very being, and at other schools the study of the Congo "developed at the margins of the centers of academic power, even if it mobilized great jurists."[29] The Ministry of Colonies designed it to train a privileged few men, and only a small number ever attended. By 1931, eleven years after its founding, the school had produced a mere 98 graduates; by 1940, 216. In all, about half of the colony's territorial administrators were formed at the school.[30] The school appealed to potential students' sense of adventure and desire to join an elite, even though by 1910 the conquest of the Congo was a fait accompli and the empire less and less could entice recruits with the prospect of colonial exploits, battles, and rapid promotion.[31] A school brochure said "strong spirits" would find in the colony "a field of action more vast" than the "inevitably limited space of our liberal professions."[32] Minister of Colonies Franck exhorted students in one of his speeches to "Become men capable of commanding, and remember always that to be a colonial functionary is not a job! *It is a mission and an honor.*"[33] While Franck and others emphasized the scientific goals of the university, its education was moral more than anything else.[34] An early school brochure indicated, "The École Coloniale Supérieure seeks to become one of the most popular schools of the Nation, not at all only by the services it renders to the Colony and to the Metropole, but more by the action that it will try to exercise on the character of its students. It will endeavor to produce more than distinguished functionaries. It wants to form MEN!"[35] To foster camaraderie, students lived and ate meals together, often sharing those meals with professors.[36] Except when military service imposed itself, all four years were lived on campus; the school restricted off-campus travel — for example, to go back home or to downtown Antwerp — in order to cultivate a sense of community and keep students out of trouble.[37]

The university's elite moral education is evident in the two men who dominated the university's administration and education, Charles Lemaire and Norbert Laude. Louis Franck appointed his personal friend Lemaire as director at the time of the school's founding in 1920, and Lemaire remained director until his death in 1925. Born in Cuesmes just outside Mons, Lemaire was a veteran of the first days in the Congo, an "authentic" colonial, better known today for his brutal actions in the conquest of the colony.[38] He first traveled to central Africa in the service of Leopold II in 1889 and advanced rapidly to become *commissaire du District de l'equateur* (commissioner of the Equatorial District) by 1890. He later served the king in the attempt to explore the EIC and expand its borders into the Bahr el-Ghazal in the Sudan.[39] Lemaire's diary recorded the regime's naked brutality, and he himself accepted that "one must cut off hands, noses and ears" in order to gather rubber.[40]

Lemaire's approach to the education of his students in the early 1920s revealed his belief in molding an elite and reflected more general postwar fears of degeneration and decline. A later commentator said that Lemaire downplayed intellectual pursuits in favor of practical knowledge: "What he wanted was less encyclopedists than men *tout court* . . . [and] to protect his students from the meanness and the vulgarity that lie in wait for the weak in a society where the fierceness to earn money makes so many tragic converts."[41] One student recorded that Lemaire told him and his classmates, "<u>Passage through the school must be a purification.</u>"[42] He also told his students he would do all in his power so that the university produced "a genuine elite, not an elite of words, no, an Elite in the flesh, in heart and mind."[43] Its products were to be rulers, bearers of civilization to central Africa, and Renaissance men conversant in many subjects, able to practice self-control and self-abnegation, and always ready to act in the best interest of their charges.[44]

Experience, not technical learning, formed the basis of Lemaire's instruction. His method was unstudied: "Lemaire had a strongly personal conception of his pedagogical mission. One would say today that it was very social, but also permeated with humanism. The scientific, the philosophical, the erudite [were equal] . . . [his] teaching aimed to develop the character, to promote the human as much as the beautiful. He would consider that the education of future territorial administrators was as important as their instruction; as he described it himself, it had to be 'gentlemen-like'; thus sportive, but also cultural."[45] Lemaire spoke to students about whatever was on his mind, covering a range of subjects from astronomy to gardening to tropical disease, dispensing tidbits of colonial wisdom, and calling their attention to things he recently had read and thought important to pass on. Students called Lemaire "papa," and he called them his "children."[46] His system of anecdotal education led him to transmit some dubious information to his students, as one recorded in 1921: "Our Commander [Lemaire] is a sworn enemy of any drug, above all <u>quinine. Here is the method he gives for treating</u>

a bout of fever: As soon as the first symptoms, stick to bed and take some cups of tea, well heated. Cover yourself very well and put up the greatest passiveness to the fever. At the end of some days: *all is finished*."[47] Firsthand knowledge from seasoned colonial veterans, such as Lemaire, and presentations over the years from a number of visiting colonial dignitaries and officials, such as French minister of colonies Albert Saurraut, Sir Frederick Lugard, and King Albert I, made students' formation moral, spiritual, and experiential rather than just technical or bookish.

The second major figure to shape the Université coloniale was Norbert Laude, who succeeded Lemaire as director in 1926, serving in that position until he was forced to retire in 1958 because of his advanced age. Although Laude lost an eye in World War I, arguably the most intense years of his life occurred during World War II when he organized resistance in Antwerp to the German occupation. The Gestapo threw him in prison; treated him viciously, including torture; caused him multiple injuries; and sentenced him to death by shooting in September 1944. He lived only because of the liberation of Antwerp that very same month.[48]

It was during Laude's twenty-plus-year tenure that the university's program developed to its fullest extent, coming to include courses covering not only "colonial" subjects but also law, geography, biology, literature, philosophy, history, and linguistics, among others.[49] There was a business program from 1925 to 1949 after colonial businessman Edouard Bunge provided the impetus and funds.[50] Practical education in the form of students growing food in their own gardens added to the diverse program, and Laude sustained the formation of a well-rounded male elite to administer the colony.[51] As Lemaire's method had been based more on experiential knowledge than technical learning, so did Laude's style have its own nonscientific bent, as seen when he presided over the induction of each year's class, or "*promotion.*" At those events, he bestowed on each class the name of a deceased pioneer, colonial official, explorer, missionary, or the like, during the course of a hagiographic speech. Playing on their emotions and injecting mysticism into the colonial calling, Laude rallied the students with the invocation of these names by saying that the spirit of that colonial lived in them.

The naming of each class was one way in which the university brought together different vectors of imperialistic propaganda. The patrons given to promotions generally hearkened back to the EIC period and reinforced the legitimacy of state rule by rooting it in the past.[52] The list of patrons contained familiar names that one also could see at numerous monuments throughout Belgium, such as famous pioneers (Dhanis and Coquilhat) and missionaries (Roelens and de Deken). Unlike monuments, patrons also included a few foreigners (Stanley), colonial ministers (Godding, Renkin, and Franck), businessmen (Edouard Bunge and Emile Banning), even World War I heroes (Gabrielle Petit).[53] The school also interconnected with the Musée du Congo Belge when students made outings to Tervuren to meet with conservators and learn about museum collections.[54] Henry Schouteden, Tervuren director 1927–46, taught a course on African zoology at the university from 1927 until 1952, demonstrating both how the museum functioned as an agent of colonial education and how different aspects of pro-empire propaganda fed off of each other.[55] The university was also a site of memorials to overseas expansion. The Ligue du souvenir congolais worked with the school to put up a monument to pioneers inside the school's main building around 1930, comprising some 1,500 names in golden lettering on those walls students saw most often (in the library, hallways, etc.).[56] The school put up numerous other memorials to colonial figures, and inaugurations became moments for solemn remembrances of deceased colonial pioneers.[57] Unsurprisingly, the university's program of study lauded Leopold II.[58]

The school, like the Musée du Congo Belge, faced budget problems at different moments in its history, such as after a destructive fire in 1929. In the early 1920s, Lemaire instigated the formation of a group called Les Élèves et anciens élèves de l'ECS (Students and Alumni of the ECS) to foster fellowship and provide funds for the school. When students started their own publication in the early 1920s—the *Bulletin des Étudiants de l'École Coloniale Supérieure*—they too ran up against the problem of inadequate funding.[59] Around 1930, students created their own Association des étudiants de l'Université coloniale de Belgique (Student Association of the Colonial University of Belgium) and its corollary for graduates, the Association des anciens étudiants de l'Université coloniale de Belgique (Alumni Association of the Colonial University of Belgium), along with their own bulletin, *Le Trait d'Union*. Reflecting the clublike atmosphere at the school, the publication included announcements of student marriages and family deaths and births, items on life at the university, news of professors and their works, lists of former students working in the Congo, and other brief notes.[60] How much money these groups raised is unclear.

Of course, not many students actually attended the university in Antwerp; incoming classes infrequently numbered more than one or two score students. Moreover, because only males could be students, the university excluded fully half of the country's population. This was not mass schooling, rather education designed to create an elite. Nonetheless, considering the proliferation of higher education programs beyond Antwerp, elite education did reach significant numbers of Belgians. And beyond an elite, the state did attempt to mobilize the masses through propaganda in the education of the majority of children in the classroom, in part through textbooks.

Of Textbooks and Triumphs

In recent decades, the school textbook has become a major tool of investigation for scholars of European overseas imperialism. Some have explored ideology in textbooks written for Africans during the colonial period, while others have focused on textbooks for use in European classrooms.[61] In the case of Britain, John MacKenzie has found that propaganda in favor of empire in textbooks of the 1890s — when history was first incorporated into the curriculum — presented a simplified version of the past that abetted a popularization of the empire. The influential *The Expansion of England* (1883) depicted Britain and its empire as the apotheosis of the nation-state, and its author, J. R. Seeley, thought history should "be deliberately employed as an uplifting moral force, to stimulate exertions, and raise the morale of the nation."[62] Classroom teaching sustained Seeley's moralizing into the post–World War II era and beyond. As early as the 1870s, textbooks in use in the Third Republic educated students about the overseas empire; by the 1930s, the French Colonial Ministry had created a special body to distribute to classes colonial textbooks that legitimized the new empire by portraying it as compensation for the loss of the first overseas empire.[63]

It is not possible to consider a transition in the depictions of empire from the late nineteenth to the early twentieth century in Belgian textbooks because there was no overseas empire until 1908; an equivalent to Seeley's *The Expansion of England* simply did not exist. Unlike higher education at the time of the reprise, elementary and secondary schools received virtually zero education on the colony, save occasional talks by groups like the Société belge des études coloniales (Belgian Society of Colonial Studies) and the Union coloniale belge and such information as a few schools received from the Ministry of Colonies.[64] One might expect this considering that people remained rather aloof from EIC affairs, taking little interest in the reports of atrocities, Morel's Congo Reform Campaign, and Leopold's own 1905 Commission of Enquiry report. One 1905 history textbook reflected this lack of engagement, its author only cursorily mentioning the Congo in connection with Leopold II and dedicating just 2 of 138 pages to the king and the Congo, including a portrait of Leopold. Nevertheless, the author did manage to convey in few words the themes that other authors would develop during the Belgian state-rule period: "Enormous areas were opened for us; our products find sales there in varied ways; slavery is abolished; civilization is improving the material and moral living conditions of the people, who just a few years ago were deeply barbarian."[65]

Inattention to the colony was the rule after the 1908 reprise, at least in the first decades, a point that Benoît Verhaegen stresses in his work on Belgian schoolbooks. Verhaegen also points out that French-language textbooks often served as models for Flemish manuals, especially in terms of relations between Belgium and the colony, and notes the striking homogeneity in treatment between French and Flemish and even secular and Catholic school manuals into the 1960s.[66] An early example is Godefroid Kurth's pro-Catholic and antisocialist history textbook *La nationalité belge* (1912), which justified the existence of the Belgian nation-state. This nearly two hundred–page history text devoted only one page to the Congo and incorrectly placed the date of annexation at 1909.[67] C. Debaere and N. Piret's 1927 *Nieuwe en nieuwste geschiedenis* set aside just seven of its 224 pages to European overseas expansion, with only one page on the Congo.[68] French-language texts of the interwar period similarly dedicated little space to the central African colonies.[69] L. Verniers and P. Bonenfant's two-part *Histoire de Belgique* (1941) needed less than three pages to cover both the history of Leopoldian involvement in Africa from 1876–1908 and Belgian colonialism to 1914.[70] Coverage increased in the post–World War II period but remained slim even into the 1950s.[71] H. Corijn's 1951 *Algemene en nationale geschiedenis*—oriented to the official teaching curriculum—dedicated a whole section to "Colonial Expansion and the European Balance," but only four pages to Belgium and its colony: "Colonial administration or colonization in the literal meaning of the words [were] practically not treated."[72] Antoon De Baets writes of an important 1959 *manuel d'histoire* (history textbook) that consecrated only one and a half pages to Leopold II and his Congo politics.[73] Frans van Kalken's texts on Belgian history that instructors used as guides, if not in classes, barely began to offer significant coverage of the colony in the 1950s.[74] De Baets, Verhaegen, and Raphael De Keyser have produced overviews of this issue that confirm that textbooks said little about the colony, and what they did came mostly in the period immediately preceding decolonization.

The time teachers spent on the colony and its history mirrored the paucity of textbook coverage. From 1919–39 teachers dedicated only about three hours total every week to history and geography, and it follows that little time could have been spent addressing the overseas possessions.[75] De Baets stresses that before 1960 the curriculum "gave priority to teaching the history of Belgium itself: one planned for only a few class hours on the subject of the Congo. Moreover these lessons on the colony were

not treated but in summary fashion, as a sort of appendage."[76]
The Belgian state was more concerned with educating children
to be citizens of the nation, and controversies in the curriculum
such as there were concerned divisions between Catholics and
Liberals. The Ministère de l'instruction publique (Ministry of
Public Education) sent few materials to schools on its own for
instruction on Congolese history or geography, even into the last
years of Belgian rule.[77]

Nonetheless, teachers and students did use history textbooks
containing messages about imperialism; therefore, what they
conveyed is important because of the effects it may have had
and because textbooks "provide an outstanding embodiment
of the educational intentions and mentality or mentalities that
prevailed among the educational opinionmakers."[78] Kurth's *La
nationalité belge* presented Belgium as a feisty colonial power
that accomplished what even larger powers could not or would
not do, namely, spread religion and civilization in central Africa
and create the possibility of a future of millions of Christians in
a large African nation that could join the ranks of the world's
great countries. Belgium not only was feisty, but it also was the
best colonizing power, paralleling what British schoolchildren
learned about themselves and their empire.[79] According to this
narrative, what set Belgium apart from other colonizing powers
was the fact that it took on the task of colonizing central Africa
with reluctance, even altruism, for which Flemish and Walloon
children could be especially proud.

Like imperial expositions, museums, and monuments, textbooks praised Leopold II and ignored the abuses of his regime. Kurth's 1912 text exclaimed, "We are today, thanks to
the generosity of our great king, a colonial power, and the Belgian flag flies over a territory that is eighty times larger than the

motherland." Kurth presented the Congo as compensation for the 1839 removal of provinces, which the reader might infer to mean that Leopold II had fulfilled the previously incomplete nation-state—this is how the king himself had viewed it.[80] Other texts presented Leopold's activity in Africa as a well-intentioned œuvre civilisatrice without asserting that he acted independently by associating his actions with the work of soldiers, merchants, entrepreneurs, financiers, and missionaries; that is, the "pioneers" of the "heroic period" in the Congo.[81] As another school text put it, those who worked with Leopold II accomplished heroic tasks when up against "innumerable obstacles," having to fight "against the hostile tribes, against the Arabs . . . against tropical diseases, against wild beasts, against the forest. Danger was everywhere." Despite praise for other pioneers, it was always the case that "the importance accorded to the sovereign plunged other [colonial] heroes into the shadows."[82] Textbook accounts of the country's second king became more "objective" in the years leading up to decolonization, but still at that late point he "was always described with grandiose praise."[83] Texts curtly dismissed any abuses: "As often in similar cases, one did some violence to the indigenous populations. Subsequently, when the occupation was solidly assured, these populations were treated with more solicitude."[84] In this way, texts alluded to problems in Leopold's regime only to dismiss them. At other times, texts excused problems in the colony by simply excluding them from the narrative.[85]

The history of the Belgian Congo in these textbooks was the period 1885–1908, especially in the first several decades of Belgian rule; textbooks infrequently addressed the post-1908 period.[86] Verhaegen identifies one standard work, H. Dorchy's *Histoire des Belges des origines à 1940* that, like so many others, basically skipped over the Belgian colonial period entirely. In Dorchy's text, edited and published in numerous editions into the 1980s, "Fifty years of colonial history are concealed."[87] In this way, textbooks did not reflect recent events on the ground in the Congo that might have unveiled problems with the colonial system. Verhaegen writes, "The Bapende revolt in 1931 and the repression that followed caused dozens of deaths, but aroused few echoes in the metropole. *Not a single history textbook reported it [Aucun manuel d'histoire n'en fait état].*" In essence, after 1908, "Not a single shadow [tarnished] the picture."[88] Of course, by occluding past events rather than informing students of them, history textbooks had the opposite result they were supposed to have, which was education. This de-emphasis also subtly tied the contemporaneous Belgian Congo to the "heroic period" of the Leopoldian state from 1885–1908 and made a tradition of colonialism part of Belgium's national self-representation. This nationalized the history of the Congo, as did textbooks that named Belgian officers and omitted foreign explorers in the conquest of the Congo.[89] Unsurprisingly, the histories of the Congo did not go back earlier than the beginnings of Leopoldian rule in central Africa, and textbooks portrayed the Congolese and central Africa as not having had a history before the arrival of the Belgians.

Like the Musée du Congo Belge, textbooks justified imperialism by claiming that Africans were inferior and needed Belgium's guidance. Even to World War II, some textbooks counterposed the Belgian presence in the Congo—civilized, solid, and secure—with Congolese, who supposedly were cannibals when the Belgians arrived and still were *barbares* (barbarians), *sauvages* (savages), and *primitives* (primitives), according to colonists and even many missionaries.[90] The image of the Congolese as "primitive savage" only gave way "to the belief in the human progress of the 'African black'" in the 1950s.[91] Textbook illustrations of only "self-assured whites" implied African backwardness, which was made explicit through juxtapositions of photographs of African hunters in the forest armed with spears and those of a Katanga copper mine.[92] By expounding on European culture without similar treatment of African culture, texts denied the latter's existence; those exceptional textbooks that did address Congolese history and culture only came out at the very end of the colonial period.[93] It was not until that same era that any hint of problems in Belgian colonial history appeared in textbooks: "To be sure, the courage, boldness, and energy of the Belgians was still always emphasized, but here and there critical words [were] also to be heard."[94] Textbooks such as Gysels and Van den Eynde's 1955 *Niewste tijden (1848–1955): Geschiedenis van België* shifted somewhat in tone, and subsequent editions of works originally printed in the 1930s and 1940s shied away from more triumphant postures.[95] The stress, such as it existed, was increasingly on Belgium's justification for possessing the Congo; texts returned to the theme of the anti-Arab, antislavery campaigns to justify Leopold II's takeover of the Congo and subsequent Belgian rule. These narratives depicted Leopold II not as a brutal exploiter but rather a protector, and of course did not broach questions of native land rights, political questions, or repression.

The Commission Coloniale Scolaire

While textbooks' messages were significant, their power to persuade school-age children was limited; this probably changed little until the last years of the colony. Because schedules were tight and there was an abundance of material to cover in geography and history classes, even if instructors spent time on the Congo, they oftentimes only briefly squeezed it in at the end of the school year.[96] Considering that the state reached out to influence school-age children at world's fairs, quinzaines coloniales, and the Musée du Congo Belge, it is unsurprising that state actors also took a more direct approach by creating a program called the Commission Coloniale Scolaire that brought state administrators directly into the classroom. In many cases, the CCS probably acted as the sole significant source of education about the Congo, and officials themselves recognized that schools did not have enough time to dedicate to the study of the colony.[97]

The highest levels of the colonial administration in Brussels viewed the CCS as a vital tool of imperial propaganda. The CCS finds its origins in two ministries, those of the colonies and of science and arts. In 1922 these two ministries created the CCS's predecessor, the Commission de Propagande Coloniale Scolaire (School Board of Colonial Propaganda).[98] Those who pushed for this new organization were administrators in the Ministry of Colonies and other imperialists who wanted to coordinate the education of both "teaching personnel and pupils" with the goal that they "get to know our colonies better" and discover and implement "the most favorable tools in order to popularize colonial problems."[99] The Commission de Propagande Coloniale Scolaire awarded prizes for student studies on the Congo and organized lessons in schools that often included film projections. It continued its work as the renamed CCS after 1937, with the only halt occurring during the German occupation of 1940–44. The program of the CCS after the war comprised sending men from a selected group of speakers, called *conférenciers*—under the direction of the CCS and its president, Colonial University director Norbert Laude—to schools throughout the country to teach students about the empire, in theory by means of a cycle of three conferences per year. By 1951 there were seven francophone or Flemish-speaking conférenciers. Even though the CCS direction put pressure on schools to accept visits from its conférenciers—they sent out hundreds if not thousands of letters each year requesting participation—involvement was voluntary, and the talks, usually accompanied by a film, were always free of charge.[100] Each of the CCS speakers gave dozens of presentations each academic year: in 1953–54 the group gave a total of 775 at 340 different schools; in the following year's cycle, they spoke at 565 schools.[101] Because textbooks barely addressed the Congo and the Belgian presence there, the CCS provided schools with books, including classics like *Notre colonie* and Pierre Ryckmans's *Dominer pour servir*, and subscribed them to numerous publications such as *La Revue Coloniale Belge*, *Revue Congolaise Illustrée*, and *Kongo-Overzee*, thereby making available hundreds of copies of colonial magazines across the country.[102] The CCS hoped not only to interest students but to incite them to get their parents engaged in colonial questions as well.[103] The Ministry of Colonies considered the program so significant that when the CCS decided not to give its regular cycle of presentations for 1958 and instead chose to focus on guided tours at that year's exposition universelle, Minister of Colonies Auguste Buisseret insisted that the 1957–58 cycle take place in addition to the tours.[104]

The CCS conférenciers were all male, although their backgrounds varied. During the 1950s there were seven or eight of them, divided between French and Flemish speakers, most of them teachers or clergymen. The CCS direction and the conférenciers themselves believed it important that they be actual colonials who had lived in the colony and therefore could speak from firsthand experience.[105] Many seem to have had such direct experience, for example, as territorial administrators or employees at colonial firms.[106] Although CCS speakers were paid, it was only a part-time job; despite the fact that it was a state effort to promote the empire through deliberate indoctrination in the classroom, speakers insisted that for the program to be effective, it was vital "to give the impression that one speaks with complete independence [*en toute indépendance*]."[107]

These representatives of the Ministry of Colonies and Ministry of Public Education conveyed a number of ideas in the classroom on a consistent basis. One conférencier, Georges Rhodius, stressed that Belgians should take pride in accomplishments in the Congo that they had achieved with an *haute conscience* (high conscience).[108] The titles of just a few of his lectures — including "Blooming of an Empire," "Birth of an Empire," and "Unknown Aspects of Our Colonial Empire" — indicate that he argued to students that Belgium's overseas possessions were in fact an *empire*, not just colonies.[109] After World War II, Rhodius time and again stressed others' jealousy in presentations like "The Congo, Envied Treasure," "Can We Keep It?," and "Are the Great Powers Not Going to Divide It Up?"[110] According to Rhodius, before Belgians arrived, central Africa had been "Terra incognita: An unknown land where the inhabitants led one of the most primitive lives in tragic conditions, exposed without defenses to the worst sicknesses and to the raids of slavers."[111] Here is a typical formulation: the populations were defenseless and primitive at the time of Europeans' arrival, and this without raising the issue of how Leopold II might have worsened conditions. He stressed the dazzling results of imperialism, including the creation of the stunning Congo, and how no other imperial power had achieved so much considering the obstacles.[112]

According to CCS presentations, it was the Saxe-Cobourg dynasty of Leopold II and his successors that had led the way in ameliorating the situation in central Africa.[113] Speakers exalted Léopold II le colonisateur (Leopold II the Colonizer), who had achieved an *œuvre gigantesque* (gigantic task), and they thereby connected the present-day colony to Leopold's EIC. Speakers explained the 1908 handover as a natural outcome, decided by Leopold II once he had accomplished all he had set out to do.[114] CCS speakers used King Baudouin's trip in 1955 to emphasize the enduring importance of the monarchy and the success of the colonial project, such as when they showed a film on Baudouin's trip and emphasized the "innumerable crowds" that expressed their "feelings of loyalty" to him at every stage through "frenetic ovations" in both the Congo and Ruanda-Urundi. The king's popularity among the populations of Ruanda-Urundi and their leaders, Bami, proved "that the commitment made by Belgium to favor the political and social evolution of the populations of Ruanda-Urundi, to assure the peace and security in their territory [had] been scrupulously fulfilled."[115]

Similar to textbooks, CCS conférenciers sometimes referred to Congolese as "primitives" right into the last decade of the colonial period.[116] Rhodius's description of Congolese homes was typical: they to him were mere huts, "raised haphazardly without the slightest symmetry." As to their mindset, he testified that "the Black does not have the faintest notion of the law. . . . The 'Negro' [*Nègre*] himself does not have a notion of time. There is for him only the day and the night."[117] Not that all schools swallowed the rhetoric from the CCS speakers unquestioningly. Some doubted the thoroughness of speakers' reports or specific aspects of the colonial system, such as the preponderant role of large capital in the colonial economy.[118] Yet overall, presentations appear to have been effective; Rhodius for one induced at least two students to enroll at the Université coloniale and persuaded school instructors to organize trips to the Tervuren museum.[119]

Even into the late 1950s, CCS presentations were simplified, boiling down the history and current affairs of the colony to a minimum in order not to lose students' attention.[120] This did not always go over well with teachers and school officials, such as one who wrote to the Ministry of Colonies in 1959: "The presentation was made with much clarity and dynamism: the students' attention (±160) was very well sustained up to the end." "At the same time," this same person regretted, "the clarity of the presentation wound up more than one time with an exaggerated simplification of the complexity of the problems."[121] Presentations may have led to unrealistic expectations among schoolchildren and their teachers. In 1959 one teacher responded to a presentation at a school in Pecq by writing the minister of colonies that it was an "Interesting speech, very much at the level of an audience composed of students of the lower middle cycle. The speaker clearly made the point of the current situation, he underlined the moral position of Belgium and showed that we do not have any reason to despair of a loyal collaboration with the native populations."[122] Panglossian interpretations might have contrasted with other information coming to teachers and students regarding the colony, because between 1955 and 1959 news coverage reported more and more developments in the colony, many of which were antithetical to the idea that the Congo was an unqualified success.[123] The year 1955, for example, marked both Baudouin's triumphant voyage to the Congo and the December publication of Jef Van Bilsen's thoughts on Congo's future independence. In the years to follow, Belgians would learn of the évolué publication of a *Manifeste de conscience africaine*, preparations for the first-ever elections in the Congo, and hear Baudouin mention the word "independence" in January 1959. With the shifting political situation in the Congo and troublesome events in 1959, interest among schools for the CCS program of speakers dropped dramatically. Yet the Ministry of Colonies did not back down and instead maintained both its messages and its resiliency as it continued to reach out to schools through the CCS, indicating that time and events were passing it by.[124]

Extracurricular Empire

Pro-empire propaganda directed toward children was not restricted to curricular activities. Many children learned about missionary activities in the colony at expositions, in films, or at mass, while others learned about colonial history at the raising of monuments and at local museums, often located at high schools or universities. As discussed, the Tervuren museum emphasized student visits and instructed school teachers through its Journées d'Études Coloniales.[125] Students learned about government actions and colonial commerce at expositions, such as when the CCS offered tours of the 1958 World's Fair or when the Office colonial enticed them to visit a quinzaine coloniale.[126]

In addition, colonial interest groups targeted schools to develop support for the colonial project. The Ligue du souvenir congolais donated five hundred French and five hundred Flemish editions of its *Livre d'or du souvenir congolais* to the government to be distributed to all schools in the country. The *Livre d'or* was a print memorial to countrymen who died in Africa from 1876 to 1908, with one newspaper noting, "The attention of the teaching personnel will be called in particular to this publication; our youth will find the most noble examples of patriotism, of pride, of abnegation and of sacrifice in the glorious past that it retraces."[127] Another group that educated schoolchildren was les Journées Coloniales (Colonial Days), which was both an organization and a festivity. Founded in 1920, les Journées Coloniales organized annual celebrations of the colony, called Koloniale Dagen or Journées Coloniales, which were similar to Empire Day, the Semaine Coloniale (Colonial Week), and the Giornata Coloniale (Colonial Day) in Britain, France, and Italy, respectively.[128] Les Journées Coloniales, alongside local branches like the Koloniale Dagen van België in Mechelen (Colonial Days of Belgium at Mechelan) and the Section Régionale des Journées Coloniales de Tirlemont (Regional Section of Colonial Days of Tienen), helped organize annual celebrations which took place toward the end of June or beginning of July each year to celebrate the anniversary of the July 1885 proclamation of the EIC.[129] These events involved school-age children when they coincided with the inauguration of memorials to local pioneers or when schools brought students out to parade alongside colonial veterans or military formations.[130] Students sometimes sold knickknacks to raise money, and even if uninvolved in formal organized activities, they often came out to watch the festivities.[131]

In addition to participating in colonial days, many students also took part in colonial essay competitions, similar to those in Britain that the Royal Colonial Institute organized annually.[132] In Belgium this essay competition was the Concours Colonial Scolaire, in which probably tens of thousands of schoolchildren participated, beginning in the 1920s. The government held at least eight contests during the interwar period, and both Catholic and secular schools participated.[133] This was a strictly metropolitan undertaking directed at the general population of students, not just those in colonial studies; the competitions excluded students attending special programs of colonial studies or living in the colony.[134] The Concours Colonial Scolaire began with a written examination on a question of history or geography chosen from a list, such as "Describe the course of the Congo River indicating the different navigable sections and demonstrate its importance for communications in the Belgian Congo (with a sketch)" or "In what circumstances was the Congo annexed to Belgium?" For those who scored a minimum number of points on the written part, there was a verbal examination on a colonial book or publication chosen from a list.[135] People at home and abroad cited these contests as a great method of propaganda: "Leopold should be satisfied with his work," *La Dépêche Coloniale de Paris* wrote about the Concours, suggesting it be replicated in France.[136] After the interruption of the war, the CCS restarted the competition in 1953–54, from which point forward it was an appendage of the CCS designed to get students interested in the colony.[137] Local groups such as the Koloniale en Maritieme Kring, Brugge; the Koloniale Kring van Leuven (Colonial Club of Leuven); and the Cercle africain borain (Borain African Club) held their own concours, often with financial and other support from the Ministry of Colonies, reaching thousands of students.[138]

Officials embraced the fact that this was important propaganda for increasing support for imperialism.[139] As with CCS talks in schools, the minister of colonies paid a great deal of attention to the working of the Concours Coloniaux Scolaires, leading him to attend its organizational meetings, serve on its juries, and sometimes personally award the prizes in a solemn ceremony.[140] The king or the heir to the throne awarded the prizes many of the years, thus associating the colonial project in students' minds with the dynasty. And speakers at award ceremonies explicitly linked the dynasty and Leopold II to ongoing colonization efforts, such as one speaker for whom Leopold II was "the great monarch" who endowed little Belgium with an empire, and who ended his remarks by "acclaiming the colony and the Dynasty."[141] This emphasis on the dynasty reinforced the connection between the colony and the Kingdom of Belgium, a connection likewise made at the Tervuren museum, at colonial expositions, monuments, and elsewhere.

Although the importance of textbooks can be overstated — they explained little about the colony, teachers covered much other history and geography, educators did not prioritize the Congo because it lay outside a nationalist history projected back in time for centuries — the messages they conveyed can tell us much about Belgian attitudes toward Africans and the empire. Looking beyond textbooks reveals other important efforts, such as the Ministry of Colonies filling the gap in education through its own initiatives, in essence making it an educating or propagandizing body. The Commission Coloniale Scolaire and the Concours Coloniaux Scolaires brought the Ministry of Colonies directly into the classroom to indoctrinate schoolchildren, and its propaganda there reinforced pro-imperial messages that students likely came across elsewhere, including love of dynasty and nation, pride in the empire, reverence for Leopold II and his colonial pioneers, and negative views of Africans. The post–World War II takeoff of the CCS, reaching hundreds of schools and tens of thousands of students, might help explain in part why Belgians were so shocked and dismayed in 1960 when the Congo so suddenly achieved its independence.

The CCS ended the Concours Coloniaux Scolaires and its conferences in 1960, just as the royal society Journées Coloniales ceased its activities in that year.[142] As both De Keyser and De Baets have noted, textbook and classroom coverage of the Congo after 1960 ceased for the time being, for all intents and purposes. Precipitous decolonization in the Congo, to use Jean Stengers's phrase, led to an abrupt end of Belgian political control in Africa that was mirrored by a sudden drop-off in research into, writing about, and promotion of imperialism in the metropole, resulting in a situation where Belgians born in the late 1950s and after 1960 knew little about their colonial past.[143] The abrupt halt to education about the Congo beginning in 1960 demonstrates that colonial education was not designed to educate students about central Africa for the sake of knowledge but rather to underpin the empire.

Five

Cast in the Mold of the EIC

The Colony in Stone and Bronze

Scholars agree that Leopold II was the driving force of Belgian imperialism, and most would concur that in general Belgians were reluctant imperialists at best during the EIC period from 1885–1908. During that time—an epoch of monument building in Europe—probably not more than ten memorials commemorating imperialism were erected: to brothers Lieven and Jozef Van de Velde (busts in 1887 and 1888 respectively, and a memorial in Ghent, 1888); Camille Coquilhat (Antwerp, 1895); local pioneer Cowé (Quiévrain, 1895); Pierre Ponthier (Marche-en-Famenne, 1897); Henri de Bruyne and Joseph Lippens (Blankenberghe, 1900); missionary Constant De Deken (Wilrijck, 1904); and arguably the Cinquantenaire Arch (Brussels, 1905). By 1960 dozens if not hundreds of imperialistic memorials had been built, meaning almost all were built after 1908.[1] They dotted the landscape across the country, varying in size, substance, manufacture, and representation. Some made explicit reference to Africa, while others celebrated colonial heroes and legitimized Belgian rule more obliquely. What follows is an examination of who went to the trouble to build these many memorials after Leopold left the imperial scene in an effort to understand why so many were built, what they say about the nature of Belgian imperialism, and what they reveal about the effects of overseas empire back at home.

On the Significance of Physical Memorials

How meaningful were statues, plaques, and memorial busts, and how much did they draw attention to themselves and thereby shape people's attitudes toward the overseas empire? Some imperial monuments were large and prominently situated, such as the Baron Dhanis memorial in Antwerp and the monuments to Leopold II in Oostende and Brussels. Yet the surrounding landscape largely obscured others; today, plaques to colonial veterans and other imperial monuments often escape tourist guidebooks and even locals' awareness.[2] Other larger monuments are tucked away in nooks off the beaten path or lost in the overgrown brush of city parks, such as the Camille Coquilhat monument in King Albert Park in Antwerp, while still others are usually not recognized as colonial monuments as such. Without knowing its origin, it is hard to link the hulking Arcade du Cinquantenaire in Brussels to Leopold II's expansion in Africa even though it was largely funded by his Congo profits. The same is true for the statue to the monarch in the Place du Trône, which appears as just another statue and whose inscription, "Leopoldo II, Regi Belgarum, 1865–1909, Patria Memor [the homeland remembers]," indicates no colonial connection.

Yet the obscurity today of some monuments does not detract from their historical significance during the colonial period. Building permanent memorials in stone necessitated time, money, and organization, and the creative process included decision making that illustrates the mentality of those involved. At the same time, they were different than other forms of propaganda in that they were more permanent. Whereas expositions were temporary, films wore out, and colonial history in textbooks changed over time, most memorials survived for decades, framing people's everyday lives. Belgians clearly recognized that monuments recounted history in physical form, as recent events illustrate. After someone effaced the words "l'Arabe" and "Arabische" on Vinçotte's Colonial Monument in Cinquantenaire Park in the late 1980s, people complained and the original words were brought back.[3] In 2005 someone again removed the words, and they were restored anew — as was the entire monument after a request to the Brussels Regional Parliament.[4] In the latest round of this public argument, someone once more had chipped out the offending words by early 2010. In 2004 a political party's local branch asked the Hal (Halle) city administration to take down the monument to Leopold II in that city's park, "because mass murderers do not deserve a monument."[5] Not long afterward, an attack on a Leopold monument in Oostende left one of its African figures missing a hand, a move that former colonials quickly moved to rectify.[6]

Of course it is possible to overstate the importance of monuments, especially considering that in Belgium, as elsewhere in Europe, memorials are to be found all over the place, including many obscure ones located off the beaten path. Yet a remarkable number of colonial monuments loomed large in everyday life, and many were central to the locales where they were built. The figure of Father De Deken, an African woman crouching at his feet, dominated Wilrijk's Grand'Place just outside Antwerp for more than a century. It was the center of attention not only at its inauguration but also in later years, such as when a large crowd celebrated its twenty-fifth anniversary.[7] Smaller memorials served as sites of inaugurations and gatherings, and newspapers covered such events enthusiastically. Photographs from Verviers in the 1930s show throngs of people gathered at the Chic-Chac steps near the train station where a local veterans group in 1931 had placed a small plaque commemorating fifteen local pioneers who died in Africa. The site served in subsequent years both as a rendezvous and as a kind of staging area for speeches commemorating the civilizing mission in Africa—likewise at dozens of other memorials across the country.[8] Because the literature on Belgian imperialism overwhelmingly argues that metropolitan "interest in the colony or colonial questions remained superficial," it is surprising to come across photographs and accounts in archives, personal collections, newspapers, and periodicals that time and again show large crowds gathered at sites such as memorials to honor colonial pioneers and the overseas empire they acquired.[9]

The fact that people quickly rebuilt a number of monuments destroyed by war reinforces the point that monuments retained their importance over time. After occupying Germans took the large Lippens–De Bruyne monument in Blankenberghe—funded by public subscription and unveiled in 1900—"during the night" in September 1918, it was rebuilt within only three years.[10] When retreating Germans destroyed Namur's statue to Leopold II at the end of World War II, a local colonial group quickly rebuilt it, and it still stands today in Place Wiertz.[11] Under cover of darkness, Germans took down a bronze bust to General E. Storms in the Square de l'Industrie in Brussels in 1943, and today a stone replacement stands in nearby Square de Meeus.[12] Pro-empire enthusiasts deliberately moved other memorials to new locations, when rebuilding or urban planning threatened them.

Colonial memorials increased their influence when they reached beyond their actual site into newspapers and other media. Local or special publications reproduced images of many, such as when the 1930 World's Fair publication *Antwerpen 1930* showed off the city's annexation monument and Dhanis statue

Ostende. — Monument à Léopold II.
Oostende. — Standbeeld aan Leopold II.
Ostend. — Monument to Leopold II.

7. Postcard of Leopold II Oostende monument (author's collection).

to readers along with other important landmarks.[13] Images of other monuments found their way into school textbooks and commemorative publications, such as Vinçotte's Colonial Monument, which became the cover of an overview of Belgian colonial history.[14] Procolonial groups reproduced physical memorials as symbols in their publications and elsewhere, putting them into circulation among a broader public than those who might only walk past a monument, and who may or may not have paid attention as they did so.[15] Postcards reproduced innumerable others, radiating pro-empire images at home and abroad.[16]

The ways in which local government, colonial veterans, and others involved the local population and national figures in the memorial-building process deepened their significance. Inaugurations not only offered opportunities for remembrance at sites across the country but also led to extended cross-class commemorations of the imperial idea.[17] A not untypical event was a

1932 inauguration in Hal that included an entire day of activities centered around the unveiling of the town's first colonial monument, dedicated to Jacques de Dixmude and local colonial pioneers. According to the schedule, it began with a morning mass followed by a wreath laying at the city's World War I monument. The inauguration procession set off by 2:30 p.m.; after winding through the city with a stop in the Grand'Place, the procession arrived at Albert Park, the site of the monument's unveiling. Speakers included the president of the Cercle colonial de Hal (Colonial Club of Hal), the president of the Ligue du souvenir congolais, the minister of colonies, and the mayor. The day ended with a concert that evening at 8:00 p.m.[18] This type of day-long celebration of Belgium's empire — sometimes days long — took place in other cities as well.[19]

Inaugurations activated a whole range of people, not just men or colonial enthusiasts or members of the bourgeoisie. Numerous individuals and groups became involved long before someone unveiled the final work, such as with Antwerp's Francis Dhanis monument, Mons's colonial memorial, and memorials to General Malfeyt and Aristide Doorme in Oostende. Dhanis made his career and his name in Leopold II's EIC by leading forces to take Kasongo in 1893 during the Arab campaign, an achievement for which he received a hero's welcome home in 1894 and a barony. When he died in 1909, Antwerp's Club africain — Cercle d'études coloniales (African Club — Colonial Study Society), of which Dhanis was a founder, began planning his monument. Although their goal was to unveil the memorial in 1913 on the twentieth anniversary of the event that had made Dhanis famous, the public's response was so enthusiastic that they reached their fundraising goal within a few months.[20] In Mons, raising a memorial to colonial pioneers involved the town's school students, who offered the material of which the plaque was made.[21] The building of a monument in Oostende to hail Aristide Doorme as a hero of the Arab and Batetela campaigns led to dozens of contributions from people from the city and elsewhere, and yet another to General Malfeyt brought out an "attractive group of students from the schools of Oostende . . . who, after the ceremony, added their flowers to the wreaths placed before the memorial."[22] Subscriptions that the publication *L'Horizon* collected funded the Doorme monument, which went up in 1929.[23] Even something as simple as raising a commemorative plaque in a colonial pioneer's native town could bring out children in an attempt to rally them to the cause.[24] As was the case also in France, these mobilizations of the local community, especially when it meant calling on them for money, necessarily involved the larger public in the project of remembering, reaching beyond the dedicated individuals who organized the event and were likely to participate in inauguration ceremonies.[25]

Not everyone was willing to join inaugural events, such as the Cuesmes section of the small Trotskyite Parti socialiste révolutionnaire (Revolutionary Socialist Party, PSR), which called on workers to abstain from the celebration for the Charles Lemaire plaque in Cuesmes in July 1937. Calling all "Workers of Cuesmes!" the PSR attacked imperialism and capitalism as well as its rival Belgian Workers' Party (POB/BWP). The PSR disparaged the POB/BWP and its leader Vandervelde for embracing imperialism by entering into a tripartite government during World War I, even if Vandervelde himself had remained anticolonial, supposedly, in principle: "Since 1918, by their participation in ministries of national union, they help the latter to maintain our unfortunate brothers of color in the Congo in slavery." The PSR concluded, "Drive everyone away from [*Faites le vide autour*] a ceremony as odious as that which is going to take place in our commune the 24 and 25 July. Down with the colonial banditry of the imperialists and the militarists! Long live the liberation of all the people of color enslaved by capitalism! *Vive l'Internationale!*"[26] Inaugural events mobilized large groups of people in favor of empire, but because they were public events, they presented opportunities for opposition as well. Nevertheless, such protests were very rare. Most evidence points to the fact that Belgians from varied backgrounds eagerly embraced the commemoration of colonial heroes in bronze and stone, and the Cuesmes protest highlights if anything the POB/BWP's acceptance of empire in Africa.[27]

Whether or not people paid attention to memorials at inaugurations, they did pay attention to them when they physically changed the landscape. As Nuala Johnson has pointed out, the physical place where memorials themselves are located needs to be examined: "The space which these monuments occupy is not just an incidental material backdrop but in fact inscribes the statues with meaning."[28] For instance, the Place du Trône Leopold II statue lies at a busy intersection on Brussels's city ring road, near the Palais Royal and busy Porte de Namur. The De Deken statue in Wilrijk formed the centerpiece of the city's center square; the benches around it—and the statue base at times—provided seating for locals passing time. Commemorative sculptures to Jacques de Dixmude and Leopold II in Hal's city park form a backdrop still today for students walking from school to the park's bus stop, and as they stand waiting for the bus.

Monuments also served, and continue to serve, as sites of remembrance and storytelling. The unveiling of the equestrian memorial to Leopold II in the Place du Trône in 1926, for instance, was an opportunity to assemble colonials and affirm the country's noble African mission. Albert I lauded his predecessor's contributions to the imperial effort in his speech to mark the event, as did the prime minister.[29] The monument served afterward as a rallying point for Belgian colonials during annual commemorations and special anniversaries, such as the one in 1958 that celebrated fifty years of Belgian state rule in Africa.[30] With the increase in tourism in Brussels, tour guides in the capital may have stopped by the monument to draw attention to Belgium's second monarch. Monuments in provincial centers served a similar purpose during the colonial period, chiefly on the annual Koloniale Dagen.[31] They continued to do so into the post-1960 period and continue to do so even today.[32]

A particularly notable memorial is Thomas Vinçotte's Colonial Monument in Cinquantenaire Park, which was the site of the 2000 remembrance discussed at the outset of the book. The Colonial Monument is explicitly imperialistic and became an important site of remembrance.[33] Planning began in 1910 at the time of the Brussels Exposition Universelle with its Section Congolaise, but the inauguration did not take place until 1921.[34] In the monument's foreground is a young African lying down, representing the Congo River. On the left a soldier combats the slave trade, while figures on the right represent a European colonial soldier tending to a wounded comrade.[35] In the central panel, "the African continent henceforth open to civilization, advances toward the group of soldiers surrounding Leopold II. Above, Belgium welcoming the black race is represented under [sous] the features of a superb young woman."[36] Like others, the memorial became a site of annual commemorations that celebrated pioneers and empire as well as a site to not only recover but exalt Leopold II's role in Belgium's glorious imperial past.[37]

At its inauguration, Minister of Colonies Louis Franck — in a speech reproduced verbatim in numerous publications — eulogized Leopold, praising him in one breath and dismissing the excesses of his regime in another, all the while turning an eye toward Belgium's future in central Africa.[38] Treated as a place of remembrance by Franck and others at its 1921 unveiling, Vinçotte's Colonial Monument is a good example of how memorials continued to serve as sites of memory for enthusiasts, veterans, and others throughout the colonial period and beyond, albeit during the latter period with a much reduced turnout.[39]

Characteristics of Colonial Monuments in Belgium

Belgian colonial monuments are to a large degree about men and the military. The one unifying aspect of all the plaques, statues, and monuments — whatever their form, age, location, material, or inauguration date — is that they commemorate men. This is not surprising and reflects the fact that public life in Belgium was for a long time dominated by men, which extended in particular to rule in the Congo in its many aspects from its first days.[40] Slightly less common but almost as universal is that imperial memorials in Belgium commemorated military figures, often expressly exalting the military. This theme is clear in a simple listing of a few memorials: General Storms (a bust in Brussels), Sergeant De Bruyne and Lieutenant Lippens (a monument in Blankenberghe), Captain Crespel, Colonel Chaltin, General Wangermée (a stela, bust, and funerary monument, respectively, in Ixelles), Commandant Laplume (a monument in Vielsalm), Lieutenant Colonel Louis Royaux (a plaque in Dinant), Commander Bia (one bust in Liège, another in Brussels), Lieutenant General Baron Tombeur de Tabora (a monument in St. Gilles), Commandant Dhanis (a plaque in Brussels and a monument in

8. Bust of Colonel Chaltin, Ixelles (photo by the author).

Antwerp); the list could continue. In many cases, monuments that did not explicitly commemorate the military nevertheless insinuated a military theme because those they memorialized began their careers in the military in Belgium or in the Congo, even if what made them famous was not directly related to armed exploits. The splendid Albert Thys monument on the edge of Cinquantenaire Park, for example, and the one to Crespel in the quiet Square du Solbosch in Ixelles celebrated men who entered into the service of Leopold II or Belgium in Africa only after a stint in the army.[41]

Some might consider the dominance of military figures strange considering Belgium is a country without a strong militarist tradition. By the time of Leopold II's reign, Belgium's navy had been abolished (1869); the king's efforts to increase military defense spending during the last years of his reign met intransigent parliamentary opposition.[42] In the years preceding the outbreak of war in 1914, Belgium was fiercely neutral; its army's capabilities against the Germans in August 1914 were surprising, not least of all to the Germans. During the interwar years, the kingdom abandoned military cooperation with France — in part because of its pacifism and its refusal to commit to an all-out defense of Belgium — and embraced neutrality in an effort to stave off a potential German attack.[43] The fact that the country's colonial tradition left a great number of monuments in stone and bronze to military figures is thus surprising. Of course, there exist in many locales monuments to the dead from the two world wars, but those commemorate resistance to foreign domination by a stronger power. Imperial monuments in Belgium celebrate the contrary: conquest, victory, and domination over weaker and militarily inferior peoples, albeit with a supposedly altruistic goal.

Geographically, many more memorials arose in Wallonia than Flanders: around half in the former, a third in the latter, and the remainder in Brussels. One might exclude memorials within or at the Musée du Congo Belge from those erected in Flanders considering the museum was a royal or national site and therefore might not demonstrate local or regional initiative to build imperial monuments. But even if one includes the several memorials at the Tervuren museum within the total for Flanders, Wallonia still has many more imperial memorials. Marking colonial memorials on a map of Belgium creates almost a belt extending from Tournai in the southwest through Mons and Charleroi to Liège and its vicinity. Yet it would seem that Wallonia's predominance as a site for imperial monument building was something that did not really begin until the latter half of the 1920s (chart 1). Despite this predominance, which probably reflects the dominance of the French-speaking bourgeoisie in the Congo, imperial memorials generally are dispersed throughout the country, in both large and small urban areas. Clusters understandably exist in larger metropolitan areas such as Antwerp and Brussels, but they are also found in smaller cities such as Namur, Arlon, and Oostende.

A periodization of memorials demonstrates that enthusiasm for building memorials endured throughout the colonial period. It is no surprise that few sprang up from 1914 to 1918 or from 1940 to 1945, when Germany occupied the country.[44] The period 1925–40 was a boom period, with eight memorials built from 1925 to 1929 and forty-seven from 1930 to 1940. Monument building picked up again beginning in 1947 when Chaltin's monument was moved from the Union colonial belge building to its current site, the Square du Solbosch, followed by the raising of a bust of Albert Thys in his hometown of Dalhem. The

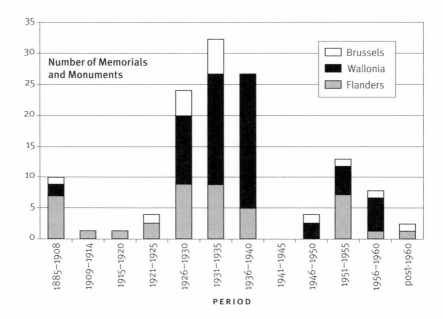

Number of Memorials
and Monuments

□ Brussels
■ Wallonia
▨ Flanders

PERIOD

Chart 1. Memorials and monuments by region and period;
Tervuren monuments included among those in Flanders.

period from 1950 to independence was another decade heavy
with imperial commemorations in stone and metal, especially
ones to Leopold II, as people built or rebuilt monuments to him
in Namur, Arlon, Ghent, Hal, Mons, and Tervuren; a plaque
inside the Arcade du Cinquantenaire in Brussels placed his image within the framework of the Saxe-Coburg dynasty. At least
seventeen memorials were raised during this period, not including the re-erection of the Leopold II monument in Namur. As
in education and the 1958 Brussels World's Fair, there were no
signs of diminishing eagerness for empire. After 1960, by contrast, memorial building for all intents and purposes came to
a halt, although most memorials remained in place, with few
exceptions.[45]

Who Built Colonial Monuments?

The overwhelming majority of monuments came into being not at the hands of the three so-called pillars of Belgian colonial rule. The government's Office colonial (later Inforcongo) expended great efforts to commission films on the Congo, organize expositions, and edit numerous official publications. Business groups reached out to children and others to a degree at expositions and were joined in doing so by Scheutists and other missionary orders, who also reached people in churches, schools, publications, cinemas, and expositions. But none of these groups took the lead to memorialize heroes with statues or other permanent memorials. During the interwar years the government refused all but the most minimal support for enterprising local groups that asked for assistance to build monuments, an attitude that continued into the immediate post–World War II period.[46] There were few monuments to colonial administrators (either those who worked in the Congo or the metropole); a plaque to Nicolas Cito in the Musée du Congo Belge and a bust to administrator Victor Denyn in Antwerp are rare exceptions.[47] Other administrators celebrated in memorials, such as Dhanis or Charles Lemaire, are men better known for their roles in the conquest of the Congo. UMHK memorialized several of its administrators, but privately in their Brussels offices.[48] None of the outstanding governors or ministers of the Congo, such as Théophile-Théodore Wahis, Pierre Ryckmans, Jules Renkin, or Henri Jaspar, found themselves publicly immortalized in stone and bronze (except for official busts of each prime minister). The only great colonial administrator commemorated publicly was Leopold II. There are likewise very few monuments to religious figures, even though missionaries figured large in European involvement in the Congo.

9. Leopold II monument in Hal (photo by the author).

Instead, the driving forces behind imperial monuments were veterans groups, local government, and local colonial interest groups seeking to create foci of dedication and devotion to keep the memory of imperial heroes alive.[49] The Cercle africain borain from the southern mining region of the Borinage, for instance, organized a Comité des mémoriaux géologue Jules Cornet et Commandant Charles Lemaire (Committee for the Geologist Jules Cornet and Commander Charles Lemaire Memorials) to erect plaques to those two in the city of Cuesmes.[50] The Association des ingénieurs de la faculté polytechnique de Mons (Association of Engineers of the Polytechnic Faculty of Mons) memorialized Jules Cornet in larger form in nearby Mons to commemorate his prospecting work in the Congo; a quote from Cornet on the monument focuses the viewer's attention on the subterranean mineral resources in the Congo.[51] The statue of Leopold II in Namur, originally built by the city's Chamber of Commerce, provides another example of local dedication to the imperial project: after retreating Germans destroyed it as the Allies advanced through Belgium in 1944, a local colonial society rebuilt it. Other local groups elsewhere put up smaller plaques with lists of the names of those who died in Africa up to 1908, resembling memorials to World War I dead that adorn so many Belgian, French, and Italian villages and towns. Subscribers to the colonial newspaper *L'Expansion Coloniale* could read in 1932 a summary of the several inaugurations that the Cercle africain des Ardennes (African Club of the Ardennes) carried out in 1930 and 1931.[52] Local groups and colonial veterans were understandably eager both to keep their comrades' memories alive as well as to frame their own pasts in a glorious, self-gratifying light.

Local groups did not always act alone; just as in other states, both contestation and cooperation between national and local and official and unofficial actors in the twentieth century drove events. In Belgium, local groups often interacted with national organizations, which sometimes spurred those group into action.[53] The two main groups that promoted the building of imperial memorials during the 1920s and 1930s were the Ligue du souvenir congolais and the Vétérans coloniaux (Colonial Veterans), both of which made it a point to commemorate the role colonial veterans played in "opening up" Africa.[54] In fact, the Ligue du souvenir congolais in 1929–30 compiled lists of all "pioneers" who died in the Congo between 1876 and 1908 with the deliberate goal of erecting memorials to local veterans in every single applicable municipality throughout the entire country.[55] The Ligue sent out lists to five hundred cities and communes to galvanize them into action on the issue, resulting in dozens of memorials.[56] Not untypical is a plaque to Commandant Pierre

Van Damme placed on barracks in Arlon for which Emmanuel Muller, colonial enthusiast and editor of the monthly *Vétérans Coloniaux*, thanked the Ligue du souvenir congolais for its support at the unveiling.[57]

The dozens of memorial plaques scattered across Belgium are testimony to efforts by veterans groups and the Ligue du souvenir congolais to commemorate fallen colleagues. Colonial enthusiasts and surviving EIC pioneers were eager to keep the memories of their departed comrades alive in the minds of their countrymen. For some of these men, memorials were not only for colonial pioneers but also for good friends.[58] More than that, they viewed this as a form of spiritual education. Colonial enthusiasts often complained that their compatriots did not have enough imperial spirit or did not know enough about the colony, and veterans asserted that their fellow citizens did not grasp the true value of the empire that Leopold had bequeathed them nor the sacrifices of the pioneers in his service. They were ready to paint their own actions in a glorious, self-gratifying light, and building memorials and making patriotic speeches at inaugurations were one way to do this.

State financing of memorials changed during the 1950s, at the very least suggesting an attempt to shore up Belgium's control of its colony in reaction to contemporaneous developments. The Comité exécutif du monument Bia (Executive Committee of the Bia Monument) in Liège contacted the Ministry of Colonies in 1949 to gain the ministry's financial support for its plans to erect a memorial, but as in years past the state took little action. Both the Ministry of Colonies and the ministry's parastatal funding group, the Fonds colonial de propagande economique et sociale (Colonial Fund for Economic and Social Propaganda), refused the committee a subsidy. This changed with the new decade, for the ministry began to provide numerous subsidies to local groups on request:

- 50,000 francs for the Fraternelle des troupes coloniales 1914–1918 (Brotherhood of Colonial Troops 1914–1918) for its monument to General Baron Tombeur de Tabora (unveiled 1951);[59]

- In 1952, 15,000 francs to the Pater Vertenten-comité (Father Vertenten Committee) in Hamme, which aimed to raise a memorial to that missionary;[60]

- 100,000 francs for a monument to Leopold II and colonial pioneers in Hasselt (unveiled 1952);[61]

- In 1953, 25,000 francs for a monument to Pionniers malinois (Mechlin Pioneers), 100,000 francs for the Victor Roelens monument in Ardooie, and 50,000 francs for the Jules Cornet monument in Mons;[62]

- At least 15,000 francs to the Koloniale Kring van Mechelen (Mechlin Colonial Club) for a monument to local pioneers (unveiled c. 1953);[63]

- 140,000 francs to the statue in Mons for Leopold II and the Hennuyers (unveiled 1958).[64]

Moreover, many *cercles* (clubs) received large subsidies from the Ministry of Colonies during the 1950s, and these funds paid in part for the building of monuments and commemorations.[65] As anticolonialism increased at the United Nations and elsewhere, and as the Gold Coast, Sudan, and others began to achieve independence, the state defended its imperialism at home by subsidizing monuments that legitimized its hold over a vast central African domain.

Material Messages

The ideas these monuments communicated to observers are as equally important as their origins, general characteristics, time-frame, and geographical distribution. Probably the most significant effect was the explicit nationalization of the exploration and conquest of central Africa. Even memorials that seemingly celebrated only exploration carried nationalistic messages by means of exclusions. Foreign nationals who played a key role in the exploration of the Congo, such as Paul and Richard Böhm, Leo Frobenius, Major Hermann von Wissmann, and Henry Morton Stanley, did not appear among colonial memorials. Instead, monuments to exploration in Africa celebrated lesser Belgian figures, such as Crespel and General Storms, giving a clearly nationalistic emphasis to this area of Eurafrican history. In terms of a message of conquest, monuments built after 1908 focused on the "heroic era" of occupation and triumph that stretched from initial endeavors in the 1870s, through the Arab campaigns and the suppression of the Batetela revolts at the end of the nineteenth century, to the turnover of the Congo to Belgium. Again, this pattern denied foreigners a role, even though "Swedish, Danish and Norwegian sea-captains, helmsmen, machinists and craftsmen . . . in reality made possible the Belgian conquest of the Congo."[66] In this category are memorials to men of household names such as Lippens, De Bruyne, and Dhanis, to the latter of whom was dedicated a plaque in the Brussels post office in addition to the large and prominent monument in Antwerp. But here also figure statues and plaques in natal towns to local sons who died by any means in Africa—obscure men such as A. F. Ardevel, whose name is inscribed on the colonial monument in Hal; Victor Sandrart, whose memorial is in Thorembais-Saint-Trond; and many others—as well as blanket monuments such as the Colonial Monument in the Cinquantenaire Park.

After the reprise, monuments repeatedly emphasized the themes of heroism, pioneering, and *mission civilisatrice* (civilizing mission) during the pre-1908 period, making them a mantra. This began as early as the 1913 Dhanis monument in Antwerp whose inscription defined his pioneering work in the Congo: "Voor de mensheid [for mankind]."[67] In the discourse of monuments, the period from 1876 or 1885 to 1908 became the heroic and glorious pioneer period to be celebrated as the noble foundation of the empire. On 14 October 1930 the Conseil communal (Communal Council) of Mons unveiled a plaque in the main entranceway of the Hôtel de Ville dedicated to the city's pioneering sons, or as one publication put it, "in memory of the *Montois* [citizens of Mons] who died for civilization before 1908."[68] Planners deliberately chose the period identified on the plaque, 1876 to 1908: perhaps not a single person from Mons died in the Congo from 1908 to when the city unveiled the plaque twenty-two years later, but it is certain that organizers chose the date 1876 with ulterior motives in mind because none of the pioneers listed on the plaque died before 1891. This was a memorial to Leopold II's rule and those who worked for him. Memorials referring similarly to the EIC period appeared in Liège and Namur, as well as smaller towns such as Ixelles, Seilles, Lens, Leuven, and Saint-Josse-ten-Noode, among others. Tervuren's Musée du Congo Belge communicated a similar message by means of a 1934 wall memorial in its salle du mémorial. Put up on the initiative of the Ligue du souvenir congolais, with the assistance of museum director Schouteden, it listed names of 1,508 Belgians killed for the African cause from 1876 to 1908.[69] Monuments in this way reflected in physical space the idea of the "heroic period," which different people at various times reproduced in so many areas of production about the Belgian Congo's history and in discourse in general about the colony after 1908. What many Belgians came to believe about their colonial rule, of course, had quite a bit to do with the portrayal of it in monuments and elsewhere in the metropole.

Other themes that memorials cultivated were the 1914–18 campaigns and the importance of the Congo to Belgium during World War I. Baron Tombeur de Tabora figured prominently in this regard—a memorial to him stands in the St. Gilles area of Brussels—as did lesser-known figures. In Arlon, for example, commemorators erected a plaque "to the memory of the Commandant Pierre Van Damme, last Belgian officer killed in the Congo at the time of the campaign 14–18," and another "to the memory of the General Philippe Molitor, child of Arlon and former commander in chief of the North Brigade of the East African Troops during the campaign of Tabora 1914–1918."[70]

There were only a few monuments that memorialized the civilizing mission, but those that did indicated the desire to represent the several aspects of Belgium's declared œuvre civilisatrice. At the 1925 inauguration of the monument to brothers Georges and Paul Le Marinel at the Université coloniale, Dr. Dryepondt stated, "The eminent sculptor Matton was admirably inspired," showing in the casts of the Le Marinel brothers "those who dedicated themselves to take the natives out of barbarism and to bring them progress and civilization."[71] The monument to geologist Jules Cornet in Mons drew attention to the rational exploitation of Africa's subterranean riches. For the extension of a judicious administration, there was in Vielsalm a monument to Laplume, who ran elephant training operations in Api. Monuments to Albert Thys implicitly celebrate his building of

10. Laplume memorial in Vielsalm-Salmchâteau (photo by the author).

Congo railways.[72] For the spread of Christianity, a startlingly infrequent theme in monuments, the town of Ardooie built a statue of Monseigneur Victor Roelens, the first bishop in the Belgian Congo.[73]

Among the many imperialistic figures in metal and stone, none stands out more or more often than Leopold II, for whom at least ten major monuments were built. In the capital alone his likeness was reproduced in stone and metal numerous times: the equestrian statue in the Place du Trône, Vinçotte's Colonial Monument in Cinquantenaire Park, his profile among those of Belgium's first five monarchs on a late–colonial period plaque within the Arcade du Cinquantenaire. A statue of him strikes a perhaps more true-to-life representation off Avenue Louise in the Jardin du Roi, where today it still stands tall and appropriately alone, overseeing the garden that was one of his many royal bequests to the nation's capital. Outside Brussels, people built statues to Leopold II in Ghent, Mons, Antwerp, Oostende, Namur, Arlon, Tervuren, and Hal. Innumerable other permanent markers invoked and honored his name and legacy, either at inaugurations or in subsequent years. For instance, at the 1921 inauguration of the Colonial Monument in the Cinquantenaire Park, which places the king in a central position, Minister of Colonies Franck gave a speech during which "he recounted in large strokes the history of our colonial effort and rendered homage to King Leopold II as well as all those pioneers who built for us a splendid empire in the heart of Africa."[74] Such monuments rehabilitated Leopold II as an advocate of civilization and benevolence in Africa and affirmed him as the prescient founder of the œuvre civilisatrice.

The form of many monuments to Leopold II indicates they were colonial monuments and not just celebrations of the king himself or the Saxe-Coburg dynasty. This was at times explicit. In the case of the rather plain Leopold II monument in Mons, the base inscription linked him to local colonial heroes and thus imperialism in the Congo: "To His Majesty Leopold II and to the colonial pioneers from Hainault." In Arlon a busy intersection just outside of town still today bears a large monument to Leopold II that carries his saying: "I embarked upon the work of the Congo in the interest of civilization and for the good of Belgium." The Cercle colonial arlonais (Arlon Colonial Club) put up this monument, which Leopold II's upright figure dominates, in 1951. Reading from left to right, the memorial's two wings comprise before-and-after depictions of Leopold's work: The left panel shows mostly naked Africans wailing, cowering, and in bondage under the control of Arabs in turbans with whips. The right shows clothed Africans at work as carpenters, scientists, blacksmiths, miners, and students, as well as one who is wearing a cross. As noted in the chapter on museums, the Tervuren Musée du Congo Belge is a memorial of a different kind to Leopold II because it has been, and continues to be, an extended homage to the king.

In other cases, statues of Leopold became imperialistic only through their use over time. Illustrating this is the temporary monument set up for the 1930 Exposition Universelle in Antwerp whose three monumental arches, one each for the three equestrian statues of the monarchs who had ruled during the country's first hundred years of independence, formed a massive Arc de Triomphe that was the principal entryway into the fair. It was at the statue of Leopold II and not at the other two that colonial veterans and others celebrated a "popular homage" to their imperial dynasty in an "exciting ceremony" that summer, complete with music played by colonial troops brought in from

Boma.[75] The monument that seems to have been the model for the 1930 Antwerp statue, the equestrian monument to Leopold in the Place du Trône in Brussels, is in and of itself not visibly colonial, yet it repeatedly served as a meeting place for commemorations to the colonial project.[76] Victor Demanet's statue to Leopold II in Namur—put up by the city in 1928 to serve as a colonial site in this "third most colonial city" in Belgium, and rebuilt after World War II—is another example of how monuments to Leopold transformed into imperial memorials and remained significant over time.[77] "Ceremonies organized at the time of the celebration of the Journées Coloniales by the CCN" took place around that monument; at that time, "diverse units of the Army formed the square and before him . . . the youth of the schools paraded, rendering a belated homage to the great, long unrecognized Monarch."[78] The Place du Trône statue of Leopold, which did not indicate an imperial theme in and of itself, also came to celebrate the empire with time. The king's former private secretary Baron Carton de Wiart largely propelled the building of the Place du Trône statue.[79] Efforts to build it began before 1914, but the war helped delay its completion until 1926. Public subscription and generous donations from the royal family funded it, including 100,000 francs from the king and 20,000 francs from Princess Stéphanie.[80] Donations from the public were so great that the total raised—equivalent to 2.5 million Euros in 2005—paid for a duplicate erected in Leopoldville in 1928, which became the subject of controversy in Kinshasa in 2005.[81]

Thus at its inauguration the Place du Trône statue was a national, not a colonial memorial, and it was not until after the inauguration that it took on an increasingly imperial meaning. Devotion to the founder of the EIC took the form of pilgrimages to the Place du Trône statue every year on 15 November, the feast day of Saint Leopold.[82] Leopold II took on a particular, almost sacred, meaning for colonial veterans and enthusiasts, and perhaps for much of the population at large. It was under his command that veterans had served, and it was his vision that had led to the founding of the empire. For some old colonial hands, erecting monuments and commemorating the king and his "African" pioneers took on a near-religious or spiritual meaning. One observer described the 1930 pilgrimage as follows:

> We went next to the Place du Trône where many other colonials were waiting. Everyone gathered in silence facing the statue of Leopold II. Then, following the gesture of General Baron Tombeur who [was] the first to place a wreath of flowers at the foot of the monument, the presidents of the different groups, the Colonial Veterans, Journées Coloniales, Mutuelle Congolaise, Entr'Aide Coloniale, etc., broke away from the rows of marchers. The flags bowed and the *"anciens"* [old soldiers], as if spontaneously, observed before the great image of the Sovereign, creator of the Belgian African Empire, a pious minute of silence.[83]

In this unscripted ceremony, religious rite took place with military discipline. In another case, Minister of Colonies Edmond Rubbens, a Catholic, said that Vinçotte's Cinquantenaire monument was "like an altar" at which he and fellow commemorators could come to praise Leopold II.[84] One activist for the colonial veteran cause characterized his enduring efforts to commemorate veterans as a "crusade" and "sacred duty."[85] Although scholars have argued that Belgians distrusted colonial theorizing more than any other European imperial power and that the government's Congo policy was above all else "pragmatic," it would be a mistake to extrapolate this to mean that Belgians were dispassionate toward the empire.[86] The reverence and emotion with which veterans and others embraced the memory of Leopold II and the EIC's heroic period show that at least some Belgians had visceral emotional attachments to the colony and revered the empire religiously.

While brochures, books, and other publications reproduced Leopold's portrait like those of other sovereigns to honor kingdom and dynasty, they repeatedly associated print images of him and his monuments with the Belgian Congo. The Ministry of Colonies' propaganda office, the OC, used the equestrian image of the king at the Place du Trône in their brochure for an Exposition des Produits du Congo.[87] Yet another instance can be found in the Ministry of Colonies' official brochure for the 1930 Wereldtentoonstelling voor Koloniën, Zeevart en Vlaamsche Kunst, whose cover had a blue background with an overlaid gold star, suggesting the flag of the EIC and the Belgian Congo. The images superimposed on this background were of the steam ship *Albertville*, what appears to be the cathedral of Antwerp, city buildings, and largest of all an image of the equestrian monument of Leopold II from the Place du Trône.[88] It is remarkable organizers did not choose an image of the current sovereign, Albert I, considering his popularity after World War I, or an image of their first king, Leopold I, for an exposition that celebrated the nation's centennial. Instead, they used the image of Leopold II as an icon, attesting to the emblematic value of the monument itself and to the fact that the statue was an important memorial to Belgium's empire in central Africa, a primary focus of the exposition and a main export destination for Antwerp.

Perhaps the greatest imperial monument in Belgium is one that is often not recognized for being one: the Arcade du Cinquantenaire, today next to the European Union in the Quartier Leopold in Brussels. When built, the arcade formed a massive gateway from Brussels out the Avenue de Tervuren toward the village of the same name and Leopold's colonial edifices being built there. The arch's figures symbolized the future for the capital and the nation. The figures facing toward Brussels represented architecture, sculpture, painting, music, engraving, and poetry — representations of Brussels's artistic past that stretched back before Belgium's independence. The opposite side of the arch spoke to a vision of modernity and triumph; figures representing science and industry, agriculture, mechanics, commerce, and a navy anticipated the city's future at the beginning of the twentieth century. The representation of the navy pointed to Leopold II's longing that his people be a seagoing and expansive people with an empire. Confined in Europe and with borders guaranteed through its neutrality and the great powers' will, Belgium had no possibility for expansion on the Continent, meaning the only expansion it and its people could achieve was outside Europe. "If the patrie remains our headquarters, the world must be our objective," Leopold said in 1888. In the late nineteenth and early twentieth centuries, this meant Africa and more specifically the Congo.[89] The triumphant arch led out to a figuratively larger and imperial world in the suburb of Tervuren, where Leopold was building his colonial museum. Which victory did this Arc de Triomphe signify, if not Leopold's conquests in central Africa? The association between Leopold II and the arc are clear. When the debate opened as to where to situate the equestrian statue of Leopold that ended up at the Place du Trône, at least one publication suggested it be placed atop the Arcade du Cinquantenaire, and the Ligue du nouveau Bruxelles (League of the New Brussels) put pressure on the city and the organizing committee to have Leopold's statue placed there.[90] Later publications associated the arc with Leopold and Africa.[91] One observer noted, "In the royal park of Tervueren, seven miles distant from Brussels, he built a magnificent museum, and laid the foundation of a colonial school, in which Belgians and natives of every country were to be instructed. . . . He made new suburbs at Brussels, in the north-east; through the great forest of Tervueren he caused a wide avenue seven miles long to be built, leading to the gate of his Colonial Museum. At the commencement of that avenue at the Cinquantenaire Museum at Brussels, he built a glorious Arch of Triumph."[92] Thus the fact that the arcade connected Brussels to Tervuren and represented imperialism was not lost on contemporaries.

Memorials also had inadvertent consequences that reveal aspects of Belgian imperialism and colonial propaganda visible only now, from a distance. The inauguration of the Place du Trône monument, for example, revealed again the deep apprehension about the presence of colonial subjects in the metropole. Writing to Mayor Adolf Max, Baron Carton de Wiart suggested bringing in a contingent of Congolese troops for the 1926 inauguration: "The presence of our black soldiers would give a completely special depth to this ceremony and would consecrate the homage rendered to the founder of our African possessions. People have made objections to this suggestion that appear to me hardly founded. From a hygienic or moral viewpoint, one can respond that the stay of these troops could be limited to the space of time between two steamship departures."[93] Despite the fact that Carton de Wiart favored bringing in the troops and that in the end no troops came because none were available on time, his note suggests not only that the colonial theme permeated the inauguration—even if not explicitly evoked—but also that Belgians feared the presence of Africans in the metropole.

Another perhaps unintended consequence of monument building is that it tied citizens more closely together within the imagined community of the Belgian nation.[94] In the case of France, William B. Cohen pointed out that the putting up of statues in the provinces in the nineteenth century indicated cities' participation in a national French culture.[95] Similarly, imperial memorials in Belgium suggest a tying of the provinces closer together within a national culture or an imagined community while simultaneously legitimizing and celebrating the imperial project. By memorializing their sons killed in Africa, local groups and city councils not only maintained the memories of native heroes but also bound themselves more tightly to the empire, which was a national project. Evidence of the unitary nature of imperialism has been provided by Francis Ramirez and Christian Rolot, students of colonial cinema who pointed out how people who made colonial films were "belgicains"; that is to say, there was only a Belgian—not Flemish or Walloon—colonial cinema.[96] Likewise, people at imperial memorials united around a single overseas empire and therefore became more "belgicain."

Monument building linked directly with nation building in Belgium, offering an interesting case to compare to France, Britain, and other nations where scholars recently have grappled with the concept of the nation. In the British case, Antoinette Burton argues against the notion of "the nation" as a fixed thing and against the idea that the empire "out there" helped solidify the nation of Britain "back home," as if the former were a uniform monolith and the latter were singular and fixed rather than what it is, something in the process of becoming.[97] In the case of the French empire, Gary Wilder has asked us to "unthink" the nation.[98] In the Belgian case, few would accept the nation as somehow "fixed" or "eternal" because of its origins and the long-standing centrifugal forces of language divisions, of which the constitutional devolutions of power to the provinces and regions of the past thirty years are only the most recent manifestation. All the same, local celebrations of national figures after 1908, such as building monuments to Leopold II in Namur and Mons, associated cities with the nation and the dynasty. When communities and local interest groups erected monuments to colonial pioneers, they joined themselves to a unitary enterprise, because empire was a national undertaking; there was no distinctly Flemish or Walloon vision of empire.[99] The most national of monuments were those to Leopold II because they both tied the locality to the shared imperial project and hailed the dynasty, a long-standing unifying force. If imperial memorials fortified the Saxe-Coburg dynasty, this might help explain in part the growth in state and other spending on colonial monument building in the 1950s because of the "manifest crisis" the dynasty had entered into after the 1945 nonreturn of Leopold III from Germany.[100] The Christian Socialist government vote in 1950 that reinstated Leopold III as sovereign unleashed a wave of strikes that only was solved after he abdicated in favor of his son Baudouin, merely twenty years old at the time.[101] Leopold III's controversial actions during and after the war, a period of regency under his brother Charles, and a young monarch's ascension to the throne all put the dynasty in need of support.

Building monuments also may be considered as the writing of a particular history and the invention of an imperialist tradition.[102] All of the various modes of imperial propaganda after 1908 told a story, consciously or not, about the so-called œuvre civilisatrice. It is ironic and amazing that colonial monuments celebrated Leopold II, thereby helping transform his figure into a great, if not the greatest symbol for imperialism: ironic because it was Leopold's exploitation and outrageous misadministration that forced him to hand the Congo over to Belgium; amazing because his rule was the opposite of what Belgium proclaimed its colonialism to be after 1908, namely, efficient, beneficial, benevolent, and civilizing. Perhaps Leopold as icon is even more appropriate than commemorators imagined, as in fact abuses continued after 1908 and Belgium's legacy was an unsuccessful, unstable independent Congo.[103] It is peculiar that Belgium would base the legitimacy of its rule in the Congo on Leopold's legacy because his administration was justified in the first place (albeit only ostensibly) by his "opening up" of central Africa to international influence, whereas Belgium struck a clear nationalist tone in its control over its expansive African territories.

The histories that colonial memorials told were glorious ones, although backing away from discourse about the "heroic" period to look in detail at those who figured in monuments paints a more muddled picture. There is, for example, the monument to Captain L. Crespel in the Square du Solbosch in the town of Ixelles, today a commune in Brussels. When built, the four-sided stela proclaimed that Crespel's friends in Ixelles had built the monument in his honor: "Captain CRESPEL, Chief of the 1st Belgian expedition in central Africa. Born at Tournai the 4th December 1838, Deceased at Zanzibar the 24th January 1878." The dedication includes the EIC's motto, "Travail et progrès [work and progress]." The monument obscures the fact that Crespel never arrived on the African continent, that he never reached the area that was to become the Congo, and that he did not work for the EIC. He and his party arrived at Zanzibar to prepare their journey to the mainland on 12 December 1877—that is years before the EIC came into existence in 1885—yet within just a few weeks Crespel was dead of fever, never having left the island.[104]

Like Crespel, Émile Rochet and Alexandre Velghe died igno-
minious deaths in Africa and were memorialized later for service
to the EIC, in their case in their shared native town of Tongres.
Rochet entered into the military service of the EIC in August
1894 under the jurisdiction of Commandant H. J. Lothaire. Just
more than a year later, in December 1895, Rochet died in Kilon-
ga-Longa of hematuria (abnormal bleeding in the genitourinary
tract), apparently having done nothing remarkable during the
period of service leading up to his premature death.[105] Velghe's
end was even more gloomy. He had left the army to join the EIC
in 1893, one year before his townsman Rochet did. By 1894 he
was the commanding officer at the post of Bomokandi, having
benefited from the swift recognition and promotion that often
came to officers in the Force publique during the Leopoldian
period, at least those who survived. Velghe made the mistake
of arming fifty Africans under his command, not knowing or
perhaps having forgotten that they had heard they soon would
be impressed into service as manual laborers under another officer's command. Because they were too far from their homes
to flee, the men took over the post, and Velghe absconded. He
became sick, recovered at the EIC capital of Boma, and in late
1894 joined Lothaire's troops—as his fellow townsman Rochet
already had—to fight in the antislavery campaign in Ituri. Yet
this opportunity for Velghe to regain some prestige slipped away,
for he died of dysentery in the forest in July 1895.[106]

Lieven Van de Velde, who along with his brother was memorialized on more than one occasion in Ghent and whose bust
resides today in the salle du mémorial at the Musée du Congo
Belge, also died in the Congo: his "boy" accidentally shot him
in the back.[107] Similarly sad endings came to many others later
commemorated as heroes at home. Batetela fighters killed F. A.

Ardevel in a surprise attack in 1898, recompense for which commemorators in his hometown added his name to their colonial
monument thirty-four years later. Followers of Tippu Tip's son
Sefu murdered Lippens, who figures on the joint Lippens–De
Bruyne monument in Blankenberghe and who at the time of his
murder was suffering from dysentery, smallpox, stomach ail-
ments, and hepatitis.[108]

Notwithstanding less than glorious heroes, colonial monuments as a whole changed the landscape of Belgium. Before the
Congo adventure, there was little to unify the nation-state in
concrete form through public memorials. Although some monuments such as those to Leopold I or the Colonne du congrès
(Congress Column) celebrated the nation, most figures represented in stone and bronze were drawn from Belgium's pre-1830
past: Habsburg rule, Dutch rule, French rule, and so forth.[109]
This changed after 1908 when Belgium gained an overseas empire around which its citizens could rally. There was no doubt
about imperial monuments: unlike virtually all other public statues and commemorations in this recently independent nation,
monuments to the empire were unambiguously Belgian.

Several themes run through Belgium's many colonial memorials,
such as the repeated focus on the pre-1908 Leopoldian period,
dated either from the 1876 Brussels Geographic Conference or
the 1885 declaration of the EIC. Many commemorated military
figures while few honored colonial administrators. Missionaries
made little effort to erect memorials in the metropole despite the
fact that they figured large in the Congo, and the fact that there
were zero memorials to women is a particularly glaring omis-
sion. Female figures that did find their way into colonial monuments were suppliants or helpless Africans. Considering the

investment made in the colony's health care system and the important role of women as wives, medical personnel, and missionaries — by 1934 there were more female than male missionaries working in the colony — this represents a major exclusion.[110]

These monuments had many effects, not least of which was the uniting of the country's provinces within the imagined community of the nation closely tied to the dynasty. They also helped write a particular history of the country's involvement in central Africa revolving around the themes of heroism, pioneering, and the civilizing mission. This invented a national tradition of imperialism that not only celebrated the imperial project but also ennobled and legitimized it by founding contemporaneous rule on the heroic era — that is, the "glorious" years of colonial pioneers from 1876 (or 1885) to 1908, during which Belgians fought and died in the service of civilization in Africa. Thus, there also was a divorce between monuments' rhetoric and reality. Like expositions of the colony in the metropole that stressed the interpénétration of the colonial and Belgian economies, public memorials in the metropole that proclaimed the greatness of the heroic period projected a narrative different from the reality on the ground in Africa.

Six

Projected Propaganda

Imperialistic Filmmaking in Belgium

Film as a means of pro-empire propaganda during the New Imperialism is different because motion pictures represented an entirely new medium. Whereas monuments, museums, expositions, and education had histories of significant state involvement dating back to the nineteenth century, the question of who was going to control film was an open one as it developed. Because colonial films did not begin to come into their own until after 1908 and television did not take off until the 1960s, Belgian state imperialism coincides with the era in which "cinema was the dominant mass medium" in Europe, making the medium all the more important to study in this context.[1] Motion pictures, unlike the Musée du Congo Belge or universal expositions, necessarily presented partial views of the colony as opposed to claiming total pictures. Take, for example, an early film, Alexandre's 1897 *Les Congolais à Tervueren*, which only addressed Congolese at the Tervuren exposition that year. Alexandre's picture simply could not aspire to show more than a snippet of one facet of Belgian involvement in central Africa. At the same time, whereas museums and expositions strove for authenticity in their presentations, moving pictures did not have to do so to the same degree because viewers believed the medium to be somehow inherently authentic. Examining Belgian colonial films and considering who produced them, what their goals were, and what people saw in them can tell us much about efforts to sell the Congo to the metropolitan population. Many in the Ministry of Colonies believed cinema to have great power and used films to promote the empire at home and later as an integral part of their defense of empire on the world stage at the United Nations in the 1950s. Missionaries, colonial businesses, and others also used films intended for a domestic target to advance their own interests.

While understanding its importance, it is essential to view colonial film production within the context of the European and Belgian film industries. Cinema was a new medium of entertainment well into the interwar period, and films about the Congo made up only a small proportion of Belgium's film industry, which itself was never very large due to powerful international competition from Britain, France, and the United States and the country's comparatively small domestic market. Before World War I, French firms led by Pathé dominated the world market, including Belgium.[2] By the late 1920s, Belgium was producing few feature films and importing the vast majority of them, primarily from the United States.[3] This was also true for film shorts, and by 1927 the U.S. market share of the Belgian short-subject film market was 80 percent.[4] By 1937 approximately 40 percent of all films shown in Wallonia and 80 percent in Flanders were American in origin.[5] Although there may have been upward of one thousand colonial films produced before 1960, giving the impression of a large production, the domestic Belgian film industry, including colonial films, remained overshadowed by imports of films from abroad. The German occupation during World War II slowed the film industry's growth, making postwar production appear comparatively large, but foreign domination continued in the late 1940s and 1950s. In this way Belgium differed from Britain, France, and Italy, where large domestic markets and robust film industries created possibilities for strong colonial cinemas. In France, for example, filmmakers made hundreds of fiction films in the Maghreb alone.[6] Although films from the United States ruled the box office in Italy during the interwar years, Italy's film industry was still strong; after the 1936 defeat of Ethiopia, directors created prize-winning films with African themes, including *Lo squadrone bianco* (1936) and *Luciano Serra pilota* (1938).[7] This was not the case in Belgium.

Despite foreign domination of their film market, Belgians created hundreds of movies on the Congo and Ruanda-Urundi and deliberately used them to bolster colonial rule by teaching Africans about the benefits of colonial rule; by building support for overseas imperialism at home; and by persuading foreign opinion, especially after World War II. Pro-empire films from the medium's first years of existence are few but significant. As discussed in the first chapter, the first-ever Belgian film production company of any kind was Optique belge, established and financed by leading imperialists with the goal of showcasing the Congo. Although colonial filmmaking was hesitant during the Leopoldian period, this was likely due not to a lack of will but rather to technological obstacles for the nascent medium. As discussed below, despite a boost from government funding during World War I, colonial filmmaking was slow to develop during the interwar years and only really intensified in the final years of Belgian colonial rule. By that time, film had become a vehicle of government propaganda par excellence; even in cases where the colonial administration did not generate the material for films, they managed to control the final product, with few exceptions. A measure of the propaganda value of this colonial cinema is that profit was not a primary objective, if a goal at all, for almost all producers of motion pictures about the colony.

Belgian colonial films can tell us much about Belgian history and colonial cinema, in particular by pairing a breakdown of production and distribution with an analysis of film content. Many films may be considered "colonial": documentary, short, and feature films; films made in the Belgian Congo; motion pictures about Belgium's colony or about other colonies; those that convey some sort of colonial theme, explicitly or implicitly; films produced for Congolese during the colonial period or those made for Belgians or those produced for both; or films about Belgium's colony produced for foreign distribution. Francis Ramirez and Christian Rolot have identified around nine hundred colonial films, and they estimate that filmmakers created upward of one thousand before independence.[8] Many scholars of African or colonial cinema treat films about Africa in a sense as a block, that is to say, as the total production of films about the colony or those filmed on location there.[9] Yet directors and producers made most films either to fashion a procolonial view in the metropole or to teach Africans aspects of European culture and inculcate a pro-Belgian attitude, as was the case with many missionary films.[10] Drawing a line between these two types of production and focusing on the former directs our attention toward films created by and for Belgians that promoted or directly addressed imperialism in central Africa.

Redirecting our view away from the moving image itself and toward the actors behind the scenes helps reveal who made colonial films, for what purposes, whom they were trying to reach, and how successful they were. A key work that focuses on the moving image itself is Ramirez and Rolot's *Histoire du cinéma colonial au Zaire au Rwanda et au Burundi*. Extraordinarily rich, Ramirez and Rolot's work, nonetheless, is to be treated with caution. The authors depended on access to the Tervuren museum's film archive for much of their research, and it was the museum that published the book in 1985. Based on the museum's history of concealing materials and toeing the official line, one should be both cognizant of potential omissions and prepared to corroborate the authors' arguments. Moreover, the authors relied little on nonfilmic primary and secondary sources and engaged in little to no archival work beyond the films themselves at the museum. Despite these shortcomings, as a whole their book is a fine and exhaustive study that analyzes in a detailed way the aesthetics of colonial films, even if the focus on comprehensiveness and film images detracts from a diachronic analysis. Yet equally if not more important is assessing how many films made it to distribution and what impact they did or did not have. A particular film might have been groundbreaking visually or textually, but if the final product departed from the intentions of its creators or if few ever saw it, its historical importance is questionable. Thus, we need to keep in mind Nicholas Reeves's point in *The Power of Film Propaganda: Myth or Reality?* — people's belief in the propaganda power of film has proven stronger than film's real persuasive power.

The Cinéma Colonial

Private investors and colonial enthusiasts pioneered the first ventures into colonial cinema, rather than either the EIC (before 1908) or the Belgian colonial administration (after 1908). Optique belge, the very first colonial film organization in Belgium, had been financially unsuccessful and, as discussed earlier, disappeared almost as soon as the 1897 Tervuren exposition closed its doors. Aside from smaller ventures and purely scientific films produced by the Ministry of Colonies and the Tervuren museum, Belgium's next significant colonial film venture, le Cinématographe des colonies—or the Cinéma colonial, as it was called—was founded in December 1908.[11] At that time, entrepreneurs were opening *salles de cinéma* (film rooms) in cities across the country in an effort to tap into the growing popularity of film, and the men behind the Cinéma colonial—and they were all men—were "businessmen with strong colonial ties."[12] The first reels from filmmaker François Evenepoel arrived from Africa on 15 April 1909, and the Cinéma colonial opened its doors in downtown Brussels on 24 April. In all, the Cinéma colonial produced dozens of shorts on the colony that it sent (after a first screening at the Cinéma colonial) to be shown to paying customers at the Tour du Monde in Brussels and the Antwerp Scala music hall; they even sold them abroad in France and Germany.[13]

Who saw the first colonial films that the Cinématographe des colonies and others showed in Belgium beginning as early as 1897? Whereas in the 1890s really only *la classe aisée* (the upper class) could afford going to the cinema, films and theaters multiplied so much that by 1908 cinemas (fixed or itinerant) had reached almost all cities and villages.[14] An ever-increasing number of movie theaters showed colonial and other films; there were around 650 theaters by 1914, representing a comparatively high density.[15] Music halls and fairs were still showing films from the 1897 exposition such as *Les Congolais à Tervueren* as late as 1908, attesting to both an interest in colonial movies and a lack of original film production in the last decade of the EIC's existence. Local groups such as the Club africain-Cercle d'études coloniales d'Anvers and the Cercle congolais de Mons (Congolese Club of Mons) hosted screenings accompanied by commentary from experienced colonials. The Cinéma colonial attracted fifty thousand theatergoers in its first year of existence. The Ministry

of Colonies incorporated screenings into its 1910 colonial exhibits at Tervuren by setting up one of the rooms of the new Musée
du Congo Belge to show motion pictures. Although the distribution of colonial films is difficult to gauge, by 1913 movie theaters
were more widespread — and therefore accessible — in Belgium
than perhaps in any other country; films made in sub-Saharan
Africa "were no longer rarities for screens." Considering that
ten years passed before colonial filmmaking restarted after the
failure of Optique belge, the lack of new films between 1897 and
1908 can be attributed more to technological challenges inherent in production and transportation than to a lack of will. And
because of Optique belge's 1897–98 failure, filmmakers really
were starting over in 1908 with the production of films about
the new colony.[16]

For one reason or another, most early films on the Congo,
like many from other areas south of the Sahara, have been lost;
any analysis of their content and messages must be tentative.[17]
What is clear is that backers of the Cinématographe des colonies
intended to interest the Belgian general public in the recently
acquired colony and to convey images of progress that had been
achieved there: to "popularize, by the 'animated' image . . . everything that has to do with our Congo."[18] In this way, procolonialists in Belgium like their counterparts in Germany, France,
and elsewhere harnessed film to promote overseas expansion
well after the Scramble for Africa came to an end.[19] Considering
the titles of these films alone, we can infer what "everything that
has to do with our Congo" meant to investors in the Cinématographe des colonies. From 1909 to 1910, filmmakers Evenepoel
and Léon Reinelt created, among others, *Matadi* and *Boma*
(demonstrating urbanization), *Le marché de Boma* (emphasizing commerce), *Le fort de Shinkakasa* and *Le défilé de la Force*

publique (showing military strength and control), *Chemin de fer des cataractes* (transportation), *Le prince Albert au centre de l'Afrique* (a focus on the dynasty), and *L'arrivée du ministre des colonies à Banana, Boma et Matadi* (highlighting the new colonial administration).[20] Although directors may not have necessarily distanced the new administration from the abuses of the past, the absence of a film on Leopold II so soon after his death, which might have commemorated him as the founder of the empire, is telling. What is more, these same themes are to be found in films shown at special sessions taking place before World War I. On the eve of war, in July 1914, the Union coloniale belge held a "film talk" (*causerie cinématographique*) that included the films *Les exploitations minières de l'Étoile du Congo et de Kambove* and *Les usines métallurgiques de la Lubumbashi,* among others.[21] Directors showed a limited interest in indigenous culture and society, focusing instead on Belgian accomplishments. Also, these were silent films, therefore neither French nor Flemish, initiating what was to be an undivided colonial cinematic praxis that would carry through to independence. The men who created colonial films were what Ramirez and Rolot call "belgicains"; that is to say, above all, they were Belgian, not Flemish or Walloon.[22]

The Interwar Years

An injection of government funding into colonial filmmaking followed World War I, and it is fair to say that the conflict and the German occupation provoked a wave of colonial motion picture making driven by the state. Financial assistance at this point and afterward contradicts the notion put forth by some that there was no state aid for short documentaries or other films before the 1950s.[23] Although the Congo remained Belgian during the war and its Force publique troops successfully fought German colonial troops—defeating them at Tabora in September 1916—most of the metropole was overrun and the Ministry of Colonies rightly feared the loss of the colony to a victorious, expansionistic Germany.[24] The exiled government produced films on the colony to show "the contribution of Belgians in the Congo to the war effort" as well as the country's "success in spreading 'civilization'" in a conflict that pitted Entente *civilisation* (civilization) against German *Kultur* (culture).[25] The Ministry of Colonies founded a documentation and popularization service in Le Havre to demonstrate both their wartime contributions to their Entente allies and the importance of the colony to their countrymen.[26] In 1916, from Le Havre, Minister of Colonies Jules Renkin sent director Ernest Gourdinne to the Congo to make motion pictures, which resulted in *Les tracés du chemin de fer établis pendant la guerre, Le minerai de cuivre du Katanga, L'installation d'un colon dans le Kasaï, Le grand centre de Lusambo et son industrie*, among others (all 1917–19). Although these films, like others from this era, are no longer to be found, one can see that Gourdinne emphasized industry, raw materials, transportation, and other key themes of the colonial endeavor, while saying little about indigenous society.

The emergency of war that boosted colonial filmmaking was followed by a serious postwar use of Gourdinne's films to promote the empire at home.[27] By 1919 Gourdinne had projected his films, especially those focusing on the colony's economy and development, around one thousand times in Belgium in a major publicity effort.[28] Luc Vints has written that "the country was literally submerged by a wave of propaganda. It targeted above all education; it addressed itself very consciously to youth."[29] It is impossible to say why there was such a big push at this particular moment, but one can conjecture three determinants. First, cinema houses had not been able to show those films produced during the harsh German occupation, resulting in pent-up demand.[30] Second, film production was a low priority in the months after the armistice and theaters had to make do with those they had on hand.[31] A third likely factor was the international situation in which Belgium found itself at the time. Peace negotiations unfolded over many months after 11 November 1918, and even the June 1919 Treaty of Versailles with Germany did not mark the end of maneuvers to divide up Germany's overseas empire. As the country's delegation fought hard for African acquisitions over many months, they came to realize the tenuousness of their position at the hands of the great powers, even if Belgium did occupy substantial portions of German East Africa.[32] The effort to develop domestic support for overseas empire put greater pressure on France and Britain to appease the populace of the ally that had fought by their side for four years. In the process, colonial cinema acted along with other media promoting the empire to unify the population around a common project, contradicting the view that film exacerbated the French-Flemish divide that Philip Mosley and others have argued.

A second burst of post–World War I filmmaking came in 1925–28 with the creation of a number of films by Ernest Genval (Ernest Thiers), who not only was the "principle artisan of colonial cinema" in the country in the 1920s but really the only artisan of colonial cinema that decade.[33] Genval was to colonial cinema in the late 1920s what Gourdinne had been during World War I and Evenepoel and Reinelt had been in the immediate post-reprise era. Unlike the film crew sent out during World War I, Genval in 1925–28 was largely financed by private companies — something not unusual for the film industry in Belgium at the time—which a sample of his film titles makes clear: *La Compagnie du Kasaï* and *Sabena: L'aviation* (both 1925–26), *La géomines* (1928), and *L'Union minière du Haut-Katanga* (1928).[34] Other industrial concerns worked through different directors in the Congo, such as Lord Leverhulme financing Baron Lambert's trip to the Congo in 1924 to produce *Un voyage au Congo*, which made the connection between Congolese raw materials (oil) and European manufactured goods (soap).[35] Genval continued to produce films for colonial businesses into the 1930s, such as *Le diamant* (1938), which he filmed for Forminière.[36] This is not to say Genval did not take orders from other groups, for in the late 1930s he made a film for Foréami (Fonds Reine Elisabeth pour l'assistance médicale aux Indigènes du Congo Belge [Queen Elizabeth Fund for Medical Assistance to Natives of the Belgian Congo]) about its activities, to be shown at the 1939 New York World's Fair and at Liège's Exposition de l'Eau.[37] Unusual was the fact that one of Genval's colonial films, *Le Congo qui s'éveille* (1927), was actually a financial success.[38]

Although motion pictures such as *Le Congo qui s'éveille* won a significant audience, there are important reasons not to overestimate their impact. Not only did foreign films rule the domestic market, but colonial films also had to compete for audiences with *ciné-clubs* and socialist film clubs that attracted movie enthusiasts and workers.[39] Moreover, the colony was not the only object of government and private filmmaking efforts, and scarce resources were spread thin.[40] Financing from private sources, such as there was, and a lack of government film crews in the 1920s attest to Paul Davay's assertion that the Belgian state was slow to incorporate cinema into information production, including that produced about the colony. A French visitor to the Musée du Congo Belge in 1924 noted disapprovingly that it possessed few films on the Congo, indicating the Ministry of Colonies could not provide a decent collection even to its flagship institution.[41] Therefore, the state-sponsored Gourdinne trek during World War I appears as an exception to the rule.[42]

While the colonial administration did not make many films between the wars, it did deliberately control and use motion pictures. The governor-general's ordinance No. 53 of 1 May 1936 governed filming in the Congo and contributed to the Ministry of Colonies' control over what was shot there.[43] The ministry used films on a number of occasions, such as when it incorporated them into on-site projections at the 1930 Antwerp international exposition by making two Cinéscope machines part of the Congo pavilion. While the content of the films remains unclear, it does seem these were at best frustrated first steps at "self-service" instructional films: one teacher in 1930 said she was humiliated in front of her students when she tried to use the self-service projectors because one of the pavilion's own watchmen (mistakenly) told her she was not allowed to use it.[44] The Office colonial maintained a film library and lent films to be shown at local expositions and conferences.[45] For the sixth Koloniale Jaarbeurs van Antwerpen, in 1932, the OC provided seven films, which organizers then showed every day from three to six o'clock in the afternoon.[46] The ministry lent out films to organizations for special showings—for example, to the Université coloniale, to which the ministry sent films every two weeks, at least during the 1920s.[47] The 1935 Brussels World's Fair colonial pavilion did not contain any film showings for a variety of more mundane reasons, including the fact that the colonial ministry's films were old and worn, indicating that although the ministry kept control over filmmaking, its own film resources were literally stretched thin.[48]

Whereas government harnessing of film propaganda during the interwar period fluctuated, missionary groups were all but absent from the scene until the late 1930s, by which time Catholic groups such as the Scheutists predominated in the Congo even if Protestants maintained a sizeable presence. It was not until 1936 that the pope issued an encyclical on cinema, its uses, and abuses; only later that decade did the Church, working through the newly founded Office catholique international du cinéma (International Catholic Office of Cinema, OCIC), recognize the ineluctable advance of cinema as a medium of entertainment and information and develop its own film movement.[49] As Monsignor Ladeuze at Leuven University put it at the time, "In order to make their voice heard in the paganized concert, it is necessary that Catholics should have a place in the orchestra."[50] But it was not until after World War II that Catholic missionaries began to make films in significant numbers.

The war itself put a stop to almost all Belgian filmmaking, colonial or otherwise, even if finished motion pictures continued to be shown.[51] An exception was André Cauvin's *Congo* (1943–44). Minister of Colonies Albert De Vleeschauwer and Foreign Minister Paul-Henri Spaak prevailed on Cauvin, who headed the cinematographic mission to London from 1940–44, to make the film in order to influence public opinion and leaders in the United States, a crucial ally.[52] It was the post–World War II years up to the Congo's independence that were to be the great yet terminal epoch of Belgian colonial cinema.

The Ultimate Years of Pro-Empire Film

When post–World War II missionary film production really took off, it was aimed, above all, toward an African audience. Catholic missionaries formed three film companies: Africa-Films, a

Pères Blancs operation headed by Father Roger De Vloo; Lu-luafilm, a Scheutist operation created by filmmaker Father Albert Van Haelst; and Edisco-Films, formed from *éduquer et distraire les Congolais* (educate and entertain the Congolese) by Scheutist Alexandre Van den Heuvel.[53] By 1946 Catholic bishops and missionaries in the Congo had set up an umbrella organization headed by Van den Heuvel called the Centre congolais d'action catholique cinématographique (Congolese Center of Catholic Cinematographic Action, CCACC), designed to coordinate their film production in and for the colony.[54] The goal was moral indoctrination and, similar to Britain's Colonial Office policy, substitution for potentially nefarious films that might reach Congolese through commercial markets.[55] Africa-Films, Luluafilm, and Edisco-Films created dozens of motion pictures between 1946 and 1960 with cineastes André Cornil (an abbot with no affiliation to any missionary congregation), Van den Heuvel, and De Vloo most prominent among directors.[56] In the brief period immediately following the war, missionaries tried to use film to popularize their activities in Africa with the metropolitan population, either producing ones specifically for that purpose or for both European and African audiences such as De Vloo's *Feu de brousse* (1947) and *Bizimana* (1950–51). Few movies for Africans—like Cornil's *Chauffeur, la mort te guette sur la route* (1953) or *Sikitu* (1953)—were shown in Belgium, and then only to demonstrate what films were being made for Congolese.[57] Yet there was a rapid change in the target audience, and when the bulk of production was turned out by missionaries during the 1950s, it overwhelmingly comprised films directed at the African population. Those intended for African and European audiences such as *Bizimana* remained exceptional.[58]

As for the colonial administration after the war, it had no

up-and-running operations nor plans in place to make new films, viewed such deficiencies unfavorably, and took steps to remedy them by producing more films beginning in the late 1940s.[59] The Ministry of Colonies entered quickly into a contract with director André Heyman to make films for Africans. But he was not Belgian, and there was an effort to have him replaced at least in part for this reason, indicating the ongoing nationalization of colonial filmmaking.[60] The Leopoldville administration's information service took over state film production in this period, yet the film crew there remained weak. At one point a functionary literally underlined, "Our film section in Africa is composed of amateurs."[61]

Nevertheless, filmmaking resumed by the end of the decade, the top priority being films to educate Congolese and shield them from films for European and U.S. audiences. The Ministry of Colonies used footage from the colony as fast as it could get it.[62] The administration in the colony controlled who saw which motion pictures through regulations prohibiting Africans from attending European theaters and maintaining state and missionary authority over theaters for Congolese (fixed and itinerant); it only needed films to show. A second need was news shorts for commercial distribution in Belgium and in movie theaters for Europeans in the colony.[63] In addition to shorter films such as *Le voyage en Angola du gouverneur général Jungers* (c. 1950), *Les éléphants au Congo Belge* (c. 1950), and *Les mines d'or de Kilo-Moto* (1950), the administration created an Images from the Belgian Congo film series between 1948 and 1954 that had as its goal "the systematic exploration of our Colony from the point of view of film."[64] In the words of Léon Pétillon, the vice governor-general of Ruanda-Urundi (later governor-general and minister of colonies), these films were less to unveil the "morals and customs of the natives" than Belgian realizations in Africa, including "important railway and road works," "the education of blacks by the whites," and "the active life of the Europeans—as much in the urban centers as in the interior, the shops, the buildings, animated public places, car traffic, the traffic of the ports, etc."[65] The series painted a reassuring image for existing and potential colonists by showing the pleasures of life in European sections of the big cities and giving "the impression that Leopoldville was an African Brussels."[66] Shown in theaters across Belgium, these films by 1949 "had conquered the Belgian public's favor," as one official put it.[67] Even if the Ministry of Colonies believed films on Africans or ethnography remained unimportant and unpopular in the metropole, this is not to say that no films about Africans were commissioned. The ministry's post–World War II propaganda division, the Centre d'information et de documentation du Congo Belge et du Ruanda-Urundi (Center for Information and Documentation of the Belgian Congo and Ruanda-Urundi, CID), did contract with Gérard De Boe in 1950–51, for example, to make a number of short films that included *Les tatouages*, *La pirogue*, and *Au pays des Bakuba*.[68] Yet the emphasis remained on European life and European-led progress in the Congo.

If views within the administration diverged, it was Brussels being more concerned with popularizing the Congo and showing off to Europeans what Belgium had achieved and was continuing to achieve there, whereas Leopoldville's information office wanted instructional films for Congolese.[69] Conflicting views about film reflected long-standing tensions between the Brussels administration, which tended to centralize, and the African administration, which was subordinate to Brussels.[70] Minister of Colonies Pierre Wigny by 1950 saw the need for imperialistic propaganda by film in Belgium and abroad, and his department had reason to tell a positive story about its accomplishments and ongoing work—for example, the 1949–59 ten-year plan.[71] Within its limited budget, the ministry sought not only to educate the African masses with films, it also sought to reach the public in the metropole with messages such as the benefits of Belgian colonial administration.[72] A main method of reaching the home audience was through brief clips of *actualités* (news) shown in movie theaters. Thus, for example, theatergoers in 1947 could have seen clips showing the "voyage of the Senatorial Commission to the Belgian Congo" or "the arrival of Marshal Montgomery at Leopoldville." The administration in Leopoldville sent both films to the Colonial Ministry, which claimed that 840 of the country's 1,000 movie theaters showed them.[73] The difference in emphasis is not to say that the central and African administrations were working at cross purposes, for they were not; the governor-general also wanted to have press accounts with photographs of the Congo in them in the metropole.[74] But Brussels increasingly turned toward swaying opinion at home and abroad while Leopoldville remained more interested in reaching Congolese audiences.

The administration directed filming in the Congo after World War II through close supervision, regulation, and control of funding.[75] Crews had to complete a request for authorization to film, subject to review by the governor-general. In some cases, the African administration directly supervised scripts and production, such as that of André Cornil during his 1950 tour of the Congo; in others, the Ministry of Colonies managed the story, structure, and tempo of films.[76] Unsurprisingly, the administration looked favorably on films destined for audiences outside the Congo (or Ruanda-Urundi) if they transmitted a positive image of Belgian efforts. This helps explain why much of the world viewed the Congo as an oasis of stability in the 1940s and 1950s, even though this was not the case considering how the state's policy of intense production during World War II put huge pressures on African workers—in 1941 UMHK mine workers struck, as they almost did again in 1944—and conflicts lay just under the surface after the war.[77] Even after decades of colonial rule, Belgium's control over the vast Congo was "highly disarticulate," as Frederick Cooper has put it. Cooper describes the Belgian colony as a "hodgepodge of zones of mineral and agricultural exploitation and zones of neglect, except for labor recruitment."[78] *Colons* who had settled in central Africa were insecure about Belgian-Congolese relations and of a divided mind as to whether or not it was best to "civilize" Africans since this resulted in empowering them.[79] The administration's control over motion pictures and other information was a way in which they could conceal conflicts and project an image of stability.

That people at the time and afterward considered the Congo of the 1950s as being unchanging and tranquil is due in no small part to the Ministry of Colonies controlling both the production and transfer of information, including filmmaking in the Congo.[80] The administration prohibited some directors from making films while permitting others to do so, suggesting the administration sensed the tenuousness of its rule, was on the defensive, and responded to events happening elsewhere in the 1950s. One clear example of the attitude toward film can be seen in the administration's reactions to an application from Dudley Pictures Corporation.[81] The Ministry of Colonies urged Leopoldville not only to approve the Dudley application but to assist them in their work: "The films of the Dudley Mission will constitute an excellent propaganda material on our civilizing action; they will be assured of a large distribution in the United States and probably in a number of other countries. Also I would be most grateful to you to be sure to attend to such that the work of this mission is facilitated in every measure possible."[82] The same willingness to assist favorable film crews held true for well-established directors like Gérard De Boe and André Cornil.[83] The administration used the power of the purse, such as when Cornil made films on order for the government in the 1950s, all based on preapproved scripts: he had to stick to his preapproved plan because if the administration rejected the final product, it would not acquire the films and would instead stick Cornil with the bill.[84] In practice, it appears neither the Ministry of Colonies nor its Leopoldville administration provided all the scripts for Cornil, De Boe, or others, but they certainly kept a close watch over the product from start to postproduction in order to make sure that, as one ministry official put it, "the presentation and commentary of the films respond to the goal of colonial propaganda that we are pursuing."[85]

Of course, how people perceived these films when shown in Belgium is an open and difficult question. A 1947 article from *La Métropole* provides an indication. Writing about films by André Heyman and De Boe, the paper called them "perfectly successful and greatly interesting," and went on to say that the films were "superb documentation, teaching us to know our marvelous colony, its rich possibilities and constitute a greatly efficacious medium of propaganda."[86] Colonial enthusiasts acclaimed De Boe's films, *La Revue Colonial Belge* stating that De Boe's *Étonnante Afrique* was "strongly appreciated" by a packed crowd at a special showing at the Royale union coloniale belge.[87] Although the reception of colonial films was far from universally positive, as discussed below—reviews in the press, colonial or otherwise, indicate favorable receptions for many of them.

The focus here on the metropole should not permit us to ignore the fact that in the 1950s the colonial administration felt increasing pressure internationally as attacks on the legitimacy of Belgian rule in the Congo mounted. Of particular concern was "*la menace onusienne*," or the threat of UN intervention, to which Belgians responded by presenting the Congo as a model colony.[88] Former governor-general Pierre Ryckmans was in charge of reports on Ruanda-Urundi Trust Territories to the UN, and in 1950 his report was accompanied by the film *Ruanda-Urundi 1949* (1948).[89] The Ministry of Colonies wanted yet another film to illustrate the next report, one more closely in line with the administration's propaganda needs; thus it dispatched De Boe to make the film and ordered the vice governor of Ruanda-Urundi to give him the direction needed on the ground. Ministry offices in Brussels indicated to the vice governor that Ryckmans insisted that a new film be made in close collaboration with those who wrote Belgium's UN report.[90] By intervening in filmmaking to promote and defend imperialism at the UN, where it had to give reports to the Trusteeship Council on Ruanda-Urundi, the administration sought to counter the "blacks," "Arabs," and others abroad that the Ministry of Colonies believed were working to undermine the empire through false rumors and negative propaganda.[91]

Films produced by the government, by missionary groups, and by private companies were, with few exceptions, works of propaganda in the sense that they either misrepresented facts on the ground in the Congo or specifically sought to instruct the audience along the lines of particular ideological goals, or both. It is unsurprising that the final products, like colonial films made in the British Empire and other colonial settings, avoided colonial problems.[92] They revealed no discussion of administrative challenges, no images of forced labor or messianic religious movements, and no signs of potential trouble with or disadvantages of colonial rule. Films on major developments in the Congo that might have shed an unfavorable light on the colonial administration simply do not exist; although films on the Catholic missions exist, there are none on the Watchtower (Kitawala) movement or Kimbanguism. Directors created pictures about the huge Congolese contribution to the war effort from 1940 to 1945, but none to represent the "presiding sense of oppression, of weariness, and of gloom" that the strain of war created, nor the 1941 mine workers' strike or the 1944 near rebellion.[93] The information services in Leopoldville and their colleagues in Brussels deliberately steered clear of reporting unfiltered facts and objective news in the interest of Belgian state control.[94]

Film propaganda's potential to mislead can be seen in Jean-Marc Landier's multifilm documentary series on education produced by the colonial administration that aimed to show "the pedagogical progress and above all the changes in mentality that had taken place in the domain of the education of Blacks."[95] The series, which reinforced propaganda in other media, showed black and white populations coming together through the mixing of African and European children at school, suggesting that schools were integrating.[96] Yet few Congolese went to schools for Europeans and the mixing of African and European schoolchildren was "purely symbolic and theoretical in the majority of the cases."[97] In fact, of the approximately 1.2 million African children in school in the Congo in 1953, European schools admitted only 21, and this number rose to only 1,493 by 1959.[98] Ramirez and Rolot describe Landier's scenes of elementary education: "On purpose, the production constructed a harmony that, in reality, was certainly not so perfect."[99] This false image of reality was useful to colonial authorities, because even if education for Africans in European schools was "too limited for the colony's needs," it was nevertheless "quite adequate from a Belgian public relations standpoint."[100]

The colonial administration, film directors, missionaries, and private capital interests recognized their own films as propaganda and debated what kinds were most subtle, and thereby most effective.[101] The administrations in Brussels and Leopoldville hid their propagandistic goals from the public, such as when a vice governor wrote to Minister of Colonies Wigny that the film *Ruanda-Urundi 1949* was adequate for the UN Trusteeship Council yet not suitable for a Belgian public because, "In the manner in which it is put together, this film does not hide at all its goal of propaganda. . . . It is exactly necessary to avoid making the public feel too much this governmental will to publicity."[102] Authorities hid their popularization efforts because they feared it would not come off well and would detract from the power of the film if the viewer realized he or she was being targeted.

An opportunity to sway Belgian public opinion arose when King Baudouin toured the Congo in 1955, which Minister of Colonies Auguste Buisseret promised would be "the occasion of a particular effort to draw the attention of the Belgian public to the Colony, to show to natives the interest that the authorities of the metropole have for them and to affirm Belgian authority and sovereignty over our territories of Africa." Buisseret emphasized the importance of covering the trip to the many press firms he contacted about the voyage: "It matters greatly that your firm integrate in its news programs — destined to Belgian and foreign publics — scenes taken on this occasion." The Ministry of

Colonies considered the opportunity so important that it intervened directly in information production by providing moving pictures, filmed expressly for the purpose, each day to news firms and television. "Each firm will receive a length [of film] much bigger than it will be able to use, in such manner that each news broadcast can be — in part at least — original." The ministry assumed virtually all costs in order to make it financially attractive for firms and thus to maximize participation, and Buisseret assured journalists wishing to travel to the Congo — most for the first time — to cover the king's visit that not only would they receive authorization to do so but they also would benefit from free transportation between Brussels and Leopoldville and free lodging.[103] In addition, André Cauvin created a film in conjunction with the trip, *Bwana kitoko* (1955), which showed that in the Belgian empire of the 1950s, "there was not the least problem and that the Congolese population was very grateful to the colonizer." Promotional posters for *Bwana kitoko* reinforced the image of a grateful, subservient Congo.[104]

Despite what seems at times a heavy hand, colonial cinema was not something always imposed on the populace from the top down. Not only did colonial groups and the press more generally appreciate colonial films, but between the wars local groups were already eager to acquire films for local showings. The Royale union coloniale belge, for example, held screenings of colonial films, and Leopold III and Minister of Colonies De Vleeschauwer even attended their 1940 showing of Cauvin's *Nos soldats d'Afrique* and *Congo, terre d'eaux vives*.[105] The Koloniale en Maritieme Kring, Brugge requested numerous films over a number of years, in the early 1950s asking for films that promoted "the work accomplished by our compatriots and the idea that the CONGO is very much ours and has to remain so."[106]

The CCS's program of films in schools was not an unwelcome initiative in the sense that many schools and groups requested films from the Ministry of Colonies and even from some colonial firms.[107] Directors like Cauvin and De Boe were willing participants, eager to portray Belgian colonialism in the best light possible.[108] After being turned down for a job for UMHK that went to De Boe, Cauvin wrote to the firm about his disappointment in not being able to work on "the creation of a film of prestige . . . that would be of a nature to serve Belgian interests abroad, and to present an interest at the same time of a general order and of a more durable nature."[109] In the 1950s André Cornil received hundreds of thousands of francs in subsidies from UMHK, from Comité spécial du Katanga, and from Compagnie du Congo pour le commerce et l'industrie; he made films for UMHK that included *Kolwezi*, *Fête Indigène à Kipushi*, and *A chacun son métier*.[110] Like colonial monuments and local museums and expositions, filmmaking and film showing demonstrate a degree of local initiative at work to spread pro-empire messages.

Another filmmaker occupied with the colonial idea was Hélène Schirren, atypical not only because she was a female director but also because she was one of the few women to play a prominent role in promoting the empire at home.[111] Schirren was distinctive also in that her focus was on the metropole rather than the colony. Working through the company Phoebus Films, she produced a number of motion pictures, including *Sous l'étoile d'or* (1939) about the Colonial University in Antwerp, *Guerir sous les tropiques* (1946, with Guillaume-Linephty) about the Institut de médecine tropicale d'Anvers, and the eponymous *Tervuren, Musée du Congo Belge* (1939–40). Another collaboration by Schirren and Guillaume-Linephty, *Sans Tam Tam* (1949) is an example of the type of covert propaganda that occurred in the last years of the Belgian Congo. For *Sans Tam Tam*, Phoebus Films received the rights to film in the Congo and at metal refineries in Belgium in return for producing a picture that remained under the creative control of the colonial companies involved.[112] Not that this was all that necessary: Guillaume-Linephty and Schirren described in a confidential *avant-projet* (project proposal) to UMHK how the film would convey upbeat messages about the company by having its positive achievements and those of the colonial administration form the "continuous backdrop" for the film's action, thereby not giving the picture an overtly propagandistic bent.[113] Thus, directors such as Schirren collaborated sub rosa and hand in glove with the main colonial interests on films, in this case *Sans Tam Tam*, in order to lead the audience toward a procolonial position. In *Africa on Film*, Kenneth Cameron argues that British and American filmmakers on the ground in Africa "were often the captives of white African advisors, hunters, and guides; they always had to satisfy colonial officials. . . . Their reliance on colonialism led them *not* to turn their cameras on colonialism."[114] In the Belgian case, many directors were willing captives of colonialism.

The questions remain as to who saw these films during the post–World War II period, where they saw them, and what sort of impact they might have had. Smaller colonial interest groups continued to screen films, such as the Société belge d'études et d'expansion (Belgian Society of Study and Expansion), which had held 336 film sessions by 1947 alone.[115] The Ministry of Colonies distributed films from its Visages du Congo Belge series to *salles d'actualités* (newsrooms) throughout the country, and visitors could at times see films at local colonial expositions.[116] In 1953 the CID sent seventeen newsreels free of charge to news firms — which increased to twenty-two in 1954 — all of which apparently were shown on television, limited as it was at the time.[117] The Colonial Ministry showed films to its personnel and invited guests to special film sessions, such as when it commemorated the EIC's foundation.[118] Movie houses in Brussels and elsewhere showed film shorts on the colony in special matinees that were successful in the 1950s.[119]

An important new arena of distribution in the post–World War II era was schools. The first application of film to a school setting may have been as early as 1908, but it appears there was no systematic emphasis on the use of films on the colony in the classroom until after 1945.[120] As discussed earlier, the CCS used films to teach schoolchildren, increasing distribution in the late 1940s and 1950s to meet the felt need to bind the nation's youth more tightly to the empire.[121] Until the end of the colonial period, members of the Ministry of Public Education expressed concern that there were not enough film resources for teaching schoolchildren about the Congo, indicating that of the 2,800 films it possessed, only around 20 were about the colony.[122] CCS conférenciers repeatedly requested certain films because of their appeal to students, according to the conférenciers; these included *Arbre de vie* (1948, De Boe and L. Deroisy), *A la conquête du Ruwenzori* (1949, G. Félix), *Le cuivre* (1951, De Boe), *Zwarte landbouwers onder de Tropen* (1951, L. Colleaux), *Charmant décor* (1952, W. De Boeck), and *Arts congolais* (1952, De Boe).[123] By the 1950s, colonial films were more readily available in Belgium than at any time in the past, even if they faced competition from many other motion pictures.

The effects these films had on audiences is difficult to measure, and it is critical not to presume their efficacy as propaganda.[124] Nevertheless, it is important to consider the themes that films transmitted during the final years of empire, which

are more accessible because the films from that period are better preserved. Films for Belgians largely focused on European
life, to the detriment of the image of African society and culture. The three pillars of the colonial system wanted to manifest
modernity, not African backwardness; few Belgians showed an
interest in Congolese culture, not even within the colonial administration.[125] Whereas films referred to the European as the
"white" or the "white man," they mentioned Africans in the plu-
ral, making them "black workers" or "natives," with exceptions
among late missionary films. Not until Cauvin's 1952 *Bongolo
en de negerprinses* did a colonial film give its African charac-
ters names on-screen, and even then the motion picture's stars
Joseph Lifela and Petronelle Abapataki were not named in the
credits.[126] Cineastes showed Africans in groups and juxtaposed
those groups with the individual white European; the white doctor, for example, became "the solitary hero working for the undifferentiated mass of natives."[127] Films for whites insinuated
there was no need for police, whereas films for Africans showed
the police, implying the comparative quality and security of life
for Europeans in the colony.[128] By showing Congolese working
as servants and showing Europeans playing individual (and thus
costly) sports while concealing their everyday *petit* (menial) occupations, films not only represented the white in the Congo as
in control but also as a member of the gentry or even aristoc-
racy.[129] In some films, depictions of colonists at work replayed
the heroic story of the white explorer in Africa. Because European businesses depended on a work force and population that
was overwhelmingly black African, the image of the solitary and
heroic white European in the colony was just as much a fiction
as the image of the intrepid, lone, and in-control white male explorer forging a new path through Africa.[130] The idea of African

improvement, the very existence even of évolués, was addressed late, and then only tentatively.[131] De Boe's *Ngiri* (1946), for instance, revealed a deep skepticism of the possibility of the "evolution" of Africans and suggested it might fail in the end, despite Belgians' best efforts.

History was not a frequent film subject, but when it was, it was unsurprisingly Eurocentric and pro-Belgian. Directors depicted exploration and conquest of the Congo as having been achieved without force or opposition.[132] The Congorama's thirty-minute movie that taught central African history from the official Belgian state point of view transported some two hundred thousand visitors at the 1958 World's Fair to Africa. Other films presented a simplified image of Leopold II that avoided any engagement with critiques of his administration.[133] Cauvin's *Bwana kitoko*, other films, and related publications tied the Congo of the present to the Leopoldian regime and the dynasty and asserted that "the Belgians administer in the Congo the heritage of Leopold II."[134] Through its title alone, Baron Y. de Brouwer's 1951 film *Rêve d'un grand roi: Léopoldville, capitale du Congo Belge* hailed the man who began Belgium's African adventure. Schirren's *Tervuren, Musée du Congo Belge* invoked the monarch's glory: "The film ends in a sort of apotheosis, by the moving evocation of figures, glorified in ivory by our best masters, of King Leopold II, founder of our colonial empire, of Albert I and of Leopold III, continuators of his work."[135] Schirren associated the dynasty with the empire and harnessed Leopold II's supposed glory to the ongoing Belgian colonial enterprise, thereby associating it with the EIC.

Films focused on the advantages of empire and reinforced Belgian certitude.[136] Benefits in the field of Congolese education, for instance, justified overseas expansion to filmgoers.[137] Although films showed how the colony was tied to the metropole economically, they skirted the fact that Belgians, the state, or private companies were the main beneficiaries of African labor and the colonial regime.[138] Guido Convents writes that André Heyman's 1948 *Cinquantième anniversaire du chemin de fer Matadi-Léopoldville* "underlined that the train benefited principally Congolese. It showed also that it was one of the most important works of infrastructure of the colony, but neglected to say that its construction had cost the lives of thousands of Africans."[139] In fact, films presented the integration of Africans into the colonial economy as something beneficial, only reinforcing Belgian confidence.[140] "This tranquil certitude of the validity of the action undertaken is moreover one of the dominant traits of the presentation of the system of values in colonial films destined for Europeans. No political stirring ever comes to trouble the sentiment of the civilizers to be the propagators of an absolute and incontestable progress."[141] Again departing from reality, films even showed the Congo and Ruanda-Urundi as vacation destinations: Kivu in *Fils d'Imana* (Eric Weymeersch, 1959) became for the viewer the "African côte d'Azur."[142]

Motion pictures also strengthened Belgians' confidence by scaling the Congo down to something manageable, classifiable, and thus comprehensible, similar to the action of the Musée du Congo Belge. "Films destined for Europeans showed the bush practically transformed into a park, where the wild animals that yesterday were menacing today were threatened while at the same time protected [by the administration]." *Kivu, jardin de l'Afrique* (G. Félix, 1954) told the audience that the colony "can be considered as the largest animal reserve [in the world]," as opposed to wild and uncontrollable. Motion pictures classified and condensed the colony with "a spirit of inventory."[143] Of course we should not presume viewers were entirely persuaded, because not all of them accepted films' premises, conclusions, or themes. One journalist criticized the film *Léopoldville* (A. R. Heyman, 1946) because it presented a superficial and overly rosy image of the capital that gave the impression of an easy life to attract people tempted by a colonial career.[144] Despite occasional criticisms, the image of an idyllic and manageable colony, so often repeated, likely contributed to the shock at the 1959 Leopoldville riots and at the rapid political decolonization in the following year.

Colonial cinema helps us understand power in the colonial setting through its articulations of authority and power relations. David Slavin has shown that, in the case of North African French colonial cinema, French authority shifted from being more open-minded to more willful after the Rif War.[145] Power and colonizer-colonized relations played out in different ways in Belgian colonial cinema. In one way, these films distanced whites and blacks in a sense by raising whites up and placing an African always between the colonizer and the colonized when it came to a rebuke or punishment. Jean-Luc Vellut has argued that colonizers felt a deep ambivalence about imperialism and their contradictory feelings came out in the self-image of the white colonizer. While this self-image rested on the ideals of the mission civilisatrice and the white as a positive force, there was among Belgians, as among other imperialists in Europe, an underlying *malaise du colonisateur*, or the feeling that they might be doing something wrong because of the negative aspects of their rule.[146] Cinema expressed at times an ambivalent picture of whites as well, as with the depiction of the white as dominant yet always hiding behind (and therefore dependent on) an African who was forced to do the dirty work.[147]

Yet the number of colonial films that assigned animal

characteristics to Africans — reflecting trends elsewhere, like in Hergé's *Tintin au Congo* — calls into question the deep ambivalence for which Vellut would like to argue.[148] *Bwana kitoko* and *La chanson du voyageur solitaire* (Cauvin, 1958) associated pygmies with chimpanzees.[149] *Les seigneurs de la forêt* (Heinz Sielmann and Henry Brandt, 1958) began with images of flora and fauna, then people (Africans), then alternated between animals (lions, hyenas, hippos) and people. About thirty minutes into the film, successive shots counterposed dancing women and birds dancing and performing a mating ritual, a linkage made explicit when narrator Max-Pol Fouchet described the women as being "like large birds." The film achieved a similar anthropomorphism regarding pygmies when the narrator called them "the lords of the forest" just before designating the ape "the absolute lord."[150] Marianne Thys explained that Fouchet was "guilty of the 'sin' of anthropomorphism and the vaguely paternalistic tone typical of the fifties" but that his text remained "intelligent throughout." But it is difficult to find unfailing intelligence in a commentary that, in conjunction with the images, dehumanized people and in which "The Africans are . . . animalized and the animals humanized."[151] *Les seigneurs de la forêt* was a nature film created with the pretense of "scientific rigor" by the Fondation internationale scientifique (International Scientific Foundation), financed by banking groups, and initiated by Leopold III and Tervuren museum director Frans Olbrechts.[152] Being a purportedly scientifically accurate film, *Les seigneurs de la forêt* like the Musée du Congo Belge was surreptitiously racist.[153] Directors, government officials, and scientists did not make films with malice toward Africans, but if anthropologists or others began to question the fundamentals of the colonial condition, they had little noticeable effect before 1960.

Apotheosis: 1956–58

The big colonial companies, with exceptions, did not view film propaganda as a priority in the 1940s and early 1950s. It is true that in the years following World War II large colonial enterprises supported the empire through cinema subtly, such as by loaning reels to colonial clubs and sending footage shot in the Congo to the administration to make news shorts for commercial movie theaters.[154] Yet the largest of the colonial concerns, UMHK, did not view the making of its own films as a priority.[155] The company, perhaps viewed as deep pockets with money to spend on film production, had to reject numerous proposals after the war, such as in 1947 when UMHK administrator-director H. Robiliart refused Hélène Schirren's offer to make a film about the firm, referring her instead to state agencies.[156] The following year, Robiliart wrote that although UMHK's companies might work on a government-sponsored film in the future, they were not particularly interested: "Most of the companies and notably the mining companies have no need for commercial publicity [*propagande commerciale*], and it is clear that a film of this type has above all publicity as its goal [*a surtout la propagande pour but*]."[157] After one exceptional film in the mid-1950s by Gérard De Boe on UMHK's African installations, discussed next, UMHK turned down additional offers with the excuse that it had just finished a film, further indicating their limited interest in film.[158]

The exception to UMHK's attitude toward cinema occurred in the early to mid-1950s when the company sought an opportunity to propagate a positive vision of itself in Belgium and abroad through the making of what became *Étonnante Afrique*.[159] UMHK, BCK, and Forminière contracted with De Boe to create four films by 1956 in time to celebrate their fiftieth anniversary—one film for each company and another for all three entitled

Étonnante Afrique. De Boe's film was one of few produced by private companies with the goal of commercial distribution aimed at publicity or propaganda. In fact, of the four films for the three companies—*Trait d'union*; *Diamant, pierre précieuse*; *Katanga, pays du cuivre*; and *Étonnante Afrique*—only *Étonnante Afrique* was to be distributed commercially, the other three being at the disposal of the respective companies to use as they wished.[160] UMHK only showed *Étonnante Afrique* to select groups, mainly procolonial ones such as Royale union coloniale belge, suggesting the company was not overly interested in swaying public opinion as a whole to its vision of African empire and UMHK's place in it.[161]

Marianne Thys has written that *Étonnante Afrique* "never descends into industrial or colonial propaganda," yet preproduction discussions at UMHK, BCK, and Forminière indicate the contrary.[162] In essence, the three companies ordered De Boe to create a propaganda film favoring the three companies and Belgian rule. They changed De Boe's original title *Mélangeur d'hommes* (*Mixer of Men*) to *Étonnante Afrique* (*Amazing Africa*) to better emphasize Belgian-led progress and modernization through industry. According to UMHK directors, the film was intended to "show by comparison with the past what the industrialization of Katanga and Kasai have done for the material and social development of the natives" and all that industry had done "to make the black leave his primitive state and lead him gradually to the stage of civilization to which he has arrived right now."[163] *Étonnante Afrique* downplayed mining and refining as it existed before the arrival of Europeans to play up the role of Belgians in the development of the natives.[164]

While *Étonnante Afrique* was about BCK, Forminière, and UMHK's production facilities, its underlying message was a justification for their operations in the Congo and thus a validation of Belgian rule. That UMHK sought out directors who would create what the company wanted to see produced was revealed in an interview with Cauvin where the company asserted they wanted a director who could make a film "capable of profoundly arousing the spectators by illustrating the grandeur of the task accomplished by Union Minière."[165] De Boe was their man because he made films his clients wanted. For instance, UMHK decided an internal tax issue against De Boe because, according to UMHK, De Boe did not have any intellectual property rights over a film he had produced for the company since he had not invested any creativity into the project. "De Boe is really less an artist . . . than a manufacturer in charge of creating, for a fixed price calculated to the meter, the films suitable for his clients," the company wrote.[166] Although one might read this evidence as a statement staking out a company's position on a contentious tax issue, UMHK, BCK, and Forminière also approved De Boe's scripts beforehand and stipulated that no significant changes be made without their approval.[167] With De Boe's 1956 creations in hand, all three companies were prepared with films for the 1958 Exposition Universelle, which placed the empire center stage.

In more ways than one, 1958 and the World's Fair was the apotheosis not of the empire but of Belgian imperial propaganda. There were dozens of films made with funding from the colonial administration in conjunction with the fair.[168] We can take a closer look at the changed tone by the late 1950s and the acceleration of propaganda by looking in-depth at *Main dans la main*, subtitled "A stroll through the section of the Belgian Congo and Ruanda-Urundi at the 1958 Brussels International Exposition."[169] Created on the initiative of Inforcongo, *Main dans la main* combines candid footage with staged scenes to take the viewer on a tour of the World's Fair, following a black child and a white child as they walk hand in hand from one pavilion to the next. With an inversion of conventional figurative superiority, the African child is noticeably taller than the European boy. The film shows the king's arrival to inspect the Congo section, the huge crowds present at his arrival, and a visit by Queen Elisabeth to the Congo pavilions, linking empire and dynasty.[170] African guards stand at attention as the king arrives; there are images and sounds of the Force publique playing and marching and images of the Troubadours du Roi, with even a few Africans in the crowd. The movie conveys the idea of cooperation, with a black couple (in an apparently staged scene) in the tropical gardens talking with a white gardener, who offers the woman a flower. The movie shows Congolese and Europeans eating together at the Café Matadi of the Grand Palais, the camera lingering on two European waiters serving dinner to an African. A scene shows blacks as tourists at the exposition itself—for example, being taxied around by whites. At the end, the narrator sums up the movie with the platitude, "White or black, we are brothers." The tone of *Main dans la main* is clearly changed from earlier films and represents an explicit attempt to bring together Africans and Europeans in a belated attempt at accommodation. It also exemplifies the Ministry of Colonies' information service's use of film for propaganda.

A third film representative of the apotheosis is the Catholic missionary picture *Tokèndé* (1957). Gérard De Boe created the film "on order from the Catholic missions of the Belgian Congo with the view toward presentation in the missions pavilion during the World's Fair of 1958 in Brussels."[171] *Tokèndé* was "a fresco of the history of the Catholic missions in the Congo," beginning with a reconstruction of the first, difficult steps of missionaries in central Africa, followed by an account of the church's realizations, particularly in education. Different than in some other colonial motion pictures, scenes from the film revered missionary work and exalted its results in the Congo without humiliating Africans in any way, and the film ended with images showing "the profession of a black sister and the ordination of a black priest. Finally, the viewer sees echoes of the preceding scenes, but the white missionary has become the black priest."[172] The film can be considered as three blocks, each of which conveys a theme: the time of pioneers, the missionaries' field of action (construction, education, and social-medical work), and finally the call of Congolese to church vocations.[173]

Although centered around a historical re-creation, the film looked as much forward as it did backward, emphasizing both what had already been realized and the foundation that had been put down to create a future full of promise. "That is expressly the case in the pieces on education ('the black people have understood that education is the key to their future' and 'the youth that tomorrow will take the fate of Africa') and on the African vocation. The film combines satisfaction with achievements with a perspective of new challenges wherein the main role now appears to be reserved for Africans."[174] In this sense the film reflected reality because the church, unlike the administration or industry management, already had been significantly Africanized by the 1950s, with Africans making up 15.5, 51, and 25 percent of priests and religious brothers and sisters, respectively.[175] The film stresses the church as an institution, not its Belgian or European nature nor its relation with the metropole, mining companies, or other components of the colonial edifice. "The church-institute" appears in the film, "in other words, as if it were isolated from the broader social tissue." The film looked forward to a date when Africans would run the church in Africa, thus necessarily discounting the necessity of colonial rule.[176] This is not to say that audiences naively believed this message or that the film was a realistic portrayal of the situation in 1958. Guido Convents writes that De Boe "gives a totally illusory image of the Congolese reality. He celebrates health services, education, and the supervision of young people within Catholic organizations [without interesting] himself whatsoever in racism, in messianic movements, in colonial apartheid, or in the disintegration of society by a colonial economy running thanks only to extremely low salaries."[177] Audiences picked up on the film's undue worship of missions, one reviewer calling it "Tokéndé [sic], Le Congo, colonies [sic] . . . des Missions!" and lamenting that the film focused only on the missions and ended up giving "an absolutely false image" of the colony. "The Blacks who work in the factories, on the construction sites, in the plantations, on the docks, where are they in all this?"[178] Like those Belgians with regrets about the Congo display at the 1958 Brussels World's Fair, those expressing reservations and doubts about films such as *Tokèndé* were few and voiced their views only late in the colonial period.

Even if the production of colonial films was limited, it is nevertheless evident that the Ministry of Colonies, missionary groups, and to a lesser extent colonial businesses used film as publicity or propaganda in the most basic sense, it being in favor of their empire. At times this was overt, at others clandestine, and it was at various moments and places directed at different targets: the Belgian public, the UN, foreign audiences, and Congolese. The administration strictly controlled filming in the colony and deliberately commissioned films to promote its goals, such as when it tried to influence world opinion at the UN Trusteeship Council. The line between international and national audiences blurred at the 1958 Brussels World's Fair where the Congorama transported fairgoers to Africa and taught an official state history of the Congo. The acceleration of this kind of propaganda by motion picture in the 1950s, alongside increased funding for colonial monuments and other propaganda, suggests that as developments in Africa and elsewhere foretold a possible conclusion of the colonial era, enthusiasts defended Belgian rule by way of a ramped-up effort. Cineastes like Cauvin, De Boe, and Schirren were only too eager to work for the government, colonial companies, and missionary groups to produce films portraying imperialism in the best light possible. The lack of any anti-imperial endeavors in this area is extraordinary: there is no record of iconoclastic, anti-imperial films having been made—for example, by socialists in Belgium or nationalists in the Congo—which might have unveiled negative aspects of Belgian rule. Instead, as a result of Belgian paternalism, at independence there was not a single Congolese director prepared to take up filmmaking when Belgian production ceased.[179]

Conclusion

As Frederick Cooper, Gary Wilder, and others have shown, the histories of Europeans and overseas imperialism are inextricably linked to the history of the world beyond Europe; therefore, before concluding, a note on Congolese reactions to pro-empire propaganda and the role they played in shaping discourses and knowledge about the colony in the metropole is in order. This is challenging both because Belgians limited Congolese contestations of their depictions by simply keeping them out of Europe, except on rare occasions, and because we know little about African experiences with and reactions to imperialistic discourse in the metropole. We know that as early as 1897 two Congolese died while voyaging to Belgium for the Tervuren exposition and that seven others died once there because of poor living conditions, making it unlikely they appreciated treatment that one contemporary described as being "parked as animals are in contests" subject to the "ferocity" of white onlookers.[1] Yet despite bad housing and rough treatment, one Belgian later reported from the colony that a returning Congolese's account of the experience of his stay and the fair was nothing but positive, although of course we have to question this reaction considering its source.[2] One scholar has noted that in certain cases, "the exhibited natives were paid very well, treated with warmth and care, and offered sightseeing tours and dinners with local prominents."³ Zana Aziza Etambala notes that Chief Masala was treated well during his visit to Belgium to become part of the displays for the 1885 Antwerp fair.⁴

Congolese reactions continued to be complex and multifarious. In terms of colonial filmmaking, Africans assisted missionary and other European directors and therefore must have influenced film production in subtle ways. Yet as the literature on African cinema in the Belgian Congo makes clear, Africans played minor roles in making such pictures; as noted earlier, there was no Congolese director prepared to take up moviemaking when Belgian filmmaking dropped off beginning in 1960. There is evidence that Africans resisted Belgian depictions of them, such as when in 1958 Changwe Yetu dancers asked the minister of colonies to extend their stay to spend more time getting to know Belgium and its people. That same year, others returned from the World's Fair to the Congo early because they were tired of the inhumane treatment at the hands of the public. Congolese also met in secret in Brussels during the 1958 exposition, helping to spread nationalist and proindependence sentiment. The very existence of a Congolese community in the metropole, if only two or three hundred in strength, resisted the official policy of exclusion; by showing up as visitors at events such as the 1958 World's Fair, those Congolese refused to conform to Belgian ideas about the colonial situation. Although small-scale, these acts of defiance contrast with the lack of Belgian opposition to colonialism after 1908. Resistance among Flemings and Walloons, such as it existed, came from a very small percentage of the population like radical leftists and others usually not opposed to imperialism as such but rather to the influence of large capital in the colonial economy and administration.

We need to explore further what Africans were thinking as

Europeans represented them and Africa to metropolitan populations. It is clear what the colonial administration wanted when it requested artisans to participate in the 1958 World's Fair Congo section, for instance, but we know little about Congolese willingness to participate or their expectations. We have a good idea what Musée du Congo Belge curators desired, but we know little what the Congolese in suits passing through the Tervuren museum with director Olbrechts in the 1950s thought as they observed sculptor Matton's casts of "types indigènes." We know that the colonial administration feared the presence of Congolese in the metropole and restricted Africans' voyages there, but little work has been done on the Congolese community in Belgium before 1960. We have an idea regarding Belgians' thoughts on the importance of the colony during World War I, but we do not know enough about those few Congolese like Paul Panda Farnana who found themselves in the metropole in August 1914 and who fought to defend the country against advancing German armies.[5] There are few accounts of Africans' encounters with Belgians in Europe before the late 1950s, and studies such as Zana Aziza Etambala's careful piecing together of the experience of Masala at the time of the 1885 Antwerp Universal Exposition are exceptional. An examination of their reactions to discourse about the colony and their contributions—conscious and otherwise—to the development of people's ideas about the colony and Africans would broaden our understanding of Congolese resistance to Belgian imperialistic discourse.

With the exception of smaller-scale acts of resistance, Walloons and Flemings largely controlled depictions of "their" Africa and Africans at home, and restrictions on travel to and from the colony led to minimal contacts between Belgians and Congolese. Metropolitan empire exhibits offered opportunities for exchange, but they were squandered. With rare exceptions, smaller expositions included no Africans. For the approximately 80 percent of the Belgian population that visited the 1958 World's Fair, the Congo section was probably their first direct observation of "Africa" other than what they might have learned in a book, at school, or from friends and family; this was probably even more true at earlier such expositions. For those brought to Belgium to live in the African "village" on the 1958 fairgrounds, contacts with visitors were so unpleasant as to drive them to return home early. Motion pictures likewise failed to move Flemings, Walloons, and Congolese in the direction of any kind of Belgo-Congolese community. Here, this study breaks with Ramirez and Rolot's study of Belgium's colonial cinema, which should have been titled *Histoires des cinémas colonials* because there really were two cinemas: one of educational films for Congolese audiences and another of motion pictures for Belgians. Rarely did films cross over from one sphere to the other. Films for Belgians more likely than not distanced their audience from the Congo by encouraging misunderstandings about it by focusing on European cities, society, missions, and industry at the expense of indigenous culture and society. Belgians learned from tendentious filmic facsimiles of central Africa and its history that treated Leopold II in an oversimplified manner to produce an undifferentiated image that emphasized his positive attributes. Colonial cinema condensed the Congo to a controllable dimension, portraying it as if it were one undifferentiated and orderly bloc. Congolese participated in filmmaking only as actors or assistants under European directors' guidance, never as screenwriters or directors. All of this suggests that there is much power left in Edward Said's interpretation as set forth in *Orientalism*. Many scholars have questioned Said's argument that imperialists dominated the culture and history of the Orient through Orientalism, or the "Western style for dominating, restructuring, and having authority over the Orient."[6] Belgians possessed their own backward "Orient" in the diversity of the Congo's territories, peoples, and histories; they exercised epistemological control over it, defining themselves against it as advanced and civilized. The Belgian case suggests that Said's interpretation retains a great deal of its analytic power.

After 1908, colonial authorities and pro-imperialists in the metropole openly recognized and embraced the mobilization of enthusiasm for empire among their fellow citizens through propaganda, and they sold the empire at home much as other imperial nation-states did. As in France and Britain, imperial propaganda continued well into the twentieth century, indeed right up to decolonization, not even diminishing during peacetime after the noxious effects of wartime propaganda during World Wars I and II. Even after two severe occupations, both of which were buttressed at least in part by German propaganda, pro-imperialists openly and eagerly attempted to induce an imperial spirit. The products of their efforts shared a great deal with pro-empire propaganda produced by Belgium's neighbors.

In terms of film, for instance, Belgium was at a basic level no different than other states with African colonies in that it used film as a medium of propaganda to promote empire.[7] Many local groups sought out films to show at local screenings, making Belgium's colonial cinema similar to those of Britain and France, which were not forcibly imposed top down on the population. In Britain empire-themed films had great success between the wars, and in both Britain and France colonial agencies fulfilled demands for films from local colonial interest groups, exhibitions, even seminaries and scientific lecturers.[8]

There also was a similarity of practice at expositions. At the 1931 Paris Colonial Exposition, the Portuguese used José dos Santos Rufino's favorable images of African labor in his *Albuns fotográficos e descrítivos da colónia de Moçambique* in an attempt to deflect criticism and shore up the Portuguese empire. At the same time, dos Santos's albums reveal insecurity about the colony resulting from long-standing criticisms of Portuguese labor practices.[9] Something similar took place at Belgian expositions, where organizers responded to imperial insecurities by asserting particular visions of empire. Belgian rule in Africa after 1908 was tenuous for a number of reasons, first and foremost because of the legacy of Leopoldian abuses. The addition of German African territories at the end of World War I and their administrative unification with the Congo in the mid-1920s provoked German irredentism. In addition, recent research has shown that conflicts lay just under the surface in central Africa in the supposedly tranquil years after World War II.[10] The Ministry of Colonies put the colony on display in the metropole in an attempt, like Rufino's albums, to buttress colonial rule and stave off criticism, such as by asserting the interpenetration of the Belgian and Congo economies or by rewriting history. Thus, Belgian efforts paralleled those at other European and U.S. expositions, where "organisers did not hide their interests, no one was ashamed of the imperial idea, [and] millions celebrated it with gusto and panache, using the exhibition site to bathe in the glory of conquest."[11] Belgian imperialism has come under criticism that stresses its brutality, but in terms of displaying empire at home, the colonial administration sold the empire much like Britain, France, Portugal, and even the United States. An atavism, the "native village" in 1958 only continued a European tradition of dehumanizing Africans by displaying them in a "primitive" state for observation.

Another similarity with Britain and France is that people in favor of empire in Belgium believed the country's children did not know enough about the colonies. "Both British imperialists and French colonialists believed that the national education of youth was woefully inadequate in terms of what students learned about the empire."[12] The Ministry of Colonies strove to instruct schoolchildren both at quinzaines coloniales in the interwar period and at world's fairs. Colonial museums showed a similar eagerness to inculcate pro-empire sentiments among children. The Tervuren museum, for instance, targeted children and their teachers by taking instructors on tours to educate them about the Congo and the museum's holdings and by hosting colonial study days for geography teachers. If attendance figures from 1957, 1960, and 1963 are indicative, school children made up a substantial plurality of visitors.[13] Considering that mandatory elementary education was in place in Belgium by the time of the reprise and that the Tervuren museum staff targeted schoolchildren, it is likely that the Musée du Congo Belge exposed girls and boys of all social classes to its collections.

Even those children who did not have the opportunity to learn about the colony in Tervuren did have the chance to learn about the Congo in school classrooms and in some cases school colonial museums. By the twentieth century all European states used education as a means to preserve the status quo; when the status quo changed dramatically for Belgium beginning in 1908, mass education changed to address the new situation. The effort that went into teaching children about the colony suggests that many viewed their colonial rule as insecure and threatened from within, which only an intense commitment to the colony could fix. Belgian imperialism was not a given but rather something always in the process of becoming, and even into the last days of empire the state and others grasped at ways to direct how it would turn out. Belgian colonial education for the masses lagged behind even French and British education, the latter two having incorporated imperial studies into public instruction programs by the 1930s in one way or another.[14] Although less research has been done on Germany, the Netherlands, Portugal, and Italy, by the first decades of the twentieth century, pro-empire education in all of them targeted youth to instill imperialistic feelings.[15] The efforts to propagate the colonial idea in schools only confirms what we already know about the importance of education as a tool of indoctrination from the late nineteenth century right through to the latter half of the twentieth century.

Discourse in imperialistic messages often paralleled French and British discourses. The quinzaines that urged people to "buy Belgian" and "buy Congo" corresponded to British and French campaigns in the 1930s, for example. Also similar was how the metropole controlled the colony figuratively. Raymond Betts has pointed out that the French Empire was a unified "empire" in rhetoric only, as it was made up of "a great number of properties scattered around the world . . . never joined in purpose or in organisation or in sentiment."[16] Neither was the Congo a unified empire in a cultural, demographic, or economic sense, even if its administration was centralized and its provinces contiguous. Yet the Tervuren museum, monuments incorporating a map of the colony, films, maps in textbooks and at expositions, and other avenues of publicity reduced it to a single integrated possession and emphasized its unity, when in fact it was a sprawling territory comprising greatly varied environments, regions, peoples, languages, and cultures.[17]

Similar to the British and French cases, propaganda in Belgium also served a state-building purpose via nationalist messages that made the overseas empire a national project, around which disparate elements in the metropole could associate. Memorials, for instance, unified Flemings, Walloons, and German speakers in the country around a shared mission and tied the provinces closer together within an imagined community while simultaneously legitimating and celebrating empire. Placing busts of monarchs in expositions' Congo pavilions and teaching the significance of monarchs' colonial actions in classrooms emphasized the importance of the Saxe-Cobourg dynasty.

Colonial films, like those in France, also unified the population around a common national undertaking. Alison Murray has argued that French viewers of films from the empire "left the theater reassured not only that the Empire was coherent and controlled, but also that despite France's internal divisions, her colonial possessions provided a space in which Frenchmen were united in a common project."[18] Colonial cinema in Belgium made little mention of the country's language divisions. French, not Flemish, was the language of production of almost all films; what is more, French was the common language of the empire according to portrayals in colonial films, viewed as a whole. Ramirez and Rolot found but one image of Flemish language instruction in a Congo classroom in *Une école au bord du lac Kivu* (W. De Boeck, 1955).[19] This did not reflect the reality on the ground in central Africa, where much Flemish was spoken if not used extensively in the administration until the 1950s. Philip Mosley has argued that after the close of the silent film era, "cinema in Belgium could now be heard in either French or Flemish," which precipitated the country's "bicultural division. A 'split screen' came into being, with audiences naturally gravitating to films in their own language" and film production being divided up similarly.[20] Yet Ramirez and Rolot have shown that even after the silent era, colonial films worked against this trend, and the men and women who created these films—whether for Congolese, foreign, or Belgian audiences—were "belgicains," that is to say Belgians above all, not Flemish or Walloon. Perhaps World War II destruction and European unification contributed to a decline in nationalism and a growth in regionalism in Belgium and elsewhere in western Europe. But the loss of the Congo conceivably reduced the possibilities for Walloons and Flemings to imagine a Belgian nation, and further work needs to be done to explore the connections between decolonization and decentralization and regionalism in Belgium after 1960.

The prevalence and striking similarities of official and unofficial imperialist propaganda across European borders suggest it not only was widespread and lasting but in fact was a vital component of overseas rule in the nineteenth and twentieth centuries. That being said, Belgian propaganda was in ways exceptional and reflected a unique situation, such as the large and perhaps to some ridiculous asymmetry between the geographic size of the metropole and the overseas territory. In addition, the country did not conquer its overseas territories but rather received them, placing it in the situation of having to justify colonial rule to the world and its own citizens. Counterbalancing themes after 1908 were that Belgium was a small but proud country and that the Congo might be taken over by bigger powers. The latter was evident even before the reprise in the underlying fear of a British, French, or German takeover. Then, during World War I, the country was overrun, and people correctly feared losing the Congo to an expansionistic Germany. Even after suffering occupation for four years, helping defeat Germany in east Africa, and occupying substantial portions of German East Africa, the country's delegation at the Versailles Treaty negotiations found

itself fighting hard for acquisitions in Africa. As a result, delegation members and the public that followed their progress came
to realize the tenuousness of their position at the hands of the
great powers. During the 1930s there were concerns about Berlin's claims for the restitution of its colonies, and perhaps even
the takeover of the Congo. After World War II the administration rejected those who might interfere in the colony, so-called
pouvoirs anti-colonialists (anticolonial powers), blaming outside
interference on jealousy of their successes and the Congo's mineral riches.

Particular media of pro-empire messages were unique, such
as colonial cinema, which was distinct from those of its neighbors in the sense that it was more purely propagandistic. For
virtually all film producers, whether governmental, missionary,
or private, making money on motion pictures was not a main
objective—if one at all—which was unusual.[21] In *Le cinéma colonial* Pierre Boulanger analyzed 210 French fiction films made
in the Maghreb, including box office successes such as Georg-
Wilhelm Pabst's adaptation of Pierre Benoit's novel *L'Atlantide*
(1932), a huge production that cost 1.8 million French francs.[22]
American film companies created numerous commercial hits,
such as *King Solomon's Mines* (Andrew Marton, 1950).[23] By
contrast, financially successful Belgian colonial films, such as
Genval's *Le Congo qui s'éveille* (1927), were rarities—as were
those that earned international renown, such as Cauvin's 1948
documentary *L'equateur aux cent visages*, winner of the Grand
Prix International du Documentaire de la Biennale de Venise.[24]
Sielmann and Brandt's *Les seigneurs de la forêt* is notable because Twentieth Century Fox distributed it across the world
in twenty-two languages.[25] There were few exceptions such as
these among the hundreds of Belgian colonial movies.

Belgian authorities also were exceptionally concerned about the presence of Africans in the metropole, resulting in a policy of control and exclusion. The short-lived attempt in the late nineteenth century to educate some Congolese in Europe contrasts sharply with the situation elsewhere. Already in the 1880s individuals from the French Empire were studying in France itself; one of these, Blaise Diagne, was elected to the French National Assembly as early as 1914. In the British case, Indians served as MPs as early as the 1890s. In the 1920s some Belgians expressed doubts about the health and moral effects of bringing Congolese troops to the metropole—for example, to unveil the Place du Trône statue to Leopold II. When the societies of Soprocol brought in Congolese for the 1935 Exposition Universelle, the prospect made government officials anxious; fears of nefarious European influences on Africans ran right up to 1960.[26] By preventing Congolese from visiting the metropole, the administration thought it could keep dangerous ideas that might undermine imperial rule from reaching the colony, and sought to maintain "a certain image of Europe" among Congolese.[27] Jean-Luc Vellut has shown how fears of anticolonialism and communist infiltration during the interwar years led to what were basically forced returns to the Congo, the surveillance of Congolese mariners who arrived in Antwerp working for commercial shipping lines, and the creation of a cordon sanitaire around the colony.[28] When officials worried in the period leading up to the 1958 Exposition Universelle as to where Congolese workers for the fair would stay, this was nothing new but rather conformed to a long-standing attitude stretching back to the Leopoldian period.

The case of Belgium perhaps is unique in terms of who was most interested in producing pro-empire propaganda to sway the population at home. Among the three pillars of Belgian empire, private companies and missionary groups were less eager to promote imperialism than the state. This can be seen most clearly in colonial film production. Private interest groups showed great interest in films on the Congo from the reprise into the 1920s, financing Evenepoel and Reinelt's 1909–10 trip and Gourdinne's films of the 1920s. Apparently, this interest waned during the later interwar period, World War II, and the postwar era, when private companies expressed comparatively little interest in promoting the colony among Belgians. Missionary groups were late to the game of filmmaking, and their abbreviated post–World War II attempts to influence public opinion at home and subsequent concentration on film for Africans affirms John Onwumelu's and Marvin D. Markowitz's arguments that missionaries not only eventually came to accept independence but worked toward securing their place in a self-governing Congo.[29] Or as a group of expert authors put it, "The Congo was for Catholics above all not a colony, but a field of missionary activity."[30] Indicative of this orientation is that some missionaries continued to make films into the postcolonial period for a time.

By contrast the state promoted imperialism vigorously and broadcast a particular vision and history of its rule in the Congo, particularly in a ramped-up effort after 1945. The fact that village priests often acclaimed the "great work" going on in the Congo to their flocks and that a recent survey unveiled a surprising number of central African ethnographic collections at Belgian missionary headquarters indicates further research is needed. But equally clear is that the state took the lead in promoting imperialism, thus informing our understanding of why the small, neutral state of Belgium, devoid of a colonial tradition, took over and ran a massive African empire for decades. Traditional interpretations have explained that Leopold II was the driving force behind imperialism and that the three pillars sustained the empire after 1908. The production of imperialistic information shows the state led the way in popularizing the empire, indicating it had the greatest stake in the status quo after 1908.

The state also centralized information production. Even though there were numerous efforts to create museums in Belgium, particularly the sometimes clamorous efforts in Namur, the administration in Brussels was able to control propaganda production in museums. The Musée du Congo Belge comprised a department within the Ministry of Colonies and received its funding from the same; throughout the colonial period, the ministry maintained the Tervuren museum as *the* museum of the Congo by rebuffing regionalists' pleas. Also, the OC could manage local permanent colonial exhibits through its control of resources and its connections with firms that could provide resources to be put on display. The OC maintained close contacts with local groups and schools that put together their own little colonial museums, even sending out staff to coordinate and direct exhibits. In this sense, the colonial administration conveyed uniform messages across time and space and downplayed if not outright suppressed potentially diverse messages regarding the empire in favor of an official pro-empire discourse. Similar investigations of information production in other European imperial states would benefit from such an analysis. By drawing permanent colonial institutions and imperial ephemera in France, Britain, Italy, Germany, and elsewhere into one analytical framework, we would be able to detect parallels and common practices and also more clearly identify in which ways local ideas contradicted or reinforced official pro-empire doctrine. For example, one could examine whether messages that colonial expositions conveyed in Italy, Britain, France, and elsewhere reinforced or contradicted themes communicated at local exhibits and museums like the Pitt-Rivers museum, the Musée des colonies et de la France extérieure, or the Museo Coloniale in Rome. By extending the analysis across borders, one could pick up on transnational currents. Even if there were significant differences among national colonial museums, for instance, it is likely there were similar practices among museum directors and curators that paralleled each other across western Europe and that may have contributed to a European colonial ethnography or museology.

Also similar to other European cases is how Belgian pro-empire propaganda had mixed results, recognized even by devotees of empire who fought against the population's supposed dearth of colonial knowledge. What exactly we know about women's — fully half the population — acquaintance with empire is unclear. Imperial propaganda was a male province, both in terms of production and subject matter. This might reflect either a desire to sustain male privilege or women's disengagement from questions of overseas expansion from the beginning. Whereas further research is clearly needed in the case of gender, the picture is clearer as to age and empire, or at least how elders perceived the country's future imperialists. Despite their hard work, the Ministry of Colonies and pro-empire enthusiasts never believed the Concours Coloniaux Scolaires and other efforts were enough to educate the nation's youth. As late as 1955 the minister of colonies stated, "It is necessary to create in Belgium a colonial education and a colonial tradition."[31] This was in part because of the ongoing need for colonial administrators to nationalize the administration. But the unease with colonial education and the feeling that there could never be enough of it reveals something deeper, namely, that the state always viewed its colonial rule as insecure and threatened from within, which only a deep-seated national faith in the colony could solve. Belgian colonial rule was never fixed; instead, it was something in the process of becoming. Even into the last days of empire, the state grasped at ways to direct how it would turn out.

One way in which propaganda had modest results was in how world's fairs and other expositions failed to bring about much interpenetration of the colonial and metropolitan economies. Quinzaines coloniales that publicized colonial exports and imports and acted as a go-between for colonial businessmen had at best a questionable impact on the interpenetration of the colonial and metropolitan economies. During the interwar years, officials noted that not only were connections between the Belgian and colonial economies lacking but that in some cases they were declining.[32] André Mommen and others have pointed out how the importance of the Congo to the Belgian economy as a whole has been overstated and that at the time of decolonization the colony contributed not more than 3 percent of gross domestic production. Only 2.7 percent of exports at the time went to the Congo, and only 5.7 percent of imports came from the colony.[33] In other words, attempts to link the colony and metropole economically did not work.

What also failed to develop was a more general understanding of Congolese. Take, for example, expositions, which lacked authenticity by not reflecting a diversity of ethnic stereotypes, as was often the case at French, British, and American world's fairs.[34] In 1894 anthropologists divided Congolese into thirteen tribal groups, and in 1897 authorities separated Africans in Tervuren into villages roughly according to ethnicity. Yet after 1908, exposition organizers simply lumped Africans together,

paralleling a pre–World War I practice in Germany where ethnographic shows' priorities shifted from science to ticket sales.[35]
In Belgium after 1908, the priority was entertainment and propaganda, Changwe Yetu being a rather extreme instance of this,
comprising as it did dancers from across the vast Congo and
Ruanda-Urundi. Although architecture at universal expositions
could be used to resist categories of Western thinking—such
as was the case of nineteenth-century Islamic architecture that
challenged "Islamic" as an all-inclusive category by stressing
national identities—European-created architecture at Belgian
world's fairs achieved the opposite by homogenizing the diversity of the Congo. The 1958 fair did not foster closer relations
despite the fact that officials brought hundreds of Congolese to
the heart of the metropole for a period of months; rather, it reinforced the otherness and foreignness of Africans, its village
indigène and pavilions dehumanizing Congolese by presenting
them as objects. In a sense, this last great colonial exhibit was
in a tradition going back to V. Jacques's anthropological study
of the Congolese on display at the 1894 fair, *Les Congolais de
l'Exposition Universelle d'Anvers*. In Tervuren in 1897 Congolese had been "parked as animals are in contests, flesh to white
onlookers."[36] More than six decades later they were "parked
like livestock and exhibited as curious beasts."[37] So much for
Belgian-led progress.

Even the grandiose displays of empire in 1958 appear to have
done little to increase feelings of loyalty or attachment for the
central African empire. Although visits to colonial pavilions
and the sheer number of national and local colonial expositions
suggest an enthusiasm for empire, expositions seem to have
done little to develop a deep attachment to it. Scholars dispute
whether major colonial displays, such as the 1931 Paris Colonial

Exposition, represented the height of metropolitan interest in empire and developed bonds between colonizer and colonized. Charles-Robert Ageron asserts that the apogee of French interest in the empire came after World War II—that is to say, many years after the 1931 event.[38] Herman Lebovics argues the 1931 Vincennes fair indicated more the enthusiasm of its organizers than the public at large, and Bernard Porter stresses that empire exhibits appealed to Britons not because of imperialism but because they were fun.[39] Contrary to the growing literature describing European culture as "imbricated" or "steeped" with empire, the evidence suggests that Ageron, Lebovics, and Porter's arguments are in certain respects correct. It is important to point out that this failure to create stronger metropole-colony bonds had important ramifications. One administration official wrote that because of the lack of public interest in empire, the administration in Brussels and Leopoldville "was for years in a state of isolation; it was obliged to act alone."[40] According to Jean Stengers, the Belgian government pursued and the three pillars acquiesced to a policy of rapid decolonization because of the public's opposition to any sort of armed intervention in central Africa. "Any possible alternative to the government's policy implied, in one way or another, the application of force. To speak of it directly was to provoke public opinion, no one dared to do so. The attitude of Belgian public opinion . . . was the major paralyzing agent which stifled any possibility of effective reaction to nationalist demands. In the Congo the protagonists of Congolese independence were the Patrice Lumumbas and the Kasavubus; in Belgium the protagonist was, more than anyone else, the man in the street."[41] For all its success in impressing on Belgians an honorable colonial history, the 1958 fair did not convert the man in the street, who opposed fighting to retain the

Congo; thus the colony became independent with little opposition only twenty months after the 1958 fair closed its doors.

Yet emigration to the Congo injects ambiguity into the picture. Belgians remained reluctant to settle in the colony throughout the colonial period, except from the end of World War II to decolonization, during which time the population of Belgians in the Congo increased 276 percent from 23,643 to 88,913. Perhaps only in the last years of the colony did all the publicity and popularization of the early decades of the twentieth century bear fruit.

Additional evidence suggests that pro-empire propaganda had significant effects since most of what the majority learned about the colony came to them in the metropole. Propaganda strengthened Belgian feelings of supremacy and otherness toward Africans by repeatedly denigrating Africans and their culture and asserting the superiority of Europeans in comparison. Colonial films unified Flemings and Walloons by visually depicting a division between blacks and whites. "The films for Whites give in effect the image of an almost absolute separation" of Europeans and Africans.[42] White supremacy was inherent to this depiction, which continued throughout the period after 1908 with the exception of a few films at the very end of the colonial period. As the Musée du Congo Belge subtly imparted superiority over Congolese through supposedly scientific—and therefore objective—depictions of Africans and Europeans, so did movies imply Africans were animal-like, such as in the purportedly scientific *Les seigneurs de la forêt*. When depicted as animal-like and helpless, and therefore requiring assistance, Congolese appeared in need of colonial rule, revealing an ideological message being touted as objectively true. In this sense, we see another intersection of race, culture, and empire that reflects those that scholars

have explored in other contexts. For example, Chandra Harris
has pointed out how the negative images of Africans and African Americans in post–World War II Italian films helped Italian audiences "maintain a sense of power" even after defeat.[43]
These visions of subservient Africans in colonial films, like those
in other metropoles, reinforced ideas of European supremacy,
lulled Belgians into complacency, and may have contributed to
a powerful disillusionment after 1960.[44] The post–World War I
effects of government wartime propaganda in Germany comes
to mind: "The news that the government was seeking an armistice — that, after all the fanfares of victory, the war was in
fact lost — [had] a universally shattering effect."[45] Knowing that
more sympathetic portrayals of Africans only arrived at the
very end of the colonial period — for example, with *Tokèndé*
and *Main dans la main* — it is more clear why the Belgian populace was so shocked when the Congo achieved independence so
quickly.

And even if propaganda did not cultivate deep emotional
bonds, it did achieve another of its organizers' goals, that of
telling a certain history of the country's involvement in central
Africa. That pro-empire enthusiasts conveyed this idea with success is all the more impressive considering their narrative often
simply did not mesh with historical reality. The nationalistic
motifs of the 1910 and 1913 world's fairs, for instance, changed
after World War I to ones that stressed a colonial history stretching back to the 1876 AIA. This continued right to the end of
the colonial period and the 1958 Congorama, which began with
Stanley's forays into Africa on behalf of Leopold II.

There were two myths in particular that propaganda depended on in order to create a tradition of empire that helped
underpin the colony after 1908. The first of these was the myth

of the heroic pioneer period of the EIC, which was staked out as occurring between either the 1876 Geographical Conference or the 1885 declaration of the EIC and the reprise of 1908. Pro-empire information transformed the international and brutal period from 1885 to 1908 into a heroic, pioneer, and *Belgian* era that became the bold and glorious foundation for a noble and justified civilizing mission. Colonial memorials subsumed all Belgians, good actors and bad, who had been in the Congo from 1876 to 1908 into one heroic narrative. Yet some "heroes" who supposedly died courageous deaths fighting for civilization in Africa instead suffered rather pathetic deaths or never even made it to the Congo. Others, such as Charles Lemaire, were vicious soldiers of conquest and exploitation. In any case, the sacrifices of the heroic period justified Belgian rule in the Congo: the country had earned the right to rule by ending the slave trade, bringing civilization to theretofore unexplored territories, and offering up its own blood sacrifice. Just as the administration made the empire Belgian after 1908, so too was the heroic period nationalized, as propaganda expunged Leopold II's legion of foreign collaborators and substituted Belgian involvement in the first hours.

As for the second myth, enthusiasts deliberately rehabilitated the image of Leopold II by falsely portraying his notorious colonial rule as glorious and honorable, even though it had little to do with Belgians or the Belgian state. Leopold ruled his Congo as an absolute monarch from a distance—to a large extent creating an administration by proxy that was designed to make money through concessionary companies, not benefit the Congo. His rule led to greatly increased mortality by exacerbating tensions in an already agitated area of the continent, and agents of state and private administrations caused literally countless deaths and brutal abuses. At the time of his death, his subjects understood him little and loved him less. Yet the deceased king took on a particularly powerful meaning for colonial veterans and enthusiasts, who were at the forefront of promoting his legend, resulting in a dramatic metamorphosis of his image.

The multifaceted and dogged effort to craft a colonial tradition manifested itself above all in the emotional attachment to Leopold II and his colonial pioneers and in a robust effort to educate children. Leopold took on special meaning for colonial veterans and enthusiasts; for some, erecting memorials and commemorating pioneers and the king assumed an almost religious significance, such as when they performed "pilgrimages" to the Place du Trône statue. They lamented the lack of a similar conviction among the population more generally. Leopold II remained central to efforts to popularize the Congo at expositions, his presence often made material through busts that figured prominently. Organizers turned exhibits into opportunities to recast Leopold's legacy into a beneficent and proud myth. The Tervuren museum paid an extended homage to Belgium's second monarch and his African imperialism that lauded Leopold II increasingly over the years as its focus shifted from economic topics toward issues of colonial history. Monuments helped build this "Leopold myth," to draw on Ian Kershaw's work. Kershaw persuasively demonstrated how propaganda created a "Hitler myth" in Germany that fostered widespread if shallow support for the Nazi regime in the 1930s and 1940s while obscuring its leaders' true aims.[46] Such historical legends exercise powerful effects on perceptions and beliefs down to the present day. Just as twenty-first-century U.S. undergraduates understand Nazism as being a movement wherein Hitler mesmerized or brainwashed the masses, many in Belgium continue to maintain a positive image of Leopold II.

The cultivation of a Leopold myth is understandable considering that every colonialism of the nineteenth and twentieth centuries relied on myths to legitimize conquest and control of foreign peoples in faraway lands. Belgium was without an imperial heritage, unlike almost every colonial power of the late nineteenth and twentieth centuries. Even the lesser powers of Spain and Portugal could count long imperial histories in their favor. As Nicola Cooper explores in *France in Indochina*, even France — a country with a history that included an empire in the Americas, the continental emperor Napoleon Bonaparte, and the Second Empire of his nephew — needed myths to legitimize its empire in Indochina.[47] The whitewashing of Leopold II's misrule in Africa à outrance supported the dynasty and nation by obviating the need to deal with ambiguity. Therefore, there was no need to question the colonial past, and the issue of atrocities was avoided altogether. The prestige of the royal lineage was important, as the Saxe-Coburg dynasty long served to unify a nation that suffered a great north-south language divide. History might even have been used in service of the royal family's legitimacy. After World War II, the dynasty entered a period of crisis due to Leopold III's questionable actions during the war, and the building of monuments to Leopold II after the war might be viewed as an attempt to bolster support for the Saxe-Coburg dynasty.[48] The use of Leopold II as a motif after 1908 rooted contemporaneous Belgian imperialism within a supposedly long-standing tradition of overseas expansion, legitimizing the young empire in central Africa. Yet this focus on Leopold II also made pro-empire propaganda in Belgium distinctive. No comparable figure is to be found in Portuguese, British, Italian, Dutch, German, or French discourses on empire.

The two myths that came into being during the Belgian

state-rule period—"the heroic period" and "Leopold II"—present ironies. Pro-imperialists reshaped the period 1885 to 1908 into a praiseworthy era of altruistic pioneering and used that narrative to sell to Belgium its "tenth province." Monuments, for instance, explicitly celebrated the period from the Association internationale africaine, or the declaration of the EIC, to the reprise with their inscriptions. Yet it was precisely because this period was so illaudable that the country received an empire at all. Leopold II became the preeminent symbol for Belgian colonialism when his exploitation and outrageous misadministration forced him to hand the Congo over to Belgium. This is also amazing because his rule was the opposite of what Belgium proclaimed its colonialism to be, which was efficient, beneficial, benevolent, and civilizing. Leopold II had created an empire despite Belgian indifference, and yet numerous people later used him and his works to mobilize that same population behind the empire he had created. Perhaps Leopold as a symbol is even more apposite than commemorators imagined because in fact the post-1908 administration continued abuses begun during the EIC period and because Belgian rule did not end in the foundation of a stable and prosperous Congolese nation-state.[49] It is also strange that so many imperialists should tie the legitimacy of their rule in the Congo to Leopold's efforts because his administration was justified in the first place (albeit only ostensibly) by his "opening up" central Africa to international influence, whereas Belgium struck a clearly nationalist tone in its jealous ownership of its huge tracts in Africa.

Polls taken toward the very end of the colonial period suggest the Ministry of Colonies effectively conveyed its version of colonial history. In a 1956 poll of around three thousand Flemings and Walloons, more than 80 percent expressed the view that their country's presence in the Congo was legitimate. Typical responses to the poll included "We inherited it from Leopold II, and inheritances are legitimate"; "Because the Congo was given to Belgium by Leopold II"; and "For the reason of the rights acquired and services rendered." In the same poll, more than 83 percent of respondents judged Belgium's presence in central Africa beneficial to the indigenous population. Again, some of the beliefs reiterated by respondents demonstrated their belief in colonialism's positive effects. Was Belgian rule beneficial? "No doubt when one sees what the Congo was 75 years ago"; "Without the Belgians the Congo would be a region ravaged by sickness, given over to superstitions and fights between tribes"; "The benefits are numerous: hygiene, the removal of superstitions, etc!"[50] That Belgians viewed their presence as valid reflects the success of the production of information in favor of empire. Adam Hochschild has argued that Belgians experienced a "Great Forgetting," through which they both neglected Leopold II's brutal misrule in the Congo and made themselves out to have been exemplary rulers in central Africa.[51] This was not by chance but due at least in part to a deliberate effort by enthusiasts, the Ministry of Colonies, missionaries, and many others.

So imperialistic propaganda stimulated visceral connections to the colony among only a few yet successfully recast Leopold II and Belgium's colonial past in profound ways, suggesting that the argument among historians as to whether or not empire impacted European metropoles is not an either-or proposition and that what Herman Lebovics terms "the back workings of colonialism and imperialism on the metropolitan countries" is a complex issue.[52] To some, such as Catherine Hall and Sonya Rose, "Empire was omnipresent in the everyday lives of 'ordinary people,'" actually being "lived" in everyday practices in the metropole.[53]

This line of inquiry extends back to John MacKenzie, who argued in *Propaganda and Empire* that Britain's empire impacted everyday British culture, not just elite culture, in significant ways. Some such as David Cannadine have deliberately set out not only to recover "the world-view and social presuppositions of those who dominated and ruled the empire" but also "to put the history of Britain back into the history of empire, and the history of the empire back into the history of Britain."[54] Bernard Porter and others maintain a contrary view: "There was no widespread imperial 'mentality.' . . . Imperial culture was neither a cause nor a significant effect of imperial*ism*."[55] It is not a question of whether European nation-states were steeped with empire or by contrast unaffected. Rather the truth lies somewhere in between. Scholars should focus on discovering in what particular ways—important and minor, expected and unexpected—imperial influences found their way into European cultures and consider the ways in which disparate messages and means of propaganda in other media reinforced or diminished similar and different pro-empire (and anti-empire) themes produced in local and national expositions, colonial museums, film, and elsewhere.

Colonial propaganda and the ensuing myths surrounding Leopold II have had a lasting impact on how Belgium's colonial past is interpreted today, as suggested in the introduction. Adam Hochschild has asserted that Belgians know nothing of their colonial past as a result of a "Great Forgetting." According to many in the popular press, the Congo "is Belgium's forgotten skeleton" in the closet.[56] Others attack today's Royal Museum for Central Africa as an example of this forgetting, calling it an imperialist artifact. As the BBC's Angus Roxburgh wrote about a more "honest" 2005 exhibition at the Tervuren museum, "Belgians are finally learning the unvarnished truth about the brutalities of their colonial past."[57] It is true that there was a great deal of forgetting of atrocities that had occurred during Leopoldian rule and that most historical scholarship on central Africa told a positive story. But this does not mean that there has been no serious investigation into the colonial past; there has been, and continues to be, serious research in Belgium into the Leopoldian and state-rule eras. When critics argue that there is today a "collective amnesia" in Belgium about the colonial past, what they mean is that there is a lack of knowledge as to what those critics believe Belgians' history *really* was—or, in the words of another Leopold, "wie es eigentlich gewesen war [as it had actually been]."[58] Yet evidence suggests there is a significant awareness of Belgium's colonial past, as Leopold II and Belgian imperialism have been, and continue to be, discussed within Belgium. There are numerous organizations in Belgium that have kept the colonial legacy alive and that revisit history in publications such as *Congorudi* and now on the Internet at sites such as those maintained by UROME.[59] It is not that Belgians have forgotten, for example, about the Royal Museum for Central Africa. Whereas in the 1950s the number of visitors at the museum never surpassed 200,000 per year, by the mid-1970s attendance exceeded 225,000 per year. Although this dropped below 200,000 again by the early 1980s, the museum continued to draw in tens of thousands of visitors every year.[60] Hochschild's book had a significant impact after it was translated into French and Flemish, evidence that it landed on fertile ground. The 2004 film *White King, Red Rubber, Black Death* caused a stir when shown in Belgium, and Foreign Minister Louis Michel pressured state television not to broadcast it.[61] A justified criticism is not that Belgians are ignorant of their past, or that people ignored the 2004 film, but rather that Belgians did not react to the film as critics would have liked them to have responded.

Rather than having forgotten the colony in their past, perhaps Belgians instead lament its loss. Here we return to a final yet important point. Imperialist propaganda reveals an unexpected level of enthusiasm among much of the population for the œuvre civilisatrice in central Africa. For example, there is the creation of multiple colonial museums. Critics of Leopoldian and Belgian imperialism often have pointed to the colonial museum in Tervuren as an outdated relic of a paternalistic and harmful imperialism out of touch with reality. Yet the overwhelming focus on the museum at Tervuren has inhibited deeper study of colonial museums more generally and obscured the fact that it was only one of several. Just as the large number of people who went to see colonial pavilions at world's fairs suggests a particular enthusiasm for the imperial project, so does the establishment of museums indicate a level of support for the œuvre civilisatrice in Africa at odds with the common interpretation that Belgians were indifferent imperialists. It is in part true, as colonial administrators themselves acknowledged, that after 1908 two foreign occupations and a major economic depression took precedence in a lot of people's minds.[62] Yet the creation of Congo museums, the viewing of colonial films, and visits to colonial museums and ethnographic exhibits suggest some not only had the time to pay attention to goings on in their faraway central African empire but also the inclination to do so. Likewise in the case of building colonial memorials. Although not accepted by everyone — for example, radical left socialists — a surprising number of memorials were erected and celebrated in Belgium after 1908. There was a post–World War I burst of monument building propelled by veterans groups, and another surge in the decade before Congolese independence that indicated an acceleration of imperialistic propaganda just as the colony was starting to slip away. In the end, the driving force behind colonial monuments came largely from the ground up—not only from local groups and colonial veterans who wanted to honor the local dead, fallen comrades, and Leopold II, but also from the many ordinary Belgians who came out at inaugurations and in subsequent years to support the work in central Africa. This counters the long-standing interpretation that Belgians were hesitant imperialists, that Leopold II was the only driving force of empire, and that Belgians—not eager to take on a foreign empire—administered the Congo only reluctantly.

When considering the propaganda of Belgian imperialism in its many forms, the issue of Belgians' appetite for empire is cast in a different light. There may not have been a deep "colonial temper" in Belgium, in contrast to France and Britain and perhaps others. It is true there was no Belgian equivalent to France's Union coloniale française or its Comité de l'Afrique française, to Germany's Gesellschaft für deutsche Kolonisation, or to Britain's Primrose League or its British Empire League—all of which whipped up enthusiasm for empire in their respective countries. Yet pro-empire propaganda, which after 1908 did not come from Leopold II, tells a different story. Colonial businesses played a role, as did missionary orders, with the state taking the lead. And local participation in the promotion of the colonial idea in Belgium shows a significant level of grassroots activity in support of overseas empire, be it for reasons of nationalistic pride, perceived economic benefits, or other reasons. The impetus may have come from only a few, but the interest generated for the imperial cause was widespread, if not in all ways profound. The acclaim heaped on Leopold II in the Belgian state-rule period suggests that Belgium's reluctance has been overstated and that there was an important level of support for the imperial enterprise.

Notes

Introduction

1. Explanatory plaque in park at the Colonial Monument, author's visit, September 2002.

2. *Cercle Royal des Anciens Officiers des Campagnes d'Afrique: Bulletin Trimestriel*, no. 3 (September 2000): 7. I discuss this event and local colonial interest groups in Stanard, "Imperialists without an Empire."

3. Ville de Namur, "Cérémonie nationale d'hommage au drapeau de Tabora."

4. Régie des bâtiments, "Place du Trône."

5. Gilbert and Large, *End of the European Era*, 119.

6. Gordon Wright, *Ordeal of Total War*, 66–72; and Judt, *Postwar*, 310–11.

7. Jowett and O'Donnell, *Propaganda and Persuasion*, 4.

8. Connelly and Welch, *War and the Media*; and Taylor, *Munitions of the Mind*.

9. Row, "Mobilizing the Nation."

10. On colonial literature, see Renders, "In Black and White"; Halen, *Petit Belge avait vu grand*; Halen and Riesz, *Images de l'Afrique et du Congo*; and Quaghebeur and Van Balberghe, *Papier blanc, encre noire*.

11. Much work has been done on Hergé, *Tintin*, and the Congo. See Hunt, "Tintin and the Interruptions of Congolese Comics."

12. On photography, see Geary, *In and Out of Focus*.

13. Davis, "Maps on Postage Stamps as Propaganda"; Schwarzenbach, *Portraits of the Nation*; de Cock, *Congo Belge et ses marques postales*; Vancraenbroeck, *Médailles de la presence belge en Afrique centrale*; and Banque nationale de Belgique, *Franc belge*, 296.

14. Aldrich, "Putting the Colonies on the Map"; and Edouard Vincke, "Discours sur le noir," 91.

15. *Au service des broussards* (Namur, 1937) and *Les Grands Ordres missionnaires. Les spécialistes du continent noir* (Paris-Namur, 1939), located in Pirotte, "Armes d'une mobilisation," 84.

16. Blanchard and Lemaire, *Culture coloniale*, 5–39.

17. A Fleming is someone from Flanders, the northern, Dutch-speaking part of Belgium; a Walloon is someone from Wallonia, the southern, French-speaking part of the kingdom.

18. Stengers, "Statesman as Imperialist," 48–51.

19. Ewans, "Belgium and the Colonial Experience."

20. Young, *Politics in the Congo*, 148.

21. Peemans, "Imperial Hangovers," 275.

22. Vellut, "Hégémonies en Construction."

23. Anstey, *King Leopold's Legacy*, 44.

24. Slade, *King Leopold's Congo*, 194.

25. Vanthemsche, "Historiography of Belgian Colonialism in the Congo."

26. Castryck, "Whose History Is History?"

27. Bate, *Congo*; and Hochschild, *King Leopold's Ghost*. Kevin C. Dunn's *Imagining the Congo* omits the Belgian state period entirely.

28. Viaene, "King Leopold's Imperialism."

29. He makes clear they are not the objects of his study. Vanthemsche, *Belgique et le Congo*, 26, passim.

30. See, for example, Gewald, "More than Red Rubber and Figures Alone."

31. Wrong, "Belgium Confronts Its Heart of Darkness"; cf. Riding, "Belgium Confronts Its Heart of Darkness."

32. Edgerton, *Troubled Heart of Africa*, xii–xiii.

33. Bell, "Leopold's Ghost," 16.

34. The "reprise" was Belgium's takeover of the colony from Leopold II on 15 November 1908.

35. Harms, "End of Red Rubber."

36. Aldrich, *Greater France*, 192–95; and Gide, *Voyage au Congo suivi de Le retour du Chad*.

37. Gründer, *Geschichte der deutsche Kolonien*, 121.

38. Ferguson, *Empire*, 39–40.

39. Thomas, Moore, and Butler, *Crises of Empire*, 29.

40. David Anderson, *Histories of the Hanged*; and Elkins, *Imperial Reckoning*.

41. Osborn, "Belgium Exhumes Its Colonial Demons."

42. Vanthemsche, "Historiography of Belgian Colonialism in the Congo." See also Stengers, "Belgian Historiography since 1945."

43. Castryck, "Whose History Is History?" 80–82.

44. Stengers, *Combien le Congo a-t-il coûté à la Belgique*; Stengers, *Belgique et Congo*; and Vellut, Loriaux, and Morimont, *Bibliographie historique du Zaïre*, 43–63.

45. De Witte, *Assassination of Lumumba*.

46. For example, Slade, *King Leopold's Congo*; Anstey, *King Leopold's Legacy*; and Emerson, *Leopold II of the Belgians*.

47. Vints, *Kongo, made in Belgium*; Jacquemin and De Moor, *"Notre Congo/Onze Kongo"*; and Wynants, *Des ducs de Brabant aux villages congolais*.

48. Viaene, Van Reybrouck, and Ceuppens, *Congo in België*.

49. Schneider, *Empire for the Masses*; MacKenzie, *Propaganda and Empire*; August, *Selling of the Empire*; and MacKenzie, *Imperialism and Popular Culture*.

50. Huxley, "Notes on Propaganda," 36–39.

51. Emerson, *Léopold II*, passim.

52. Gann and Duignan, *Rulers of Belgian Africa*, 59.

53. Vellut, "European Medicine in the Congo Free State (1885–1908)," 77.

54. See, for example, Union minière du Haut-Katanga, *Union minière du Haut-Katanga 1906–1956*, 82–237, esp. 112.

55. Fetter, *Creation of Elisabethville 1910–1940*; and Fetter, "Martin Rutten (1876–1944)."

56. Aschmann, *Gefühl und Kalkül*.

57. Vellut, "Préface," 18.

58. Stengers, "Precipitous Decolonization," 305–35.

59. MacKenzie, *Propaganda and Empire*, 118, 193, 224, 253; and Porter, *Absent-Minded Imperialists*.

60. Bennett, "Exhibitionary Complex," 80–81.

61. Pratt, *Imperial Eyes*, 6.

62. Van Bilsen, "Een dertigjarenplan voor de politieke ontvoogding van Belgisch Afrika." For more on Van Bilsen, see Kwanten, "Go-between tussen twee culturen."

63. Mitchell, *Colonising Egypt*, 149, 164, 166.

64. Prakash, "Subaltern Studies," 1479, 1483.

65. Stoler and Cooper, "Between Metropole and Colony."

66. Cooper calls post–World War II France an "empire-state," a term Wilder rejects in favor of "imperial nation-state." Frederick Cooper, *Colonialism in Question*, 153; and Wilder, *Imperial Nation-State*.

67. Betts, *France and Decolonisation 1900–1960*, 7.

68. Vanthemsche, *Belgique et le Congo*, 353–54.

69. It was difficult for Belgians to go to the colony because only highly capitalized persons or skilled workers were permitted to relocate. Foutry, "Belgisch-Kongo tijdens het Interbellum." Even the Office de colonisation, which the Ministry of Colonies set up in 1937, was intended less to foster colonization than to stop the jobless from seeking employment in the colony. "Colonisation blanche."

70. Vellut, "Belgians in the Congo (1885–1960)."

71. Louis, *Ends of British Imperialism*, 39–40.

72. Talbott, *War without a Name*, 14; Judd, *Empire*, 332; and Louis, *Ends of British Imperialism*, 40.

73. Slade, *King Leopold's Congo*, 46; Storme, "Engagement de la propagande"; Union minière du Haut-Katanga, *Union minière du Haut-Katanga*, 173; and Jewsiewicki, "Colonat agricole européen au Congo Belge."

74. Gillot, *Vie des Belges au Congo*, 20, 69, 85, 105, 131, 198; and Young, *Politics in the Congo*, 89.

75. In 1931 less than 30 percent of 22,300 Europeans in the Congo were female. *Congo: Revue Générale de la Colonie Belge/Algemeen Tijdschrift van de Belgische Kolonie* 1, no. 1 (January 1932): 134; and Wesseling, *European Colonial Empires, 1815–1919*, 20–24.

76. Folder 470, UMHK archives, AGR; and *Service postal rapide*, 87–88. I thank Phyllis Martin for calling my attention to the similarity with other colonies.

77. *Le Soir* (Brussels), 30 July 1958.

78. Onwumelu, "Congo Paternalism," 52.

79. Jacquemyns, "INSOC à quinze années d'activité," 90.

80. Debrunner, *Presence and Prestige*; and Yates, "Educating Congolese Abroad."

81. Vellut, "Episodes anticommunistes dans l'ordre colonial belge (1924–1932)"; and Ketels, *Culte de la race blanche*, 90.

82. Porter, *Absent-Minded Imperialists*, 33–34.

83. Fogarty, *Race and War in France*; and Kongolo, "Paul Panda Farnana (1888–1930)," 2–3.

84. *Évolués* is a condescending and erroneously applied term used by Belgians and other Europeans to specify Africans who were "civilized" and European educated—literally "evolved." See entry for "évolués" in *Dictionnaire d'histoire de Belgique: Les hommes, les institutions, les faits, le Congo belge et le Ruanda-Urundi*. Regarding the frequency of Congolese visitors, see, for example, Lonehay, *Notables congolais en Belgique*; *Het Laatste Nieuws* (Brussels), 30 May 1953; *De Nieuwe Gazet* (Antwerp), 31 May 1953; and *La Dernière Heure* (Brussels), 28 June 1953. One estimate put the number of Congolese in the metropole in 1947 at only 10, and the number of all Africans from anywhere (including north Africa and Ruanda-Urundi) at no more than 1,848. Kagné, "Immigration d'origine subsaharienne avant 1960." Many Congolese who made their way to Belgium did so illegally. R. P. Stanislas Van de Velde in Agence Belga press release, 12 July 1952, liasse *Portefeuille no. 373b. Documentation historique coloniale. 8) Manifestations*, portefeuille 125 Infopresse, AA.

85. Potter, "Empire, Cultures and Identities"; Gascoigne, "Expanding Historiography of British Imperialism"; and Berenson, "Making a Colonial Culture?"

86. Chafer and Sackur, *Promoting the Colonial Idea*.

87. Blanchard and Lemaire, *Culture coloniale*; and Blanchard and Lemaire, *Culture impériale 1931–1961*.

88. Aldrich, *Vestiges of the Colonial Empire in France*.

89. Nicola Cooper, *France in Indochina*.

90. Palumbo, *Place in the Sun*; Andall and Duncan, *Italian Colonialism*; and Ames, Klotz, and Wildenthal, *Germany's Colonial Pasts*.

91. Stanard, "Interwar Pro-Empire Propaganda"; and MacKenzie, *European Empires and the People*.

92. August, *Selling of the Empire*, 56.

93. Hall, *Cultures of Empire*; and Codell and Macleod, *Orientalism Transposed*.

94. Burton, *After the Imperial Turn*.

95. Porter, *Absent-Minded Imperialists*, 320.

96. Lebovics, *Imperialism and the Corruption of Democracies*, xix.

97. Wils, "Introduction."

98. It might be more accurate to speak of Belgium as a nation in a state of unbecoming, for it has dismantled itself as a unitary nation-state. Sometime–prime minister Yves Leterme has said that the country was "an accident of history" and that Belgians had little in common except "the king, a football team, some beers." Navarro, "Entrevista a Yves Leterme"; and Quatremer, "Leterme à la tête d'un 'accident de l'histoire.'"

99. Fox, *Film Propaganda in Britain and Nazi Germany*.

100. Cole, *Propaganda in Twentieth Century War and Politics*.

101. Welch, "Introduction," xii.

1. The Inheritance

1. Biographies of Leopold II include Dumont, *Léopold II*; Emerson, *Leopold II of the Belgians*; Ascherson, *King Incorporated*; Stinglhamber and Dresse, *Léopold II au Travail*; Ludwig Bauer, *Leopold the Unloved*; de Lichtervelde, *Léopold of the Belgians*; and MacDonnell, *King Leopold II*.

2. Viaene, "King Leopold's Imperialism," 741–90.

3. Quoted in Wesseling, *European Colonial Empires*, 137.

4. Vandersmissen, *Koningen van de wereld*.

5. Quoted in Emerson, *Léopold II*, 78.

6. It was considered "independent" because it was not a colony of a European state. Emerson, *Léopold II*, 73–151.

7. The literature on violence and the EIC is extensive. For a good introduction, see Roes, "Towards a History of Mass Violence."

8. Slade, *King Leopold's Congo*, 178.

9. Vanthemsche, "Belgische Socialisten en Congo," 32–33.

10. Burton, *After the Imperial Turn*, 5.

11. Slade, *King Leopold's Congo*, 195–97.

12. Van den Wijngaert, Beullens, and Brants, *Pouvoir et Monarchie*, 335; and Long, "Russian Manipulation of the French Press, 1904–1906."

13. Anstey, *King Leopold's Legacy*, 15n3.

14. Ranieri, *Léopold II*, 123–40; and Stinglhamber and Dresse, *Léopold II au Travail*, 241–44.

15. On the colonial party, see Viaene, "King Leopold's Imperialism." For details on annexationist publications, see Poncelet, *Invention des sciences coloniales belges*, 83–93.

16. Poncelet, *Invention des sciences coloniales belges*, 47–51.

17. Viaene, "King Leopold's Imperialism," 764.

18. Invitations in Papiers André Van Iseghem, MRAC archives; and Shattuck, *Banquet Years*.

19. J.-M. Jadot, "Iseghem (Van)," in *Biographie coloniale belge/Belgische koloniale biografie*, vol. 5, cols. 464–68. *Biographie coloniale belge/Belgische koloniale biografie* will be listed hereafter as BCB.

20. *Dictionnaire d'Histoire de Belgique: Vingt siècles d'institutions, les hommes, les faits*, s.v. "Thys, Albert."

21. Léon Anciaux, "Thys," in BCB, vol. 4, cols. 875–81.

22. Hennebert to Henry de la Lindi, 17 July 1935, document 254, dossier 62.40 "Correspondence 1927–," Papiers Josué Henry de la Lindi, MRAC archives.

23. Stengers, *Congo, mythes et réalités*, 9–40.

24. Findling and Pelle, *Encyclopedia of World's Fairs and Expositions*.

25. Etambala, "Carnet de route d'un voyageur congolais: Masala à l'Exposition Universelle d'Anvers, en 1885; Première partie"; and Etambala, "Carnet de route d'un voyageur congolais: Masala à l'Exposition Universelle d'Anvers, en 1885; Suite et fin."

26. Vandersmissen, *Koningen van de wereld*, 224–27; and Couttenier, *Congo tentoongesteld*, 89–96.

27. Etambala, "Antwerp and the Colony," 185; Corneli, *Antwerpen und die Weltausstellung 1885*, 164; and Couttenier, *Congo tentoongesteld*, 94.

28. Bancel et al., *Zoos humains*; and Rothfels, "Bring 'Em Back Alive."

29. Larson, *Devil in the White City*, 121, 133–34, 160, 209, 222–23.

30. Bradford and Blume, *Ota*, 97–99; and *New York Times*, 10–13, 18 September 1906.

31. Greenhalgh, *Ephemeral Vistas*, 52.

32. Minder, "Construction du colonisé dans une métropole sans empire."

33. Cockx and Lemmens, *Expositions Universelles*, 50.

34. *Le Mouvement Antiesclavagiste* (Brussels: J. Goemaere, Imprimeur du Roi), 25 April 1894, 179; July–August 1894, 291; and October 1894, 389.

35. Wynants, *Des ducs de Brabant*, 120.

36. De Burbure, "Expositions et sections congolaises," 27–28; *Congo à l'Exposition Universelle d'Anvers 1894*, 58n1; Jacques, *Congolais de l'Exposition Universelle d'Anvers*; and *Souvenir de l'Exposition Universelle 1894 et d'Anvers*, views 3 and 4.

37. Cockx and Lemmens, *Expositions Universelles*, 50.

38. *Le Mouvement Antiesclavagiste* (Brussels: J. Goemaere, Imprimeur du Roi), September 1894, 367.

39. Flynn, "Taming the Tusk," 188.

40. Wynants, *Des ducs de Brabant*, 116.

41. Debrunner, *Presence and Prestige*, 340–42; and Wynants, *Des ducs de Brabant*, 120–21, 125.

42. De Burbure, "Expositions et sections congolaises," 27–28; and Jacquemin and De Moor, "*Notre Congo/Onze Kongo*," 15.

43. Ndaywel è Nziem, *Histoire générale du Congo*, 531; Dujardin, *Boma–Tervuren*; and Corbey, "Ethnographic Showcases, 1870–1930," 348.

44. *Le National*, 7 July 1897, quoted in Luwel, "Congolezen op de Tentoonstelling van 1897," 44.

45. Dewulf to Van Iseghem, 14 November 1897, folder "Van Iseghem, A. Correspondence 1896, 1897. BW Dewulf, opstand ven de voorwecht ven de Batetela," box 1, Papiers André Van Iseghem, MRAC archives.

46. Convents, "Film and German Colonial Propaganda"; Deocampo, "Imperialist Fictions"; MacKenzie, *Propaganda and Empire*, 83; and Fremaux, *Lumière Brothers' First Films*.

47. Ramirez and Rolot, *Histoire*, 19.

48. Convents, *Préhistoire*, 65–68; Convents, "Film als politiek instrument"; and Onclincx, "Milieux coloniaux," 300–301.

49. *Le Petit Bleu Exposition*, 13 August 1897, quoted in Onclincx, "Milieux coloniaux," 305n124.

50. Convents, "Apparition du cinéma en Belgique (1885–1918)," 17.

51. Thys, *Belgian Cinema*, 37; and Convents, *Préhistoire*, 65–66.

52. Onclincx, "Milieux coloniaux," 306.

53. Convents, *Préhistoire*, 67.

54. On the museum's early history, stressing anthropology, see Couttenier, *Congo tentoongesteld*.

55. Van Schuylenbergh, "Découverte et vie des arts plastiques," 4; and Bouttiaux, "Des mises en scène de curiosités."

56. See, for example, Rahier, "Ghost of Leopold II," 62.

57. Van Hoecke and Jacquemin, *Africa Museum Tervuren*.

58. Van Hoecke and Jacquemin, *Africa Museum Tervuren*, 14–15. On Masui's and Coart's classification schemes, see Couttenier, *Congo tentoongesteld*, 196–223.

59. Luwel, "Histoire du Musée royal du Congo Belge à Tervuren," *Congo-Tervuren*, 39–40.

60. Attendance at the 1905 Exposition Universelle et Internationale de Liège was surpassed only by that at Paris in 1900. Cockx and Lemmens, *Expositions Universelles*, 62.

61. Poncelet, *Invention des sciences coloniales belges*, 105; and de Burbure, "Expositions et sections congolaises," 28.

62. Drèze, *Livre d'or*, 88, 316, 320.

63. Emerson, *Léopold II*, 235.

64. Louis, *Ends of British Imperialism*, 157.

65. Louis and Stengers, *E. D. Morel's History of the Congo Reform Movement*; and Cattier, *Étude sur la situation de l'État Indépendant du Congo*.

66. See, for example, Rahier, "Ghost of Leopold II," 61.

67. Including catalogs such as Lemaire, *Congo et Belgique*, 206–18; and Masui, *Guide de la Section de l'État Indépendant du Congo*.

68. Viaene, "King Leopold's Imperialism."

69. Degrijse, "Belgique et les missions."

70. Pirotte, "Armes d'une mobilisation," 60–64; and Cleys et al., "België in Congo, Congo in België," 151.

71. Vanthemsche, "Belgische Socialisten en Congo," 33–35.

72. Viaene, "King Leopold's Imperialism," 761.

73. *Le Congo à l'Exposition Universelle d'Anvers, 1894*, 3–6; *New York Times*, 28 July 1903; *Notice sur l'État Indépendant du Congo*; and Drèze, *Livre d'or*, 352.

2. Denying African History

1. The tombs are empty; the dead were buried in a common grave.

2. *Mémorial Officiel de l'Exposition*, 236.

3. Nicola Cooper, *France in Indochina*, 65; and Moncel, "Il y a 50 ans."

4. Ageron, "Exposition Coloniale de 1931," 584–85.

5. Lebovics, *True France*, 93.

6. Porter, *Absent-Minded Imperialists*, 213–14, 261.

7. For example, Schroeder-Gudehus and Rasmussen's *Les fastes du progrès: Le guide des expositions universelles 1851–1992* omits the 1885, 1894, and 1930 world's fairs.

8. Hochschild, *King Leopold's Ghost*, 292–306.

9. Çelik, *Displaying the Orient*, 3.

10. Said, *Orientalism*.

11. De Burbure, "Expositions et sections congolaises," 28.

12. "Next Exposition to Be in Brussels."

13. *1935: Bulletin Officiel de l'Exposition Universelle et International de Bruxelles/Officieel Blad der Algemeene Wereldtentoonstelling van Brussel*, no. 11 (15 June 1934): 381.

14. Van der Linden, "Congo Belge à l'Exposition," 444.

15. *Bruxelles et l'Exposition — 1910*.

16. *Exposition Internationale Bruxelles 1910*; de Burbure, "Expositions et sections congolaises," 28; Ministère de l'industrie et du travail, Commissariat général du Gouvernement, *Exposition Universelle et Internationale de Bruxelles 1910*, 110–12; and liasse *205.812.22 Expos et foires diverses organisées en Belgique. Exposition Universelle de Bruxelles en 1910. 1) Section Coloniale de Tervuren*, portefeuille OC 417, AA.

17. *Bruxelles et l'Exposition — 1910*; and Rossell, *Livre d'or*, 163, 263, 346–47. Quote from either Arnold or Olyff in "Procès-verbal de la séance du 17 juillet 1912," p. 4, groupe XIX, classe 117, liasse *205.812.22. Expos. et foires diverses organisées en Belgique. Expos univ et intern. de Gand. 1913*, portefeuille 418 OC, AA.

18. Van der Linden, "Congo Belge à l'Exposition," 444; and Ministère de l'industrie et du travail, Commissariat général du gouvernement, *Exposition Universelle et Internationale de Bruxelles 1910*, 571–84.

19. Dujardin, *Boma–Tervuren*.

20. *Bruxelles et l'Exposition—1910*, unnumbered page.

21. Luwel, "Histoire du Musée royal du Congo Belge à Tervuren," *Belgique d'Outremer*; de Haulleville, *Musée du Congo Belge à Tervueren*; and Wynants, *Des ducs de Brabant*, 161–66.

22. Cockx and Lemmens, *Expositions Universelles*, 76–77.

23. *Bruxelles et l'Exposition—1910.*

24. *Geïllustreerde gids van Gent.*

25. *Groupe XIX, Commerce, colonisation* was divided into four classifications: 116 (*commerce*); 117 (*procédés de colonisation*); 118 (*matériel colonial*); and 119 (*produits spéciaux destinés à l'exportation dans les colonies*).

26. *Exposition Universelle et Internationale de Gand en 1913: Programme Général*, 6. Emphasis in original.

27. *Exposition Universelle et Internationale de Gand 1913. Commissariat général du Gouvernement*, 4.

28. "Procès-verbal de la séance du 17 juillet 1912," groupe XIX, classe 117, liasse *205.812.22. Expos. et foires diverses organisées en Belgique. Expos univ et intern. de Gand. 1913*, portefeuille 418 OC, AA. Quote from *Bulletin de la Société d'Études d'Intérêts Coloniaux de Namur*, no. 5 (May 1913): 50.

29. Capiteyn, *Gent in weelde herboren*, 147, 149; and Parmentier, *Exposition Universelle et Internationale de Gand en 1913*. Attendance figure drawn from "La Section Coloniale Belge de l'Exposition de Gand," 19 January 1914, [signature illegible], liasse *205.812.22. Expos. et foires diverses organisées en Belgique. Expos univ et intern. de Gand. 1913*, portefeuille 418 OC, AA.

30. "La Section Coloniale Belge de l'Exposition de Gand," 19 January 1914, [signature illegible]; and "Exposition universelle et internationale de Gand en 1913. Groupe XIX, Classe 117, Procès-verbal de la séance du 17 juillet 1912." Both at liasse *205.812.22. Expos. et foires diverses organisées en Belgique. Expos univ et intern. de Gand. 1913*, portefeuille 418 OC, AA. On exhibitors, see *Exposition Universelle et Internationale de Gand en 1913*.

31. Scheler, *Gand et son exposition*, 33–34; *Exposition Universelle et Internationale de Gand en 1913*; and photographs at liasse *205.812.22. Expos. et foires diverses organisées en Belgique. Expos univ et intern. de Gand. 1913*, portefeuille 418 OC, AA.

32. Note on organization of *classe 117*, liasse *205.812.22. Expos. et foires*

diverses organisées en Belgique. Expos univ et intern. de Gand. 1913, portefeuille 418 OC, AA.

33. *Bulletin de la Société d'Études d'Intérêts Coloniaux de Namur*, no. 5 (May 1913): 50.

34. Capiteyn, *Gent in weelde herboren*, 150. It had a circumference of around 377 feet and a height of 42–46 feet. See also Scheler, *Gand et son exposition*, 33.

35. Stanard, "Interwar Pro-Empire Propaganda," 44–45.

36. Stanard, "Selling the Empire."

37. *Exposition Internationale Coloniale, Maritime et d'Art Flamand: Anvers 1930*, liasse *205.812.22. Expos et foires diverses organisées en Belgique. Exposition internationale d'Anvers 1930. 7) Conférences, publicité, presse. 1) Brochures 1927–1930*, portefeuille 425 OC, AA.

38. Findling, *Historical Dictionary*, 259; and Secretary General, Ministry of Colonies, to Minister of Industry, 13 April 1929, liasse *205.812.22 Expos et foires diverses organisées en Belgique. Exposition internationale, coloniale, maritime et d'art flamand d'Anvers 1930. 1) organisation 1) généralités-corresp. 1927–1931*, portefeuille OC 420, AA.

39. "Het grootsche Paviljoen van Italië," cover page; "Het Paviljoen van Portugal, dat heden wordt ingehuldigd," cover page.

40. Doom, "World Exhibitions and Colonial Propaganda," 206; and *Livre d'or de l'Exposition Internationale Coloniale*, 370.

41. Debit for Dr. Duren, 24 May 1930, portefeuille R92 Office Colonial, AA; and *Antwerpen 1930*, 30 July 1930, 4.

42. "Administration du Congo Belge à l'Exposition d'Anvers"; and Executive Committee, "Note pour Monsieur le Secrétaire Général," 19 July 1929, liasse *205.812.22. Expos et foires diverses organisées en Belgique. Foire internationale d'Anvers 3) Construction et Aménagement 2) Contrats, 1929–1930*, portefeuille OC 423, AA.

43. "Inauguration du Palais du Congo," 7–8; and form letter from Cayen to colonial companies, 30 April 1929, liasse *Exposition d'Anvers*, portefeuille OC 2030, AA.

44. Charles to van der Burch, 26 April 1929, no. 1670, liasse *Expos et foires diverses organisés en Belgique. 205.812.22. Expos. internationale d'Anvers 1930. 1) Organisation. 2) Correspondence échangée entre le*

Ministère des Colonies et le Commissariat Général du Gouvernement près l'exposition inter. d'Anvers 1928–1930, portefeuille OC 420, AA; and "Pavillon du Congo Belge, Participation Officielle," portefeuille OC 426, AA.

45. Cockx and Lemmens, *Expositions Universelles*, 104; and *Officieel Maandschrift van de Wereldtentoonstelling voor Koloniën, Zeevaart en Vlaamsche Kunst: Antwerpen 1930/Bulletin Officiel de l'Exposition Internationale Coloniale, Maritime et d'Art Flamand: Anvers 1930*, no. 3 (1928): 2.

46. *Livre d'or de l'Exposition Internationale Coloniale*, 123.

47. Matton to Minister of Colonies, 19 December 1929; and Secrétaire-Général des Colonies to Matton, 3 January 1930, no. 330. Both at liasse *205.812.22. Expos et foires diverses organisées en Belgique. Foire internationale d'Anvers 3) Construction et Aménagement 2) Contrats, 1929–1930*, portefeuille OC 423, AA. See also 17th meeting, 22 August 1929, liasse *Registre II des Procès-Verbaux des Séances*, portefeuille 420 OC, AA.

48. *Exposition Internationale Coloniale, Maritime et d'Art Flamand Anvers 1930: Palais du Congo Belge: Guide officiel*, 39.

49. "Bij de opening van het Congopaleis," 4.

50. *Antwerpen 1930*, 24 May 1930, 5.

51. *Antwerpen 1930*, 24 May 1930, 6.

52. *Exposition Internationale Coloniale, Maritime et d'Art Flamand Anvers 1930: Palais du Congo Belge: Guide officiel*, 38.

53. *Exposition Internationale Coloniale, Maritime et d'Art Flamand Anvers 1930: Palais du Congo Belge: Guide officiel*, 38, 40.

54. Nicola Cooper, *France in Indochina*, 20.

55. "Inauguration du Palais du Congo," 7–8.

56. 51st meeting, 14 July 1930, liasse *Registre II des Procès-Verbaux des Séances*, portefeuille 420 OC, AA; and "Pavillon du Congo Belge à l'Exposition Internationale d'Anvers," 580.

57. Camus to Secretary General, 15 November 1928, liasse *205.812.22. Expos et foires diverses organisées en Belgique. Foire internationale d'Anvers 3) Constructions et Aménagement 4) Constructions. corresp., notes. 1928–1931*, portefeuille OC 423, AA.

58. Reper to Koller, 25 November 1929, liasse *205.812.22. Expos et foires diverses organisées en Belgique. Foire internationale d'Anvers 3)*

Construction et Aménagement 1) Offres de Services non acceptées, porte-feuille OC 423, AA; and liasse *205.812.22. Expos et foires diverses organisées en Belgique. Exposition internationale d'Anvers 1930. 5) Personnel de sur-veillance*, portefeuille 425 OC, AA.

59. *Antwerpen 1930*, 2 September 1930, 12–13.

60. Nauwelaerts, *Panoramische droom*, 65; and 31st meeting, 19 December 1929, liasse *Registre II des Procès-Verbaux des Séances*, portefeuille 420 OC, AA. See also Director General, "Note pour Monsieur le Secrétaire Gé-néral," 9 April 1930; and correspondence. Both at liasse *205.812.22. Expos et foires diverses organisées en Belgique. Foire internationale d'Anvers 3) Construction et Aménagement 2) Contrats, 1929–1930*, portefeuille OC 423, AA.

61. Morton, *Hybrid Modernities*, 255.

62. *Livre d'or de l'Exposition Internationale Coloniale*, 121; "Procès-verbal, 57e séance," 26 November 1930, Registre III, liasse *Foires et expos. diverses organisées en Belgique. 205.812.22. Expos internationale d'Anvers 1930. 1) Organisation 3) Commission exécutive en département*, portefeuille 420 OC, AA.

63. Çelik, *Displaying the Orient*, 3.

64. Findling, *Historical Dictionary*, 275; Mattie, *World's Fairs*, 167; and Deville, "Exposition Universelle et Internationale du Heysel de 1935," 130–41.

65. Comité exécutif de l'Exposition, *Livre d'or*, 25, 42.

66. *1935: Bulletin Officiel de l'Exposition Universelle et International de Bruxelles/Officieel Blad der Algemeene Wereldtentoonstelling van Brussel*, no. 11 (15 June 1934): 382.

67. Liasse *205.812.22 Expositions et foires diverses organisées en Bel-gique. Exposition universelle et internationale de Bruxelles 1935. 6) Visi-teurs d) réceptions, festivités*, portefeuille 439 OC, AA; and "Procès-verbal de la 2ème séance du Comité Exécutif du Département pour la Participation du Ministère des Colonies à l'Exposition de Bruxelles 1935," 2nd meeting, 27 April 1933, liasse *205.812.22. Expos et foires diverses organisée en Belgique. Exposition universelle et internationale de Bruxelles 1935. 1) organisation 5) Commission du Ministère des Colonies près l'exposition de Bruxelles a) procès verbaux des séances*, portefeuille 433 OC, AA.

68. *Exposition Universelle et Internationale de Bruxelles, 1935*, 8–9; and Comité exécutif de l'Exposition, *Livre d'or*, 361–68.

69. Comité exécutif de l'Exposition, *Livre d'or*, 361; and "Procès-verbal de la 30ème séance de la Commission du Département près l'Exposition de Bruxelles en 1935," 25 January 1935, p. 2, liasse *205.812.22. Expos et foires diverses organisées en Belgique. Exposition universelle et internationale de Bruxelles 1935. 1) organisation 5) Commission du Ministère des Colonies près l'exposition de Bruxelles a) 41 procès verbaux des séances*, portefeuille 433 OC, AA.

70. Photos in envelope 27, box "Expo. de Brux. 1935 No. 186A, No. 26–33," Archives de l'Exposition Universelle de Bruxelles 1935, AGR.

71. Blueprint, liasse *205.812.22. Expos et foires diverses organisées en Belgique. Exposition universelle et internationale de Bruxelles 1935. 1) organisation 1) Généralités*, portefeuille 433 OC, AA; Comité exécutif de l'Exposition, *Livre d'or*, 363; and "Office colonial à Bruxelles 1935," 6250–51.

72. *L'Illustration Congolaise*, no. 146 (1 November 1933): 4711–13.

73. "Exposition Universelle et Internationale de Bruxelles 1935. Société auxiliaire de propagande coloniale (Soprocol) et Collectivité des entreprises coloniale. Activités comparées," 13 September 1934, portefeuille 439 OC, AA; and "Congo à l'Exposition de 1935," 5110.

74. See *Service postal rapide*; and Nicoll, *Catalogue officiel*, 155–59.

75. *L'Illustration Congolaise*, no. 196 (January 1938): 6707; and "Exportation au Congo vue de l'Exposition de Bruxelles," 5476–77.

76. "Exposition Universelle et Internationale de Bruxelles 1935. Société auxiliaire de propagande coloniale (Soprocol) et Collectivité des Entreprises coloniales. Activités comparées," 13 September 1934, portefeuille 438 OC, AA; and blueprint of Pavillon des Entreprises, liasse *205.812.22 Expos et foires diverses organisés en Belgique. Exposition universelle et internationale de Bruxelles 1935. 1) organisation 6) Groupe XXV: Colonisation*, portefeuille 433 OC, AA.

77. Janssen to Administrateur Général des Colonies, 19 March 1936, OC 859, liasse *205.816.0. Propagande commerciale au Congo. Correspondence générale*, portefeuille 483 OC, AA.

78. "Extrait du procès verbal d'une séance tenue d'urgence à Mondorf"

[Soprocol], undated, portefeuille 438 OC, AA; "Procès-Verbal de la 13ème séance de la Commission du Département pour la Participation à l'Exposition de Bruxelles 1935," 27 February 1934, liasse *205.812.22. Expos et foires diverses organisées en Belgique. Exposition universelle et internationale de Bruxelles 1935. 1) organisation 5) Commission du Ministère des Colonies près l'exposition de Bruxelles a) 41 procès verbaux des séances*, portefeuille 433 OC, AA; and *"Doit"* from Van Segvelt to Gouvernement de la Colonie, 4 July 1935, liasse *Comptabilité particulière Expo de Bruxelles 1935. oc 220.103.31. Bordereaux de payement. 1/Bruxelles à 95/Bruxelles, 9 février 1934–2 janvier 1937*, portefeuille R97 OC, AA.

79. Liebrecht, "Congo au Heysel," 382.

80. Project of note to be inserted into "Guide de l'Exposition," 18 February 1935, p. 3, liasse *205.812.22. Expos et foires diverses organisées en Belgique. Exposition universelle et internationale de Bruxelles 1935. 1) organisation 6) Groupe XXV: Colonisation*, portefeuille 433 OC, AA.

81. "Procès-verbal de la réunion des personnalités membres de la classe 152, du 23 octobre 1934," liasse *205.812.22. Expos et foires diverses organisées en Belgique. Exposition universelle et internationale de Bruxelles 1935. 1) organisation 6) Groupe XXV: Colonisation*, portefeuille 433 OC, AA.

82. Liebrechts to Janssen, 17 May 1934, portefeuille 433 OC, AA.

83. Invoices from Imprimerie Disonaise, 29 May and 10 June 1935, and from *L'Illustration Congolaise*, 4 July 1935, liasse *Comptabilité particulière Expo de Bruxelles 1935. oc 220.103.31. Bordereaux de payement. 1/Bruxelles à 95/Bruxelles, 9 février 1934–2 janvier 1937*, portefeuille R97 OC, AA; Minister of Colonies to Director of OC, 10 January 1935, liasse *Expos. et foires diverses organisées en Belgique. 205.812.22. Expos. universelle et internationale de Bruxelles 1935 7) Publicité, conférences, presse b) Guide et catalogue*, portefeuille 440 OC, AA; liasse *Expos. et foires diverses organisées en Belgique. 205.812.22. Expos. universelle et internationale de Bruxelles 1935 7) Publicité, conférences, presse a) publicité dans la presse et dans les revues*, portefeuille 440 OC, AA; and "Procès-Verbal de la 30ème Séance . . . ," p. 4, liasse *205.812.22 Expos et foires diverses organisées en Belgique. Exposition universelle et internationale de Bruxelles 1935. 1) organisation 5) Commission du Ministère des Colonies près l'exposition de Bruxelles a) Généralités*, portefeuille 433 OC, AA.

84. Morton, *Hybrid Modernities*, 96–129; cf. Bancel, Blanchard, and Vergès, *République coloniale*, 112, 115.

85. Photos in envelope 27, box "Expo. de Brux. 1935 No. 186A, nos. 26–33," Archives de l'Exposition Universelle de Bruxelles 1935, AGR.

86. "35ème Séance de la Commission du Département pour la Participation du Département à l'Exposition de Bruxelles 1935," 29 March 1935, p. 1, liasse *205.812.22 Expos et foires diverses organisées en Belgique. Exposition universelle et internationale de Bruxelles 1935. 1) organisation 5) Commission du Ministère des Colonies près l'exposition de Bruxelles a) Généralités*, portefeuille 433 OC, AA.

87. Morton, *Hybrid Modernities*, 7, 216–71.

88. Undated communication, portefeuille 433 OC, AA; and Directeur Chef du Service to Minister of Colonies, 26 June 1935, no. 43, liasse *205.812.22 Expos et foires diverses organisées en Belgique. Exposition universelle et internationale de Bruxelles 1935. 2) Participation 1) du Département. 4e Direction. Générale*, portefeuille 434 OC, AA.

89. *Bruxelles 1935*, 18; *Exposition Universelle de Bruxelles 1935*, 66, 71–75; and Comité exécutif de l'Exposition, *Livre d'or*, 368.

90. *Bruxelles 1935*, 21–23; and Nicoll, *Catalogue officiel*, 155–59.

91. "35ème Séance de la Commission du Département pour la Participation du Département à l'Exposition de Bruxelles 1935," 29 March 1935, p. 2, liasse *205.812.22. Expos et foires diverses organisées en Belgique. Exposition universelle et internationale de Bruxelles 1935. 1) organisation 5) Commission du Ministère des Colonies près l'exposition de Bruxelles a) 41 procès verbaux des séances*, portefeuille 433 OC, AA.

92. Stanard, "Bilan du monde."

93. *Objectif 58*, no. 29 (August 1957): 3.

94. Findling, *Historical Dictionary*, 315.

95. Stanard, "Bilan du monde," 268.

96. "L'hotellerie congolaise."

97. D'Ydewalle, "Tout le Congo au Heysel."

98. *Objectif 58*, no. 26 (May 1957): 2–3, 35; and *Section du Congo Belge et du Ruanda-Urundi, 1957*.

99. Baron Moens de Fernig, interview with *Le Soir* (Brussels), 21 May 1958, quoted in *Inforcongo Bulletin de Presse* (Brussels: Office de l'information et des relations publiques pour le Congo Belge et le Ruanda-Urundi), 26 May 1958.

100. Kruseman, director of the Belgian Congo and Ruanda-Urundi section for the Commissariat général, interview with *Objectif 58*, no. 10 (December 1955): 8.

101. Meeting minutes, 6th meeting, 29 May 1956, liasse *Procès verbal de la Comité permanent de la Section du Congo belge et du Ruanda-Urundi*, portefeuille 796, AA; 9th meeting of the Commission des Arts de la Section du Congo Belge et du Ruanda-Urundi, 4 July 1957, liasse *Exposition 1958, Président, Section du Congo belge et du Ruanda-Urundi, 1957*, portefeuille 440, AA; and *Mémorial Officiel de l'Exposition*, 245.

102. *Mémorial Officiel de l'Exposition*, 236.

103. Stanard, "Bilan du monde," 268.

104. "La, fut un jardin exotique"; *Objectif 58*, no. 12 (February 1956): 17; and "Voici les quatre 'jardins choc' de l'Exposition 1958."

105. Meeting minutes, 1st meeting, 20 December 1954, liasse *Procès verbal de la Comité permanent de la Section du Congo belge et du Ruanda-Urundi*, portefeuille 796, AA. For the conversion, see Antweiler, "Pacific Exchange Rate Service," especially s.v. "per 1 British Pound," http://fx.sauder.ubc.ca/etc/GBPpages.pdf (accessed 20 April 2011); and the Federal Reserve Bank of Minneapolis's Web site, http://m.minneapolisfed.org/.

106. Stanard, "Bilan du monde," 270–72; and Thonnon, *Main dans la main*.

107. Stanard, "Bilan du monde," 270–74.

108. Solesmes, "En regardant vivre le Congo," 24, 26; *Revue Congolaise Illustrée*, no. 7 (July 1958): 18; and *Mémorial Officiel de l'Exposition*, 250.

109. Solesmes, "En regardant vivre le Congo," 26.

110. Stanard, "Bilan du monde," 271.

111. Such ersatz transportation at expositions was not particular to 1958. Miller, *Nationalists and Nomads*, 67–71; and Breckenridge, "Aesthetics and Politics of Colonial Collecting."

112. *Frankfurter Allgemeine Zeitung* (Frankfurt), 26 April 1958, quoted in *Inforcongo Bulletin de Presse* (Brussels: Office de l'information et des relations publiques pour le Congo Belge et le Ruanda-Urundi), 5 May 1958.

113. *Pourquoi Pas? Congo* (Léopoldville), 10 May 1958, quoted in *Inforcongo Bulletin de Presse* (Brussels: Office de l'information et des relations publiques pour le Congo Belge et le Ruanda-Urundi), 19 May 1958.

Numerous reviews expressed similar sentiments. See, for example, "In dreissig Minuten erzählt CONGORAMA fünfundsiebzig Jahre Kongo-Geschichte," 6; and *Elseviers Weekblad* (Netherlands), 17 May 1958, quoted in *Inforcongo Bulletin de Presse* (Brussels: Office de l'information et des relations publiques pour le Congo Belge et le Ruanda-Urundi), 26 May 1958. See also *Inforcongo présente Congorama: L'histoire du Congo racontée en 30 minutes*, p. 1, liasse *Gascht*, portefeuille 67 Infopresse, AA.

114. "CONGORAMA."

115. *Inforcongo présente Congorama: L'histoire du Congo racontée en 30 minutes*, p. 1, liasse *Gascht*, portefeuille 67 Infopresse, AA.

116. For more on the discussion in this paragraph, see Stanard, "Bilan du monde."

117. Meeting minutes, 15th meeting, 3 July 1957, p. 2, liasse *Procès verbal de la Comité permanent de la Section du Congo belge et du Ruanda-Urundi*, portefeuille 796, AA.

118. Xpo58, *Expo 58 (16)*; and Xpo58, *Expo 58 (17)*.

119. "Une blonde hôtesse du pavillon des mines se souviendra longtemps de la visite du Roi à la section du Congo," 5.

120. Mitchell, *Colonising Egypt*.

121. Stanard, "Bilan du monde," 274–75.

122. *Mémorial Officiel de l'Exposition*, 240–41.

123. "Pavillon du Commerce du Congo," 7.

124. De Meyer, *Introducing the Belgian Congo and the Ruanda-Urundi*, 26.

125. Robins, "A travers mes lunettes solaires . . . ," 1.

126. Stanard, "Bilan du monde," 281.

127. Vanthemsche, "Belgische Socialisten en Congo," 47.

128. Jacquemyns and Jacquemyns, "Exposition de 1958," 43.

129. Quoted in "Artisans du village Congolais sont retournés chez eux . . . ," 5.

130. Hodeir, "Épopée de la décolonisation," 310.

131. Stanard, "Bilan du monde," 285–86.

132. Ndaywel è Nziem, *Histoire générale du Congo*, 531; and "Au palais."

133. Stanard, "Bilan du monde," 275–76.

134. "Changwe Yetu war das Ereignis des 77," front page, 6; and *De*

Standaard (Brussels), 3 July 1958, quoted in *Inforcongo Bulletin de Presse* (Brussels: Office de l'information et des relations publiques pour le Congo Belge et le Ruanda-Urundi), 7 July 1958.

135. Delegates of Changwe Yetu to Minister of Colonies, in *Le Soir* (Brussels), 9 August 1958.

136. Ceuppens, "Een Congolese kolonie in Brussel," 242.

137. Stanard, "Bilan du monde," 275–79.

138. Codell and Macleod, *Orientalism Transposed.*

139. L., "Première au Palais du Congo."

140. Michel, "Activité de l'Office colonial dans les années trente."

141. "Vétérans Coloniaux," 71. *Les Vétérans Coloniaux 1876–1908* was alternatively titled during the colonial and postcolonial years as *Bulletin de l'Association des Vétérans Coloniaux*; *Vétérans Coloniaux*; *Bulletin Mensuel de l'Association des Vétérans Coloniaux*; and *Revue Belgo-Congolaise Illustrée*, all published in Brussels. See also J.-M. Jadot, "Janssen," in *Biographie Belge d'Outre-mer/Belgische Overzeese Biografie*, vol. 6, cols. 534–37.

142. Vanthemsche, *Belgique et le Congo*, 157–209.

143. Judd, *Empire*, 187–200, 287–96; and Marseille, *Empire colonial et capitalisme français.*

144. Janssen to Martin, 24 April 1928, no. 588, liasse *205.812.11. Les expositions de Quinzaine. 10) le tabac, le cacao, le café, le sucre, du 15 au 31 mai 1928*, portefeuille 413 OC, AA.

145. "M. Tscoffen a inauguré mercredi matin l'exposition coloniale des produits textiles"; [Ministère des colonies, Office colonial], *Exposition Coloniale du Textile*, 9; and H. W. Bauer, *Kolonien im Dritten Reich*, 2:78.

146. Stanard, "Selling the Empire between the Wars," 166.

147. [Ministère des colonies, Office colonial], *Exposition des Produits du Congo*, 7.

148. [Ministère des colonies, Office colonial], *Exposition des Produits du Congo*, 6. See also [Ministère des colonies, Office colonial], *Exposition Coloniale du Textile*, 5; and [Ministère des colonies, Office colonial], *Exposition Coloniale des Produits Alimentaires*, 5.

149. [Ministère des colonies, Office colonial], *Exposition Coloniale du Textile*, 13.

150. Stanard, "Selling the Empire between the Wars," 166–67.

151. *L'Étoile Belge* (Brussels), 17 May 1927, liasse *205.812.11. Les expositions de Quinzaine. 7) La coutellerie et le petit outillage du 16 mai au 15 juin
1927*, portefeuille OC 413, AA.

152. Stanard, "Selling the Empire between the Wars," 167–68.

153. See, for example, *Avenir du Luxembourg* (Arlon), 15 March 1927; *La
Meuse* (Liège), 15 March 1927; and *Vers l'Avenir* (Namur), 15 March 1927.

154. Speech by Landeghem, liasse *portefeuille 205.812.11. Expositions
de Quinzaine. 15) Exposition des produits textiles. 15/10–22/11/1933*, portefeuille OC 415, AA.

155. Stanard, "Selling the Empire between the Wars," 167.

156. *Indépendance Belge* (Brussels), 24 March 1926.

157. "Exposition à l'OC," 1, at liasse *Exposition de Quinzaine 205.812.22.
Le Matériel électrique. 10 au 25 mars 1926*, portefeuille OC 412, AA.

158. Bevel, "Causerie," 241.

159. See Istace to Minister of Colonies, 29 April 1926, liasse *Exposition de
Quinzaine 205.812.11. Les appareils de Mines 18/10 au 6/11/26*, portefeuille
OC 412, AA; Minister of Colonies to President and Members of the Salon de
la Chaussure Executive Committee, 16 November 1925, no. 1253, liasse *Exposition de Quinzaine 205.812.22. La chaussure, du 15 au 31 octobre 1925*,
portefeuille OC 412, AA; Minister of Colonies to de Heuvel, undated, liasse
*Exposition de Quinzaine 205.812.22. Les vêtements et les accessoires, du 4
au 19 mai 1926*, portefeuille OC 412, AA; and Secretary General to Jeanjean,
2 February 1927, no. 147, liasse *205.812.11. Les expositions de Quinzaine.
7) La coutellerie et le petit outillage du 16 mai au 15 juin 1927*, portefeuille
OC 413, AA.

160. Stanard, "Selling the Empire between the Wars," 167–68.

161. Stanard, "Selling the Empire between the Wars," 167–68.

162. Grinnaerl to Director of OC, 11 January 1934, liasse *205.812.11 Expositions de Quinzaine. 15) Exposition des produits textiles 15/10–22/11/1933.
1) Correspondence générale 1933–1934*, portefeuille OC 415, AA.

163. [Ministère des colonies, Office colonial], *Exposition Coloniale du
Textile*, frontispiece. See also [Ministère des colonies, Office colonial], *Exposition Coloniale des Produits Alimentaires*, frontispiece.

164. *L'Expansion Coloniale* (Brussels), 5 November 1933; and "Discours de M. MOREL, Président de la Fédération Nationale des Chambres de

Commerce et d'Industrie de Belgique," liasse *205.812.11. Expositions de Quinzaine. 16) Exposition Produits Alimentaires du 7 au 21 mars 1936*, portefeuille OC 416, AA.

165. "Expositions permanentes en Belgique et à l'Étranger," undated list, liasse *205.812.00 E. Propagande, Publicité, relations avec la Presse, Généralités. Classement des dossiers. Expositions permanentes en Belgique et à l'Étranger*, portefeuille 412 OC, AA.

166. *Eerste Koloniale Boekententoonstelling Antwerpen*; *Notre Congo peint par nos livres: Exposition du 6 au 27 février 1937*, liasse *205.812.22 Expos et foires diverses organisées en Belgique*, portefeuille 444 OC, AA; and *L'Avenir Belge*, 26 December 1936.

167. N'Doki, "Coup de Bambou." *Mukanda* was the "*Organe mensuel de défense des intérêts coloniaux belges* [monthly organ for the defense of Belgian colonial interests]."

168. *Transit: Revue Belge de Commerce International*, January 1940, 79.

169. "Foire Industrielle et Commerciale de la Louvière du 28 juillet au 16 août."

170. "Exposition Coloniale de Namur." Similar results were had at other expositions. See Dubois to Janssen, 31 July 1935, liasse *205.812.22. Expos et foires diverses organisées en Belgique. Foire Commerciale de Jemappes du 21 juillet au 6 août 1935*, portefeuille 442 OC, AA; "Dans les cercles coloniaux"; and *La Province* (Mons, Belgium), 25 July 1936.

171. Liasse *205.812.22. Expos et foires diverses organisées en Belgique. 10e 12. Foire coloniale d'Anvers. du 8 au 30 septembre 1928*, portefeuille OC 419, AA. On the 1925 fair, see Van Schuylenbergh, "Découverte et vie des arts plastiques," 14.

172. *Congo Paleis.*

173. *Bulletin Mensuel* [Cercle Africain Borain] (Frameries, Belgium), no. 7 (June 1937): 2.

174. *Mémorial de l'Exposition Missionnaire.*

175. Cercle Africain Borain to Closet, 17 November 1936, portefeuille OC 445, AA.

176. S. A. Bunge to Director of OC, 17 July 1928; and Janssen to Samyn, 16 July 1928, no. 1044. Both at liasse *205.812.22. Expos. et foires diverses organisées en Belgique. 10e 4. Exposition de la Louvière. 28/7–15/8, 1928*, portefeuille 418 OC, AA.

177. Janssen to Administrateur Général, 13 March 1937, no. OC 866, liasse *205.812.22. Expos et foires diverses organisées en Belgique. Exposition de Jemappes. Juillet 1937*, portefeuille 445 OC, AA.

178. OC Director to Briels (NOVA), 29 October 1932, liasse *205.812.42. Expositions permanentes. Expositions permanentes. Anvers Nova*, portefeuille 548 OC, AA.

179. OC Director to President of Middenstandsvereeniging, 19 June 1928, no. 895, liasse *205.812.22. Expos. et foires diverses organisées en Belgique. 10e 3) Exposition de Ledeberg. 14 au 23 juillet 1928*, portefeuille 418 OC, AA. See also Van Lommel to Simar, 16 August 1946; and Sister Marie-Lutgar du Sacre Cœur to OC, 16 August 1946. Both at portefeuille 417 OC, AA.

180. Janssen to Commissiare Général du Comité des Expositions de la Brasserie et des Industries Connexes, 27 April 1937, nos. OC 1566, 1567, 1568, liasse *205.812.22 Expos et foires diverses organisées en Belgique. Exposition de la Brasserie de Gand, 14 mai au 28 mai 1937*, portefeuille 445 OC, AA. See also liasse *205.812.22. Expos. et foires diverses organisées en Belgique. 10e 4. Exposition de la Louvière 28/7–15/8 1928*, portefeuille 418 OC, AA.

181. Liasse *205.812.22. Expos et foires diverses organisées en Belgique. Foire Coloniale de Bruxelles 1948*, portefeuille 504 OC, AA; note from A. Polchet, 5 December 1949, no. 2/I/I-II/1961, liasse *Centre d'Information et de Documentation du Congo Belge et du Ruanda-Urundi. OC 205.812.0. Foires-Expositions-Congrès*, portefeuille 412 OC, AA; and Michel, "Activité de l'Office colonial dans les années trente," 43.

182. Comité Régional de Mons to Minister of Colonies, 16 October 1928, liasse *205.812.22. Expos. et foires organisées en Belgique. 10e 11. Exposition de Mons. 15 novembre–15 décembre 1928*, portefeuille OC 419, AA.

183. "Les produits du Congo Belge," "Exportations," and "L'Exposition des Bois du Congo à la Foire Coloniale," all in *5me [Cinquième] Foire Coloniale*.

184. "A la foire commerciale," copy at liasse *205.812.22. Expos. et foires diverses organisées en Belgique. 10e 4. Exposition de la Louvière 28/7–15/8 1928*, portefeuille 418 OC, AA; "Questions economiques," quoting Prime Minister Georges Theunis from *Revue Belge*, 15 April [1924]; and "Fédération pour la colonisation nationale," 372.

185. "Au Palais du Congo—La 6me Foire Coloniale d'Anvers."

186. August, *Selling of the Empire*, 71–87; and MacKenzie, *Propaganda and Empire*, 121–46.

187. "Procès-verbal de la réunion du 30 janvier 1940. Organisation de la Section Coloniale," 30 January 1940, folder "Foire Internationale de Bruxelles 1940/Exposition 1897/Stand Un. Min. H.-Kat. à l'Exp. Inter. d'Anvers 1930," Papiers André Van Iseghem, MRAC archives.

188. "IIe [Deuxième] Foire Coloniale."

189. Note from Leplae to 4ème Direction, 1 March 1928; and Janssen to President and Members of the Comité de l'Exposition Internationale du Café et Industries connexes, 14 April 1928, no. 533. Both at liasse *205.812.22 Expos. et foires diverses organisées en Belgique. 10e 10. Exposition internationale du Café 22 septembre–7 octobre 1928*, portefeuille OC 419, AA.

190. Gorlia to Burgemeester van Dendermonde, 21 June 1946, no. KB/4079, liasse *205.812.22. Expos et foires diverses organisées en Belgique. Exposition de Termonde. 1946*, portefeuille 504 OC, AA.

191. "Foire coloniale."

192. "Foire Coloniale d'Anvers," 25.

193. *Exposition Coloniale d'Arlon.*

194. *Congo Paleis*; and "Foire Commercial d'Anvers," undated, liasse *205.412.22 Expos et foires diverses organisées en Belgique. Foire internationale d'Anvers 28 mars–28 avril 1936*, portefeuille 443 OC, AA.

195. For example, Carrol, "1924 Colonial Exhibition in Strasbourg."

196. Stovall, *Paris Noir*; and Rose, "Sex, Citizenship, and the Nation."

197. Woodham, "Images of Africa and Design," 28; and Morton, *Hybrid Modernities*, 5–6.

3. Curators and Colonial Control

1. The Tervuren museum has been known variously as Musée du Congo (1898–1908), Musée du Congo Belge (1908–52), Musée royal du Congo Belge (1952–60), and Musée royal de l'Afrique centrale (since 1960). For the sake of simplicity, the chapter uses Musée du Congo Belge throughout.

2. Olbrechts, *Ethnologie.*

3. Maesen, "Notes sur la vie et la pensée."

4. For a sympathetic account of his life and work, see Petridis, *Frans M. Olbrechts 1899–1958.*

5. "Impressions congolaises."

6. Macdonald, "Exhibitions of Power and Powers of Exhibition," 3.

7. Legrand, "Le Musée de Tervuren fête ses 100 ans."

8. Rahier, "Ghost of Leopold II," 67.

9. See Couttenier, *Si les murs pouvaient parler.*

10. Pratt, *Imperial Eyes*, 6.

11. Prakash, "Subaltern Studies."

12. Couttenier, "De impact van Congo in het Museum van Belgisch Congo in Tervuren," 121. Leopold II paid 8,300,000, and the Belgian government paid the rest. Ranieri, *Léopold II*, 141–54.

13. Vincart, "Een paar uurtjes," 374.

14. Schouteden, *Guide illustré du Musée du Congo Belge*, 5th ed., 15.

15. Ranieri, *Léopold II*, 141.

16. P. Pirenne, "Projets de Léopold II et réalisations actuelles"; and Luwel, "Histoire du Musée royal du Congo Belge à Tervuren," *Congo-Tervuren*, 40.

17. Undated invitation, Papiers André Van Iseghem, MRAC archives.

18. Van den Wijngaert, Beullens, and Brants, *Pouvoir et Monarchie*, 340.

19. Schouteden, *Guide illustré du Musée du Congo Belge*, 7th ed., 11.

20. Luwel, "Histoire du Musée royal du Congo Belge à Tervuren," *Belgique d'Outremer*, 212.

21. Both quoted in Cockx and Lemmens, *Expositions Universelles*, 76–77.

22. Luwel, "Histoire du Musée royal du Congo Belge à Tervuren," *Belgique d'Outremer*, 212.

23. Stoerk, "Review of Alphonse de Haulleville."

24. De Haulleville, "Musée du Congo Belge à Tervueren," 211.

25. Maes, *Musée du Congo Belge à Tervuren*, 11.

26. The essential work is Couttenier, *Congo tentoongesteld.*

27. Couttenier, "De impact van Congo in het Museum van Belgisch Congo in Tervuren," 122–25.

28. Van Keuren, "Museums and Ideology," 173.

29. Coombes, *Reinventing Africa*, 43–44.

30. Philip Wright, "Quality of Visitors' Experiences in Art Museums."

31. Nicholas Thomas, "Material Culture and Colonial Power," 53n5.

32. Vincart, "Een paar uurtjes," 373.

33. Vincart, "Een paar uurtjes," 376–77n1.

34. Coombes, "Museums and the Formation of National and Cultural Identities," 64.

35. Couttenier, "De impact van Congo in het Museum van Belgisch Congo in Tervuren," 119; and de Haulleville, "Musée du Congo Belge," 217.

36. Luwel, "Histoire du Musée royal du Congo Belge à Tervuren," *Congo-Tervueren*, 46.

37. Communication with museum staff, 18 May 2005.

38. Hall and Rose, *At Home with the Empire*.

39. "Bezoeken aan het museum," 123.

40. To draw, of course, on Joan Scott, "Gender: A Useful Category of Historical Analysis," in Scott, *Gender and the Politics of History*, 28–50.

41. Rahier, "Ghost of Leopold II"; and Hochschild, *King Leopold's Ghost*, 292–93.

42. Van Hoecke and Jacquemin, *Africa Museum Tervuren*; and Marechal, "Musée royal de l'Afrique centrale."

43. Comité exécutif de l'Exposition, *Livre d'or*, 176.

44. Jewsiewicki, "Colonat agricole européen"; Luwel, "Histoire du Musée royal du Congo Belge à Tervuren," *Congo-Tervuren*, 41; and de Haulleville, "Musée du Congo Belge."

45. De Meersman and Vangroenweghe, *Royal Museum for Central Africa*, 8; and Schouteden, *Guide illustré du Musée du Congo Belge*, 7th ed., 17.

46. Cahen, "Musée dans le présent et dans l'avenir."

47. Rahier, "Ghost of Leopold II," 75–76.

48. Van Hoecke and Jacquemin, *Africa Museum Tervuren*, 20; and Verswijver and Burssens, "Hidden Treasures of the Tervuren Museum."

49. Excerpt from "Rapport de la Commission des colonies," 406–8.

50. Schouteden to Minister of Colonies Rubbens, 10 December 1935, no. 35/4989, portefeuille 549 OC, AA.

51. Janssen, "Note pour Monsieur le Ministre," 31 July 1932, no. OC 2150, portefeuille 433 OC, AA.

52. Couttenier, "De impact van Congo in het Museum van Belgisch Congo in Tervuren," 119; and Secretary and Mayor of Tervuren town council to Minister of Colonies, 3 March 1932, no. 4982, portefeuille 433 OC, AA.

53. Couttenier, *Congo tentoongesteld*, 252.

54. Biebuyck, "Olbrechts and the Beginnings of Professional Anthropology in Belgium," 104.

55. Van Hoecke and Jacquemin, *Africa Museum Tervuren*, 20.

56. *Les amis du Musée du Congo Belge; en néerlandais: De vrienden van het Museum van Belgisch Congo: Constitution.*—*Nominations* (Copie *in extenso* de l'acte no. 2173 publié aux annexes au *Moniteur belge* du 25 août 1951), 3.

57. Wastiau, *ExitCongoMuseum*, 25, 37; and Benedict Anderson, *Imagined Communities*, 184.

58. Royal decree of 1 January 1910, quoted in Luwel, "Histoire du Musée royal du Congo Belge à Tervuren," *Congo-Tervuren*, 40.

59. Binkley and Darish, "'Enlightened but in Darkness,'" 49.

60. Stocking, *Objects and Others*, 4–5.

61. Rahier, "Ghost of Leopold II," 66.

62. Wastiau, *ExitCongoMuseum*, 18. See also Wastiau, "Violence of Collecting"; and Couttenier, *Congo tentoongesteld*, 264–67.

63. Stanard, "Interwar Pro-Empire Propaganda," 27–48.

64. Corbey, "EXITCONGOMUSEUM," 26; and Vincart, "Een paar uurtjes," 376.

65. L., "Ce que le visiteur ne voit pas . . . ," 215–16. By the 1990s the museum held more than twelve million insect specimens, the largest such collection in the world. De Meersman and Vangroenweghe, *Royal Museum for Central Africa*, 35.

66. Luwel, "Histoire du Musée royal du Congo Belge à Tervuren," *Belgique d'Outremer*, 212.

67. Clifford, *Routes*, 121.

68. Schouteden, *Guide illustré du Musée du Congo Belge*, 7th ed., 39–44.

69. Document 62.40.2521, dossier "Lettres de Henry," Papiers Josué Henry de la Lindi, MRAC archives.

70. Metzger, "D'une puissance coloniale à un pays sans colonies."

71. "Allemands et la question coloniale"; and Onwumelu, "Congo Paternalism," 94. Still useful on German post-Versailles overseas imperialism is Schmokel, *Dream of Empire*.

72. Aschmann, *Gefühl und Kalkül*.

73. De Haulleville, *Musée du Congo Belge à Tervuren*, 7, 12–14, 17, 51–52, 55–64.

74. Janssen to Administrateur Général des Colonies, 11 December 1935, no. OC 3163, liasse 205.812.22. *Expos et foires diverses organisées en Belgique. Exposition universelle et internationale de Bruxelles 1935. 3)*

Construction 3) Décoration 38) Baron Vinçotte, portefeuille 438 OC, AA; and Schouteden, *Guide illustré du Musée du Congo Belge*, 5th ed., 15.

75. Schouteden, *Guide illustré du Musée du Congo Belge*, 5th ed., 21.

76. Rahier, "Ghost of Leopold II," 65.

77. Rahier, "Ghost of Leopold II," 65.

78. Schouteden, *Guide illustré du Musée du Congo Belge*, 7th ed., 9.

79. "Au Musée de Tervuren."

80. Schouteden, *Guide illustré du Musée du Congo Belge*, 7th ed., 35–38.

81. *Une Promenade historique/Een historische wandeling/A Historical Stroll*, temporary exposition shown at Musée royal de l'Afrique centrale/ Koninklijk Museum voor Midden-Afrika, 2003; and "Au Musée du Congo Belge."

82. O. Boone to de San, 14 April 1950, folder 490, UMHK archives, AGR; "Hommage aux pionniers luxembourgeois du Congo"; and author's visits 2002–3.

83. Kavanagh, "Museum as Memorial."

84. Inspecteur Général, Chef de Service (Ministère des Colonies), to Henry, 5 July 1927, no. 7627, dossier "correspondence 1927–," Papiers Josué Henry de la Lindi, MRAC archives.

85. Van Hoecke and Jacquemin, *Africa Museum Tervuren*, 242.

86. Van Hoecke and Jacquemin, *Africa Museum Tervuren*, 242.

87. De Haulleville, "Musée du Congo Belge à Tervuren," 211.

88. Wilder, *Imperial Nation-State*.

89. Couttenier, "De impact van Congo in het Museum van Belgisch Congo in Tervuren," 125.

90. Cahen, "Musée dans le présent et dans l'avenir," 214.

91. Lepersonne, "Lucien Cahen," 8.

92. Lepersonne, "Lucien Cahen"; and van den Audenaerde, "In Memoriam Lucien Cahen."

93. Nicholas Thomas, "Material Culture and Colonial Power," 51.

94. De Jonghe, "Note sur le Musée d'Art Colonial à Namur," 18 December 1935, no. 22/7631, portefeuille 549 OC, AA; and Wastiau, *ExitCongoMuseum*, 43.

95. L., "Ce que le visiteur ne voit pas . . . ," 215.

96. See Van Schuylenbergh, "Découverte et vie des arts plastiques," 15.

97. Jacquemin and De Moor, *"Notre Congo/Onze Kongo,"* 16.

98. Rahier, "Ghost of Leopold II," 62.

99. Morris, "Both Temple and Tomb," 1–86.

100. Saunders, "Congo-Vision," 79–89.

101. Clifford, *Predicament of Culture*, 198–200, 213.

102. Schouteden, *Guide illustré du Musée du Congo Belge*, 5th ed., 15, 34, 47, 56, 57, 60, 64; "Œuvres d'art du Congo à Tervueren"; "Exposition du peintre Pierre de Vaucleroy"; and CoBelCo, "Questions aux écrivains."

103. Schildkrout and Keim, "Objects and Agendas," 4; and Bouttiaux, "Un siècle de pillage culturel à Tervuren?" 2.

104. Lepersonne, "Lucien Cahen"; van den Audenaerde, "In Memoriam Lucien Cahen"; and Maesen, "Notes sur la vie et la pensée."

105. Saunders, "Photological Apparatus and the Desiring Machine," 25.

106. Arnoldi, "Where Art and Ethnology Met," 202.

107. Stocking, *Race, Culture, and Evolution*, 192.

108. Photograph at CoBelCo, "Questions aux écrivains."

109. Nicholas Thomas, "Material Culture and Colonial Power," 47.

110. Maes, *Musée du Congo Belge à Tervuren*, 5.

111. De Haulleville, "Musée du Congo Belge," 217; Maes, *Musée du Congo Belge à Tervuren*, 5–6; and *Congo-Tervuren*, nos. 1–2 (January–April 1956): 51.

112. Regnault, "Une visite au Musée du Congo Belge," 65.

113. Schedule "Journées d'Études Coloniales"; form letter from Vandenborre; Van Den Haute to Vandenborre, 9 February 1951, no. 1505/CCS; and photographs. All at liasse *Journées d'études coloniales, Rôle français: mercredi 6 décembre 1950. Koloniale Studiedagen. Vlaamse Rol: Donderdag 7 December 1950*, portefeuille Infopresse 17, AA.

114. Undated note, liasse *C.C. Scolaire. Conférences. Généralités 1950/53/55/59*, portefeuille 8 Infopresse, AA; and Rhodius to A. Gascht, 14 April 1955, dossier "Mr. Rhodius No 1," Papiers Georges Rhodius, MRAC archives.

115. Bennett, "Exhibitionary Complex," 93.

116. One can take a virtual tour at Musée africain de Namur, "Le Musée et ses salles," 2004, www.museeafricainnamur.be/en/musee.php.

117. See "Notre programme"; "Inauguration du Musée commercial et

colonial de Namur"; and "Procès-verbaux des Séances de la société: A. Séance du 7 janvier 1913."

118. Musée africain de Namur, *Petit guide*, 9–11; also Arnaut, "Belgian Memories, African Object."

119. OC to Président, Association des Anciens Élèves de l'École Industrielle de Namur, 28 December 1933, no. 32923, liasse *205.814.5 Musées coloniaux scolaires. Musée d'art colonial de Namur 1) Divers*, portefeuille 549 OC, AA. See also "Note pour Monsieur le Chef du Cabinet," 8 April 1930; and Closet to Chevalier and attachment, 30 October 1940. Both at liasse *205.814.5 Propagande scolaire. Musées coloniaux scolaires. Musée industriel et colonial de l'école industrielle de Namur*, portefeuille 548 OC, AA.

120. Adam and van Stappen to Rodigas, 24 December 1931, liasse *205.814.5 Propagande scolaire. Musées coloniaux scolaires. Musée industriel et colonial de l'école industrielle de Namur*, portefeuille 548 OC, AA.

121. "Note pour Monsieur l'Administrateur général," 25 October 1934, liasse *205.814.5 Musées coloniaux scolaires. Musée d'art colonial de Namur 1) Divers*, portefeuille 549 OC, AA. Gérard and his associates soon renamed the museum the Musée national d'art africain. Musée africain de Namur, *Petit guide*, 9–11.

122. Janssen to Monsieur le Ministre, 20 November 1935, no. 32922, portefeuille 549 OC, AA.

123. Schouteden to Minister of Colonies Rubbens, 10 December 1935, no. 35/4989, portefeuille 549 OC, AA.

124. De Jonghe, "Note sur le Musée d'Art Colonial à Namur," 18 December 1935, no. 22/7631, portefeuille 549 OC, AA.

125. Directeur-Chef de Service to Minister, 18 October 1937, no. 34033, liasse *205.814.5 Musées coloniaux scolaires. Musée d'art colonial de Namur 1) Divers*, portefeuille 549 OC, AA.

126. "Relevé des sommes payées par la Loterie Coloniale du 24.8.1934 au 30.9.1939 au Musée d'Art Colonial, à Namur," undated, liasse *205.814.5 Musées coloniaux scolaires. Musée d'art colonial de Namur 2) Publicité de la Loterie Coloniale*, portefeuille 549 OC, AA.

127. Janssen, "Note," 21 August 1937, no. OC 3310, liasse *205.814.5 Musée d'art colonial Belge à Namur 3) Question Gérard 1934–1940, 1942, 1946, 1948*, portefeuille 549 OC, AA.

128. "Note pour Monsieur l'Administrateur général," 25 October 1934; and Heyerick, "Musée d'Art colonial de Namur," undated note [c. late 1934, early 1935]. Both at liasse *205.814.5 Musées coloniaux scolaires. Musée d'art colonial de Namur 1) Divers*, portefeuille 549 OC, AA.

129. Gérard, "Cercle d'etude et de propagande coloniale de Namur."

130. Nepper to Yanssens [*sic*], 24 February 1936, liasse *205.814.5 Musées coloniaux scolaires. Musée d'art colonial de Namur 1) Divers*, portefeuille 549 OC, AA.

131. Président of the Cercle to Charles, 22 September 1930, liasse *205.812.42. Expositions permanentes. Exposition du Cercle colonial et maritime de Bruges*, portefeuille 548 OC, AA.

132. Morton, *Hybrid Modernities*, 274.

133. Nepper to Janssens, 7 July 1936, liasse *205.814.5 Musées coloniaux scolaires. Musée d'art colonial de Namur 1) Divers*, portefeuille 549 OC, AA.

134. Janssen to Gorlia, 17 August 1936, liasse *205.814.5 Musées coloniaux scolaires. Musée d'art colonial de Namur 1) Divers*, portefeuille 549 OC, AA; Janssen to Deridder, 5 March 1936, liasse *205.814.5 Musée d'art colonial Belge à Namur 3) Question Gérard 1934–1940, 1942, 1946, 1948*, portefeuille 549 OC, AA; and note from Père Cambier, 3 February 1936, and Major Weber to Janssen, 3 March 1936, liasse *205.814.5 Musée d'art colonial Belge à Namur 3) Question Gérard 1934–1940, 1942, 1946, 1948*, portefeuille 549 OC, AA.

135. "Note pour Monsieur l'Administrateur général," 25 October 1934, liasse *205.814.5 Musées coloniaux scolaires. Musée d'art colonial de Namur 1) Divers*, portefeuille 549 OC, AA.

136. Quote from Gérard to Minister of Colonies, 8 November 1937, liasse *205.814.5 Musées coloniaux scolaires. Musée d'art colonial de Namur 1) Divers*, portefeuille 549 OC, AA. See also Gérard to Minister of Colonies, 1 February 1938, liasse *205.814.5 Musées coloniaux scolaires. Musée d'art colonial de Namur 1) Divers*, portefeuille 549 OC, AA.

137. "Note pour Monsieur l'Administrateur général," 25 October 1934, liasse *205.814.5 Musées coloniaux scolaires. Musée d'art colonial de Namur 1) Divers*, portefeuille 549 OC, AA.

138. Correspondence between Musée d'art colonial belge and the Loterie Coloniale, especially Directeur de la Loterie Coloniale, "Note pour Monsieur

le Chef de Cabinet," 31 October 1935, liasse *205.814.5 Musées coloniaux scolaires. Musée d'art colonial de Namur 2) Publicité de la Loterie Coloniale*, portefeuille 549 OC, AA. See also report #479/341/S.A., 5 January 1940, liasse *Gérard, Weber, Neppens*, portefeuille 549 OC, AA.

139. De Jonghe, "Note pour Monsieur le Ministre," 24 December 1935, no. 22/7641, liasse *205.814.5 Musée d'art colonial Belge à Namur 3) Question Gérard 1934–1940, 1942, 1946, 1948*, portefeuille 549 OC, AA; and "Musée d'Art Colonial Belge-Namur," October 1935, and Gérard to Ministre de l'Instruction Publique, 8 November 1935, liasse *205.814.5 Musée d'art colonial Belge à Namur 3) Question Gérard 1934–1940, 1942, 1946, 1948*, portefeuille 549 OC, AA.

140. *Vers l'Avenir* (Namur, Belgium), 4 April 1939, 27 April 1939, and 5 May 1939; and "Note pour Monsieur le Directeur," 4 August 1939, liasse *205.814.5 Musées coloniaux scolaires. Musée d'art colonial de Namur 2) Publicité de la Loterie Coloniale*, portefeuille 549 OC, AA.

141. Musée africain de Namur, *Petit guide*, 9–11; and Toussaint to Director of OC, 3 September 1946, liasse *205.814.5 Propagande scolaire. Musées coloniaux scolaires. Musée industriel et colonial de l'école industrielle de Namur*, portefeuille 548 OC, AA.

142. Gérard to Minister of Colonies, 23 January 1948, liasse *Gérard, Weber, Neppens*, portefeuille 549 OC, AA.

143. Musée africain de Namur, *Petit guide*, 9–11.

144. T., "Inauguration du Musée scolaire"; and Prinz to Van den Haute, 11 July 1951, and photographs, liasse *15a. Musées coloniaux scolaires de Jambes*, portefeuille Infopresse 17, AA.

145. "Inauguration du Musée commercial et colonial de Namur," 3–4.

146. T., "Inauguration du Musée scolaire." Its present-day successor on Rue du 1er Lancier displays at least two busts to Leopold II. Author's visit, 16 March 2003.

147. Arnaut, "Belgian Memories, African Objects," 32; and Arnoldi, "Where Art and Ethnology Met," 195.

148. Van Damme-Linseele, "From Mission 'Africa Rooms'"; Van Damme and Sweygers, *Lubuka! Lubuka!*; and Centrum voor Religieuze Kunst en Cultuur, "Etnografie."

149. Mantels, *Geleerd in de tropen*, 42–48, passim.

150. "Preparer pour Université de Bruxelles," undated note; and Vauthier and Secrétaire de l'Université (ULB) to Minister of Colonies Houtart, 25 May 1926. Both at liasse *205.814.5. Musées coloniaux scolaires. Université de Bruxelles corresp. 1926; 1935*, portefeuille 548 OC, AA.

151. This "museum" comprised a hallway of framed photographs, maps, and charts, as well as a small Bibliothèque du musée colonial (Colonial Museum Library). Monsieur le Préfet de l'Athénée Royal to Minister of Colonies, 8 March 1933, liasse *205.814.5 Musées coloniaux scolaires. Musée scolaire de Athénée Royal Ixelles*, portefeuille 548 OC, AA; and *La Meuse* (Liège), 28 October 1933.

152. *Bulletin de l'Association des Vétérans Coloniaux*, October 1933.

153. Père Brunin, Collège Saint-Michel, to Director of OC, 20 October 1935, liasse *205.814.5 Musées coloniaux scolaires. Musée Collège St. Michel*, portefeuille 549 OC, AA.

154. Inspecteur Général to Préfet du Collège St. Michel, 30 October 1935; Janssens to Administrateur Général des Colonies, 30 October 1935, no. OC 2683, and 27 January 1936, no. OC 256; OC to Pynaert, Director of Jardin Colonial de Laeken, 20 June 1936, no. 1854; Pynaert to Janssen, 23 June 1936, no. 201; Janssen to Brunincx, Recteur du Collège St-Michel, 8 July 1936, no. 2076; and Collège Saint-Michel to Director, undated (c. 22 July 1936) and 10 September 1936. All at liasse *205.814.5 Musées coloniaux scolaires. Musée Collège St. Michel*, portefeuille 549 OC, AA.

155. See liasse *205.814.5 Musées coloniaux scolaires. Musée scolaire de Gand 1927; 1929–1934; 1932*, portefeuille 549 OC, AA.

156. "Rapport sur la visite au Musée Colonial installé à la Section Commerciale de l'Université de Liège, le 15 avril"; "Rapport sur la visite au Musée Colonial installé à la Section Commerciale de l'Université de Liège," 15 November 1930; and OC to Wittmeur, 19 November 1930, 15 November 1932, 17 July 1935, and 9 December 1936. All at liasse *205.814.5 Musées coloniaux scolaires. Musée à l'Université de Liège 1930–1933; 1935–1939*, portefeuille 548 OC, AA.

157. Directeur-Chef de Service to Minister, 18 October 1937, no. 34033, liasse *205.814.5 Musées coloniaux scolaires. Musée d'art colonial de Namur 1) Divers*, portefeuille 549 OC, AA. NOVA's itinerary included Malines, Diest, and Tirlemont, among others. Janssen to Briels, 12 November 1928; undated photograph; undated note; and Briels to Janssen, 14 May 1934. All at liasse

205.812.42. Expositions permanentes. Expositions permanentes. Anvers Nova, portefeuille 548 OC, AA.

158. Correspondence between Janssen and Van Damme, liasse *205.812.42. Expositions permanentes. Exposition du Cercle colonial et maritime de Bruges*, portefeuille 548 OC, AA.

4. Educating the Imperialists of Tomorrow

1. A colonial school may have been set up in Brussels as early as 1904. *École Coloniale; fondée en 1904*; and Depaepe, *Order in Progress*, 86.

2. Ranieri, *Léopold II*, 141–54; and Luwel, "Histoire du Musée royal du Congo Belge à Tervuren," *Congo-Tervuren*, 40.

3. Cornevin, *Histoire du Congo*, 195.

4. Bernault, "Fin des etats coloniaux."

5. Hamerow, *Birth of a New Europe*, 167.

6. Closet to Janssens, 9 August 1932, folder 205.816.3 R 1925–49, portefeuille R61 OC, AA.

7. Leplae, "Nécessité d'une propagande agricole coloniale," 284–85, emphasis in original.

8. "Association de la presse coloniale," mispaginated; *Bulletin de l'Association des Vétérans Coloniaux*, no. 1, new series (August 1945): 11–12; Vandevelde, "Ignorance des Belges," 17; N. Arnold, *L'Illustration Congolaise*, no. 131 (1 August 1932): 4113; and Arnold, "Propagande coloniale à l'école."

9. Van Hecke to Laude, quoting Laude, 17 January 1950, no. 55/Inf., portefeuille 23 Infopresse, AA; and Laude, "A propos de l'enseignement colonial."

10. Depaepe, "Belgian Images of the Psycho-pedagogical Potential of the Congolese," 711–12.

11. The British recruited colonial civil servants from universities. Wesseling, *European Colonial Empires*, 45–49; and Couttenier, *Congo tentoongesteld*, 122–23.

12. Mantels, *Geleerd in de tropen*, 28–35.

13. Couttenier, *Congo tentoongesteld*, 121–24.

14. Gann and Duignan, *Rulers of Belgian Africa*, 100.

15. *Communication faite par M. Orts à la séance du 20 Novembre 1908: De la formation des fonctionnaires coloniaux* (n.p., 1908), 4; and Institut

Solvay, Institut de sociologie, Groupe d'études coloniales, "Documentation. Commission instituée en vue de rechercher les meilleurs moyens de formation aux carrières coloniales," report, RG 981. Both at Papiers Pierre Orts, MRAC archives. See also Gann and Duignan, *Rulers of Belgian Africa*, 180.

16. Renamed Institut universitaire des territoires d'outre-mer (University Institute of the Overseas Territories, INUTOM) in 1949.

17. *Fondation de l'université coloniale*; and *Université coloniale de Belgique*.

18. *Brochure de propagande: Ecole coloniale supérieure*, p. 5, *Textes législatifs et réglementaires relatifs à l'Institut I*, portefeuille 4 INUTOM, 2e DG 2/4 no. 4 (3864), AA; "Note pour Monsieur le Ministre," 27 January 1950, and Van den Abeele to President of the Conseil d'Administration de l'INUTOM, 18 August 1950, portefeuille 91 INUTOM, 2e DG 2/4 no. 111 (3898) 91 Elèves mulâtres, AA; and Fondation royale des amis de l'Institut universitaire des territoires d'outre-mer/Vriendenfonds van het Universitair Instituut voor de Overzeese Gebieden (hereafter FRAIUTO), *Middelheim*.

19. Poncelet, *Invention des sciences coloniales belges*, 168–69.

20. G. Ferir, *Bulletin de l'Association Coloniale Liégeoise, Edition Spéciale du Bulletin de l'ACL Dédié à la Mémoire du Colonel Louis Haneuse, 1853–1938*, no. 50 (January–February 1939): 16–17; and Minister of Colonies De Vleeschauwer's speech, *Congo: Revue Générale de la Colonie Belge/ Algemeen Tijdschrift van de Belgische Kolonie* 2, no. 2 (July 1939): 223–24. Also "Rapport sur le Fonctionnement de l'Ecole coloniale de Tournai pour la periode 1958–1959," 25 March 1959; and "Rapport sur le Fonctionnement de l'Ecole coloniale de Tournai pour la periode 1958–1959," 2 May 1960. Both at liasse *Centre d'Expansion économique et coloniale du Tournaisis*, portefeuille 62 Infopresse, AA.

21. Union coloniale belge, *Cours de préparation coloniale*, 5.

22. *La Revue Colonial Belge*, no. 12 (1 April 1946): 15.

23. Minister of Colonies Wiart in "Semaine coloniale interuniversitaire."

24. Poncelet, *Invention des sciences coloniales belges*.

25. Pirotte, "Armes d'une mobilisation," 62, 74–79, quote from 78.

26. Monheim, *Croisade antiesclavagiste*; and Monheim, *Passé colonial de la Belgique*.

27. With one exception: François Zuza studied at the university starting in 1940. Mantels, *Geleerd in de tropen*, 142, 158–63.

28. Mantels and Tollebeek, "Highly Educated Mission," 379–83.

29. Poncelet, *Invention des sciences coloniales belges*, 388.

30. "Université coloniale et l'ecole coloniale"; speech by Arthur Wauters in *Koloniale Hoogeschool van België*, 14; and Van Grieken-Taverniers, *Inventaire des archives*, 1.

31. Gann and Duignan, *Rulers of Belgian Africa*, 68–69.

32. *Brochure de propagande: Ecole coloniale supérieure*, pp. 3–4, *Textes législatifs et réglementaires relatifs à l'Institut I*, portefeuille 4 INUTOM, 2e DG 2/4 no. 4 (3864), AA.

33. "Discours de M. le Ministre des Colonies," emphasis in original; cf. Delafosse, "Une opinion française."

34. *Fondation de l'Université coloniale*; and *Université coloniale de Belgique*, 12.

35. *Brochure de propagande: Ecole coloniale supérieure*, p. 10, *Textes législatifs et réglementaires relatifs à l'Institut I*, portefeuille 4 INUTOM, 2e DG 2/4 no. 4 (3864), AA.

36. "C.A. de l'Universite Coloniale séance du 8/2/27," portefeuille 94 INUTOM 2e DG 2/4 no. 115 (3899) 94-Requètes-Réclamations des étudiants, AA.

37. N. Laude, 23 September 1926, dossier "I.U.C. 1925/1929. Dossier Personnel," Papiers Robert Moriamé, MRAC archives.

38. Vangroenweghe, *Du sang sur les lianes*, 27–47.

39. Couttenier, *Congo tentoongesteld*, 178–96.

40. Vangroenweghe, "Journal de Charles Lemaire."

41. Speech by Arthur Wauters in *Koloniale Hoogeschool van België*, 11.

42. Journal entry, 23 January 1922, Papiers Jean Fivé, MRAC archives.

43. Journal entry, 8 October 1922, Papiers Jean Fivé, MRAC archives. See also Depoorter, *Commandant Charles Lemaire*.

44. Journal entry, 6 November 1921, Papiers Jean Fivé, MRAC archives.

45. Roger Depoorter, biographical note in FRAIUTO, *Middelheim*, 31–34.

46. Jean Fivé, journal, Papiers Jean Fivé, MRAC archives.

47. Journal entry, 13 October 1921, Papiers Jean Fivé, MRAC archives.

48. FRAIUTO, *Middelheim*, 35–38.

49. "Injuste agression contre l'Université coloniale d'Anvers." See also FRAIUTO, *Middelheim*.

50. *L'Illustration Congolaise*, no. 22 (15 January 1925): 249; and Van Grieken-Taverniers, *Inventaire des archives*, 2.

51. Delafosse, "Une opinion française"; Norbert Laude, "La formation des administrateurs territoriaux du Congo Belge par l'Université coloniale de Belgique," quoted in *Trait d'Union: Organe de l'Association des Étudiants de l'Université Coloniale de Belgique* (Antwerp), 1934; and Laude, "Service territorial."

52. Laude, *Discours/Redevoeringen*.

53. FRAIUTO, *Middelheim*, passim.

54. Journal entry, 31 March 1922, Papiers Jean Fivé, MRAC archives.

55. Paulus to Minister of Colonies, 17 December 1952, no. 224/2996/ INUTOM 29, portefeuille 186 INUTOM, 2e DG 2/4 no. 45 (3886) 186-Monsieur H. Schouteden, AA.

56. *L'Illustration Congolaise*, no. 178 (1 July 1936): 5944; "Mémorial des vétérans coloniaux," 146–47; and "Conférences et manifestations coloniales," copy at Portefeuille 101 Presse, AA.

57. Such memorials included those for Georges and Paul Le Marinel (1925), Albert Thys (1926), Charles Lemaire (1927), and Victor Denyn (1931), among others. *L'Illustration Congolaise*, nos. 41–42 (1 and 15 November 1925): 629; "Inauguration du monument Le Marinel à l'Université coloniale d'Anvers"; speech by N. Arnold, 23 October 1926, dossier "II. U.C. 1925/1929. Discours. Réceptions. Fonds des Amis 1966," Papiers Robert Moriamé, MRAC archives; *L'Illustration Congolaise*, no. 70 (1 July 1927): 1482; *L'Illustration Congolaise*, no. 69 (1 June 1927): 1457; Norbert Laude, *Commandant Charles Lemaire: Discours prononcés à l'inauguration des mémoriaux du Commandant Charles Lemaire et de Jules Cornet à Cuesmes le 25 juillet 1937 et à la Séance Académique de l'Université coloniale le 23 octobre 1925*, quoted in *Le Trait d'Union: Organe de l'Association des Étudiants de l'Université Coloniale de Belgique* (Antwerp), [1937]; "Une cérémonie à l'Université coloniale d'Anvers," 4263; Laude, *Discours/Redevoeringen*, 67, 74; and E. De Jonghe, "Denyn," in *BCB*, vol. 1, cols. 294–300.

58. Journal entry, 23 May 1922, Papiers Jean Fivé, MRAC archives.

59. Journal entry, 6 November 1921, Papiers Jean Fivé, MRAC archives.

60. *Le Trait d'Union: Bulletin Trimestriel de l'Association des Étudiants de l'Université Coloniale de Belgique* (Antwerp), 1934–36.

61. For the Belgian Congo, see Vinck, "Livrets scolaires coloniaux"; and Nóvoa, Depaepe, and Johanningmeier, *Colonial Experience in Education*.

62. Seeley, *The Expansion of England*, quoted in MacKenzie, *Propaganda and Empire*, 179. See also MacKenzie, *Propaganda and Empire*, chap. 7.

63. Rioux, "Colonie ça s'apprend à l'école!"; August, *Selling of the Empire*, 122–23, and chap. 5n67; and Nicola Cooper, *France in Indochina*, 11–28.

64. "Documentation. Commission instituée en vue de rechercher les meilleurs moyens de formation aux carrières coloniales," documents "Enseignment Général Colonial. Degré primaire" and "Enseignement Colonial Général. Degré Moyen," RG 981, Papiers Pierre Orts, MRAC archives.

65. Kardenne-Kats, *Vielles histoires de ma patrie*, quoted in De Keyser, "Belgisch-Kongo in den belgischen Geschichtslehrbüchern," 154.

66. Verhaegen, "Colonisation et la décolonisation," 336, 348–49, 351–52.

67. Kurth, *Nationalité belge*, 120.

68. Debaere and Piret, *Nieuwe en nieuwste geschiedenis*, 180–87, quoted in De Keyser, "Belgisch-Kongo in den belgischen Geschichtslehrbüchern," 155–56.

69. Van Kalken, *Cours d'histoire générale à l'usage de l'enseignement moyen*; and Piret, *Cours d'histoire générale à l'usage de l'enseignement moyen et de l'enseignement normal primaire*.

70. Verniers and Bonenfant, *Manuel d'histoire de Belgique*; and Verniers and Bonenfant, *Histoire de Belgique dans le cadre de l'histoire générale*, rev. 3rd ed.

71. Verniers and Bonenfant, *Histoire de Belgique dans le cadre de l'histoire générale*, 4th ed., 220–23, quoted in De Keyser, "Belgisch-Kongo in den belgischen Geschichtslehrbüchern," 158.

72. Corijn, *Algemene en nationale geschiedenis*, quoted in De Keyser, "Belgisch-Kongo in den belgischen Geschichtslehrbüchern," 159.

73. De Baets, "Metamorphoses d'une epopée," 47. See also De Baets, *De figuranten van de geschiedenis*.

74. Van Kalken, *Histoire de Belgique des origines à nos jours*; and van Kalken, *Histoire de la Belgique et de son expansion coloniale*.

75. Monseur, "Colonisation Belge," 18–19, 22–24, 88.

76. De Baets, "Metamorphoses d'une epopée," 47.

77. Procès-verbal, CCS, 9 February 1950, p. 5, portefeuille 23 Infopresse, AA.

78. Depaepe, "Belgian Images of the Psycho-pedagogical Potential of the Congolese," 712.

79. MacKenzie, *Propaganda and Empire*, 194.

80. Kurth, *Nationalité belge*, 120, 189; and Viaene, "King Leopold's Imperialism," 753.

81. De Keyser, "Belgisch-Kongo in den belgischen Geschichtslehrbüchern," 164.

82. Monseur, "Colonisation belge," 126.

83. De Keyser, "Belgisch-Kongo in den belgischen Geschichtslehrbüchern," 164.

84. Verniers and Bonenfant, *Histoire de Belgique dans le cadre de l'histoire générale*, rev. 3rd ed., 221–23.

85. Verhaegen, "Colonisation et la décolonisation," 355–58; and Monseur, "Colonisation belge," 120–24, 171.

86. Monseur, "Colonisation belge," 107–8.

87. Verhaegen, "Colonisation et la décolonisation," 352, 361–62. See also Dorchy, *Histoire des Belges des origines à 1940*; and Dorchy, *Histoire des Belges des origines à 1981*.

88. My emphasis. He discusses numerous developments that "were never cited" in textbooks (e.g., Kimbanguism, Congolese participation in World War II, the 1944 Kitawala insurrection, and strikes in Matadi and Katanga). Verhaegen, "Colonisation et la décolonisation," 344, 362–63.

89. Verhaegen, "Colonisation et la décolonisation," 353; and Verschaffel, "Congo in de Belgische zelfrepresentatie," 72.

90. O'Brien, *To Katanga and Back*, 159–61; De Baets, "Metamorphoses d'une epopée," 48; Monseur, "Colonisation belge," 143; and Edouard Vincke, *Géographes et hommes d'ailleurs*, 65–79.

91. Depaepe, "Belgian Images of the Psycho-pedagogical Potential of the Congolese," 724.

92. De Keyser, "Belgisch-Kongo in den belgischen Geschichtslehrbüchern," 164; and Dierickx, *Geschiedenis van België*, plate 11.

93. Dierickx, *Geschiedenis van België*, 6.

94. De Keyser, "Belgisch-Kongo in den belgischen Geschichtslehrbüchern," 165.

95. Gysels and Van den Eynde, *Niewste tijden (1848–1955)*, quoted in De

Keyser, "Belgisch-Kongo in den belgischen Geschichtslehrbüchern," 159–60; and De Baets, "Metamorphoses d'une epopée," 48.

96. "Objet: Concours colonial scolaire," Ministère de l'Instruction Publique, 9 July 1955, liasse *Prémiers Prix du Concours Colonial Scolaire 1938, 1955 et 1956*, portefeuille 6 Infopresse, AA.

97. Correspondence at portefeuilles 8 Infopresse and 9 Infopresse, AA; and speech by Norbert Laude, liasse *20. Prix aux lauréats*, portefeuille 7 Presse, AA.

98. "Commission de propagande coloniale scolaire," 6242.

99. Michiels, Laude, and Carton de Wiart, *Notre Colonie*, 236, quoted in Vints, *Kongo, made in Belgium*, 50.

100. Liasse *Conférences C.C.S. 1956–57*, portefeuille 10 Infopresse, AA.

101. Liasse *Établissements à visiter en 1954–55 par les conférenciers*, portefeuille 10 Infopresse, AA; and liasse CB *Information presse-organisme d'education populaire Mouvements de la jeunesse*, portefeuille 8 Infopresse, AA.

102. Letter from J. Van den Haute, 23 February 1952, dossier "Conférences coloniales scolaires C.C.S. 1952/1953," box 3, Papiers Georges Rhodius, MRAC archives; and procès-verbal, CCS, 9 February 1950, portefeuille 23 Infopresse, AA.

103. Procès-verbal, CCS, 11 July [1953], liasse *Concours Colonial Scolaire 1954. Monsieur le Ministre 1953–1954*, portefeuille 6 Infopresse, AA.

104. Procès-verbal, CCS, 5 September 1957, and Buisseret to Laude, 17 October 1957, no. 899/Inf., portefeuille 10 Infopresse, AA.

105. "Observations sur les Conférences organisées par la Commission Coloniale Scolaire au Cours de l'Exercice 1949/1950," box 3, Papiers Georges Rhodius, MRAC archives; and Laude to Dupont, 1 March 1949, liasse *C.C.S. Conférenciers (divers) 1949–1950*, AA.

106. Undated, untitled note, liasse *C.C. Scolaire. Conférences. Généralités 1950/53/55/59*, portefeuille 8 Presse, AA.

107. "Observations sur les Conférences organisées par la Commission Coloniale Scolaire au Cours de l'Exercice 1949/1950," box 3, Papiers Georges Rhodius, MRAC archives.

108. "Congo, trésor envié," *Feuille d'Annonces*.

109. Dossier "Conférences coloniales scolaires 1951/1952 Août à décembre

1951," box 3, and dossier "Correspondence s/Conférences Congo," box 5, Papiers Georges Rhodius, MRAC archives.

110. Dossier "Conférences Coloniales postscolaires et C.L.E.O. 1951–1952–1953," box 3, and Rhodius to Louis, 12 January 1954, dossier "Mr. Rhodius No 1," Papiers Georges Rhodius, MRAC archives.

111. "Avant-projet de thème de conférence sur l'action sociale de la Belgique dans sa colonie," dossier "C.C.S. Honoraires," Papiers Georges Rhodius, MRAC archives.

112. "Très grand succès de la première conférence"; "Congo, trésor envié," *L'Écho du Centre*; and "Avant-projet de thème de conférence sur l'action sociale de la Belgique dans sa colonie," dossier "C.C.S. Honoraires," Papiers Georges Rhodius, MRAC archives.

113. "Avant-projet du texte," dossier "C.C.S. Honoraires," Papiers Georges Rhodius, MRAC archives.

114. Perlee, "Vue rétrospective sur le Congo Belge"; and V., "Vues actuelles sur le Congo."

115. "Avant projet de texte," liasse *C.C. Scolaire. Conférences. Généralités 1950/53/55/59*, portefeuille 8 Infopresse, AA.

116. "Très grand succès de la première conférence."

117. *La Nouvelle Gazette* (Charleroi, Belgium), 29 November 1949.

118. Rhodius to Laude, 31 March 1955, dossier "Mr. Rhodius No 1," Papiers Georges Rhodius, MRAC archives.

119. Thierron to Director of the CCS, 25 March 1952, and Marès to Rhodius, 22 May 1952, dossier "Conférences Coloniales Scolaires — 1951/1952 1°-1 à fin juillet 1952," Papiers Georges Rhodius, MRAC archives.

120. "Observations sur les Conférences organisées par la Commission Coloniale Scolaire au Cours de l'Exercise 1949/1950," 10 May 1950, box 3, Papiers Georges Rhodius, MRAC archives.

121. Note from École Normale de l'État "L. Degoppe" (Liège), 25 February 1959, liasse *Conférences en 1959*, portefeuille 10 Infopresse, AA.

122. Note from École moyenne de l'État pour Garçons (Pecq), 20 April 1959, liasse *Conférences en 1959*, portefeuille 10 Infopresse, AA.

123. Piniau, *Congo-Zaïre 1874–1981*.

124. Gondola, *History of Congo*, 107.

125. "Commission Coloniale Scolaire: Les journées Coloniales," meeting minutes, 27 October 1950, liasse *Journées d'études coloniales, Rôle français:*

mercredi 6 décembre 1950. Koloniale Studiedagen Vlaamse Rol: Donderdag 7 December 1950, portefeuille 17 Infopresse, AA.

126. Liasse *205.812.11 Expositions de Quinzaine. 15) Exposition des produits textiles 15/10–22/11/1933. 1) Correspondence générale 1933–1934*, portefeuille OC 415, AA; and liasse *Conférences en 1958. Réponses des Écoles*, portefeuille 10 Infopresse, AA.

127. *L'Étoile Belge*, 10 March 1931.

128. Judd, *Empire*, 201–213; August, *Selling of the Empire*, 107–9; "Celebrazione della Giornata Coloniale," 84, 86–87; "Giornata Coloniale," 109–10; and "'Giornata Coloniale,'" 117.

129. Ville de Charleroi, *L'Étoile*, 5–6.

130. "Cercle africain des Ardennes"; liasse *205.812.11. Expositions de Quinzaine. 13) Expositions des produits coloniaux. du 12 au 20 mars 1932*, portefeuille 414 OC, documents 205.812.1 Expositions de Quinzaine (1932–1933), AA; and "Troupes et les enfants des écoles," 4098.

131. Journées Coloniales, *Rapport au Roi*; and "Journées Coloniales de Belgique," 9.

132. August, *Selling of the Empire*, 109.

133. In 1925, 1,056 students participated in the competition. *L'Illustration Congolaise*, nos. 37–38 (15 September 1925): 565, and no. 17 (1 November 1924): 137; and Ministère des colonies/Ministerie van Koloniën and Ministère de l'instruction publique/Ministerie van Openbaar Onderwijs, *Concours Colonial Scolaire 1953–1954/Koloniale Schoolwedstrijd 1953–1954*. This competition involved 2,489 schoolchildren from across the country in 1930; in 1957, by contrast, only 1,382 students took part. *Bulletin Mensuel de l'Association des Vétérans Coloniaux*, no. 6 (March 1930): 13; and Ministère des colonies/Ministerie van Koloniën and Ministère de l'instruction publique/Ministerie van Openbaar Onderwijs, *Concours Colonial Scolaire 1956–1957/Koloniale Schoolwedstrijd 1956–1957*.

134. Gascht to École Moyenne d'Agriculture, Section Coloniale, 7 February 1957, no. 78/CCS; Gascht to Institut Technique Agricole, 7 February 1957, no. 79/CCS; and Gascht to Croegaert, 14 January 1957, no. 24/CCS. All at liasse *Concours colonial scolaire 1957*, portefeuille 7 Presse, AA.

135. Undated Commission Coloniale Scolaire note, "Questions du Concours Colonial Scolaire 1954," liasse *Concours Colonial Scolaire 1954. Monsieur le Ministre 1953–1954*, portefeuille 6, Infopresse, AA.

136. Quoted in *L'Illustration Congolaise*, no. 29 (May 1925): 401.

137. A. Gascht, "Note pour Monsieur J. Cuyvers," 12 May 1955, liasse *Prémiers Prix du Concours Colonial Scolaire 1938, 1955 et 1956*, portefeuille 6 Infopresse, AA.

138. Vandermotten and Bailly to Minister of Colonies, 30 September 1953, liasse *Koloniale Kring van Leuven en omliggende*, portefeuille 62 Infopresse, AA; "Koloniale Schoolwedstrijd 1957," liasse *Koloniale- en Zeevaartkring, Brugge*, portefeuille 62 Infopresse, AA; and *Bulletin Mensuel* (Cercle Africain Borain), no. 7 (June 1937), attached report pp. 1–3.

139. Bruneel to Laude, 21 February 1958, liasse 20. *Concours Colonial Scolaire 1957. Donateurs*, portefeuille 7 Infopresse, AA.

140. Liasse *Concours Colonial Scolaire 1954. Monsieur le Ministre 1953–1954*, portefeuille 6 Infopresse, AA. On awarding prizes, see *Le Soir* (Brussels), 16 July 1955; *Le Peuple* (Brussels), 15 July 1955; and *Het Laatste Nieuws* (Brussels), 16 July 1955.

141. De Paeuw, director general at the Ministry of Sciences and Arts, quoted in "Concours Colonial Scolaire 1931–1932."

142. Note from Ugeux to Rhodius, 19 September 1960, box 10, Papiers Georges Rhodius, MRAC archives; and *La Libre Belgique* (Brussels), 27 June 1960.

143. Stengers, "Precipitous Decolonization"; Vanthemsche, "Historiography of Belgian Colonialism in the Congo"; and Castryck, "Whose History Is History?" 78–79.

5. Cast in the Mold of the EIC

1. Imperialistic memorials in the metropole reveal more in this context than those in the Congo because few Belgians ever went there; it was at home that the majority received information about the colony. There were numerous monuments in the colony, evident in *L'Illustration Congolaise* in the 1930s.

2. Author's visits, 2002–3. The map of Mons, Belgium, distributed by Maison du Tourisme/Huis voor Toerisme, lists thirty-four sites but not a Hôtel de Ville plaque to veterans nor monuments to Jules Cornet and Leopold II.

3. Note in *Le Soir* (Brussels), 21 August 1989, by R. Bats, D. Cluytens, G. Keuster, A. Delannoy, A. Orlans, and J.-J. Symoens, quoted in Jacquemin, *Racisme, continent obscur*, 118. See also Edouard Vincke, "Image du noir dans les espaces publics."

4. Catherine, "Jubelpark"; Brussels Hoofdstedelijk Parlement, *Bulletin van de interpellaties en mondelinge vragen*, no. 46 (2004–5): 38–41; and Kelly Petronis, personal communication with the author, 1 March 2010.

5. Quoted in "Standbeeld Leopold II mag blijven."

6. AVRUG, "Sikitiko"; M. Lenain to Général Paelinck, 12 April 2005, at AVRUG, "Concerne: Monument du Roi Léopold II," Afrika-Vereniging van de Universiteit Gent, http://cas1.elis.ugent.be/avrug/erfgoed/pdf/cercle_2.pdf (accessed 26 May 2010); and Imbach, "Monuments publics coloniaux, lieux de mémoires contestés."

7. *L'Illustration Congolaise*, no. 97 (1 October 1929): 2665.

8. Léon Nyssen of the Royale amicale des anciens d'Afrique de Verviers, e-mail to the author, 20 March 2003; and Alain Noirfalisse of the Royale amicale des anciens d'Afrique de Verviers, letter to the author, 21 March 2003. I would like to thank Mr. Noirfalisse for sharing with me photographs of Verviers from the 1930s.

9. Quote from Markowitz, *Cross and Sword*, 19.

10. "Monument De Bruyne," 8; and "Monument Lippens-De Bruyne."

11. "Monument Léopold II," 21; and author's visit, 16 March 2003.

12. M. Coosemans, "Storms," in BCB, vol. 1, cols. 899–903; author's visit, 18 September 2002; and Fuks, *Héros et personnages*, 175.

13. *Antwerpen 1930*, 27 May 1930, back cover; and *Antwerpen 1930*, 30 July 1930, back cover.

14. Henri Pirenne, *Geschiedenis van België*, 103, cited in Barbry, Dewilde, and Van Rompaey, *Kongo, een tweede vaderland*, 47–48; and *Congo Belge/ Belgisch-Congo*.

15. Form letter from André Van Iseghem, R. de Meulemeester, Anatole De Bauw, and [signature illegible], 9 September 1937, Papiers André Van Iseghem, MRAC archives; *L'Illustration Congolaise*, no. 196 (January 1938): 6674; and *Congo Belge et ses coloniaux/Belgisch Kongo en zijn kolonialen.*

16. AVRUG, "Blankenberge."

17. Cf. Wingfield, "Statues of Emperor Joseph II."

18. "Hal honore ses enfants morts pour la civilisation," 1.

19. *Programme. Dimanche 19 juin 1932*; and Colonel E. Muller to Eugène Flagey, Bourgmestre d'Ixelles, 13 November 1946, document 5268.84, Papiers Emmanuel Muller, MRAC archives.

20. "Histoire du Congo par les monuments"; "Inhuldiging van het Geden-kteeken Baron Dhanis te Antwerpen"; and "Monument à la Mémoire du Baron Dhanis."

21. "Histoire du Congo par les monuments."

22. *L'Illustration Congolaise*, no. 97 (1 October 1929): 2655.

23. *Bulletin Mensuel de l'Association des Vétérans Coloniaux*, no. 3 (March 1931): supplement; *Bulletin Mensuel de l'Association des Vétérans Coloniaux*, no. 5 (May 1931): 7; and *Bulletin Mensuel de l'Association des Vétérans Coloniaux*, no. 6 (June 1931): 15.

24. "Souvenir Crespel à Tournai."

25. Cohen, "Symbols of Power," 509.

26. Jean Casterman, PSR leaflet (Cuesmes, 1937), liasse *205.812.22 Expos et foires diverses organisées en Belgique. Exposition de Cuesmes 24 et 25 juillet 1937*, portefeuille 445 OC, AA.

27. Vanthemsche, "Belgische Socialisten en Congo."

28. Johnson, "Cast in Stone," 51.

29. "Inauguration de la statue de Léopold II," *L'Illustration Congolaise*; and "Inauguration de la statue de Léopold II," *Congo: Revue Générale de la Colonie Belge/Algemeen Tijdschrift van de Belgische Kolonie*.

30. *La Nouvelle Gazette* (Charleroi, Belgium), 22 October 1958; Stinglhamber, "Discours prononcé"; and *XXVe [Vingt-cinquième] anniversaire de l'annexion du Congo par la Belgique*, 6.

31. "Les Journées Coloniales. La Grandiose Manifestation en l'Honneur du général major Henry," document 62.40.2269, Papiers Josué Henry de la Lindi, MRAC archives; "Journée Coloniale: A Verviers, A Arlon, A Seraing"; and *Bulletin de l'Association des Vétérans Coloniaux*, no. 3 (27 December 1940): 2.

32. "15 [quinze] novembre, au Monument Léopold II, à Bruxelles"; "Herdenkingsplechtigheid te Hasselt"; *Congorudi*, no. 47 (January 1979): 9; *Congorudi*, no. 50 (October 1979): 14; Ville de Namur, "Cérémonie nationale d'hommage au drapeau de Tabora"; and *Cercle Royal des Anciens Officiers des Campagnes d'Afrique: Bulletin Trimestriel*, no. 1 (2000): 9.

33. Edouard Vincke, "Discours sur le Noir."

34. "Exposition 1910, Section Congolaise, Fêtes sportives," folder RG 765, Papiers Félix Fuchs, MRAC archives; and "Inauguration du monument national."

35. The figures are of De Bruyne and Lippens. "Exposition 1910, Section Congolaise, Fêtes sportives," folder RG 765, Papiers Félix Fuchs, MRAC archives.

36. Explanatory plaque in park at the Colonial Monument, author's visit, September 2002.

37. Speech by J. Henry, 26 June 1927, document 6240.2646 A, Papiers Josué Henry de la Lindi, MRAC archives; and "A Bruxelles, au Parc du Cinquantenaire," 5063.

38. *L'Étoile Belge* (Brussels), 12 May 1921, edition C; *La Dernière Heure* (Brussels), 12 May 1921, 2nd (morning) edition; and *Inauguration du monument national élevé à la mémoire des Belges morts pour l'œuvre coloniale*, 5–6.

39. "Trentième anniversaire de l'inauguration du Monument aux Troupes des Campagnes d'Afrique"; *Cercle Royal des Anciens Officiers des Campagnes d'Afrique. Bulletin Trimestriel*, no. 3 (September 2000): 7; and *Cercle Royal des Anciens Officiers des Campagnes d'Afrique: Bulletin Trimestriel*, no. 3 (September 1985): 12–13.

40. Gann and Duignan, *Rulers of Belgian Africa*.

41. Guy Malengreau, "Crespel," in BCB, vol. 3, cols. 171–73; and Léon Anciaux, "Thys," in BCB, vol. 4, cols. 875–81.

42. Ascherson, *King Incorporated*, 285–89.

43. Colton, *Léon Blum*, 205–7; and Weber, *Hollow Years*.

44. *Bulletin de l'Association des Vétérans Coloniaux*, no. 2 (3 December 1940); and H. Buttgenbach, "Bia," in BCB, vol. 2, cols. 58–62.

45. In contrast to the post-1989 tearing down of monuments in Eastern Europe. James, "Fencing in the Past."

46. Général Major Hon. P. Jacques (Président, Comité Executif du Monument Bia) to Ministre des Colonies, 22 June 1949; M. Van den Abeele to Jacques, 18 July 1949, no. OC 2/1372; and R. Bagage and A. Moeller de Laddersous (Fonds Colonial de Propagande Economique et Sociale) to Van den Abeele, Administrateur Général des Colonies, 27 July 1949, no. 1038/49. All at portefeuille 483 OC, AA.

47. "Victor Denyn (1867–1924)."

48. Folder 484, UMHK archives, AGR.

49. On local colonial interest groups, see Stanard, "Imperialists without an Empire."

50. Correspondence at portefeuille R61 OC, AA.

51. Author's visit, 15 December 2002.

52. *L'Expansion Coloniale* (Brussels), 15 March 1932, première numéro.

53. Bodnar, *Remaking America*.

54. "Œuvre du souvenir congolais."

55. Closet and Arnold, "A la mémoire de nos morts."

56. "A la Ligue du souvenir congolais."

57. Document 5268.44, box 1, box 52.68, Papiers Emmanuel Muller, MRAC archives.

58. L. Fremault, undated letter, liasse *L'Action Nationale 1924–1939*, Papiers André Van Iseghem, MRAC archives.

59. R. Lavendhomme to President of Fraternelle des Troupes Coloniales 1914–18, 9 February 1951, no. 132/Inf, liasse *29a. Subsides divers 1951*, portefeuille 59 Infopresse, AA.

60. A. Dequae to Pater Vertenten-Comité, 28 May 1951, no. 499/Voorl, liasse *29a. Subsides divers 1952*, portefeuille 59 Infopresse, AA.

61. R. Lavendhomme to Minister of Colonies, 20 November 1951, no. III/10504/1869, liasse *22. Monument Léopold II-Hasselt, Subside de frs. 100,000-B.E. 1952-Art. 5*, portefeuille 59 Infopresse, AA.

62. Arrêté Royal, 18 August 1953, liasse *29a. Subsides 1953. Généralités*, portefeuille 59 Infopresse, AA.

63. F. Mariens and A. Poortman to J. Van den Haute, 10 July 1953, liasse *29a. Subsides 1953. Généralités*, portefeuille 59 Infopresse, AA.

64. Minister of Colonies Buisseret to Major Hon. H. Marquette, 26 July 1956, no. 661/Inf, liasse *32a. Subside Monument Léopold II à Mons*, portefeuille 59 Infopresse, AA. The term "Hennuyers" is one noun used to designate the people from the province of Hainaut, where Mons is located.

65. Portefeuille 62 Infopresse, AA; and C. Duponcheel to Ministry of Colonies, 31 December 1958, liasse *Cercle Colonial Namurois*, portefeuille 62 Infopresse, AA.

66. Axelson, *Culture Confrontation in the Lower Congo*, 218, quoted in Gann and Duignan, *Rulers of Belgian Africa*, 60.

67. "Inhuldiging van het Gedenkteeken Baron Dhanis te Antwerpen."

68. Author's visit, 15 December 2002; *L'Illustration Congolaise*, no. 128 (1 May 1932): 3993; "Journées Coloniales à Mons"; and *L'Illustration Congolaise*, no. 128 (1 May 1932): 3993.

69. Author's visit, 20 February 2003; and "A la Ligue du souvenir congolais."

70. "Histoire du Congo par les monuments."

71. *L'Illustration Congolaise*, nos. 41 and 42 (1 and 15 November 1925): 629; and "Inauguration du monument Le Marinel à l'Université coloniale d'Anvers," quoting *L'Essor Colonial et Maritime.*

72. "Histoire du Congo par les monuments"; and Administration communale, "Musée du Général Thys."

73. Fuks, *Héros et personnages*, 182; and "Histoire du Congo par les monuments."

74. "Inauguration du monument national."

75. *Livre d'or de l'Exposition Internationale Coloniale*, 26, 31, 359.

76. "Ceux qui se souviennent"; Stinglhamber, "Discours prononcé"; "Vingtième anniversaire de la prise de Tabora"; and meeting minutes of the *Commission pour la Commemoration du 50ème Anniversaire de la Fondation de l'État Indépendant du Congo*, 3rd meeting, 12 June 1935, document 57.49.31, Papiers Josué Henry de la Lindi, MRAC archives.

77. *L'Illustration Congolaise*, no. 86 (1 November 1928): 2177.

78. *Congo-Namur*, no. 1 (1947): 21.

79. Carton de Wiart to Joseph de Biolley, 30 October 1926, dossier 235, Fonds cabinet du bourgmestre, Archives de la ville de Bruxelles.

80. *Moniteur Belge*, 12 June 1954, 3729–33.

81. Régie des bâtiments, "Place du Trône"; and Vasagar, "Leopold Reigns for a Day."

82. "Hommage à Léopold II."

83. "Journée du 15 Novembre."

84. Rubbens quoted in *Congo: Revue Générale de la Colonie Belge/Algemeen Tijdschrift van de Belgische Kolonie* 2, no. 1 (June 1937): 99.

85. "Quelques articles parus dans *La Tribune Congolais*," document 5268.3, Papiers Emmanuel Muller, MRAC archives; and Emmanuel Muller to J. Bruneel, 27 January 1947, document 5268.87, Papiers Emmanuel Muller, MRAC archives.

86. Anstey, *King Leopold's Legacy*, 40; and von Albertini, *Decolonization*, 500.

87. [Ministère des colonies, Office colonial], *Exposition des Produits du Congo*, 3.

88. Commissariat général du gouvernement, *Centenaire de l'indépendance.*

89. Ranieri, *Léopold II*, 124.

90. *Cercle des intérêts matériels du Quartier de Linthout Nord-Est*, no. 13 (July 1914): 3; and Houbar and Chevalier Lagasse de Locht to Ministre de l'Agriculture et des Travaux Publics Baron Ruzette, 27 February 1925, no. 9199, dossier 235, Fonds cabinet du bourgmestre, Archives de la ville de Bruxelles.

91. Desonay, *Léopold II, ce géant.*

92. MacDonnell, *Belgium, Her Kings, Kingdom and People*, 286.

93. Carton de Wiart to A. Max, 16 October 1926, dossier 235, Fonds cabinet du bourgmestre, Archives de la ville de Bruxelles.

94. Benedict Anderson, *Imagined Communities.*

95. Cohen, "Symbols of Power."

96. Ramirez and Rolot, "Cinéma colonial belge," 5.

97. Burton, "Who Needs the Nation?"

98. Wilder, "Unthinking French History."

99. Ceuppens, *Congo Made in Flanders?*

100. For literature on the Leopold III controversy, see van den Wijngaert, Beullens, and Brants, *Pouvoir et Monarchie*, 429–31.

101. Mabille, *Histoire politique de la Belgique*, 309–12.

102. Hobsbawm and Ranger, *Invention of Tradition.*

103. Young, "Zaire."

104. Guy Malengreau, "Crespel," in BCB, vol. 3, col. 171.

105. M. Coosemans, "Rochet," in BCB, vol. 2, col. 816.

106. M. Coosemans, "Velghe," in BCB, vol. 1, col. 931.

107. A. Verlinden, "Vandevelde," in BCB, vol. 3, cols. 875–76.

108. A. Lacroix, "Ardevel," in BCB, vol. 1, cols. 28–29; and M. Coosemans, "Lippens," in BCB, vol. 2, cols. 638–40.

109. Meirsschaut, *Sculptures de plein air à Bruxelles.*

110. Pirotte, "Armes d'une mobilisation," 73.

6. Projected Propaganda

1. Reeves, *Power of Film Propaganda*, 4; and Mosley, *Split Screen*, 79.

2. Mosley, *Split Screen*, 31. On Belgian cinema, see Paul Thomas, *Siècle de cinéma belge.*

3. Canty, "European Motion-Picture Industry"; and Mosley, *Split Screen*, 35.

4. Golden, "Short-Subject Film Market of Europe."

5. Golden, *Review of Foreign Film Markets during 1937*, 27, quoted in Trumpbour, "'Death to Hollywood,'" 451.

6. Boulanger, *Cinéma colonial*.

7. Harris, "Who's Got the Power?"

8. The number of films on Ruanda-Urundi pales in comparison to those about the Congo. Ramirez and Rolot, *Histoire*, 227–56.

9. Convent, *Afrique? Quel cinéma!*

10. Haffner, "Entretien avec le Père Alexandre Van den Heuvel."

11. Convents, *Préhistoire*, 94; and Convents, "Jungles van België," 34.

12. Thys, *Belgian Cinema*, 65; and Convents, "Apparition du cinéma en Belgique (1895–1918)," 21–22.

13. Convents, *Préhistoire*, 136; Bolen, *Quand des Belges contaient l'Afrique centrale*, 9; and Thys, *Belgian Cinema*, 65.

14. Convents, "Apparition du cinéma en Belgique (1895–1918)," 18.

15. Convents, "Apparition du cinéma en Belgique (1895–1918)," quoted in Convents, "Des images non occidentales," 54.

16. Convents, *Préhistoire*, 52, 60–61, 76–78, 79, 96.

17. Convents, "Film als politiek instrument," 134; and Convents, "Documentary and Propaganda before 1914," 104.

18. *L'Expansion Belge*, 1909, quoted in Convents, *Préhistoire*, 95; and Thys, *Belgian Cinema*, 65.

19. Convents, *Préhistoire*, 70–76; and Convents, "Film and German Colonial Propaganda."

20. Thys, *Belgian Cinema*, 65–66.

21. Convents, *Préhistoire*, 77–79.

22. Ramirez and Rolot, "Cinéma colonial belge," 5.

23. See, for example, Sojcher, *Kermesse héroïque du cinéma belge*, 25.

24. Fischer, *Germany's Aims in the First World War*, 95–119.

25. Thys, *Belgian Cinema*, 95; and Eksteins, *Rites of Spring*, 76–77.

26. Vints, "Cinéma et propagande," 36.

27. Vints, "Kongo, made in Belgium"; and Vints, "Jungles van België."

28. Ramirez and Rolot, *Histoire*, 20; and Thys, *Belgian Cinema*, 95.

29. Vints, "Cinéma et propagande," 36.

30. Convents, "Apparition du cinéma en Belgique (1895–1918)," 24; and Zuckerman, *Rape of Belgium*.

31. Mosley, *Split Screen*, 35.

32. MacMillan, *Paris*, 98–106; and Sharp, "Mandate System."

33. Ramirez and Rolot, *Histoire*, 21.

34. Mosley, *Split Screen*, 27–65.

35. Thys, *Belgian Cinema*, 187.

36. "Les Films Industriels, Exposé introductif par M. Gustave L. Gérard, Administrateur-directeur général du Comité Central Industriel de Belgique," 5 February 1940, no. GG/HC/884, folder "Foire Internationale de Bruxelles 1940/Exposition 1897/Stand Un. Min. H.-Kat. à l'Exp. Inter. d'Anvers 1930," Papiers André Van Iseghem, MRAC archives.

37. "*Doit*," Schirren to Belgian Congo Colony, 30 May 1939; and Ministry of Colonies, *Bordereau des paiements*, no. 251/Liège. Both at liasse *documents 220.103.31. Paris 1937 Paris-Liege-New York*, portefeuille R98 OC, AA.

38. Thys, *Belgian Cinema*, 189.

39. Mosley, *Split Screen*, 41.

40. Sojcher, *Kermesse héroïque du cinéma belge*, 30–31.

41. Regnault, "Une visite au Musée du Congo Belge," 66.

42. Davay, *Cinéma de Belgique*; and Sojcher, *Kermesse héroïque du cinéma belge*, 31.

43. Lavendhomme to 6e Direction Générale, 2e Direction, Personnel d'Afrique, 5 June 1952, no. 519/Inf, liasse *10a Ciné-Photo 1950*, portefeuille 67 Infopresse, AA; and Diawara, "Sub-Saharan African Film Production."

44. "Note pour le Comité Exécutif," 26 June 1930, liasse *205.812.22. Expos et foires diverses organisées en Belgique. Exposition internationale d'Anvers 1930. 5) Personnel de surveillance*, portefeuille OC 425, AA.

45. André to Van den Haute, 29 October 1952, portefeuille 67 Infopresse, AA.

46. Dobbelaere to Janssen, 14 September 1932, liasse *205.812.22. années 1931–1933. VI Foire Coloniale d'Anvers du 3 au 25 septembre 1932*, portefeuille 432 OC, AA.

47. Journal entries for 16 January 1922 and 13 February 1922, Papiers Jean Fivé, MRAC archives.

48. "Procès-Verbal de la 31ème séance de la Commission du Département près l'Exposition de Bruxelles en 1935," 31 January 1935, p. 2; and "Procès-Verbal de la 33ème séance de la Commission du Département pour la Participation à l'Exposition de Bruxelles en 1935," 7 March 1935, pp. 2–3. Both at liasse *205.812.22. Expos et foires diverses organisées en Belgique. Exposition universelle et internationale de Bruxelles 1935. 1) organisation 5) Commission du Ministère des Colonies près l'exposition de Bruxelles a) procès verbaux des séances*, AA.

49. Trumpbour, *Selling Hollywood to the World*, 213–22; Pius XI, "Vigilanti Cura"; and Brohée and Cartuyvels, *Centre Catholique d'Action Cinématographique*, vii, 31.

50. Quoted in Trumpbour, *Selling Hollywood to the World*, 218.

51. Vints, "Cinéma et propagande," 36; and Mosley, *Split Screen*, 63.

52. Davay, *Cinéma de Belgique*, 84; and Trumpbour, "'Death to Hollywood,'" 504.

53. Ayemba, "Kino in Kongo."

54. Diawara, *African Cinema*, 13–14; and CCACC to Cornil, 22 June 1949, liasse *Information presse. Films en couleurs. Dossier relatif à l'Abbé Cornil très bon cinéaste*, portefeuille 64 Infopresse, AA. The CCACC in turn was tied to the OCIC, which was headquartered in Belgium. OCIC, *Catholiques parlent du cinéma*, 301.

55. Ramirez and Rolot, *Histoire*, 264; OCIC, *Catholiques parlent du cinéma*, 296–301; and Smyth, "Development of British Colonial Film Policy, 1927–1939."

56. Cornil received church support. Archbishop of Mechelen Leclef to Van den Abeele, 19 July 1949, portefeuille 64, AA.

57. Ramirez and Rolot, *Histoire*, 267; Thys, *Belgian Cinema*, 307, 320; invitation for screening at the Palais des Beaux-Arts, liasse *Information presse. Dossier relatif aux activités de Cornil. Le cinéma africain. Projection de films. 1954*, portefeuille 64 Infopresse, AA; and B., "M. l'Abbé Cornil présente ses films."

58. Ramirez and Rolot, *Histoire*, 267; Otten, *Cinéma dans les pays des grands lacs*, 18–21; and OCIC, *Catholiques parlent du cinéma*.

59. J. Magotte, "Note pour Monsieur le Ministre," 7 March 1946, no. OC/1620, liasse *Films Heyman*, portefeuille 64 Infopresse, AA; and Inspecteur

Royal des Colonies C. Dupont, "Note pour Monsieur le Ministre," 27 April 1950, no. 396/Inf., liasse *Mission G. De Boe. Octobre 1950*, portefeuille 64 Infopresse, AA.

60. "Contrat d'Engagement" with André Heyman, liasse *Films Heyman*, portefeuille 64 Infopresse, AA; and Dupont, "Note pour Monsieur le Secrétaire Général," 18 January 1949, p. 1, no. 154/Inf., portefeuille 64 Infopresse, AA. Also Colot to Minister of Colonies, 28 October 1950; Verriest to Ministère des Affaires Étrangères et du Commerce Extérieur, 14 November 1950, no. 1052/Inf.; and Colot to Minister of Colonies, 7 December 1950. All at portefeuille 67 Infopresse, AA.

61. Dupont, "Note pour Monsieur le Secrétaire Général," 18 January 1949, p. 2, no. 154/Inf., portefeuille 64 Infopresse, AA. Also Ramirez and Rolot, *Histoire*, 23.

62. Liasse *Mission G. De Boe. Octobre 1950*, portefeuille 64 Infopresse, AA.

63. Dupont, "Note pour Monsieur le Secrétaire Général," 18 January 1949, no. 154/Inf., portefeuille 64 Infopresse, AA; and "Cinéma pour Indigènes au Congo Belge."

64. Dupont and Bagage to Van den Haute, 13 June 1950, no. 2714/50, liasse *10a Ciné-Photo 1950*, portefeuille 67 Infopresse, AA; and Van Hecke to Governor General, Belgian Congo, 28 October 1949, marked urgent, liasse *Mission G. De Boe*, portefeuille 64 Infopresse, AA.

65. Note by Pétillon, Vice-Gouverneur Général, writing for the Minister, 16 February 1949, no. 489/Inf, liasse *Mission G. De Boe. Octobre 1950*, portefeuille 64 Infopresse, AA.

66. Ramirez and Rolot, *Histoire*, 25, 125.

67. Van Hecke to Governor General of the Congo, 28 October 1949, liasse *Mission G. De Boe. Octobre 1950*, portefeuille 64 Infopresse, AA.

68. Contract for *Mission Cinématographique G. De Boe (1950–1951)*, 29 September 1950, p. 2, portefeuille 64 Infopresse, AA.

69. Gorlia to Governor General of the Congo, 7 March 1947, no. 398/Inf., portefeuille 64 Infopresse, AA.

70. Vanthemsche, *Belgique et le Congo*, 45.

71. Wigny to Governor General, 9 May 1950, no. 431/Inf., portefeuille 64 Infopresse, AA; Davidson, *African Awakening*; and Vanthemsche, *Genèse et portée*.

72. Van den Haute to Administrateur-Directeur, 21 June 1952, no. 550/ Inf., portefeuille 67 Infopresse, AA.

73. Simar to Governor General, 1 December 1947, liasse *Films coloniaux d'Actualités ~ Travaux de Laboratoire Tarifs*, portefeuille 65 Infopresse, AA.

74. Jungers to Minister of Colonies, 5 August 1949, no. 921/32/1839/ 249/I/27, liasse *12a. Photos documentaires et d'actualité. Accords avec Belga + correspondence avec [illegible] 1948 à 1953*, portefeuille 87 Infopresse, AA.

75. Diawara, *African Cinema*, 12–13.

76. Governor General to Minister of Colonies, 10 June 1950, no. 922/16/1523/214/I; Van den Abeele to Cornil, 31 January 1950; and Gorlia to Governor General, 7 March 1947, no. 398/Inf. All at liasse *Information presse. Films en couleurs. Dossier relatif à l'Abbé Cornil très bon cinéaste*, portefeuille 64 Infopresse, AA. Also Bagage and Bours to De Boe, 26 January 1954, folder "C.I.D. Mission G. De Boe," liasse *Mission G. De Boe. Octobre 1950*, portefeuille 64 Infopresse, AA.

77. Higginson, *Working Class in the Making*; and Bernault, "Fin des etats coloniaux."

78. Frederick Cooper, *Africa since 1940*, 63.

79. Engelen, "Een Congolees aan de Franse Rivièra," 268.

80. On colonial information control, see Castryck, "Binnenste-buitenland."

81. Dudley to Gascht, 1 July 1955; Governor General to Minister of Colonies, 16 June 1955, no. 456/Inf.; and Lemborelle to Dudley Pictures Corporation, 31 August 1955, no. M 512/2738. All at liasse *Dudley Pictures Corporation*, portefeuille 65 Infopresse, AA. Also liasse *Film "The African Queen" Romulus Films-Londres*, portefeuille 65 Infopresse, AA.

82. Lemborelle to Governor General, 7 September 1955, no. M 512/2837, liasse *Dudley Pictures Corporation*, portefeuille 65 Infopresse, AA.

83. Van den Abeele to Governor General, 16 June 1950, no. 570/Inf.; and Van den Abeele to Governor General, 8 September 1950, no. 8400/Inf. Both at liasse *Mission G. De Boe. Octobre 1950*, portefeuille 64 Infopresse, AA.

84. See liasse CB. *Information presse. Mission à Léopoldville. M. l'abbé André Cornil. Subsides et frais. Contrat. 1949–1954*, portefeuille 64 Infopresse, AA.

85. Van den Haute, "Note pour Monsieur le Secrétaire Général," 27

September 1946, portefeuille 64 Infopresse, AA. See also Van den Haute to De Boe, 26 October 1946, liasse *Mission De Boe. Travaux complémentaires pour [illegible] montage films*, portefeuille 64 Infopresse, AA.

86. "Films congolais."

87. "'Etonnante Afrique.'"

88. Vanthemsche, *Belgique et le Congo*, 146.

89. Norton, "Pierre Ryckmans (1891–1959)," 405–8.

90. Van den Abeele to Vice Governor General, 8 September 1950, no. 839/ Inf.; and Dupont to Van den Abeele, 3 May 1950, no. 112/64104/652. Both at portefeuille 64 Infopresse, AA.

91. Note by Pierre Fannoy, c. 2 May 1957, liasse *Film "Razzias" de Pierre Fannoy*, portefeuille 65 Infopresse, AA; and J. Van den Haute, "Note pour Monsieur l'Administrateur-Directeur du C.I.D.," 25 May 1950, no. 494/Inf., liasse *Mission G. De Boe. Octobre 1950*, portefeuille 64 Infopresse, AA.

92. Cameron, *Africa on Film*, 56.

93. Ramirez and Rolot, *Histoire*, 105; and Anstey, *King Leopold's Legacy*, 134, 155.

94. Ramirez and Rolot, *Histoire*, 126.

95. Ramirez and Rolot, *Histoire*, 171, 211.

96. *Enseignement et Éducation*, 6; and Gingrich, "Belgian Education Policy," 250.

97. Erny, "Aspects de l'evaluation de l'enseignement colonial belge," 101.

98. Brausch, *Belgian Administration in the Congo*, 27.

99. Ramirez and Rolot, *Histoire*, 212. Ramirez and Rolot quote figures from Coquery-Vidrovitch, "Décolonisation et indépendance en Afrique centrale."

100. Gingrich, "Belgian Education Policy," 249–50.

101. Colot to Minister of Colonies, 28 October 1950, no. 4500/France; and Verriest to Minister of Foreign Affairs, 14 November 1950, no. 1052/Inf. Both at portefeuille 67 Infopresse, AA.

102. Vice Governor of Belgian Congo to Minister of Colonies, 24 February 1950, no. 922/12/416 68/I, portefeuille 64 Infopresse, AA.

103. Buisseret to press firm directors, 6 April 1955, liasse 32. *Belgavox*, portefeuille 87 Infopresse, AA; and Piniau, *Congo-Zaïre 1874–1981*.

104. Convents, *Afrique? Quel cinéma!* 110–11.

105. *Congo: Revue Générale de la Colonie Belge/Algemeen Tijdschrift van de Belgische Kolonie* 1, no. 1 (January 1940): 104.

106. "Note pour le Service de Propagande," 26 January 1931, liasse *205.812.42. Expositions permanents. Exposition du Cercle colonial et maritime de Bruges*, portefeuille 548 OC, AA. Also André to M. l'Administrateur, 6 April 1952; and André to Van den Haute, 29 October 1952. Both at portefeuille 67 Infopresse, AA.

107. CIMES (Cinéma instructif moyen d'éducation STREE) to UMHK, 10 March 1955, folder 476, UMHK archives, AGR; and R. M. Prefete to UMHK, 9 September 1953, folder 475, UMHK archives, AGR.

108. Davay, *Cinéma de Belgique*, 84, 88.

109. Cauvin to Robiliart, 13 November 1954, folder 470, UMHK archives, AGR.

110. Cornil, "Contrat de trois ans avec la Colonie pour la production de films éducatifs pour indigènes," 3 January 1954, liasse *Dossier relatif aux activités de Cornil. Le cinéma africain. Projection de films*, portefeuille 64 Infopresse, AA; and Lombar and Verdussen to Cornil, 19 May 1953, UMHK archives, AGR.

111. Ramirez and Rolot, *Histoire*, 23; and Mosley, *Split Screen*, 57.

112. Paret and Terwagne to Phoebus Films, 16 December 1948, folder 474, UMHK archives, AGR.

113. "Projet de Réalisation de Films dans le Katanga/Kasaï par la Phoebus Films Productions, S.A.," 25 June 1947, folder 474, UMHK archives, AGR.

114. Cameron, *Africa on Film*, 56.

115. Excerpt from *La Gazette de Liège*, 18 April 1947, at portfeuille 64 Infopresse, AA; and André to Monsieur l'Administrateur, 6 April 1952, portefeuille 67 Infopresse, AA.

116. *La Revue Coloniale Belge*, no. 250 (1 March 1956): 159.

117. "Question Parmentaire [sic] No. 24 de M. Dequae, à Monsieur le Ministre des Colonies," 21 June 1955, portefeuille 87 Infopresse, AA.

118. A. De Vleeschauwer, *Ordre de Service/Dienstorder* no. 158, 24 June 1953, liasse *Ciné-Photo 1951–1952–1953*, portefeuille 67 Infopresse, AA; and Bours invitation to Polchet for 20 October 1953, liasse *205.9 III Relations avec les services ou avec l'extèrieur. Divers. Centre d'Information et de Documentation du Congo Belge et du Ruanda-Urundi*, portefeuille 483 OC, AA.

119. *La Revue Coloniale Belge*, no. 247 (15 January 1956): 55; and *La Revue Coloniale Belge*, no. 249 (15 February 1956): 128. See also Simar to Governor General, 25 January 1947, no. 129/Inf; and Simar to Governor General, 6 February 1947, no. 200/Inf. Both at liasse *Films Heyman*, portefeuille 64 Infopresse, AA.

120. Convents, "Des images non occidentales," 66–68; Vints, *Kongo, made in Belgium*, 50–51; and Sluys, *Manuel de la cinématographie scolaire et éducatif*, 7, 60.

121. "Projection de films coloniaux pour les élèves des établissements d'instruction en Belgique," undated, liasse *15a. Projection de films cinématographiques*, portefeuille 17 Infopresse, AA.

122. "Compte-rendu de l'entretien de L. Gillet avec M. Rigot, Directeur du Service Cinématographique du Ministère de l'Instruction Publique," 28 December 1956, folder 476, UMHK archives, AGR.

123. Portefeuille 8 Presse, AA.

124. Reeves, *Power of Film*, 241; and Murray, "Framing Greater France," 239.

125. Ramirez and Rolot, *Histoire*, 56–57. See also Castryck, "Binnenste-buitenland."

126. Engelen, "Een Congolees aan de Franse Rivièra."

127. Ramirez and Rolot, *Histoire*, 135, 216n19.

128. Ramirez and Rolot, *Histoire*, 113.

129. Ramirez and Rolot, *Histoire*, 190–97.

130. Fabian, *Out of Our Minds*.

131. Ramirez and Rolot, *Histoire*, 169–84.

132. Ramirez and Rolot, *Histoire*, 92.

133. Ramirez and Rolot, *Histoire*, 90.

134. Quoted in Ramirez and Rolot, *Histoire*, 101. See also Cauvin, *Bwana kitoko*.

135. "Manifestations coloniales," 584.

136. Ramirez and Rolot, *Histoire*, 133.

137. Ramirez and Rolot, *Histoire*, 171.

138. Ramirez and Rolot, *Histoire*, 103.

139. Convents, *Afrique? Quel cinéma!* 109. The film does show the inauguration of a monument to porters who lost their lives. Ramirez and Rolot, *Histoire*, 93.

140. Ramirez and Rolot, *Histoire*, 147.

141. Ramirez and Rolot, *Histoire*, 99.

142. Quoted in Ramirez and Rolot, *Histoire*, 120.

143. Ramirez and Rolot, *Histoire*, 103–4.

144. Excerpt from *La Gazette de Liège*, 18 April 1947, at portefeuille 64 Infopresse, AA.

145. Slavin, *Colonial Cinema and Imperial France, 1919–1939*, 13.

146. Vellut, "Matériaux pour une image du blanc," 97; Delavignette, *Paysans noirs*; and Betts, *France and Decolonisation*, 30.

147. Ramirez and Rolot, *Histoire*, 136.

148. See also Guy Bara's *Max the Explorer* comic strip in *Le Soir* (Brussels), 5, 17, and 20 June, and 3 July 1958.

149. Ramirez and Rolot, *Histoire*, 200.

150. Sielmann and Brandt, *Seigneurs de la forêt*.

151. Sielmann and Brandt, *Seigneurs de la forêt*. On commentator Max-Pol Fouchet, cf. Thys, *Belgian Cinema*, 374; quote from Convents, *Afrique? Quel cinéma!* 73.

152. Convents, *Afrique? Quel cinéma!* 72–73; Davay, *Cinéma de Belgique*, 51; and De Roover and Weemaes to Buisseret, 17 December 1957, liasse *Fondation Internationale Scientifique*, portefeuille 65 Infopresse, AA.

153. De Roover and Weemaes to Minister of Colonies Buisseret, 17 December 1957, liasse *Fondation Internationale Scientifique*, portefeuille 65 Infopresse, AA.

154. Marlière to Director General of UMHK, 31 May 1945; Boulanger and Jacques to UMHK, 25 March 1947; Cercle Colonial & Maritime (Bruges) to UMHK, 24 October 1949; and Paret to Dubuisson, 25 August 1954, no. 25064. All at folder 475, UMHK archives, AGR.

155. Folders 475 and 476, UMHK archives, AGR.

156. H. Robiliart to H. Schirren, 5 May 1947, and other correspondence in folder 475, UMHK archives, AGR.

157. H. Robiliart to Secretary General, AICB, 2 February 1948, folder 474, UMHK archives, AGR.

158. Folder 476, UMHK archives, AGR.

159. A. Paret and H. Robiliart, "Films sur l'activité sociale de l'U.M.H.K.," 28 November 1953, folder 475, UMHK archives, AGR.

160. M. Fischer and G. Lombar (UMHK Brussels) to Direction Générale d'Afrique, 7 November 1956, folder 471, UMHK archives, AGR.

161. "Film 'Étonnante Afrique,' Diffusion au 31/5/57," folder 471, UMHK archives, AGR.

162. Thys, *Belgian Cinema*, 358.

163. "Remarques concernant le scénario du film à caractère social, commun aux trois sociétés Union Minière-B.C.K.-Forminière" (Elisabethville), 17 March 1955; Comité permanent, "Extrait du Procès-verbal de la 159ème Réunion tenue à Bruxelles le jeudi 24 février 1955," item V.1.a.; and note from UMHK Brussels to UMHK Africa, 8 January 1954. All at folder 470, UMHK archives, AGR.

164. Meeting minutes, Comité du Cinquantenaire, 4 February 1955, folder 470, UMHK archives, AGR.

165. "Entrevue avec Monsieur A. CAUVIN," 10 July 1954, folder 470, UMHK archives, AGR.

166. Service du Contentieux of UMHK, "Note pour le secrétariat de la direction," folder 471, UMHK archives, AGR.

167. Contract, folder 471, UMHK archives, AGR.

168. Detry to colonial minister, 30 December 1959, liasse *Film/divers*, portefeuille 67 Infopresse, AA.

169. Thonnon, *Main dans la main*.

170. Queen Elisabeth, widow of King Albert I.

171. Blondeel, "'Tokende,'" 72.

172. Vints, "Le film missionnaire," 92–105, quote from 101–2, quoted in Blondeel, "'Tokende,'" 73.

173. Blondeel, "'Tokende,'" 75–76.

174. Blondeel, "'Tokende,'" 76–77.

175. Paternostre, *A Work of Civilisation by the Belgians in the Congo*, 49, quoted in Onwumelu, "Congo Paternalism," 152–53.

176. Blondeel, "'Tokende,'" 76–78.

177. Convents, *Afrique? Quel cinéma!* 52.

178. "Tokéndé," 9.

179. Vieyra, *Le cinéma africain*, 104–5, quoted in Diawara, *African Cinema*, 15.

Conclusion

1. *Le National*, 7 July 1897, quoted in Luwel, "Congolezen op de Tentoonstelling van 1897," 44.

2. Dewulf to Van Iseghem, 14 November 1897, folder "Van Iseghem, A. Correspondence 1896, 1897. BW Dewulf, opstand ven de voorwecht ven de Batetela," box 1, Papiers André Van Iseghem, MRAC archives.

3. Corbey, "Ethnographic Showcases," 349.

4. Etambala, "Carnet de route d'un voyageur congolais: Masala à l'Exposition Universelle d'Anvers, en 1885; Première partie"; and Etambala, "Carnet de route d'un voyageur congolais; Masala à l'Exposition Universelle d'Anvers, en 1885; Suite et fin."

5. Mumengi, *Panda Farnana*.

6. Said, *Orientalism*, 3.

7. August, *Selling of the Empire*, 101–5, 160–61.

8. Richards, "Boy's Own Empire"; Murray, "Framing Greater France," 46; and Constantine, "'Bringing the Empire Alive,'" 210.

9. Allina, "'Fallacious Mirrors.'"

10. Bernault, "Fin des etats coloniaux."

11. Greenhalgh, "Education, Entertainment and Politics," 94.

12. August, *Selling of the Empire*, 111.

13. De Batist, "Statistiek overzicht van het museumbezoek en activiteit van de opvoedende dienst."

14. August, *Selling of the Empire*, 117.

15. See MacKenzie, *European Empires and the People*.

16. Betts, *France and Decolonisation*, 7.

17. Poncelet, *Invention des sciences coloniales belges*, 63.

18. Murray, "Framing Greater France," 56–57, 93.

19. Mosley, *Split Screen*, 94–95; and Ramirez and Rolot, *Histoire*, 123.

20. Mosley, *Split Screen*, 43, 45–46.

21. Contract for *Mission Cinématographique G. De Boe (1950–1951)*, 29 September 1950, portefeuille 64 Infopresse, AA.

22. Pabst was German. Boulanger, *Cinéma colonial*, 15, 37.

23. Cameron, *Africa on Film*, passim.

24. "Expédition cinématographique au Congo Belge."

25. Mosley, *Split Screen*, 70.

26. "Note pour Monsieur le Ministre," 27 May 1957, folder "Presse," Papiers Georges Brausch, MRAC archives.

27. Vellut, "Matériaux pour une image du blanc," 99.

28. Vellut, "Episodes anticommunistes."

29. Onwumelu, "Congo Paternalism," 344; and Markowitz, *Cross and Sword*, passim.

30. Cleys et al., "België in Congo, Congo in België," 157. See also Ramirez and Rolot, *Histoire*, 284.

31. Universitair Instituut voor de Overzeese Gebieden/Institut universitaire des territoires d'outre-mer, *Séance Académique/Academische Zitting*, 15–16.

32. Van der Straeten, "Rapport sur les travaux de la Commission d'interpénétration économique de la Belgique."

33. Mommen, *Belgian Economy in the Twentieth Century*, 114; Peemans, "Imperial Hangovers," 257; and Vanthemsche, *Belgique et le Congo*, passim.

34. Benedict, "Rituals of Representation."

35. Penny, "Cosmopolitan Visions and Municipal Displays," 217.

36. *Le National*, 7 July 1897, quoted in Luwel, "Congolezen op de Tentoonstelling van 1897," 44.

37. Jacquemyns and Jacquemyns, "Exposition de 1958," 43.

38. Ageron, "Exposition coloniale de 1931," 584–85.

39. Lebovics, *True France*, 93; and Porter, *Absent-Minded Imperialists*, 213–14.

40. Brausch, *Belgian Administration in the Congo*, 66.

41. Stengers, "Precipitous Decolonization," 335.

42. Ramirez and Rolot, *Histoire*, 123.

43. Harris, "Who's Got the Power?" 222.

44. Boulanger, *Cinéma colonial*, 9.

45. Craig, *Germany 1866–1945*, 397. Of course, other belligerents engaged in film propaganda during World War I as well. On Britain, see Reeves, *Power of Film*, 14–42.

46. Kershaw, *"Hitler Myth."*

47. Nicola Cooper, *France in Indochina*, 20.

48. I would like to thank Jim Diehl for this insight.

49. While improvements were made after 1908, change was slow, and

Belgium received a League of Nations censure in 1926 for inhumane labor practices. Higginson, *Working Class in the Making*, 68. On administrative problems, see Turnbull, *Lonely African*; and Geeraerts, *Gangrene*. On the Congo after 1960, see Young, "Zaire."

50. Jacquemyns, "Congo Belge devant l'opinion publique."

51. Hochschild, *King Leopold's Ghost*, 292–306.

52. Lebovics, *Imperialism and the Corruption of Democracies*, xix.

53. Hall and Rose, "Introduction," 22.

54. Cannadine, *Ornamentalism*, xx.

55. Emphasis in original. Porter, *Absent-Minded Imperialists*, 320.

56. Osborn, "Belgium Exhumes Its Colonial Demons."

57. Roxburgh, "Belgians Confront Colonial Past."

58. Roxburgh, "Belgians Wake Up to the Horror of Colonial Past."

59. UROME/KBUOL, "Site d'étude de la colonisation belge/Site voor de studie van de Belgische colonisatie."

60. Figures from Luwel, "Histoire du Musée royal du Congo Belge à Tervuren," *Congo-Tervueren*, 46; Cuypers, "Museumbezoek in 1977/Visiteurs au musée en 1977," 4; "Statistieken van de bezoeken aan het museum in 1972"; "Statistieken van de bezoeken aan het museum in 1973"; "Statistieken van de bezoeken aan het museum in 1974"; "Statistieken van de bezoeken aan het museum in 1975"; "Statistieken van de bezoeken aan het museum in 1976"; "Statistieken van de bezoeken aan het museum in 1978"; "Statistieken van de bezoeken aan het museum in 1980"; and "Statistieken van de bezoeken aan het museum in 1981."

61. Belien, "King Leopold's Shadow."

62. Mabille, *Histoire politique de la Belgique*, 285; and Brausch, *Belgian Administration in the Congo*, 66.

Bibliography

Archives and Libraries

Archives de la ville de Bruxelles (Brussels)
    Fonds cabinet du bourgmestre, file 235

Archives générales du royaume/Algemeen Rijksarchief (Brussels)
    Archives de l'Exposition Universelle de Bruxelles 1935
    Archives du groupe de l'Union minière

Berry College Memorial Library (Mount Berry, Georgia)

Bibliothèque royale de Belgique Albert Ier/Koninklijke Bibliotheek van België Albert Ier (Brussels)
    Bibliothèque publique
    Section des journaux et périodiques

Cinémathèque royale de Belgique (Brussels)

Indiana University–Bloomington Libraries (Bloomington, Indiana)
    Business/SPEA Library
    Fine Arts Library
    Geography and Map Library
    Herman B. Wells Library
    Kinsey Institute Library

Ministère des affaires économiques de Belgique/Ministerie van Economische Zaken van België (Brussels)

Ministère des affaires étrangères/Ministerie van Buitenlandse Zaken. Archives africaines (Brussels)

4 INUTOM, 2e DG 2/4 no. 4 (3864)

91 INUTOM, 2e DG 2/4 no. 111 (3898) 91

94 INUTOM, 2e DG 2/4 no. 115 (3899) 94

186 INUTOM, 2e DG 2/4 no. 45 (3886) 186

Bibliothèque africaine

D (4675) no. 24

Fonds 3e DG portefeuilles 439–40, Dossier du Président, 546, 658, 796,
     Exposition 1958, 439 Exposition 1958, Président

Info 64

Infopresse 6, 8, 9, 10, 17, 23, 59, 62, 64, 65, 67, 87, 125

OC 396, 412–20, 423, 425, 426, 432–34, 438–40, 442–45, 483, 485, 504,
     548–49, 714, 2030, R61, R92, R97, R98

OC 431 205.812.22. années 1931–33

Presse 7, 17, 118

Musée royal de l'Afrique centrale/Koninklijk Museum voor Midden-Afrika.
Archives historiques privées (Tervuren)
     Papiers André Van Iseghem
     Papiers Emmanuel Muller
     Papiers Félix Fuchs
     Papiers Georges Brausch
     Papiers Georges Rhodius
     Papiers Jean Fivé
     Papiers Josué Henry de la Lindi
     Papiers Paul Closet
     Papiers Pierre Orts
     Papiers Robert Moriamé

Stadsarchief Halle (Hal)
     Baron J. de Dixmude Papers

Wolfsonian-Florida International University (Miami Beach, Florida)

Published Sources

"A Bruxelles, au Parc du Cinquantenaire." *L'Illustration Congolaise*, no. 155
     (1 August 1934).

Administration communale de Dalhem. "Musée du Général Thys." *Site officiel de l'Administration communale.* http://www.dalhem.be/WEBSITE/ BEFR/o9/Tourismeo3.php (accessed 25 April 2011).

"L'Administration du Congo Belge à l'Exposition d'Anvers." *L'Illustration Congolaise*, no. 110 (1 November 1930): 3205–36.

Ageron, Charles-Robert. "L'Exposition Coloniale de 1931: Mythe républicain ou mythe impérial?" In *Les lieux de mémoire*, edited by Pierre Nora, 561–91. Paris: Gallimard, 1984.

"A la foire commerciale: L'exposition coloniale: Des réalisations pratiques." *Les Nouvelles* (La Louvière, Belgium), August 1928.

"A la Ligue du souvenir congolais." *L'Indépendance Belge* (Brussels), 19 February 1931.

Aldrich, Robert. *Greater France: A History of French Overseas Expansion.* New York: St. Martin's Press, 1996.

———. "Putting the Colonies on the Map: Colonial Names in Paris Streets." In Chafer and Sackur, *Promoting the Colonial Idea*, 211–23.

———. *Vestiges of the Colonial Empire in France: Monuments, Museums and Colonial Memories.* Houndsmill, UK: Palgrave, 2005.

"Les Allemands et la question coloniale." *Congo: Revue Générale de la Colonie Belge/Algemeen Tijdschrift van de Belgische Kolonie* 2, no. 1 (June 1927): 81–82.

Allina, Eric. "'Fallacious Mirrors': Colonial Anxiety and Images of African Labor in Mozambique, ca. 1929." *History in Africa* 24 (1997): 9–52.

Ames, Eric, Marcia Klotz, and Lora Wildenthal, eds. *Germany's Colonial Pasts.* Lincoln: University of Nebraska Press, 2005.

Andall, Jacqueline, and Derek Duncan, eds. *Italian Colonialism: Legacy and Memory.* Oxford: Peter Lang, 2005.

Anderson, Benedict. *Imagined Communities: Reflections on the Origin and Spread of Nationalism.* Rev. ed. London: Verso, 1991.

Anderson, David. *Histories of the Hanged: Britain's Dirty War in Kenya and the End of Empire.* London: Weidenfeld and Nicolson, 2005.

Anstey, Roger. *King Leopold's Legacy: The Congo under Belgian Rule 1908–1960.* London: Oxford University Press, 1966.

Antweiler, Werner. "Pacific Exchange Rate Service." University of British Colombia, Sauder School of Business. http://fx.sauder.ubc.ca/ (accessed 20 April 2011).

Arnaut, Karel. "Belgian Memories, African Objects: Colonial Re-collections at the Musée Africain in Namur." *Ateliers* 23 (2001): 29–48.

Arnold, N. "Propagande coloniale à l'école." *La Dernière Heure* (Brussels), 24 July 1932.

Arnoldi, Mary Jo. "Where Art and Ethnology Met: The Ward African Collection at the Smithsonian." In Schildkrout and Keim, *Scramble for Art in Central Africa*, 193–216.

"Les artisans du village Congolais sont retournés chez eux . . ." *La Cité* (Brussels), 27 July 1958.

Ascherson, Neal. *The King Incorporated: Leopold the Second and the Congo.* 1963. Reprint, London: Granta Books, 1999.

Aschmann, Birgit, ed. *Gefühl und Kalkül: Der Einfluss von Emotionen auf die Politik des 19. und 20. Jahrhunderts.* Stuttgart: Franz Steiner, 2005.

"Association de la presse coloniale." *L'Illustration Congolaise*, no. 116 (1 May 1931).

August, Thomas Geoffrey. *The Selling of the Empire: British and French Imperialist Propaganda, 1890–1940.* Westport CT: Greenwood Press, 1985.

"Au Musée de Tervuren: M. Van Hemelryck inaugure l'exposition de documents et archives historiques." *Le Soir* (Brussels), 15 November 1958.

"Au Musée du Congo Belge, in Tervueren, le Mémorial des campagnes antiesclavagistes perpétuera la grande œuvre humanitaire de Léopold II." *La Dernière Heure* (Brussels), 17 October 1959.

"Au palais." *Le Soir* (Brussels), 3 July 1958.

"Au Palais du Congo—La 6me Foire Coloniale d'Anvers." *La Métropole* (Antwerp), 4 September 1932.

AVRUG (Afrika-Vereniging van de Universiteit Gent). "Blankenberge: De Leopoldstraat en het monument van De Bruyne en Lippens." http://cas1.elis .ugent.be/avrug/erfgoed/blankenb/blankenb.htm (accessed 26 May 2010).

———. "Sikitiko: Het ruiterstandbeeld van Leopold II in Oostende." http:// cas1.elis.ugent.be/avrug/erfgoed/sikitiko/sikitiko.htm (accessed 26 May 2010).

Axelson, Sigbert. *Culture Confrontation in the Lower Congo.* Falköping: Gummessons Boktryckeri, 1970.

Ayemba, Julien Enoka. "Kino im Kongo—eine ziemlich lange Geschichte . . ." *AfricAvenir: International African Renaissance, Development,*

International Cooperation and Peace, 2009. http://www.africavenir .org/publications/e-dossiers/koloniale-gespenster/filmgeschichte.html (accessed 16 July 2010).

B., A. "M. l'Abbé Cornil présente ses films." *Courrier d'Afrique*, 12 February 1952.

Balthazar, H., and J. Stengers, eds. *La dynastie et la culture en Belgique*. Antwerp: Fonds Mercator, 1990.

Bancel, Nicolas, Pascal Blanchard, and Françoise Vergès. *La république coloniale*. Paris: Albin Michel, 2003.

Bancel, Nicolas, Pascal Blanchard, Gilles Boëtsch, Éric Deroo, and Sandrine Lemaire, eds. *Zoos humains: De la vénus hottentote aux reality shows*. Paris: La Découverte, 2002.

Banque nationale de Belgique. *Le Franc belge: Monnaies et billets belges depuis 1830*. [Brussels]: Banque nationale de Belgique, 1994.

Barbry, Robert, Jan Dewilde, and Lies Van Rompaey. *Kongo, een tweede vaderland: De kolonie in het onderwijs en het onderwijs in de kolonie (1908–1960)*. Ypres, 1994.

Barringer, Tim, and Tom Flynn, eds. *Colonialism and the Object: Empire, Material Culture, and the Museum*. London: Routledge, 1998.

Bate, Peter. *Congo: White King, Red Rubber, Black Death*. New York: Art Mattan, 2006. DVD.

Bauer, H. W. *Kolonien im Dritten Reich*. 2 vols. Köln-Deutz: Gauverlag Westdeutscher Beobachter, 1936.

Bauer, Ludwig. *Leopold the Unloved: King of Belgians and of Wealth*. Translated by Eden and Cedar Paul. Boston: Little, Brown, 1935.

Belien, Paul. "King Leopold's Shadow." *Wall Street Journal Europe*, 8–11 April 2004, A7.

Bell, David A. "Leopold's Ghost: Belgium's Delusions of Grandeur." *New Republic*, 10 September 2001, 16.

Benedict, Burton. "Rituals of Representation: Ethnic Stereotypes and Colonized Peoples at World's Fairs." In Rydell and Gwinn, *Fair Representations*, 28–61.

Bennett, Tony. "The Exhibitionary Complex." *New Formations* 4 (1988): 73–102.

Berenson, Edward. "Making a Colonial Culture? Empire and the French

Public, 1880–1940." *French Politics, Culture, and Society* 22, no. 2 (Summer 2004): 127–49.

Bernault, Florence. "Fin des etats coloniaux et nouvelles donnes du politique en Afrique équatoriale française." *Itinerario* 23, nos. 3–4 (1999): 136–44.

Betts, Raymond. *France and Decolonisation 1900–1960.* New York: St. Martin's Press, 1991.

Bevel, Maurice Louis. "Causerie." *Le Conseiller Congolais*, September 1933.

"Bezoeken aan het museum." *Congo-Tervuren*, nos. 3 and 4 (July–October 1956): 123.

Biebuyck, Daniel P. "Olbrechts and the Beginnings of Professional Anthropology in Belgium." In Petridis, *Frans M. Olbrechts 1899–1958*, 102–13.

"Bij de opening van het Congopaleis." *Antwerpen 1930*, 24 May 1930.

Binkley, David A., and Patricia J. Darish. "'Enlightened but in Darkness': Interpretations of Kuba Art and Culture at the Turn of the Twentieth Century." In Schildkrout and Keim, *Scramble for Art in Central Africa*, 37–62.

Biographie belge d'outre-mer/Belgische overzeese biografie. 2 vols. Brussels: Académie royale des sciences d'outre-mer/Koninklijk Academie voor Overzeese Wetenschappen, 1968, 1973.

Biographie coloniale belge/Belgische koloniale biografie. 3 vols. Brussels: Institut royal colonial belge/Koninklijk Belgisch Koloniaal Instituut, 1948–52.

Biographie coloniale belge/Belgische koloniale biografie. 2 vols. Brussels: Académie royale des sciences coloniales/Koninklijk Academie voor Koloniale Wetenschappen, 1955, 1958.

Birmingham, David, and Phyllis M. Martin, eds. *History of Central Africa: The Contemporary Years since 1960.* London: Longman, 1998.

Blanchard, Pascal, and Sandrine Lemaire, eds. *Culture coloniale: La France conquise par son empire 1871–1931.* Paris: Autrement, 2003.

———, eds. *Culture impériale 1931–1961: Les colonies au cœur de la république.* Paris: Autrement, 2004.

Blondeel, W. "'Tokende': Een missie-beeld voor Expo '58." In *Recueil d'études "Congo 1955–1960"/Verzameling studies "Congo 1955–1960,"* 71–80. Brussels: Académie royale des sciences d'outre-mer/Koninklijke Academie voor Overzeese Wetenschappen, 1992.

"Une blonde hôtesse du pavillon des mines se souviendra longtemps de la visite du Roi à la section du Congo." *La Meuse* (Liege), 13 May 1958.

Bodnar, John. *Remaking America: Public Memory, Commemoration, and Patriotism in the Twentieth Century*. Princeton NJ: Princeton University Press, 1992.

Bolen, Francis. *Quand des Belges contaient l'Afrique centrale*. Paris: Agence de cooperation culturelle et technique (ACCT), n.d.

Boulanger, Pierre. *Le cinéma colonial de "l'Atlantide" à "Lawrence d'Arabe."* Paris: Éditions Seghers, 1975.

Bouquet, Mary, ed. *Academic Anthropology and the Museum: Back to the Future*. New York: Berghahn Books, 2001.

Bouquet, Mary, and Nuno Porto, eds. *Science, Magic, and Religion: The Ritual Processes of Museum Magic*. New York: Berghahn Books, 2005.

Bouttiaux, Anne-Marie. "Des mises en scène de curiosités aux chefs-d'œuvre mis en scène: Le Musée royal de l'Afrique à Tervuren; Un siècle de collections." *Cahiers d'Études Africaines, Nos. 155–56* 39, nos. 3–4 (1999): 595–616.

———. "Un siècle de pillage culturel à Tervuren?" Belgium's Africa Conference. http://africana.rug.ac.be/texts/Belgiumsafrica/Programme2.htm (accessed 15 April 2004).

Bradford, Phillips Verner, and Harvey Blume. *Ota: The Pygmy in the Zoo*. New York: St. Martin's Press, 1992.

Brausch, Georges. *Belgian Administration in the Congo*. London: Oxford University Press, 1961.

Breckenridge, Carol. "The Aesthetics and Politics of Colonial Collecting: India at World Fairs." *Comparative Studies in Society and History* 31, no. 1 (January 1989): 195–216.

Brohée, Chanoine, and Abbé Cartuyvels. *Centre catholique d'action cinématographique*. Brussels: Secrétariat général, Imprimerie Saint-Alphonse, n.d.

Bruxelles et l'Exposition — 1910 — Brussel en de Tentoonstelling. Antwerp: Van Os/De Wolf, n.d.

Bruxelles 1935. Uccle-Brussels: René Lyr/Éditions nationales, 1935.

Bucur, Maria, and Nancy M. Wingfield, eds. *Staging the Past: The Politics of Commemoration in Habsburg Central Europe, 1848 to the Present*. West Lafayette IN: Purdue University Press, 2001.

Burton, Antoinette, ed. *After the Imperial Turn: Thinking with and through the Nation*. Durham NC: Duke University Press, 2005.

———. "Who Needs the Nation? Interrogating 'British' History." In Hall, *Cultures of Empire*, 137–53.

Cahen, L. "Le musée dans le présent et dans l'avenir." *Belgique d'Outremer*, no. 289 (April 1959): 213–14.

Cameron, Kenneth M. *Africa on Film: Beyond Black and White*. New York: Continuum, 1994.

Cannadine, David. *Ornamentalism*. Oxford: Oxford University Press, 2001.

Canty, George R. "The European Motion-Picture Industry in 1.928 [*sic*]." In Department of Commerce, Bureau of Foreign and Domestic Commerce, *Trade Information Bulletin*, no. 617. Washington DC: U.S. Government Printing Office, 1929.

Capiteyn, André. *Gent in weelde herboren: Wereldtentoonstelling 1913*. Ghent: Stadsarchief [City Archives], Gent, 1988. Published in conjunction with an exhibition shown at the Center for Arts and Culture, St. Peter's Abbey, Ghent, 7 October–11 December 1988.

Carrol, Alison. "The 1924 Colonial Exhibition in Strasbourg." Paper presented at the annual meeting of the French Colonial Historical Society, San Francisco CA, 29 May 2009.

Castryck, Geert. "Binnenste-buitenland: De Belgische kolonie en de Vlaamse buitenlandberichtgeving." In Viaene, Van Reybrouck, and Ceuppens, *Congo in België*, 271–81.

———. "Whose History Is History? Singularities and Dualities of the Public Debate on Belgian Colonialism." In Lévai, *Europe and the World in European Historiography*, 71–88.

Catherine, Lucas. "Jubelpark: Het Congo-monument van Vinçotte." Afrika-Vereniging van de Universiteit Gent. http://cas1.elis.ugent.be/avrug/erf goed/jubel/lc.htm (accessed 20 May 2010).

Cattier, Félicien. *Étude sur la situation de l'État Indépendant du Congo*. 2nd ed. Brussels: Vve F. Larcier, 1906.

Cauvin, André. *Bwana kitoko: Un livre réalisé au cours du voyage du Roi des Belges au Congo et dans le Ruanda-Urundi*. Paris: Elsevier, 1956.

"La Celebrazione della Giornata Coloniale." *L'Italia Coloniale*, no. 5 (May 1926): 84.

Çelik, Zeynep. *Displaying the Orient: Architecture of Islam at Nineteenth-Century World's Fairs*. Comparative Studies on Muslim Societies 12. Berkeley: University of California Press, 1992.

Centrum voor Religieuze Kunst en Cultuur. "Etnografie." http://www.crkc
.be/site/128.html (accessed 31 May 2010).

"Cercle africain des Ardennes." *L'Expansion Coloniale* (Brussels), 15 March
1932, première numéro.

"Une cérémonie à l'Université coloniale d'Anvers." *L'Illustration Congolaise*,
no. 135 (December 1932).

Ceuppens, Bambi. *Congo Made in Flanders? Koloniale Vlaamse visies op
"blank" en "zwart" in Belgisch Congo*. Ghent: Academia Press, 2003.

———. "Een Congolese kolonie in Brussel." In Viaene, Van Reybrouck, and
Ceuppens, *Congo in België*, 231–50.

"Ceux qui se souviennent: L'hommage à Léopold II." *L'Essor Colonial et
Maritime* (Brussels), 22 November 1936.

Chafer, Tony, and Amanda Sackur. *Promoting the Colonial Idea: Propaganda and Visions of Empire in France*. Basingstoke, UK: Palgrave, 2001.

"Changwe Yetu war das Ereignis des 77. Expo-Tages." *Grenz-Echo* (Eupen),
2 July 1958.

"Le cinéma pour Indigènes au Congo Belge." *Echo du Kivu*, 9 June 1950.

*5me [Cinquième] Foire Coloniale/5de Koloniale Jaarbeurs/5th Colonial Fair
of Antwerp: Catalogue officiel*. [Antwerp]: Foire Coloniale d'Anvers,
[1928].

Cleys, Bram, Jan De Maeyer, Carine Dujardin, and Luc Vints. "België in
Congo, Congo in België: Weerslag van de missionering op de religieuze
instituten." In Viaene, Van Reybrouck, and Ceuppens, *Congo in België*,
147–66.

Clifford, James. *The Predicament of Culture: Twentieth-Century Ethnography, Literature, and Art*. Cambridge MA: Harvard University Press, 1988.

———. *Routes: Travel and Translation in the Late Twentieth Century*. Cambridge MA: Harvard University Press, 1997.

Closet, Paul, and N. Arnold. "A la mémoire de nos morts." *L'Essor Colonial*,
31 December 1933.

CoBelCo. "Questions aux écrivains: Boris Wastiau." http://www.cobelco
.info/Interviews/interviewsfs.htm (accessed 25 April 2011).

Cockx, A., and J. Lemmens. *Les Expositions Universelles et Internationales
en Belgique de 1885 à 1958*. Brussels: Editorial Office, 1958.

Codell, Julie F., and Dianne Sachko Macleod, eds. *Orientalism Transposed:*

The Impact of the Colonies on British Culture. Aldershot, UK: Ashgate, 1998.

Cohen, William B., ed. *European Empire Building: Nineteenth-Century Imperialism.* Arlington Heights IL: Forum Press, 1980.

———. "Symbols of Power: Statues in Nineteenth-Century Provincial France." *Comparative Studies in Society and History* 31, no. 3 (July 1989): 491–513.

Cole, Robert. *Propaganda in Twentieth Century War and Politics: An Annotated Bibliography.* Lanham MD: Scarecrow Press, 1996.

"Colonisation blanche." *Congo: Revue Générale de la Colonie Belge/Algemeen Tijdschrift van de Belgische Kolonie* 1, no. 4 (April 1937): 456–57.

Colton, Joel. *Léon Blum: Humanist in Politics.* New York: Alfred A. Knopf, 1966.

Comité exécutif de l'Exposition, ed. *Le livre d'or de l'Exposition Universelle et Internationale de Bruxelles 1935.* [Brussels]: Société de l'Exposition Universelle et Internationale de Bruxelles 1935, n.d.

Commissariat général du gouvernement. *Centenaire de l'indépendance: Exposition Internationale, Coloniale, Maritime et d'Art Flamand Anvers 1930: Réglement de la Section Belge.* Antwerp: E. Stockmans, 1928.

"La Commission de propagande coloniale scolaire." *L'Illustration Congolaise,* no. 185 (1 February 1936): 6242.

"Le Concours Colonial Scolaire 1931–1932." *La Métropole* (Antwerp), 27 July 1932.

"Conférences et manifestations coloniales." *L'Essor Colonial et Maritime* (Brussels), 1930.

"Le Congo, trésor envié." *L'Écho du Centre,* no. 2817 (29 January 1954): 4.

"Le Congo, trésor envié." *Feuille d'Annonces,* no. 5 (31 January 1954): 2.

"Le Congo à l'Exposition de 1935." *L'Illustration Congolaise,* no. 156 (1 September 1934).

Le Congo à l'Exposition Universelle d'Anvers, 1894: Catalogue de la Section de l'État Indépendant du Congo. Brussels: O. de Rycker et Cie, [1894].

Le Congo Belge: Résumé historique, économique et géographique: Préparation aux carrières coloniales/Belgisch-Congo: Beknopt geschiedkundig, economisch en aardrijkskundig overzicht: Voorbereiding tot de koloniale loopbanen. Brussels: Lesigne, 1923.

Le Congo Belge et ses coloniaux: Livre d'or/Belgisch Kongo en zijn kolonialen: Gulden boek. Léopoldville, Belgian Congo: Editions Stanley, 1953.

Congo Paleis; Antwerpen, Anvers; VI Koloniale Jaarbeurs/Foire Coloniale 3 tot/à 25 September/Septembre 1932: Kataloog/Catalogue. [Antwerp, 1932].

"CONGORAMA: Nous fait vivre dans l'Afrique mystérieuse." *Le Soir* (Brussels), 10 July 1958.

Connelly, Mark, and David Welch, eds. *War and the Media: Reportage and Propaganda, 1900–2003.* London: I. B. Tauris, 2005.

Constantine, Stephen. "'Bringing the Empire Alive': The Empire Marketing Board and Imperial Propaganda, 1926–33." In MacKenzie, *Imperialism and Popular Culture*, 192–231.

Convents, Guido. *L'Afrique? Quel cinéma! Un siècle de propagande coloniale et de films africains.* Antwerp: EPO, 2003.

———. "L'apparition du cinéma en Belgique (1895–1918)." *Les Cahiers de la Cinémathèque: Revue d'Histoire du Cinéma*, no. 41 (Winter 1984): 14–26.

———. "Des images non occidentales au cœur de l'Europe avant la Première Guerre Mondiale: En Belgique, par example." In Cosandey and Albera, *Cinéma sans frontières 1896–1918/Images across Borders*, 50–72.

———. "Documentary and Propaganda before 1914." *Framework*, no. 35 (1988): 104–13.

———. "Film als politiek instrument: Een medium in handen van kolonialen en katholieken in België, 1896–1914." In Kleijer, Knotter, and van Vree, *Tekens en teksten*, 131–43.

———. "Film and German Colonial Propaganda for Black African Territories to 1918." Translated by Barrie Ellis-Jones. In Usai and Codelli, *Before Caligari*, 58–77.

———. "Jungles van België: Film en koloniale propaganda 1897–1918." *Skrien*, May–June 1982, 32–37.

———. *Préhistoire du cinéma en Afrique 1897–1918: A la recherche des images oubliées.* Brussels: OCIC, 1986.

Coombes, Annie E. "Museums and the Formation of National and Cultural Identities." *Oxford Art Journal* 11, no. 2 (1988): 57–68.

———. *Reinventing Africa: Museums, Material Culture and Popular*

Imagination in Late Victorian and Edwardian England. New Haven CT: Yale University Press, 1994.

Cooper, Frederick. *Africa since 1940: The Past of the Present.* Cambridge: Cambridge University Press, 2002.

———. *Colonialism in Question: Theory, Knowledge, History.* Berkeley: University of California Press, 2005.

Cooper, Nicola. *France in Indochina: Colonial Encounters.* Oxford: Berg, 2001.

Coquery-Vidrovitch, Catherine. "Décolonisation et indépendence en Afrique centrale." In Deschamps, *Histoire générale de l'Afrique noire,* 515–50.

Corbey, Raymond. "Ethnographic Showcases, 1870–1930." *Cultural Anthropology* 8, no. 3 (August 1999): 338–69.

———. "*EXITCONGOMUSEUM*: The Travels of Congolese Art." *Anthropology Today* 17, no. 3 (June 2001): 26–28.

Corijn, H. *Algemene en nationale geschiedenis. I–II: De nieuwe en niuewste tijden.* Liège: Dessain, 1951.

Corneli, René. *Antwerpen und die Weltausstellung 1885.* German edition by Adolf Liederwald and Karl Fr. Pfau. Leipzig: Verlag von Karl Fr. Pfau, 1887.

Cornevin, Robert. *Histoire du Congo (Léopoldville).* Paris: Éditions Berger-Levrault, 1963.

Cosandey, Roland, and François Albera, eds. *Cinéma sans frontières 1896–1918/Images across Borders: Aspects de l'internationalité dans le cinéma mondial: Représentations, marchés, influences et réception/Internationality in World Cinéma: Representations, Markets, Influences and Reception.* Quebec: Nuit Blanche Editeur/Payot Lausanne, 1995.

Couttenier, Maarten. *Congo tentoongesteld: Een geschiedenis van de Belgische antropologie en het Museum van Tervuren (1882–1925).* Leuven: Acco, 2005.

———. "De impact van Congo in het Museum van Belgisch Congo in Tervuren (1897–1946)." In Viaene, Van Reybrouck, and Ceuppens, *Congo in België,* 115–30.

———. *Si les murs pouvaient parler: Le Musée de Tervuren 1910–2010.* Tervuren: Royal Museum of Central Africa, 2010.

Craig, Gordon A. *Germany 1866–1945.* New York: Oxford University Press, 1978.

Cuypers, J.-B. "Het museumbezoek in 1977/Les visiteurs au musée en 1977." *Africa-Tervuren* 24, no. 1 (1978): 1–5.

"Dans les cercles coloniaux: Cercle africain Borain." *L'Expansion Coloniale* (Brussels), 10 August 1936.

Davay, Paul. *Cinéma de Belgique*. Gembloux, Belgium: J. Duculot, 1973.

Davidson, Basil. *The African Awakening*. London: Jonathan Cape, 1955.

Davis, Bruce. "Maps on Postage Stamps as Propaganda." *Cartographic Journal* 22, no. 2 (December 1985): 125–30.

Debaere, C., and N. Piret. *Nieuwe en nieuwste geschiedenis. Met talrijke platen, kaarten, leesstukken en toepassingen. Leerboek der algemeene geschiedenis ten gebruike van het middelbaar onderwijs en het lager normaalonderwijs. III.* 2nd ed. Liège: H. Dessain, 1927.

De Baets, Antoon. *De figuranten van de geschiedenis: Hoe het verleden van andere culturen wordt verbeeld en in herinnering gebracht*. Berchem: EPO, 1994.

———. "Metamorphoses d'une epopée: Le Congo dans les manuels d'histoire employés dans nos écoles." In Jacquemin, *Racisme, continent obscur*, 45–58.

De Batist, G. "Statistiek overzicht van het museumbezoek en activiteit van de opvoedende dienst." *Africa-Tervuren* 11, no. 1 (1965): 3, 10.

Debrunner, Hans W. *Presence and Prestige, Africans in Europe: A History of Africans in Europe before 1918*. Basel, Switzerland: Basler Afrika Bibliographien, 1979.

de Burbure, A. "Expositions et sections congolaises." *Belgique d'Outremer*, no. 286 (January 1959): 27–29.

de Cock, André. *Le Congo Belge et ses marques postales*. 1931. 2nd ed., reprint Antwerp: R-Editions, 1986.

Degrijse, O. "La Belgique et les missions." *Eglise et Mission* 237 (March 1985): 3–9.

de Haulleville, Baron A. *Le Musée du Congo Belge à Tervuren*. Brussels: A. Lesigne, 1910.

———. "Le Musée du Congo Belge à Tervueren." *La Revue Congolaise* 1, no. 5 (1910): 208–25.

De Keyser, R. "Belgisch-Kongo in den belgischen Geschichtslehrbüchern." In Fürnrohr, *Afrika im Geschichtsunterricht europäischer Länder*, 152–71.

Delafosse, M. "Une opinion française sur l'Université coloniale d'Anvers." *Congo: Revue Générale de la Colonie Belge/Algemeen Tijdschrift van de Belgische Kolonie* 1, no. 1 (January 1925): 127–28.

Delavignette, Robert. *Les paysans noirs*. Paris, 1946.

de Lichtervelde, Comte Louis. *Léopold of the Belgians*. Translated by Thomas H. Reed and H. Russell Reed. New York: Century, 1929.

Delwit, Pascal, and José Gotovitch, eds. *La peur du rouge*. Brussels: Université de Bruxelles, 1996.

De Meersman, M., and D. Vangroenweghe. *The Royal Museum for Central Africa, Tervuren*. [Tervuren, Belgium: Musée royal de l'Afrique centrale], 1992.

de Meyer, Roger. *Introducing the Belgian Congo and the Ruanda-Urundi*. Brussels: Office de publicité, 1958.

Deocampo, Nick. "Imperialist Fictions: The Filipino in the Imperialist Imaginary." *Bulletin of the American Historical Collection* 27, no. 4 (1999): 47–60.

Depaepe, Marc. "Belgian Images of the Psycho-pedagogical Potential of the Congolese during the Colonial Era, 1908–1960." *Paedagogica Historica* 45, no. 6 (December 2009): 707–25.

————. *Order in Progress: Everyday Educational Practice in Primary Schools–Belgium, 1880–1970*. In cooperation with K. Dams, M. De Vroede, B. Eggermont, H. Lauwers, F. Simon, R. Vandenberghe, and J. Verhoeven. Leuven: Leuven University Press, 2000.

Depoorter, Roger. *Le Commandant Charles Lemaire: Pionnier et pedagogue 1863–1926/Kommandant Charles Lemaire: Pionier en pedagoog 1863–1926*. Antwerp: Fondation royale des amis de l'INUTOM/Koninklijk vriendenfonds van het UNIVOG, 1985.

Deschamps, Hubert, ed. *Histoire générale de l'Afrique noire*. Vol. 2. Paris: PUF, 1971.

Desonay, Fernand. *Léopold II, ce géant*. Paris: Casterman, 1936.

"La IIe [Deuxième] Foire Coloniale." *Le Matin* (Antwerp), 13 June 1949.

Deville, Françoise. "L'Exposition Universelle et Internationale du Heysel de 1935, ensorcellement des masses." In *Bruxelles: Art déco 1920–1930*, 130–41. Brussels: Fondation pour l'architecture, [1996]. Exhibition catalog.

De Witte, Ludo. *The Assassination of Lumumba.* Translated by Ann Wright and Renée Fenby. London: Verso, 2001.

Diawara, Manthia. *African Cinema: Politics and Culture.* Bloomington: Indiana University Press, 1992.

———. "Sub-Saharan African Film Production: Technological Paternalism." *Jump Cut: A Review of Contemporary Media,* no. 32 (April 1987): 61–65. http://www.ejumpcut.org/archive/onlinessays/JC32folder/Subsaharan FilmDiawara.html (accessed 27 May 2010).

Dictionnaire d'histoire de Belgique: Les hommes, les institutions, les faits, le Congo belge et le Ruanda-Urundi. Under direction of Hervé Hasquin. 2nd ed. Namur: Didier Hatier, 2000.

Dictionnaire d'histoire de Belgique: Vingt siècles d'institutions, les hommes, les faits. Under direction of Hervé Hasquin. Brussels: Didier Hatier, 1988.

Dierickx, M. *Geschiedenis van België.* 4th ed. Antwerp: De Nederlandsche Boekhandel, 1960.

"Un discours de M. le Ministre des Colonies." *Congo: Revue Générale de la Colonie Belge/Algemeen Tijdschrift van de Belgische Kolonie* 2, no. 2 (December 1920): 374–76.

Doom, Ruddy. "De wereldtentoonstellingen en de koloniale propaganda" and "The World Exhibitions and Colonial Propaganda." In *De panoramische droom/The Panoramic Dream: Antwerpen en de wereldtentoonstellingen/Antwerp and the World Exhibitions 1885, 1894, 1930,* 195–207. Antwerp: Antwerp 93, 1993.

Dorchy, H. *Histoire des Belges des origines à 1940.* Brussels: A. De Boeck, 1948.

———. *Histoire des Belges des origines à 1981.* 6th ed. Brussels: A. De Boeck, 1982.

Drèze, Gustave. *Le livre d'or de l'Exposition Universelle et Internationale de Liège 1905: Histoire complète de l'Exposition de Liège.* Vol. 2. Liège: Imp. Aug. Bénard, 1907.

Dujardin, Francis. *Boma–Tervuren, le voyage (de juin à septembre 1897).* Brussels: COBRA Films, 1999. DVD.

Dumont, Georges-Henri. *Léopold II.* N.p.: Fayard, 1990.

Dunn, Kevin C. *Imagining the Congo: The International Relations of Identity.* New York: Palgrave Macmillan, 2003.

d'Ydewalle, Charles. "Tout le Congo au Heysel." *Le Soir* (Brussels), 3 August 1958.

École coloniale; fondée en 1904. Brussels: Ministère des colonies, 1957.

Edgerton, Robert B. *The Troubled Heart of Africa: A History of the Congo.* New York: St. Martin's Press, 2002.

Eerste Koloniale Boekententoonstelling Antwerpen/Première Exposition du Livre Colonial Anvers. 1932. Antwerp: E. Stockmans, [1932].

Eksteins, Modris. *Rites of Spring: The Great War and the Birth of the Modern Age*. Boston: Houghton Mifflin, 1989.

Elkins, Caroline. *Imperial Reckoning: The Untold Story of Britain's Gulag in Kenya*. New York: Henry Holt, 2005.

Emerson, Barbara. *Léopold II: Le royaume et l'empire*. Translated by Hervé Douxchamps and Gérard Colson. Paris: Éditions Duculot, 1980.

———. *Leopold II of the Belgians: King of Colonialism*. New York: St. Martin's Press, 1979.

Emmer, P. C., and H. L. Wesseling, eds. *Reappraisals in Overseas History*. Translated by Frank Perlin. The Hague: Leiden University Press, 1979.

Engelen, Leen. "Een Congolees aan de Franse Rivièra: Het 'succesverhaal' van *Bongolo en de negerprinses* (1952)." In Viaene, Van Reybrouck, and Ceuppens, *Congo in België*, 253–70.

Enseignement et éducation au Congo Belge et au Ruanda-Urundi. Brussels: Exposition Universelle et Internationale de Bruxelles, 1958.

Erny, Pierre. "Aspects de l'evaluation de l'enseignement colonial belge." *Revue Zaïroise de Psychologie et de Pédagogie* 3, no. 1 (July 1974): 93–106.

Etambala, Zana Aziza. "Antwerp and the Colony, from 1885 until ca. 1920." In *De panoramische droom/The Panoramic Dream: Antwerpen en de wereldtentoonstellingen/Antwerp and the World Exhibitions 1885, 1894, 1930*. Antwerp: Antwerp 93, 1993.

———. "Carnet de route d'un voyageur congolais: Masala à l'Exposition Universelle d'Anvers, en 1885; Première partie." *Afrika Focus* 9, no. 3 (1993): 215–37.

———. "Carnet de route d'un voyageur congolais: Masala à l'Exposition Universelle d'Anvers, en 1885; Suite et fin." *Afrika Focus* 10, nos. 1–2 (1994): 3–28.

"'Etonnante Afrique,' un film de Gerard De Boe." *La Revue Coloniale Belge*, no. 262 (December 1956): 912.

Ewans, Martin. "Belgium and the Colonial Experience." *Journal of Contemporary European Studies* 11, no. 2 (November 2003): 167–80.

"Une expédition cinématographique au Congo Belge." *Courrier d'Afrique*, 20 October 1950.

"L'exportation au Congo vue de l'Exposition de Bruxelles." *L'Illustration Congolaise*, no. 166 (1 July 1935).

"Exposition à l'oc du matériel électrique de construction belge." *Electricité, Eau, Éclairage, Chauffage, TSF Revue Mensuelle*, no. 3 (March 1926).

Exposition Coloniale d'Arlon. Arlon: J. Fasbender, [1935].

"Exposition Coloniale de Namur." *Vers l'Avenir* (Namur, Belgium), 29 May 1925.

"L'exposition du peintre Pierre de Vaucleroy." *La Revue Coloniale Belge*, no. 256 (1 June 1956): 402.

Exposition Internationale Bruxelles 1910. Brussels: Éditions H. Waldman and E. Defroidment, [1910].

Exposition Internationale Coloniale, Maritime et d'Art Flamand Anvers 1930: Palais du Congo Belge: Guide officiel. Brussels: Établissements généraux d'imprimerie, [1930].

Exposition Universelle de Bruxelles 1935: Guide officiel, officiel gids: Brussel 1935. Brussels: Marcel van der Donck, 1935.

L'Exposition Universelle et Internationale de Bruxelles, 1935. Quelques données, quelques chiffres. Algemeene Wereldtentoonstelling Brussel 1935: Enkele inlichtigen, enkele cijfers. Allgemeine und Internationale Weltausstellung Brussel 1935: Einige Angaben, einige Zahlen. The Brussels Universal and International Exhibition 1935: Some Facts and Figures. Brussels: Impr. E. Guyot, 1935.

Exposition Universelle et Internationale de Gand en 1913: Catalogue-Guide de la Section Coloniale Belge et du Panorama du Congo/Wereld- en Internationale Tentoonstelling te Gent in 1913: Catalogus-Leidraad voor de Belgische Koloniale Afdeeling en voor het Panorama van Congo. Brussels: Imp. A. Lesigne, 1913.

Exposition Universelle et Internationale de Gand en 1913. Programme général. Appel aux producteurs. Règlement-classification. Brussels: Imprimerie moderne, E. et H. Mertens, 1911.

Exposition Universelle et Internationale de Gand 1913. Commissariat général du gouvernement. Section Belge. Appel aux producteurs. Règlement spécial. Classification/Algemeene Wereldtentoonstelling te Gent in 1913. Algemeen commissariaat der regeering. Belgische Afdeeling. Oproep tot de voortbrengers. Bijzondere verordering. Klasse-indeeling. Brussels: L. Wintraecken, 1912.

Fabian, Johannes. *Out of Our Minds: Reason and Madness in the Exploration of Central Africa.* Berkeley: University of California Press, 2000.

"La fédération pour la colonisation nationale." *Congo: Revue Générale de la Colonie Belge/Algemeen Tijdschrift van de Belgische Kolonie* 1, no. 3 (March 1923): 372.

Ferguson, Niall. *Empire: The Rise and Demise of the British World Order and the Lessons for Global Power.* New York: Basic Books, 2002.

Fetter, Bruce. *The Creation of Elisabethville 1910–1940.* Stanford: Hoover Institution Press, 1976.

———. "Martin Rutten (1876–1944)." In Gann and Duignan, *African Proconsuls,* 374–90.

"Films congolais." *La Métropole* (Antwerp), 23 April 1947.

Findling, John E., ed. *Historical Dictionary of World's Fairs and Expositions, 1851–1988.* New York: Greenwood Press, 1990.

Findling, John E., and Kimberly D. Pelle, eds. *Encyclopedia of World's Fairs and Expositions.* Jefferson NC: MacFarland, 2008.

Fischer, Fritz. *Germany's Aims in the First World War.* New York: W. W. Norton, 1967.

Flynn, Tom. "Taming the Tusk: The Revival of Chryselephantine Sculpture in Belgium during the 1890s." In Barringer and Flynn, *Colonialism and the Object,* 188–204.

Fogarty, Richard S. *Race and War in France: Colonial Subjects in the French Army, 1914–1918.* Baltimore: Johns Hopkins University Press, 2008.

"La foire coloniale." *L'Echo de la Bourse,* 11–13 June 1949.

"La Foire Coloniale d'Anvers." *La Revue Coloniale Belge,* no. 222 (1 January 1955).

"Foire Industrielle et Commerciale de la Louvière du 28 juillet au 16 août." *Les Nouvelles* (La Louvière, Belgium), 29–30 July 1928.

Fondation de l'Université coloniale/Stichting van de Koloniale Hoogeschool. [Brussels]: Ministère des Colonies, 1923.

Fondation royale des amis de l'Institut universitaire des territoires d'outre-mer/Vriendenfonds van het Universitair Instituut voor de Overzeese Gebieden. *Middelheim: Mémorial de l'Institut universitaire des territoires d'outre-Mer/Gedenkboek van het Universitair Institut van de Overzeese Gebieden.* N.p.: Rossel Edition, 1987.

Foutry, Vita. "Belgisch-Kongo tijdens het interbellum: Een immigratie-beleid gericht op sociale controle." *Belgisch Tijdschrift voor Nieuwste Geschiedenis/Revue Belge d'Histoire Contemporaine* 14, nos. 3–4 (1983): 461–88.

Fox, Jo. *Film Propaganda in Britain and Nazi Germany: World War II Cinema.* Oxford: Berg, 2007.

Fremaux, Thierry, ed. *The Lumière Brothers' First Films.* Lyon: Kino International, Lumière Brothers Association, Institut Lumière/Association Frères Lumière, 1996.

Fuks, René. *Héros et personnages de chez nous racontés par leur statues.* Brussels: Meddens, 1986.

Fürnrohr, W., ed. *Afrika im Geschichtsunterricht europäischer Länder: Von der Kolonialgeschichte zur Geschichte der Dritten Welt.* Munich: n.p., 1982.

Gann, L. H., and Peter Duignan, eds. *African Proconsuls: European Governors in Africa.* New York: Free Press, 1978.

———. *The Rulers of Belgian Africa, 1884–1914.* Princeton NJ: Princeton University Press, 1979.

Gascoigne, John. "The Expanding Historiography of British Imperialism." *Historical Journal* 49, no. 2 (2006): 577–92.

Geary, Christraud M. *In and Out of Focus: Images from Central Africa, 1885–1960.* London: Philip Wilson, 2002.

Geeraerts, Jef. *Gangrene.* Translated by Jon Swan. London: Weidenfeld and Nicolson, 1975.

Geïllustreerde gids van Gent en de Internationale Tentoonstelling 1913. Rotterdam: H. W. Dusault, 1913.

Gérard, Adolphe. "Le Cercle d'etude et de propagande coloniale de Namur, nous a transmis la lettre que nous insérons ci-dessous." *Bulletin de l'Association Coloniale Liègeoise* (Liège), no. 2 (February 1936).

Gewald, Jan-Bart. "More than Red Rubber and Figures Alone: A Critical

Appraisal of the Memory of the Congo Exhibition at the Royal Museum for Central Africa, Tervuren, Belgium." *International Journal of African Historical Studies* 39, no. 3 (2006): 471–86.

Gide, André. *Voyage au Congo suivi de Le retour du Chad: Carnets de route.* [Paris]: Gallimard, 1928.

Gifford, Prosser, and Wm. Roger Louis, eds. *The Transfer of Power in Africa: Decolonization 1940–1960.* New Haven CT: Yale University Press, 1982.

Gilbert, Felix, and David Clay Large. *The End of the European Era: 1890 to the Present.* 5th ed. New York: W. W. Norton, 2002.

Gillot, Jean-Louis. *La vie des Belges au Congo.* Brussels: Daniel Van Eeckhoudt, 1983.

Gingrich, Newton Leroy. "Belgian Education Policy in the Congo 1945–1960." PhD diss., Tulane University, 1971.

"La Giornata Coloniale." *L'Italia Coloniale*, no. 6 (June 1927).

"La 'Giornata Coloniale.'" *L'Italia Coloniale*, no. 6 (June 1928): 117.

Golden, Nathan D. *Review of Foreign Film Markets during 1937.* Washington DC: U.S. Government Printing Office, 1938.

———. "Short-Subject Film Market of Europe." In Department of Commerce, Bureau of Foreign and Domestic Commerce, *Trade Information Bulletin*, no. 522. Washington DC: U.S. Government Printing Office, 1927.

Gondola, Ch. Didier. *The History of Congo.* Westport CT: Greenwood Press, 2002.

Greenhalgh, Paul. "Education, Entertainment and Politics: Lessons from the Great International Exhibitions." In Vergo, *New Museology*, 74–98.

———. *Ephemeral Vistas: The Expositions Universelles, Great Exhibitions, and World's Fairs, 1851–1939.* Manchester: Manchester University Press, 1988.

Gründer, Horst. *Geschichte der deutsche Kolonien.* 4th ed. Paderborn, Germany: Ferdinanc Schöningh, 2000.

Gysels, G., and M. Van den Eynde. *Niewste tijden (1848–1955): Geschiedenis van België.* Liège: Sciences et Lettres, 1955.

Haffner, Pierre. "Entretien avec le Père Alexandre Van den Heuvel, pionnier d'un cinéma missionnaire au Congo." *L'Afrique Littéraire et Artistique* 48 (1978): 86–95.

Halen, Pierre. *Le petit Belge avait vu grand: Une littérature coloniale.* Brussels: Archives du future, 1993.

Halen, Pierre, and János Riesz, eds. *Images de l'Afrique et du Congo/Zaïre dans les lettres françaises de Belgique et alentour: Actes du colloque international de Louvain-la-Neuve (4–6 février 1993)*. Brussels: Textyles-éditions, 1993.

"Hal honore ses enfants morts pour la civilisation." *L'Expansion Coloniale* (Brussels), 29 May 1932, numéro spécial [special issue].

Hall, Catherine, ed. *Cultures of Empire: Colonizers in Britain and the Empire in the Nineteenth and Twentieth Centuries; A Reader*. New York: Routledge, 2000.

Hall, Catherine, and Sonya Rose, eds. *At Home with the Empire: Metropolitan Culture and the Imperial World*. Cambridge: Cambridge University Press, 2006.

———. "Introduction: Being at Home with the Empire." In Hall and Rose, *At Home with the Empire*, 1–31.

Hamerow, Theodore S. *The Birth of a New Europe: State and Society in the Nineteenth Century*. Chapel Hill: University of North Carolina Press, 1983.

Harms, Robert. "The End of Red Rubber: A Reassessment." *Journal of African History* 16, no. 1 (1975): 73–88.

Harris, Chandra M. "Who's Got the Power? Blacks in Italian Cinema and Literature, 1910–1948." PhD diss., Brown University, 2004.

"Herdenkingsplechtigheid te Hasselt." *Revue Belgo-Congolaise Illustrée*, no. 3 (July 1966).

Hermans, Theo, ed. *The Flemish Movement: A Documentary History, 1780–1990*. London: Athlone Press, 1992.

"Het grootsche Paviljoen van Italië." *Antwerpen 1930*, 16 May 1930.

"Het Paviljoen van Portugal, dat heden wordt ingehuldigd." *Antwerpen 1930*, 17 May 1930.

Higginson, John. *A Working Class in the Making: Belgian Colonial Labor Policy, Private Enterprise, and the African Mineworker, 1907–1951*. Madison: University of Wisconsin Press, 1989.

"Histoire du Congo par les monuments." *Cercle Royal des Anciens Officiers des Campagnes d'Afrique. Bulletin Trimestriel*, no. 2 (1985): 34.

Hobsbawm, Eric, and Terence Ranger, eds. *The Invention of Tradition*. Cambridge: Cambridge University Press, 1984.

Hochschild, Adam. *King Leopold's Ghost: A Story of Greed, Terror, and Heroism in Colonial Africa*. Boston: Houghton Mifflin, 1998.

Hodeir, Catherine. "L'épopée de la décolonisation à travers les expositions universelles du XXe siècle." In *Livre des expositions universelles 1851–1989*, 305–12. Paris: Union centrale des arts décoratifs, 1983.

"Hommage à Léopold II." *La Tribune Congolaise*, 30 November 1930.

"Hommage aux pionniers luxembourgeois du Congo." *Le Soir* (Brussels), 27 September 1953.

"L'hotellerie congolaise." *Le Soir* (Brussels), 12 July 1958.

Hunt, Nancy Rose. "Tintin and the Interruptions of Congolese Comics." In Landau and Kaspin, *Images and Empires*, 90–123.

Huxley, Aldous. "Notes on Propaganda." *Harper's Magazine*, December 1936, 32–41.

Imbach, Pauline. "Les monuments publics coloniaux, lieux de mémoires contestés." Comité pour l'annulation de la dette du tiers monde, 29 September 2008. http://www.cadtm.org/Les-monuments-publics-coloniaux (accessed 26 May 2010).

"Les impressions congolaises de M. le professor Olbrechts." *La Revue Coloniale Belge*, no. 241 (15 October 1955): 722.

"L'inauguration de la statue de Léopold II." *Congo: Revue Générale de la Colonie Belge/Algemeen Tijdschrift van de Belgische Kolonie* 2, no. 4 (November 1926): 562–64.

"L'inauguration de la statue de Léopold II." *L'Illustration Congolaise*, no. 63 (15 November and 1 December 1926): 1216–17.

"L'inauguration du monument Le Marinel à l'Université coloniale d'Anvers." *Congo: Revue Générale de la Colonie Belge/Algemeen Tijdschrift van de Belgische Kolonie* 2, no. 4 (November 1925): 584–85.

"L'inauguration du monument national." *Congo: Revue Générale de la Colonie Belge/Algemeen Tijdschrift van de Belgische Kolonie* 2, no. 5 (May 1921): 772.

Inauguration du monument national élevé à la mémoire des Belges morts pour l'œuvre coloniale: Discours de M. le Ministre des Colonies. 11 mai 1921. Brussels: M. Hayez, 1921.

"Inauguration du Musée commercial et colonial de Namur." *Bulletin de la Société d'Études d'Intérêts Coloniaux de Namur*, nos. 1–2 (January–February 1913): 2–7.

"L'inauguration du Palais du Congo." *L'Essor Colonial et Maritime* (Brussels), 29 May 1930, 7–8.

"In dreissig Minuten erzählt CONGORAMA fünfundsiebzig Jahre Kongo-Geschichte." *Grenz-Echo* (Eupen), 8 May 1958.

"Inhuldiging van het Gedenkteeken Baron Dhanis te Antwerpen." *Ons Volk Ontwaakt*, 18 October 1913. http://users.skynet.be/ovo/BDhanis.html (accessed 31 May 2010).

"L'injuste agression contre l'Université coloniale d'Anvers." *L'Indépendance Belge* (Brussels), 29 November 1930.

Jacquemin, Jean-Pierre. *Racisme, continent obscur: Clichés, stéréotypes, phantasmes à propos des noirs dans le Royaume de Belgique.* Brussels: Coopération par l'éducation et la culture—Le Noir du blanc/Wit over Zwart, 1991.

Jacquemin, Jean-Pierre, and Françoise De Moor. *"Notre Congo/Onze Kongo": La propagande coloniale belge: Fragments pour une étude critique.* N.p.: Coopération par l'éducation et la culture, 2000.

Jacquemyns, G. "Le Congo Belge devant l'opinion publique." In *Institut Universitaire d'Information Sociale et Économique "INSOC,"* nos. 2–3. Brussels: Parc Léopold, 1956.

———. "L'INSOC à quinze années d'activité: Les sondages d'opinion; Questions posées; Principaux résultats." In *Institut Universitaire d'Information Sociale et Économique "INSOC,"* nos. 3–4. Brussels: Parc Léopold, 1960.

Jacquemyns, G., and E. Jacquemyns. "L'Exposition de 1958: Son succès auprès des Belges, opinions et vœux des visiteurs." In *Institut Universitaire d'Information Sociale et Économique "INSOC,"* nos. 1–2. Brussels: Parc Léopold, 1959.

Jacques, V. *Les Congolais de l'Exposition Universelle d'Anvers: Communication faite à la société d'anthropologie de Bruxelles, dans la séance du 24 septembre 1894.* Brussels: F. Hayez, 1894.

James, Beverly. "Fencing in the Past: Budapest's Statue Park Museum." *Media, Culture, and Society* 21 (1999): 291–311.

Janssens, P. G., M. Kivits, and J. Vuylsteke, eds. *Health in Central Africa since 1885: Past, Present, and Future.* Brussels: King Baudouin Foundation, 1997.

Jewsiewicki, B. "Le colonat agricole européen au Congo Belge, 1910–1960:

Questions politiques et économiques." *Journal of African History* 20, no. 4 (1979): 559–71.

Johnson, Nuala. "Cast in Stone: Monuments, Geography, and Nationalism." *Environment and Planning D: Society and Space* 13 (1995): 51–65.

"La Journée Coloniale: A Verviers, a Arlon, a Seraing." *L'Illustration Congolaise*, no. 179 (1 August 1936): 5984–85.

"La Journée du 15 Novembre." *L'Essor Colonial et Maritime* (Brussels), 20 November 1930.

Les Journées Coloniales. *Rapport au Roi sur les Journées Coloniales de 1924*. Brussels-Ixelles: R. Louis, 1925.

"Les Journées Coloniales à Mons." *L'Illustration Congolaise*, no. 131 (1 August 1932): 4103.

"Les Journées Coloniales de Belgique." *Bulletin de l'Association des Vétérans Coloniaux*, n.s., no. 1 (August 1945): 9–10.

Jowett, Garth S., and Victoria O'Donnell. *Propaganda and Persuasion*. 2nd ed. Newbury Park CA: Sage Publications, 1992.

Judd, Denis. *Empire: The British Imperial Experience, from 1765 to the Present*. New York: Basic Books, 1996.

Judt, Tony. *Postwar: A History of Europe since 1945*. New York: Penguin, 2005.

Kagné, Bonaventure. "L'immigration d'origine subsaharienne avant 1960: La Belgique découvre 'l'Africain.'" CRISP 15, no. 1721, complément [supplement] (August 2001). http://www.crisp.be/Documents/Article_Kagne.pdf (accessed 24 July 2003; site now discontinued).

Kardenne-Kats. *Vielles histoires de ma patrie: Récits historiques*. Brussels: J Lebègue, [c. 1905].

Kavanagh, Gaynor. "Museum as Memorial: The Origins of the Imperial War Museum." *Journal of Contemporary History* 23, no. 1 (January 1988): 77–97.

Kershaw, Ian. *The "Hitler Myth": Image and Reality in the Third Reich*. Oxford: Oxford University Press, 1987.

Ketels, Robert. *Le culte de la race blanche: Criterium et directive pour notre temps*. Brussels: Le Racisme paneuropéen, 1935.

Keylor, William R., ed. *The Legacy of the Great War: Peacemaking, 1919*. Boston: Houghton Mifflin, 1998.

Kleijer, Henk, Ad Knotter, and Frank van Vree, eds. *Tekens en teksten: Cultuur, communicatieen maatschappelijke veranderingen vanaf de late middeleeuwen.* Sociaal Wetenschappelijke Studies. Amsterdam: Amsterdam University Press, 1992.

Koloniale Hoogeschool van België/Université coloniale de Belgique, 1920–1945: Plechtige heropening der leergangen/Séance académique de reprise des Cours 18-X-1945. [Antwerp: Koloniale Hoogeschool van België/Université coloniale de Belgique, 1945].

Kongolo, Antoine Tshitungu. "Paul Panda Farnana (1888–1930): Panafricaniste, nationaliste, intellectuel engagé; Une contribution à l'étude de sa pensée et de son action." *L'Africain*, no. 211 (October–November 2003): 1–7.

Koos, Cheryl, and Cora Granata, eds. *The Human Tradition in Modern Europe.* Lanham MD: Rowman and Littlefield, 2008.

Kurth, Godefroid. *La nationalité belge.* Namur: Picard-Balon, 1913.

Kwanten, Godfried. "Go-between tussen twee culturen: Jef Van Bilsen en de overgang van een koloniaal naar een ontwikkelingsbeleid." In Viaene, Van Reybrouck, and Ceuppens, *Congo in België,* 283–98.

L., C. L. "Ce que le visiteur ne voit pas . . ." *Belgique d'Outremer,* no. 289 (April 1959): 215–17.

L., L. "Première au Palais du Congo: M. Buisseret: 'Nos combats d'Afrique ont toujours été ceux de croisade de libération.'" *La Cité* (Brussels), 19 April 1958.

"La, fut un jardin exotique." *Le Phare-Dimanche* (Brussels), 19 October 1958.

Landau, Paul S., and Deborah D. Kaspin, eds. *Images and Empires: Visuality in Colonial and Postcolonial Africa.* Berkeley: University of California Press, 2002.

Larson, Erik. *The Devil in the White City: Murder, Magic and Madness at the Fair that Changed America.* New York: Crown Publishers, 2003.

Laude, Norbert. "A propos de l'enseignement colonial en Belgique." *Institut Royal Colonial Belge Bulletin des Séances/Koninklijk Belgisch Koloniaal Instituut Bulletijn der Zittingen* 16, no. 2 (1945): 280–82.

———. *Discours/Redevoeringen.* Antwerp: Universitair Instituut voor de Overzeese Gebieden/Institut universitaire des territoires d'outre-mer, 1960.

————. "Le service territorial." *Belgique d'Outremer*, no. 286 (January 1959): 26.

Lebovics, Herman. *Imperialism and the Corruption of Democracies*. Durham NC: Duke University Press, 2006.

————. *True France: The Wars over Cultural Identity, 1900–1945*. Ithaca: Cornell University Press, 1992.

Legrand, Dominique. "Le Musée de Tervuren fête ses 100 ans." *Le Soir*, 20 April 2010. http://www.lesoir.be/culture/airs_du_temps/2010-04-20/le-musee-de-tervuren-fete-ses-100-ans-765393.php (accessed 26 May 2010).

Lemaire, Ch. *Congo et Belgique: A propos de l'Exposition d'Anvers*. With the assistance of Th. Masui, A.-J. Wauters, et al. Brussels: Imprimerie scientifique Ch. Bulens, 1894.

Lepersonne, J. "Lucien Cahen: Le directeur de Musée." *Africa-Tervuren* 28, no. 4 (1982): 7–10.

Leplae, E. "Nécessité d'une propagande agricole coloniale dans nos universités." *Congo: Revue Générale de la Colonie Belge/Algemeen Tijdschrift van de Belgische Kolonie* 1, no. 2 (February 1924): 284–85.

Lévai, Csaba, ed. *Europe and the World in European Historiography*. Pisa: Pisa University Press, 2006.

Liebrecht, Charles. "Le Congo au Heysel." Interview by PLF. *1935: Bulletin Officiel de l'Exposition Universelle et International de Bruxelles/Officieel Blad der Algemeene Wereldtentoonstelling van Brussel*, no. 11 (15 June 1934).

Le livre d'or de l'Exposition Internationale Coloniale, Maritime et d'Art Flamand: Anvers 1930. Antwerp: La Propagande commerciale, 1930.

Lonehay, P. *Notables congolais en Belgique*. [Brussels], 1956. Short film.

Long, James William. "Russian Manipulation of the French Press, 1904–1906." *Slavic Review* 31, no. 2 (June 1972): 343–54.

Louis, Wm. Roger. *Ends of British Imperialism: The Scramble for Empire, Suez, and Decolonization*. London: I. B. Tauris, 2006.

Louis, Wm. Roger, and Jean Stengers. *E. D. Morel's History of the Congo Reform Movement*. Oxford: Clarendon Press, 1968.

Luwel, Marcel. "De Congolezen op de Tentoonstelling van 1897." *Revue Congolaise Illustrée*, no. 4 (1954): 41–44.

————. "Histoire du Musée royal du Congo Belge à Tervuren." *Belgique d'Outremer*, no. 289 (April 1959): 209–12.

————. "Histoire du Musée royal du Congo Belge à Tervuren." *Congo-Tervuren* 6, no. 2 (1960): 30–49.

Mabille, Xavier, *Histoire politique de la Belgique: Facteurs et acteurs de changement*. Édition complétée [revised edition]. Brussels: CRISP, 1992.

Macdonald, Sharon. "Exhibitions of Power and Powers of Exhibition: An Introduction to the Politics of Display." In Macdonald, *Politics of Display*, 1–21.

————, ed. *The Politics of Display: Museums, Science, Culture*. London: Routledge, 1998.

MacDonnell, John de Courcy. *Belgium, Her Kings, Kingdom and People*. Boston: Little, Brown, 1914.

————. *King Leopold II: His Rule in Belgium and the Congo*. 1905. Reprint, New York: Negro Universities Press, 1969.

MacKenzie, John M., ed. *European Empires and the People: Popular Responses to Imperialism in France, Britain, the Netherlands, Belgium, Germany and Italy*. Manchester: Manchester University Press, 2011.

————, ed. *Imperialism and Popular Culture*. Manchester: Manchester University Press, 1986.

————. *Propaganda and Empire: The Manipulation of British Public Opinion, 1880–1960*. Manchester: Manchester University Press, 1984.

MacMillan, Margaret. *Paris: Six Months that Changed the World*. New York: Random House, 2003.

Maes, J. *Le Musée du Congo Belge à Tervuren: Guide illustré du visiteur*. Antwerp: De Sikkel, 1925.

Maesen, A. "Notes sur la vie et la pensée de Frans M. Olbrechts." *Congo-Tervuren* 3–4 (1957–58): 7–22.

"Manifestations coloniales." *Congo: Revue Générale de la Colonie Belge/ Algemeen Tijdschrift van de Belgische Kolonie* 2, no. 5 (December 1939).

Mantels, Ruben. *Geleerd in de tropen: Leuven, Congo, en de wetenschap, 1885–1960*. Leuven: Leuven University Press, 2007.

Mantels, Ruben, and Jo Tollebeek. "Highly Educated Mission: The University of Leuven, the Missionary Congregations and Congo, 1885–1960." *Exchange: A Journal of Missiological and Ecumenical Research* 36, no. 4 (2007): 359–85.

Marechal, P. "Le Musée royal de l'Afrique centrale." In Balthazar and Stengers, *Dynastie et la culture en Belgique*, 331–40.

Markowitz, Marvin D. *Cross and Sword: The Political Role of Christian Missions in the Belgian Congo, 1908–1960*. Stanford: Hoover Institution Press, 1973.

Marseille, Jacques. *Empire colonial et capitalisme français: Histoire d'un divorce*. Paris: Albin Michel, 1984.

Masui, Th. *Guide de la Section de l'État Indépendant du Congo à l'Exposition de Bruxelles–Tervueren en 1897*. Brussels: Veuve Monnom, 1897.

Mattie, Erik. *World's Fairs*. New York: Princeton Architectural Press, 1998.

Meirsschaut, Pol. *Les sculptures de plein air à Bruxelles: Guide explicatif*. Brussels: Émile Bruylant, 1900.

Mémorial de l'Exposition Missionnaire: Mons–Borinage 23–30 avril 1933. Hornu, Belgium: Léon Preux, [1933].

"Mémorial des vétérans coloniaux." *Le Trait d'Union: Bulletin Trimestriel de l'Association des Etudiants de l'Université Coloniale de Belgique*, no. 4 (August 1936).

Le Mémorial Officiel de l'Exposition Universelle et Internationale de Bruxelles: Les participations étrangères et belges. Brussels: Etablissements généraux d'imprimerie, 1961.

Metzger, Chantal. "D'une puissance coloniale à un pays sans colonies: L'Allemagne et la question coloniale (1914–1945)." *Revue d'Allemagne et des Pays de Langue Allemande* 38, no. 4 (October–December 2006): 555–69.

Michel, Florence. "L'activité de l'Office colonial dans les années trente: La participation du Ministère des colonies aux foires et aux expositions." Master's thesis, Université libre de Bruxelles, 1999.

Michiels, Albert, Norbert Laude, and H. Carton de Wiart. *Notre Colonie*. 5th ed. Brussels, 1922.

Miller, Christopher. *Nationalists and Nomads: Essays on Francophone African Literature and Culture*. Chicago: University of Chicago Press, 1998.

Minder, Patrick. "La construction du colonisé dans une métropole sans empire: Le cas de la Suisse (1880–1939)." In Bancel, Blanchard, Boëtsch, Deroo, and Lemaire, *Zoos humains*, 227–34.

Ministère de l'industrie et du travail, Commissariat général du gouvernement. *Exposition Universelle et Internationale de Bruxelles 1910: Catalogue spécial officiel de la Section Belge.* Brussels: E. Guyot, 1910.

[Ministère des colonies, Office colonial]. *Exposition Coloniale des Produits Alimentaires de Fabrication Belge et de Produits Coloniaux organisée dans les locaux de l'Office colonial du Ministère des colonies, du 7 au 21 mars 1936.* [Brussels, 1936].

————. *Exposition Coloniale du Textile organisée dans les locaux de l'Office colonial du Ministère des colonies à Bruxelles du 25 octobre au 15 novembre 1933: Catalogue.* [Brussels, 1933].

————. *Exposition des Produits du Congo. Organisée dans les locaux de l'Office colonial du Ministère des colonies. Du 12 au 20 mars 1932. A l'occasion de la Semaine Bruxelloise du Commerce.* [Brussels, 1932].

Ministère des colonies/Ministerie van Koloniën and Ministère de l'instruction publique/Ministerie van Openbaar Onderwijs. *Concours Colonial Scolaire 1953–1954/Koloniale Schoolwedstrijd 1953–1954: Palmarès/Palmares.* Brussels: Editions Cuypers, [1954].

————. *Concours Colonial Scolaire 1956–1957/Koloniale Schoolwedstrijd 1956–1957: Palmarès/Palmares.* Brussels: Imprimerie Wellens-Pay, [1957].

Mitchell, Timothy. *Colonising Egypt.* Cambridge: Cambridge University Press, 1988.

Mommen, André. *The Belgian Economy in the Twentieth Century.* London: Routledge, 1994.

Moncel, Monique. "Il y a 50 ans: L'exposition coloniale, apogée de l'Empire." *Historia* 414 (May 1981): 62–68.

Monheim, Christian. *La croisade antiesclavagiste: Le Cardinal Ch. M. Lavigerie; S. M. Leopold, souverain de l'État Indépendant.* Brochure no. 8. Leuven: AUCAM, 1928.

————. *Le passé colonial de la Belgique.* Brochure no. 13. Leuven: Éditions de AUCAM, n.d. First published in *Bulletin d'Études et d'Informations de l'École Supérieure de Commerce St. Ignace* (Antwerp), January 1930.

Mons Belgium. Mons: Maison du Tourisme/Huis voor Toerisme, n.d. Tourist map.

Monseur, L. "La colonisation belge: Une certaine image officielle (les manuels: 1919–1939)." Master's thesis, Université de Liège, 1984–85.

"Le Monument à la Mémoire du Baron Dhanis." *Bulletin de la Société d'Études d'Intérêts Coloniaux de Namur*, no. 9 (September 1913): 111–12.

"Le Monument De Bruyne." *Le Congo Belge* (Brussels), 1 January 1898.

"Monument Léopold II." *Congo-Namur*, no. 1 (1947).

"Le Monument Lippens-De Bruyne." *Congo: Revue Générale de la Colonie Belge/Algemeen Tijdschrift van de Belgische Kolonie* 2, no. 4 (November 1921): 578–79.

Morris, Wendy Ann. "Both Temple and Tomb: Difference, Desire and Death in the Sculptures of the Royal Museum for Central Africa." Master's thesis, University of South Africa, 2003.

Morton, Patricia A. *Hybrid Modernities: Architecture and Representation at the 1931 Colonial Exposition, Paris*. Cambridge MA: MIT Press, 2000.

Mosley, Philip. *Split Screen: Belgian Cinema and Cultural Identity*. Albany: State University of New York Press, 2001.

"M. Tscoffen a inauguré mercredi matin l'exposition coloniale des produits textiles." *Le XXe Siècle*, 26 October 1933.

Mumengi, Didier. *Panda Farnana: Premier universitaire congolais (1888–1930)*. Paris: L'Harmattan, 2005.

Murray, Alison Joan. "Framing Greater France: Images of Africa in French Documentary Film, 1920–1940." PhD diss., University of Virginia, 1998.

Musée africain de Namur. "Musée africain de Namur." 2004. http://www.museeafricainnamur.be/ (accessed 31 May 2010).

———. *Petit guide du Musée africain de Namur*. [Namur]: L'Imprimerie provinciale, n.d.

Nauwelaerts, Mandy, ed. *De panoramische droom/The Panoramic Dream: Antwerpen en de wereldtentoonstellingen/Antwerp and the World Exhibitions 1885, 1894, 1930*. Antwerp: Antwerp 93, 1993.

Navarro, Beatriz. "Entrevista a Yves Leterme, presidente de Flandes y vencedor de las elecciones belgas." *La Vanguardia*, 26 June 2007.

Ndaywel è Nziem, Isidore. *Histoire générale du Congo: De l'héritage ancien à la république démocratique*. Paris: De Boeck et Larcier, 1998.

N'Doki. "Coup de Bambou: Il y a foire et foire." *Mukanda*, 29 March 1925.

"Next Exposition to Be in Brussels: Preparations Completed for Its Opening on April 23, 1910." *New York Times*, 14 November 1909, C4.

Nicoll, Edna L. *Catalogue officiel de la Section Française à l'Exposition Universelle et Internationale de Bruxelles 1935.* Paris: Éditions Edna Nicoll, 1935.

Norton, William B. "Pierre Ryckmans (1891–1959)." In Gann and Duignan, *African Proconsuls*, 391–411.

Notice sur l'État Indépendant du Congo: Les missions. N.p., 1905.

"Notre programme." *Bulletin de la Société d'Études d'Intérêts Coloniaux de Namur*, nos. 1–2 (January–February 1913): 1–2.

Nóvoa, António, Marc Depaepe, and Erwin V. Johanningmeier, eds. *The Colonial Experience in Education: Historical Issues and Perspectives.* Paedagogica Historica 1. Ghent: CSHP, 1995.

O'Brien, Conor Cruise. *To Katanga and Back: A UN Case History.* New York: Simon and Schuster, 1962.

"L'Œuvre du souvenir congolais." *L'Illustration Congolaise*, no. 96 (1 September 1929): 2626.

"Œuvres d'art du Congo à Tervueren." *La Revue Coloniale Belge*, no. 260 (November 1956): 840.

Office catholique international du cinéma. *Les catholiques parlent du cinéma.* Paris: Éditions universitaires, 1948. Published in conjunction with the 4me Congrès International, June 1947.

"L'Office colonial à Bruxelles 1935." *L'Illustration Congolaise*, no. 185 (1 February 1936).

Olbrechts, Frans M. *Ethnologie: Inleiding tot de studie der primitieve beschaving.* Zutphen: W. J. Thieme, 1936.

Onclincx, G. "Milieux coloniaux et cinématographie à l'Exposition Internationale de Bruxelles de 1897." *Cahiers bruxellois: Revue Trimestrielle d'Histoire Urbaine* 3, no. 4 (October–December 1958): 287–309.

Onwumelu, John A. "Congo Paternalism: An Isolationist Colonial Policy." PhD diss., University of Chicago, 1966.

Osborn, Andrew. "Belgium Exhumes Its Colonial Demons." *The Guardian* (London), 13 July 2002.

Otten, Rik. *Le cinéma dans les pays des grands lacs: Zaïre, Rwanda, Burundi.* With the collaboration of Victor Bachy. Brussels: OCIC/L'Harmattan, 1984.

Palumbo, Patrizia, ed. *A Place in the Sun: Africa in Italian Colonial Culture from Post-unification to the Present.* Berkeley: University of California Press, 2003.

Parmentier, Gustave. *Exposition Universelle et Internationale de Gand en 1913: Plan général.* Ghent: Lith. Vanderpoorten, n.d.

Paternostre, Marcel. *A Work of Civilisation by the Belgians in the Congo.* Brussels: Committee for Christian Civilization in the Belgian Congo, 1950.

"Le pavillon du Commerce du Congo." *La Cité* (Brussels), 24 April 1958.

"Le pavillon du Congo Belge à l'Exposition Internationale d'Anvers." *Congo: Revue Générale de la Colonie Belge/Algemeen Tijdschrift van de Belgische Kolonie* 2, no. 4 (November 1930): 580.

Peemans, J.-P. "Imperial Hangovers: Belgium—the Economics of Decolonization." *Journal of Contemporary History* 15, no. 2 (April 1980): 257–86.

Penny, H. Glenn, III. "Cosmopolitan Visions and Municipal Displays: Museums, Markets, and the Ethnographic Project in Germany, 1868–1914." PhD diss., University of Illinois at Urbana–Champaign, 1999.

Perlee, Y. "Vue rétrospective sur le Congo Belge." *Journal de Bruges* (Bruges), 8 March 1952.

Petridis, Constantine, ed. *Frans M. Olbrechts 1899–1958: In Search of Art in Africa.* Antwerp: Antwerp Ethnographic Museum, 2001.

Piniau, Bernard. *Congo-Zaïre, 1874–1981: La perception du lointain.* Paris: L'Harmattan, 1992.

Pirenne, Henri. *Geschiedenis van België.* Brussels, 1928.

Pirenne, P. "Projets de Léopold II et réalisations actuelles." *Congo-Tervuren* 6, no. 2 (1960): 50–56.

Piret, N. *Cours d'histoire générale à l'usage de l'enseignement moyen et de l'enseignement normal primaire. III. Temps modernes et temps contemporains.* 10th ed. Liège: H. Dessain, 1937.

Pirotte, Jean. "Les armes d'une mobilisation: La littérature missionnaire de la fin du XIXe siècle à 1940." In Quaghebeur and Van Balberghe, *Papier blanc, encre noire,* 1:55–104.

———, ed. *Stéréotypes nationaux et préjugés raciaux aux XIXe et XXe siècles: Sources et méthodes pour une approche historique.* Louvain-la-Neuve: Collège Érasme, 1982.

Pius XI, Pope. "Vigilanti Cura." Holy See, 29 June 1936. http://www.vatican

.va/holy_father/pius_xi/encyclicals/documents/hf_p-xi_enc_29061936 _vigilanti-cura_en.html (accessed 31 May 2010).

Poncelet, Marc. *L'invention des sciences coloniales belges.* Paris: Karthala, 2008.

Porter, Bernard. *The Absent-Minded Imperialists: Empire, Society, and Culture in Britain.* Oxford: Oxford University Press, 2004.

Potter, Simon J. "Empire, Cultures and Identities in Nineteenth- and Twentieth-Century Britain." *History Compass* 5, no. 1 (2007): 51–71.

Prakash, Gyan. "Subaltern Studies as Postcolonial Criticism." *American Historical Review* 99, no. 5 (1994): 1475–90.

Pratt, Mary Louise. *Imperial Eyes: Travel and Transculturation.* London: Routledge, 1992.

"Procès-verbaux des Séances de la société: A. Séance du 7 janvier 1913." *Bulletin de la Société d'Études d'Intérêts Coloniaux de Namur,* nos. 1–2 (January–February 1913): 7–8.

Programme. Dimanche 19 juin 1932. XXVe anniversaire du Cercle congolais organisé avec le concours des Vétérans coloniaux (Section de Mons) et des Journées Coloniales. Mons: Imprimerie Léon Leborgne, [1932].

Quaghebeur, Marc, and Émile Van Balberghe, eds. *Papier blanc, encre noire: Cent ans de culture francophone en Afrique centrale (Zaïre, Rwanda et Burundi).* With Nadine Fettweis and Annick Vilain. 2 vols. Brussels: Éditions Labor, 1992.

Quatremer, Jean. "Leterme à la tête d'un 'accident de l'histoire.'" *Libération,* 12 June 2007.

"Questions economiques: L'importance des richesses congolaises pour le relèvement financier de la Belgique." *Congo: Revue Générale de la Colonie Belge/Algemeen Tijdschrift van de Belgische Kolonie* 1, no. 4 (April 1924): 560–62.

"Le 15 [quinze] novembre, au Monument Léopold II, à Bruxelles." *Revue Belgo-Congolaise Illustrée,* no. 1 (January 1966): 68.

Rahier, Jean Muteba. "The Ghost of Leopold II: The Belgian Royal Museum of Central Africa and Its Dusty Colonialist Exhibition." *Research in African Literatures* 34, no. 1 (Spring 2003): 58–84.

Ramirez, Francis, and Christian Rolot. "Le cinéma colonial belge: Archives d'une utopie." *Revue Belge du Cinéma,* no. 29 (Spring 1990): 1–63.

———. *Histoire du cinéma colonial au Zaïre au Rwanda et au Burundi.* Tervuren, Belgium: Musée royal de l'Afrique centrale, 1985.

Ranieri, Liane. *Léopold II: Urbaniste.* Brussels: Hayez, 1973.

"Rapport de la Commission des colonies, chargée de l'examen du budget du Ministère des colonies pour l'année 1931." *Congo: Revue Générale de la Colonie Belge/Algemeen Tijdschrift van de Belgische Kolonie* 1, no. 3 (March 1931): 406–12.

Reeves, Nicholas. *The Power of Film Propaganda: Myth or Reality?* London: Cassell, 1999.

La Régie des bâtiments. "Place du Trône: Statue du roi Léopold II." 3 September 2007. http://www.regiedesbatimenten.be/realisatieberichten _fr.cfm?key=84 (accessed 30 July 2009).

Regnault, Félix. "Une visite au Musée du Congo Belge." *Bulletins et Mémoires de la Société d'Anthropologie de Paris*, 7th ser., 5 (1924): 65–67.

Renders, Luc. "In Black and White: A Bird's Eye Overview of Flemish Prose on the Congo." *Tydskrif vir Letterkunde* 46, no. 1 (2009): 109–22.

Richards, Jeffrey. "Boy's Own Empire: Feature Films and Imperialism in the 1930s." In MacKenzie, *Imperialism and Popular Culture*, 140–64.

Riding, Alan. "Belgium Confronts Its Heart of Darkness." *New York Times*, 21 September 2002.

Rioux, Jean-Pierre. "La colonie ça s'apprend à l'école!" *Histoire* (France) 69 (1984): 49–55.

Robins, Bill. "A travers mes lunettes solaires . . ." *Le Soir pour les Enfants* (Brussels), no. 146 (26 June 1958).

Roes, Aldwin. "Towards a History of Mass Violence in the Etat Indépendant du Congo, 1885–1908." *South African Historical Journal* 62, no. 4 (2010): 634–70.

Rose, Sonya O. "Sex, Citizenship, and the Nation in World War II Britain." In Hall, *Cultures of Empire*, 246–77.

Rossell, Em. *Le livre d'or de l'Exposition Universelle et Internationale de Bruxelles en 1910.* [Brussels]: Em. Rossell, n.d.

Rothfels, Nigel T. "Bring 'Em Back Alive: Carl Hagenbeck and Exotic Animal and People Trades in Germany, 1848–1914." PhD diss., Harvard University, 1994.

Row, Thomas. "Mobilizing the Nation: Italian Propaganda in the Great

War." *Journal of Decorative and Propaganda Arts* 24 (Spring 2002): 141–69.

Roxburgh, Angus. "Belgians Confront Colonial Past." BBC *News*, 9 March 2005. http://news.bbc.co.uk/1/hi/world/africa/4332605.stm (accessed 6 May 2005).

———. "Belgians Wake Up to the Horror of Colonial Past." *Sunday Herald*, 6 March 2005. http://www.sundayherald.com (accessed 6 May 2005).

Rydell, Robert W., and Nancy Gwinn, eds. *Fair Representations: World's Fairs and the Modern World*. Amsterdam: VU University Press, 1994.

Said, Edward W. *Orientalism*. New York: Vintage Books, 1979.

Saunders, Barbara. "Congo-Vision." In Bouquet and Porto, *Science, Magic, and Religion*, 75–94.

———. "The Photological Apparatus and the Desiring Machine: Unexpected Congruences between the Koninklijk Museum, Tervuren and the Umistà Centre, Alert Bay." In Bouquet, *Academic Anthropology and the Museum*, 18–35.

Scheler, Edmond. *Gand et son exposition, 1913: Guide de poche illustré de Gand et l'Exposition Universelle et Internationale, contenant un plan pratique de l'exposition et du parc*. Brussels: Administration des guides Scheler; Namur: Imprimeries Jacques Godenne, 1913.

Schildkrout, Enid, and Curtis A. Keim. "Objects and Agendas: Re-collecting the Congo." In Schildkrout and Keim, *Scramble for Art in Central Africa*, 1–36.

———, eds. *The Scramble for Art in Central Africa*. Cambridge: Cambridge University Press, 1998.

Schmokel, Wolfe W. *Dream of Empire: German Colonialism, 1919–1945*. New Haven CT: Yale University Press, 1964.

Schneider, William Howard. *An Empire for the Masses: The French Popular Image of Africa, 1870–1900*. Westport CT: Greenwood Press, 1982.

Schouteden, H. *Guide illustré du Musée du Congo Belge*. 5th ed. Tervuren, Belgium: Musée du Congo Belge, 1943.

———. *Guide illustré du Musée du Congo Belge*. 7th ed. Tervuren, Belgium: Musée du Congo Belge/Brussels: Veuve Monnom, 1947.

Schroeder-Gudehus, Brigitte, and Anne Rasmussen. *Les fastes du progrès: Le guide des expositions universelles 1851–1992*. Paris: Flammarion, 1992.

Schwarzenbach, Alexis. *Portraits of the Nation: Stamps, Coins and Banknotes in Belgium and Switzerland 1880–1945.* Bern: Peter Lang, 1999.

Scott, Joan Wallach. *Gender and the Politics of History.* New York: Columbia University Press, 1988.

Section du Congo Belge et du Ruanda-Urundi, 1957; Règlement de la section du Congo Belge et du Ruanda-Urundi. Exposition universelle et internationale. Brussels: Commissariat général du gouvernement, 1955.

Seeley, J. R. *The Expansion of England.* London: Macmillan, 1883.

"La semaine coloniale interuniversitaire." *Congo: Revue Générale de la Colonie Belge/Algemeen Tijdschrift van de Belgische Kolonie* 1, no. 5 (May 1924): 767–78.

Le service postal rapide entre Anvers et le Congo de la Compagnie belge maritime du Congo. Antwerp, [1929].

Sharp, Alan. "The Mandate System in the Colonial World." In Keylor, *Legacy of the Great War,* 169–86.

Shattuck, Roger. *The Banquet Years: The Origins of the Avant-Garde in France, 1885 to World War I; Alfred Jarry, Henri Rousseau, Erik Satie, Guillaume Apollinaire.* Rev. ed. New York: Vintage Books, 1968.

Sielmann, Heinz, and Henry Brandt. *Les seigneurs de la forêt.* N.p.: Fondation internationale scientifique, 1958. Filmstrip.

Slade, Ruth M. *King Leopold's Congo: Aspects of the Development of Race Relations in the Congo Independent State.* London: Oxford University Press, 1962.

Slavin, David Henry. *Colonial Cinema and Imperial France, 1919–1939: White Blind Spots, Male Fantasies, Settler Myths.* Baltimore: Johns Hopkins University Press, 2001.

Sluys, A. *Manuel de la cinématographie scolaire et éducatif.* Series union des villes et communes belges 19. Brussels: Union des villes et communes belges, n.d.

Smyth, Rosaleen. "The Development of British Colonial Film Policy, 1927–1939, with Special Reference to East and Central Africa." *Journal of African History* 20, no. 3 (1979): 437–50.

Sojcher, Frédéric. *La Kermesse héroïque du cinéma belge, tome I: 1896–1965; Des documentaires et des farces.* Paris: L'Harmattan, 1999.

Solesmes, G. "En regardant vivre le Congo et le Ruanda-Urundi." *Revue Congolaise Illustrée*, no. 6 (June 1958): 23–27.

"Le Souvenir Crespel à Tournai." *La Revue Coloniale Belge*, no. 256 (1 June 1956): 404.

Souvenir de l'Exposition Universelle 1894 et d'Anvers. Antwerp, n.d.

Stanard, Matthew G. "'Bilan du monde pour un monde plus déshumanisé': The 1958 Brussels World's Fair and Belgian Perceptions of the Congo." *European History Quarterly* 35, no. 2 (2005): 267–98.

———. "Imperialists without an Empire: *Cercles coloniaux* and Colonial Culture in Belgium after 1960." In Koos and Granata, *Human Tradition in Modern Europe*, 155–69.

———. "Interwar Pro-empire Propaganda and European Colonial Culture: Toward a Comparative Research Agenda." *Journal of Contemporary History* 44, no. 1 (2009): 27–48.

———. "Selling the Empire between the Wars: Colonial Expositions in Belgium 1920–1940." *French Colonial History* 6 (2005): 159–78.

"Standbeeld Leopold II mag blijven." *Het Nieuwsblad Online*, 29 October 2004. http://www.nieuwsblad.be/Article/Detail.aspx?articleID=gg39s7nv (accessed 28 July 2009).

"Statistieken van de bezoeken aan het museum in 1972/Statistiques des visites au musée en 1972." *Africa-Tervuren* 19, no. 1 (1973): 25.

"Statistieken van de bezoeken aan het museum in 1973/Statistiques des visites au musée en 1973." *Africa-Tervuren* 20, no. 1 (1974): 2.

"Statistieken van de bezoeken aan het museum in 1974/Statistiques des visites au musée en 1974." *Africa-Tervuren* 21, nos. 1–2 (1975): 24.

"Statistieken van de bezoeken aan het museum in 1975/Statistiques des visites au musée en 1975." *Africa-Tervuren* 22, nos. 1–4 (1976).

"Statistieken van de bezoeken aan het museum in 1976/Statistiques des visites au musée en 1976." *Africa-Tervuren* 23, nos. 1–4 (1977): 22.

"Statistieken van de bezoeken aan het museum in 1978/Statistiques des visites au musée en 1978." *Africa-Tervuren* 25, no. 1 (1979): 18.

"Statistieken van de bezoeken aan het museum in 1980/Statistiques des visites au musée en 1980." *Africa-Tervuren* 28, no. 1 (1982): 16.

"Statistieken van de bezoeken aan het museum in 1981/Statistiques des visites au musée en 1981." *Africa-Tervuren* 28, no. 1 (1982): 16.

Stengers, Jean. "Belgian Historiography since 1945." Translated by Frank Perlin. In Emmer and Wesseling, *Reappraisals in Overseas History*, 161–81.

———. *Belgique et Congo: L'elaboration de la charte coloniale*. Brussels: La Renaissance du livre, 1963.

———. *Combien le Congo a-t-il coûté à la Belgique?* Brussels: Académie royale des sciences d'outre-mer, 1957.

———. *Congo, mythes et réalités: 100 ans d'histoire*. Paris and Louvain-la-Neuve: Duculot, 1989.

———. "Precipitous Decolonization: The Case of the Belgian Congo." In Gifford and Louis, *Transfer of Power in Africa*, 305–35.

———. "The Statesman as Imperialist." In Cohen, *European Empire Building*, 48–51. First published as Jean Stengers, "La place de Léopold II dans l'histoire de la colonisation," *Nouvelle Clio* 1 and 2 (1949–50): 517–22, 524, 527–28, 533, 536.

Stinglhamber, Colonel B. E. M. "Discours prononcé au pied de la Statue equestre de Léopold II, le 16 décembre 1934." [Brussels, 1934].

Stinglhamber, Gustave, and Paul Dresse. *Léopold II au Travail*. Brussels: Éditions du Sablon, 1945.

Stocking, George W., Jr., ed. *Objects and Others: Essays on Museums and Material Culture*. History of Anthropology 3. Madison: University of Wisconsin Press, 1985.

———. *Race, Culture, and Evolution: Essays in the History of Anthropology*. Chicago: University of Chicago Press, 1968.

Stoerk, Felix. "Review of Alphonse de Haulleville, *Les aptitudes colonisatrices des Belges, et la question coloniale en Belgique* (Brussels: Lebègue and Leipzig: Dieterich, 1898)." *Archiv für öffentliches Recht* 14, no. 4 (1899): 584–85.

Stoler, Ann Laura, and Frederick Cooper. "Between Metropole and Colony: Rethinking a Research Agenda." In Stoler and Cooper, *Tensions of Empire*, 1–56.

———, eds. *Tensions of Empire: Colonial Cultures in a Bourgeois World*. Berkeley: University of California Press, 1997.

Storme, Marcel. "Engagement de la propagande pour l'organisation territoriale des missions au Congo." In *Sacrae Congregationis de Propaganda Fide Memoria Rerum, 350 ans au service des missions, 1622–1972, vol. III: 1818–1972*, 256–94. Rome-Fribourg-Vienna, n.d.

Stovall, Tyler. *Paris Noir: African Americans in the City of Light*. New York: Houghton Mifflin, 1996.

T., J.-L. "Inauguration du Musée scolaire colonial à Jambes." *Vers l'Avenir* (Namur, Belgium), 24 June 1951.

Talbott, John. *The War without a Name: France in Algeria, 1954–1962*. London: Faber and Faber, 1980.

Taylor, Philip M. *Munitions of the Mind: A History of Propaganda from the Ancient World to the Present Era*. Manchester: Manchester University Press, 1995.

Thomas, Martin, Bob Moore, and L. J. Butler. *Crises of Empire: Decolonization and Europe's Imperial States, 1918–1975*. London: Hodder Education, 2008.

Thomas, Nicholas. "Material Culture and Colonial Power: Ethnological Collecting and the Establishment of Colonial Rule in Fiji." *Man*, n.s., 24, no. 1 (March 1989): 41–56.

Thomas, Paul. *Un siècle de cinéma belge*. Ottignies, Belgium: Quorum, 1995.

Thonnon, Marcel. *Main dans la main*. [Brussels]: Office de l'information et des relations publiques pour le Congo Belge et le Ruanda-Urundi, 1958. Filmstrip.

Thys, Marianne, ed. *Belgian Cinema/Le cinéma belge/De Belgische film*. Brussels: Royal Belgian Film Archive/Ghent: Flammarion, 1999.

"Tokéndé: Le Congo, colonie . . . des missions!" *D.R.-Magazine*, 5 April 1958.

"Trentième anniversaire de l'inauguration du Monument aux Troupes des Campagnes d'Afrique." *Cercle Royal des Anciens Officiers des Campagnes d'Afrique. Bulletin Trimestriel*, no. 3 (September 2000): 10.

"Très grand succès de la première conférence organisée par 'L'Amitié par delà les frontières' en collaboration avec 'La Royale amicale des coloniaux et anciens coloniaux.'" *Bulletin de Notariat*, 6–12 [February] 1959.

"Les troupes et les enfants des écoles, sur la Grand'Place, devant le drapeau de Tabora." *L'Illustration Congolaise*, no. 131 (1 August 1932): 4098.

Trumpbour, John. "'Death to Hollywood': The Politics of Film in the United States, Great Britain, Belgium, and France, 1920–1960." PhD diss., Harvard University, 1995.

———. *Selling Hollywood to the World: U.S. and European Struggles for*

Mastery of the Global Film Industry, 1920–1950. Cambridge: Cambridge University Press, 2002.

Turnbull, Colin M. *The Lonely African.* New York: Simon and Schuster, 1962.

Union coloniale belge. *Cours de préparation coloniale: Session 1912–1913.* Brussels: Imprimerie de "L'Expansion belge," 1912.

Union minière du Haut-Katanga. *Union minière du Haut-Katanga, 1906–1956.* 2nd ed. Brussels: Éditions L. Cuypers, 1956.

Universitair Instituut voor de Overzeese Gebieden/Institut universitaire des territoires d'outre-mer. *Séance académique/Academische zitting.* Antwerp, 1955.

Université coloniale de Belgique: Faculté des sciences politiques et administration/Koloniale Hoogeschool van België: Faculteif der staats- en bestuurlijke wetenschappen. Antwerp: Neptun, n.d.

"L'Université coloniale et l'ecole coloniale." *L'Essor Colonial et Maritime,* 8 March 1931.

UROME/KBUOL (Union royale belge pour les pays d'outre-mer/Koninklijke Belgische Unie voor de Overzeese Landen). "Site d'etude de la colonisation belge/Site voor de studie van de Belgische colonisatie." http://www.urome .be (accessed 31 May 2010).

Usai, Paolo Cherchi, and Lorenzo Codelli, eds. *Before Caligari: German Cinema, 1895–1920/Prima di Caligari: Cinema tedesco, 1895–1920.* Pordenone, Italy: Edizioni Biblioteca dell'Immagine, 1990.

V., R. "Vues actuelles sur le Congo." *La Flandre Libérale* (Ghent), 28 February 1952.

Van Bilsen, A. A. J. "Een dertigjarenplan voor de politieke ontvoogding van Belgisch Afrika." *De Gids op Maatschappelijk Gebied,* December 1955, 999–1028.

Vancraenbroeck, Marc. *Les médailles de la presence belge en Afrique centrale 1876–1960.* Brussels: Bibliothèque royale de Belgique, 1996.

Van Damme, Annemieke, and Annelies Sweygers. *Lubuka! Lubuka! "Gevaar in Afrikacollecties—Afrikacollecties in gevaar."* Herverlee: Centrum voor Religieuze Kunst en Cultuur, 2005.

Van Damme-Linseele, Annemieke. "From Mission 'Africa Rooms': Frans M. Olbrecht's Rediscovered African Collection." *African Arts* 41, no. 2 (Summer 2008): 38–49.

van den Audenaerde, D. Thys. "In Memoriam Lucien Cahen." *Africa-Tervuren* 28, no. 4 (1982): 3–4.

van den Wijngaert, Mark, Lieve Beullens, and Dana Brants. *Pouvoir et Monarchie: La Belgique et ses rois.* Translated by Anne-Laure Vignaux. Brussels: Luc Pire, 2002.

Van der Linden, Fred. "Le Congo Belge à l'Exposition de Bruxelles en 1910." *Belgique d'Outremer*, no. 280 (July 1958): 444.

Vandersmissen, Jan. *Koningen van de wereld: Leopold II en de aardrijkskundige beweging.* Leuven: Acco, 2009.

Van der Straeten, E. "Rapport sur les travaux de la Commission d'interpénétration économique de la Belgique, du Congo Belge et du Ruanda-Urundi." *Congo: Revue Générale de la Colonie Belge/Algemeen Tijdschrift van de Belgische Kolonie* 1, no. 4 (April 1935): 520–70.

Vandevelde, Major. "L'ignorance des Belges en ce qui concernent leur colonie." *Les Vétérans Coloniaux*, no. 3 (March 1946): 17.

Van Grieken-Taverniers, M. *Inventaire des archives de la 2e direction générale, 2e direction, 4e section: Activités scientifiques. Archives de l'Université des territoires d'outre-mer d'Anvers.* INUTOM. Brussels: Ministère des affaires étrangères du commerce exterieur, Archives africaines, 1975.

Vangroenweghe, Daniel. *Du sang sur les lianes: Léopold II et son Congo.* Brussels: Didier Hatier, 1986.

———. "Le journal de Charles Lemaire à l'equateur 1891–1893." Centre Æquatoria. http://www.aequatoria.be/French/CoqLemaireEquateur.html (accessed 27 June 2007). First published in *Annales Aequatoria* 7 (1986): 7–73.

Van Hoecke, Sony, and Jean-Pierre Jacquemin. *Africa Museum Tervuren 1898–1998.* Tervuren, Belgium: Musée royal de l'Afrique centrale, 1998.

van Kalken, Frans. *Cours d'histoire générale à l'usage de l'enseignement moyen.* Brussels: Office de publicité, 1926–27.

———. *Histoire de Belgique des origines à nos jours.* 5th ed. Brussels: Office de publicité, 1946.

———. *Histoire de la Belgique et de son expansion coloniale.* Brussels: Office de publicité, 1954.

van Keuren, David K. "Museums and Ideology: Augustus Pitt-Rivers, Anthropological Museums, and Social Change in Later Victorian Britain." *Victorian Studies* 28 (Autumn 1984): 171–89.

Van Schuylenbergh, Patricia. "Découverte et vie des arts plastiques du bassin du Congo dans la Belgique des années, 1920–1930." In Van Schuylenbergh and Morimont, *Rencontres artistiques Belgique-Congo, 1920–1950*, 1–62.

Van Schuylenbergh, Patricia, and Françoise Morimont, eds. *Rencontres artistiques Belgique-Congo, 1920–1950*. Enquêtes et documents d'histoire africaine 12. Louvain-la-Neuve: Université catholique de Louvain, 1995.

Vanthemsche, Guy. *La Belgique et le Congo: Empreintes d'une colonie 1885–1980*. Brussels: Complexe, 2007.

———. "De Belgische Socialisten en Congo 1895–1960." *Brood en Rozen: Tijdschrift voor de Geschiednis van Sociale Bewegingen* 2 (1999): 31–65.

———. *Genèse et portée du "Plan décennal" du Congo Belge (1949–1959)*. Mémoires/Verhandelingen in-80, n.s., 51, no. 4. Brussels: Académie royale des sciences d'outre-mer, Classe des sciences morales et politiques/Koninklijke Academie voor Overzeese Wetenschappen, Klasse voor Morele en Politieke Wetenschappen, 1994.

———. "The Historiography of Belgian Colonialism in the Congo." In Lévai, *Europe and the World in European Historiography*, 89–119.

Vasagar, Jeevan. "Leopold Reigns for a Day in Kinshasa." *Guardian.co.uk*, 4 February 2005. http://www.guardian.co.uk/world/2005/feb/04/congo.jeevanvasagar (accessed 30 July 2009).

Vellut, Jean-Luc. "Belgians in the Congo (1885–1960)." In *150 Years of Communities and Cultures in Belgium: 1830–1980*, edited by Albert d'Haenens, 260–62. Brussels: Ministry of Foreign Affairs, 1980.

———. "Episodes anticommunistes dans l'ordre colonial belge (1924–1932)." In Delwit and Gotovitch, *Peur du rouge*, 183–90.

———. "European Medicine in the Congo Free State (1885–1908)." In Janssens, Kivits, and Vuylsteke, *Health in Central Africa since 1885*, 67–87.

———. "Hégémonies en construction: Articulations entre etat et entreprises dans le bloc colonial belge (1908–1960)." *Canadian Journal of African Studies* 16, no. 2 (1982): 313–30.

———. "Matériaux pour une image du blanc dans la société coloniale du Congo Belge." In Pirotte, *Stéréotypes nationaux et préjugés raciaux aux XIXe et XXe siècles*, 91–116.

———. "Préface." In Vanthemsche, *Belgique et le Congo*, 11–22.

Vellut, Jean-Luc, Florence Loriaux, and Françoise Morimont. *Bibliographie historique du Zaïre à l'époque coloniale (1880–1960): Travaux publiés en 1960–1996.* Under the direction of Jean-Luc Vellut. Louvain-la-Neuve: Centre d'histoire de l'Afrique/Tervuren, Belgium: Musée royal de l'Afrique centrale, 1996.

Vergo, Peter, ed. *The New Museology.* London: Reaktion Books, 1989.

Verhaegen, Benoît. "La colonisation et la décolonisation dans les manuels d'histoire en Belgique." In Quaghebeur and Van Balberghe, *Papier blanc, encre noire,* 2:333–79.

Verniers, L., and P. Bonenfant. *Histoire de Belgique dans le cadre de l'histoire générale: Deuxième partie, du XVe siècle à 1914.* Rev. 3rd ed. Brussels: De Boeck, 1943.

———. *Histoire de Belgique dans le cadre de l'histoire générale à l'usage des écoles primaires à quatre degrés, des écoles moyennes, des sections préparatoires aux écoles normales et des classes inférieures des athénées et lycées. Tome II: De la fin du XIVe siècle à nos jours.* 4th ed. Brussels: De Boeck, 1948.

———. *Manuel d'histoire de Belgique dans le cadre de l'histoire générale à l'usage des écoles primaires à quatre degrés, des écoles moyennes, des sections préparatoires aux écoles normales et des classes inférieures des athénées et des lycées: Première partie, Des origines au XIVe siècle.* 2nd ed. Brussels: De Boeck, 1941.

Verschaffel, Tom. "Congo in de Belgische zelfrepresentatie." In Viaene, Van Reybrouck, and Ceuppens, *Congo in België,* 63–80.

Verswijver, Gustaff, and Herman Burssens. "Hidden Treasures of the Tervuren Museum." *African Arts* 28, no. 3 (Summer 1995): 22–31.

"Les Vétérans Coloniaux." Numéro spécial [special issue], *Revue Congolaise Illustrée,* no. 10 (October 1948).

Viaene, Vincent. "King Leopold's Imperialism and the Origins of the Belgian Colonial Party, 1860–1905." *Journal of Modern History* 80 (December 2008): 741–90.

Viaene, Vincent, David Van Reybrouck, and Bambi Ceuppens, eds. *Congo in België: Koloniale cultuur in de metropool.* Leuven: Leuven University Press, 2009.

"Victor Denyn (1867–1924)." *Congo: Revue Générale de la Colonie Belge/ Algemeen Tijdschrift van de Belgische Kolonie* 2, no. 4 (November 1924).

Vieyra, Paulin S. *Le cinéma africain: Des origines à 1973*. Paris: Présence africaine, 1975.

Ville de Charleroi. *L'Étoile: Organe de la Fédération Provinciale des Cercles Coloniaux du Hainaut. Numéro spécial des Journées Coloniales organisées par les Cercles Africains de Charleroi-Thuin et du Châtelet-Châtelineau*. N.p., 1935.

Ville de Namur. "Cérémonie nationale d'hommage au drapeau de Tabora." http://www.ville.namur.be (accessed 16 March 2003).

Vincart, L. "Een paar uurtjes in het Koloniaal Museum." *Onze Kongo* 1 (1910–11): 373–84.

Vincke, Edouard. "Discours sur le noir: Images dans les espaces urbains de Bruxelles." In Halen and Riesz, *Images de l'Afrique et du Congo/Zaïre dans les lettres françaises de Belgique et alentour*, 89–99.

———. *Géographes et hommes d'ailleurs: Analyse critique de manuels scolaires*. Brussels: Centre bruxellois de recherche et de documentation pédagogiques, 1985.

———. "L'image du noir dans les espaces publics." Université catholique de Louvain. http://www.anso.ucl.ac.be/anthropovis/vincke/noimp.htm (accessed 4 March 2003; site now discontinued). First published in *L'autre et nous, "Scènes et types,"* edited by Nicolas Bancel, Pascal Blanchard, Stéphane Blanchoin, Hubert Gerbeau, and Gilles Boëtsch, 253–59. Paris: ACHAC, 1995.

Vincke, Honoré. "Livrets scolaires coloniaux: Méthodes d'analyse—approche herméneutique." *History in Africa* 26 (1999): 379–408.

XXVe [Vingt-cinquième] anniversaire de l'annexion du Congo par la Belgique: Séance solennelle du 21 octobre 1933 dans le grand auditoire de l'Union coloniale belge/XXVste verjaring van Congo's aanhechting door België: Plechtige zitting op 21 Oktober 1933 in het groot auditorium van de "Union Coloniale Belge." Brussels: Les Anciennes imprimeries Van Gompel, n.d.

"Le vingtième anniversaire de la prise de Tabora." *L'Illustration Congolaise*, no. 181 (1 October 1936): 6065.

Vints, Luc. "Cinéma et propagande coloniale (1895–1960)." Translated by Monik Dierckx. In *Zaïre 1885–1985*, 33–39.

———. "Le film missionnaire: Histoire, conservation, analyse." In *Icono-*

graphie, catéchisme et missions: Actes du Colloque d'Histoire mission-naire (Louvain-la-Neuve, 5–8 septembre 1983). Lyon: CREDIC, 1984.

———. "Jungles van België: Film en koloniale propaganda 1918–1940." *Skrien*, 1982, 38–43.

———. *Kongo, made in Belgium: Beeld van een kolonie in film en propaganda.* Leuven: Kritak, 1984.

———. "Kongo, made in Belgium: De propagandagolf van de jaren twintig en dertig." *De Nieuwe Maand* 27 (1984): 525–36.

"Voici les quatre 'jardins choc' de l'Exposition 1958: Pour inspirer le jardin congolais, le velours du Kasaï." *La Meuse* (Liège), 30 July 1958.

von Albertini, Rudolf. *Decolonization: The Administration and Future of the Colonies, 1919–1960.* Translated by Francisca Garvie. Garden City NY: Doubleday, 1971.

Wastiau, Boris. *ExitCongoMuseum 2000: An Essay on the "Social Life" of the Masterpieces of the Tervuren Museum.* Tervuren, Belgium: Royal Museum for Central Africa, 2000.

———. "The Violence of Collecting: Objects, Images and People from the Colony." Paper presented at the annual meeting of the American Historical Association, New York NY, 4 January 2009.

Weber, Eugen. *The Hollow Years: France in the 1930s.* New York: Norton, 1994.

Welch, David. "Introduction: 'Winning Hearts and Minds'; The Changing Context of Reportage and Propaganda, 1900–2003." In Connelly and Welch, *War and the Media*, ix–xxi.

Wesseling, H. L. *The European Colonial Empires, 1815–1919.* Translated by Diane Webb. Harlow, England: Pearson Education, 2004.

Wilder, Gary. *The Imperial Nation-State: Negritude and Colonial Humanism between the Two World Wars.* Chicago: University of Chicago Press, 2005.

———. "Unthinking French History: Colonial Studies beyond National Identity." In Burton, *After the Imperial Turn*, 125–43.

Wils, Lode. "Introduction: A Brief History of the Flemish Movement." Translated by Jane Fenoulhet and Theo Hermans. In Hermans, *Flemish Movement*, 1–39.

Wingfield, Nancy M. "Statues of Emperor Joseph II as Sites of German Identity." In Bucur and Wingfield, *Staging the Past*, 178–205.

Woodham, Jonathan. "Images of Africa and Design at the British Empire Exhibitions between the Wars." *Journal of Design History* 2, no. 1 (1989): 15–33.

Wright, Gordon. *The Ordeal of Total War: 1939–1945*. New York: Harper and Row, 1968.

Wright, Philip. "The Quality of Visitors' Experiences in Art Museums." In Vergo, *New Museology*, 119–48.

Wrong, Michela. "Belgium Confronts Its Heart of Darkness." *The Independent*, 23 February 2005.

Wynants, Maurits. *Des ducs de Brabant aux villages congolais: Tervuren et l'Exposition Coloniale 1897*. Translated by Chantal Kesteloot. Tervuren, Belgium: Musée royal de l'Afrique centrale, 1997.

Xpo58. *Expo 58 (16)*. 28 December 2007. 8mm film. http://www.youtube.com/watch?v=uO4hmYJC5Hw&feature=related (accessed 31 May 2010).

———. *Expo 58 (17)*. 28 December 2007. 8mm film. http://www.youtube.com/watch?v=cp7ewthbdNg (accessed 31 May 2010).

Yates, Barbara. "Educating Congolese Abroad: An Historical Note on African Elites." *International Journal of African Historical Studies* 14, no. 1 (1981): 34–64.

Young, Crawford. *Politics in the Congo: Decolonization and Independence*. Princeton NJ: Princeton University Press, 1965.

———. "Zaire: The Anatomy of a Failed State." In Birmingham and Martin, *History of Central Africa*, 97–129.

Zaïre 1885–1985: Cent ans de regards Belges. Brussels: Coopération par l'education et la culture, 1985.

Zuckerman, Larry. *The Rape of Belgium: The Untold Story of World War I*. New York: New York University Press, 2004.

Index

250, 253; and occupation of Belgium, 146, 204; propaganda during, 245

youth, 152, 192, 255; education and, 42, 98, 131, 137–38, 141, 155–56, 160,

247–48; as target of propaganda, 13, 65, 81, 120–21, 155–56, 160, 161–64, 211, 247

Zoographe, 39